D0878226

ORDER AND DISORDER IN
EARLY MODERN ENGLAND

ORDER AND DISORDER IN EARLY MODERN ENGLAND

edited by

ANTHONY FLETCHER

and

JOHN STEVENSON

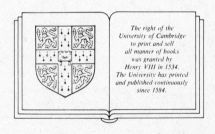

The right of the
University of Cambridge
to print and sell
all manner of books
was granted by
Henry VIII in 1534.
The University has printed
and published continuously
since 1584.

CAMBRIDGE UNIVERSITY PRESS

Cambridge

London   New York   New Rochelle
Melbourne   Sydney

Published by the Press Syndicate of the University of Cambridge
The Pitt Building, Trumpington Street, Cambridge CB2 1RP
32 East 57th Street, New York, NY 10022, USA
10 Stamford Road, Oakleigh, Melbourne 3166, Australia

First published 1985
First paperback edition 1987

Printed in Great Britain at the University Press, Cambridge

Library of Congress catalogue card number: 84-29379

British Library Cataloguing in Publication Data

Order and disorder in early modern England.
1. England – Social conditions – 16th century
2. England – Social conditions – 17th century
3. England – Social conditions – 18th century
I. Fletcher, Anthony J. II. Stevenson, John, *1946–*
942 HN385

ISBN 0 521 25294 6 hardcovers
ISBN 0 521 34932 X paperback

Contents

Notes on Contributors

SUSAN AMUSSEN is Associate Professor of History at Connecticut College, New London, Connecticut. She is preparing her thesis on 'Governors and Governed: Class and Gender Relations in English Villages 1590–1725' for publication.

C.S.L. DAVIES is a Fellow of Wadham College, Oxford. He is the author of *Peace, Print and Protestantism* and of a number of articles in learned journals. He is writing the volume on the period 1485–1547 in the New Oxford History of England.

ANTHONY FLETCHER is a Reader in History at the University of Sheffield. He is the author of *Tudor Rebellions*, *A County Community in Peace and War* and *The Outbreak of the English Civil War*. He is working on a book on *Reform in the Provinces*.

CLIVE HOLMES is Professor of History at Cornell University. He is the author of *The Eastern Association in the English Civil War* and *Seventeenth Century Lincolnshire* and he has edited *The Suffolk Committees for Scandalous Ministers*.

JOHN MORRILL is a Fellow of Selwyn College, Cambridge. He is the author of *Cheshire 1630–1660* and *The Revolt of the Provinces* and editor of *Reactions to the English Civil War*. He is writing a general study of the period 1637–1662 and the volume on the period 1643–1689 in the New Oxford History of England.

MARGARET SPUFFORD is a Fellow of Newnham College, Cambridge. She is the author of *Contrasting Communities*, *Small Books and Pleasant Histories* and

The Great Reclothing of Rural England. She is writing the volume on the seventeenth century in the Pelican Social History of Britain.

JOHN STEVENSON is a Reader in History at the University of Sheffield. He is the author of *The Slump* (with Chris Cook), *Popular Disturbances in England, 1700–1870* and *British Society, 1914–1945.* He is currently working on a study of the life and times of William Cobbett.

DAVID UNDERDOWN is Professor of History at Brown University. He is the author of *Royalist Conspiracy in England, Pride's Purge* and *Somerset in the Civil War and the Interregnum.* He has just completed a new book, *Revel, Riot and Rebellion.*

JOHN WALTER is a Lecturer in History at Essex University. He is the author of two articles in *Past and Present* and contributed to the volume edited by John Brewer and John Styles, *An Ungovernable People.* He is working on popular disorder and popular political culture in early modern England.

Abbreviations

APC	*Acts of the Privy Council*
BIHR	*Bulletin of the Institute of Historical Research*
BL	British Library
Brewer and Styles	J. Brewer and J. Styles (eds.), *An Ungovernable People: The English and their Law in the Seventeenth and Eighteenth Centuries* (London, Hutchinson, 1980)
CJ	*Commons Journals*
Cockburn	J.S. Cockburn (ed.), *Crime in England 1550–1800* (London, Methuen, 1977)
Collinson	P. Collinson, *The Religion of Protestants* (OUP, 1982)
CSPD	*Calendar of State Papers Domestic*
CUL	Cambridge University Library
Dodds	M.H. and R. Dodds, *The Pilgrimage of Grace 1536–37 and the Exeter Conspiracy 1538* (2 vols., CUP, 1915)
ECHR	*Economic History Review*
EHR	*English Historical Review*
Hay, Linebaugh, Thompson	D. Hay, P. Linebaugh, E.P. Thompson (eds.), *Albion's Fatal Tree: Crime and Society in Eighteenth Century England* (London, Allen Lane, 1975)
HLRO	House of Lords Record Office
HMC	*Historical Manuscripts Commission*

Lindley	K. Lindley, *Fenland Riots and the English Revolution* (London, Heinemann, 1982)
LJ	*Lords Journals*
LP	J.S. Brewer and J. Gairdner (eds.), *The Letters and Papers of Henry VIII* (21 vols., London, 1862–1910)
NRO	Norfolk Record Office
PRO	Public Records Office
RO	Record Office
Sharp	B. Sharp, *In Contempt of all Authority: Rural Artisans and Riot in the West of England 1586–1660* (Berkeley, University of California Press, 1980)
Sharpe	J. Sharpe, *Crime in Early Modern England* (London, Longman, 1984)
Spufford	M. Spufford, *Contrasting Communities: English Villagers in the Sixteenth and Seventeenth Centuries* (CUP, 1974)
Thomas	K.V. Thomas, *Religion and the Decline of Magic* (London, Weidenfeld, 1971)
TRHS	*Transactions of the Royal Historical Society*
VCH	*Victoria County History*
Wrightson	K. Wrightson, *English Society 1580–1680* (London, Hutchinson, 1982)
Wrightson and Levine	K. Wrightson and D. Levine, *Poverty and Piety in an English Village: Terling 1525–1700* (New York, Academic Press, 1979)

Preface

The social history of early modern England has recently become a lively area of publication and debate. We chose the theme of order and disorder, both for a seminar course which we have taught jointly for several years and for this volume, because we believe it encapsulates much of what is at present at issue between historians working in the field. The theme is much too large for us to have attempted to treat it in a comprehensive manner. To some extent this book is necessarily disparate, but we hope and our introduction seeks to suggest that it is not wholly so.

We are grateful to our students who have stimulated our thinking and to colleagues, particularly Michael Bentley, Patrick Collinson, Mark Greengrass and Daniel Szechi, who have commented upon introductory material in draft. We are grateful to our fellow contributors who have faithfully produced their essays on schedule. And finally we wish to record our gratitude to the departmental secretaries, Patricia Holland, Jane Stone and Lynda Harrison, who have been unfailingly tolerant of and patient with our demands.

June 1984   A.J.F.
                                                                       J.S.

Acknowledgements

Margaret Spufford would like to thank Mrs Dorothy Owen, Dr Zvi Razi and Dr Richard Smith not only for items mentioned in the footnotes but for more general help. She is particularly grateful to Mrs Owen for her generous guidance on sources for the medieval section of her essay and acknowledges that errors of fact or judgement remaining are, of course, her own. Dr Smith lent her an unpublished typescript of his own and gave her access to other material which was of great assistance. Dr Razi was kind enough to spend time going through his material for Halesowen, breaking down leyrwite fines by date, and thereby supplying an invaluable case study for the late thirteenth century and early fourteenth century. Dr Kenneth Parker made the publication of her essay in this volume possible by checking the footnotes when she was unable to do so.

C.S.L. Davies wishes to thank Dr G. Bernard and Dr D.M. Palliser for a critical reading of his essay. Anthony Fletcher wishes to thank John Morrill and Conrad Russell for their useful comments on his essay. Research for David Underdown's essay was assisted by a fellowship from the National Endowment for the Humanities. Earlier versions of it were presented in the Early Modern History Seminar at Harvard, the Western Societies Program at Cornell, the History Honours and Pembroke Centre Seminars at Brown: he is grateful to all those whose questions helped him to sharpen and clarify the argument. He wishes to record special thanks to Grey Osterud, Joan Scott and Rachel Weil for their helpful comments and to Susan Amussen for unfailingly creative criticism; most of the Norfolk references in his essay were generously supplied by her. A generous grant from the American Bar Foundation enabled Clive Holmes to undertake the research for his essay. It was first presented at the seminar for early modern social history at Oxford and he wishes to thank those present on that occasion, particularly Dr Joan Thirsk and Dr Felicity Heal, for their comments.

The research for Susan Amussen's essay was carried out with the assistance of the Andrew R. Mellor Foundation. An earlier version was presented to the Cornell University History Department Europeanists' Colloquium. She is grateful for the advice given there and especially to Clive Holmes and David Underdown for their helpful suggestions.

Introduction

A.J. FLETCHER and J. STEVENSON

(i) A POLARISED SOCIETY?

It has become a commonplace to refer to early modern English society as imbued with rank, hierarchy and degree. But this commonplace is an indispensable starting-point. We cannot usefully consider the means of order and the sources of disorder until we have established the context of men's personal, social, economic and cultural relationships in this period. So the first section of this introduction is concerned with social structure. Tudor and Stuart society was highly stratified. Our problem, as Keith Wrightson has pointed out, is how to bring together contemporary perceptions of its nature and the view of social developments which is emerging from the thinking of early modern historians over the last few years.[1] The criteria of social rank included birth, wealth, occupation and the life style that accompanied their gradations. Historians do not agree, any more than did contemporary commentators, on the precise weight to be given to these various criteria.[2]

In Elizabeth's reign William Harrison distinguished four 'degrees of people': gentlemen, the citizens and burgesses of the cities, yeomen in the countryside and finally those who had 'neither voice nor authority in the commonwealth but are to be ruled and not to rule other'. About 1600 Sir Thomas Wilson listed nobles, gentry, citizens, yeomen, artisans and rural labourers as the main social categories, taking care to make distinctions within the gentry between titled and professional men. Gregory King in 1695 followed Wilson in his insistence on the importance of distinguishing levels of gentility but, moving down the social scale, used a ladder of occupations rather than status terminology to characterise the

[1] Wrightson, pp. 17–38.
[2] A. Sharpe, 'Edward Waterhouse's View of Social Change in Seventeenth-Century England', *Past and Present*, LXII (1974), 27–46.

mass of the people. The most striking feature of this society, recognised by these writers and others, was social inequality.[3] There was a broad consensus among contemporaries about the pattern of inequality, though there was room for emphasis on different criteria of status. When Oliver Cromwell told parliament in 1654 that the distinctions between a nobleman, a gentleman and a yeoman were 'a good interest and a great one' he was expounding an assumption so fundamental that in more settled times there was no need for it to be said.[4]

What gave abiding strength to these perceptions of the social order was that they were based upon an old cosmology in which the concepts of a 'Great Chain of Being' and of a 'body politic' held sway. While these concepts prevailed, an ideal of harmony, of society as a living organism in which each man and woman had an allotted role, underpinned the complex reality of a system of hierarchical relationships. These relationships were mediated by the vertical ties of patronage and clientage and softened by additional horizontal ties of kin and neighbourhood. The nobility's exercise of 'good lordship' was still evident in the dealings with their tenants of some great families, like the Percies and the Stanleys, between 1500 and 1640, while it may have been declining in others. This was one expression of the traditional view of order.[5] The ceremonial which still punctuated the lives of citizens in the larger towns in the early sixteenth century was another. Examining the Corpus Christi celebrations in towns like Coventry, York, Wakefield and Chester, Mervyn James has argued that 'the concept of body provided urban societies with a mythology and ritual in terms of which the opposites of social wholeness and social differentiation could be both affirmed and also brought into a creative tension one with the other.'[6] Charles Phythian-Adams has shown in detail what civic ceremonial, and particularly the hierarchical ordering of communal processions, meant in the life of Coventry's citizens at the end of the middle ages. The town's 'history was expressed in myth; the ideal of its contemporary structure in ritual . . . both were mediums of celebration . . . both were lived rather than studied or articulated analytically'. Myth and ritual, taken together, 'served to identify and explain what made Coventry different from anywhere else'.[7] The traditional concept of order was suited to a localised

[3] D. Cressy, 'Describing the Social Order of Elizabethan and Stuart England', *Literature and History*, III (1976), 29–44.
[4] T. Carlyle, *Letters and Speeches of Oliver Cromwell* (1871), vol. III, p. 21.
[5] M.E. James, 'The Concept of Order and the Northern Rising', *Past and Present*, LX (1973), 49–83; B. Coward, 'A "Crisis of the Aristocracy" in the Sixteenth and Seventeenth Centuries? The Case of the Stanleys, Earls of Derby, 1504–1642', *Northern History*, XVII (1982), 72–3.
[6] M.E. James, 'Ritual, Drama and Social Body in the Late Medieval English Town', *Past and Present*, XCVIII (1983), 4.
[7] C. Phythian-Adams, 'Ceremony and the Citizen: the Communal Year at Coventry 1450–1550', in P. Clark and P. Slack (eds.), *Crisis and Order in English Towns 1500–1700* (London, Routledge, 1972), pp. 57–85; C. Phythian-Adams, *Desolation of a City* (CUP, 1979), pp. 112, 130, 170; see also D.M. Palliser, 'Civic Mentality and the Environment in Tudor York', *Northern History*, XVIII (1982), 79–85.

society in which hierarchy, together with obligation to those below and deference to those above, made sense of people's lives.

This mental world did not suddenly collapse at some point during the period
between 1500 and 1800 but, in face of changes in thinking about man, God,
science and the natural environment, it was slowly being dissolved.[8] Furthermore
the forces of social change interacted in such a way as to produce two crucial
developments. Local communities were penetrated ever more deeply by a process
of administrative and cultural integration which brought into them national
standards and fashions. At the same time a polarisation was occurring that
detached the gentry and some of the middling ranks from labourers and the poor,
finally leaving the traditional culture, a culture imbued with symbolism, magic
and superstition, high and dry.[9] Peter Burke has shown that this polarisation was
a European phenomenon, which led eventually in the late eighteenth and early
nineteenth centuries to the self-conscious rediscovery of popular culture by
intellectuals as part of a 'movement of cultural primitivism in which the ancient,
the distant and the popular were all equated'.[10] By the end of our period a chasm
had opened between the mentality of the gentry and the people that was not
apparent at its beginning. Yet, stated thus, this crucial development in English
society is almost certainly made to appear too simple. There were many in the
middling ranks who belonged neither wholly to the patrician culture nor wholly
to the plebeian one.[11] Their attitudes, customs and life style cry out for an
investigation that is not imprisoned by a view of society which supposes a rigid
dichotomy between classes. In any case our understanding of many aspects of
English culture in the early modern period is still at a very primitive stage.

John Morrill and John Walter in their essay in this volume draw attention to 'a
developing conflict between the beneficiaries and victims of economic change'.
Margaret Spufford comments on the fate of smaller farmers in the open arable
areas during the disastrous decade of the 1590s.[12] Prosperity came to those with
surplus produce that they could sell and the improvement in the facilities for
inland and coastal trade during the sixteenth and seventeenth centuries brought
into being a much more sophisticated system of marketing.[13] Local studies have
shown how at the same time, in certain areas like districts of Cambridgeshire,
Essex and Oxfordshire at least, the growth of a rural proletariat was proceeding

[8] For these changes see Thomas pp. 641–68; P.M. Harman, *The Scientific Revolution* (London, Methuen, 1983); M. Hunter, *Science and Society in Restoration England* (CUP, 1981); K.V. Thomas, *Man and the Natural World* (London, Allen Lane, 1983).
[9] Wrightson, pp. 13–14, 222–8.
[10] P. Burke, *Popular Culture in Early Modern Europe* (London, Temple Smith, 1978), pp. 3–10.
[11] E.P. Thompson, 'Patrician Society, Plebeian Culture', *Journal of Social History*, VII (1974), 382–405.
[12] Below, pp. 48, 152.
[13] J.A. Chartres, *Internal Trade in England 1500–1700* (London, Macmillan, 1977).

swiftly.[14] Thus there was a gradual pushing apart of the social groups described by commentators like Harrison and King. A critical aspect of this process was the alliance between the gentry and groups among the middling ranks, an alliance eased, as John Morrill and John Walter put it, 'by an identity of economic interests in service of the market'. The old pattern of hierarchy and local loyalties was at the same time complicated by new forms of association, based for instance on religious affiliation and the particularism of certain groups of workers. E.P. Thompson has argued that the riots or strikes of eighteenth-century workers and the behaviour of London's labouring poor at the gallows tree were 'fleeting expressions of solidarities' foreshadowing a class society.[15] This may be so, but a class society had not in our period yet arrived.

The nobility and gentry's assimilation of a national culture which distinguished them, and those of the middling ranks who aped their ways, from the mass of the people was a slow process that took many decades to complete. In some respects it had begun before the civil war; yet in many other respects the process was still at its height in the mid-eighteenth century. We can start with people's homes. Between the accession of Elizabeth and the civil war, the gentry's reception of classical principles of architecture was piecemeal and often muted. Many did rebuild in a new style, adopting a symmetry in their designs that showed the impact of the Renaissance.[16] But it was only after the Restoration that the vernacular tradition and timber framing went decisively out of fashion. This was when stone and brick came into their own, not just for the mansions of the wealthiest men but for unpretentious manor houses and town houses as well. A home in the classical style had become a prerequisite of social respectability.[17]

London's dominance of English cultural and social standards, secure at the beginning of our period, was even more deeply rooted by its end. The metropolis increasingly set the tone of the gentry's life; it became the criterion by which all other environments were judged. The residences of local gentry and of professional men, together with the allurements of the shops that lined the main streets, brought the fashions of the capital to provincial cities. The Glamorganshire gentry, for example, began to make regular visits to Bath and Bristol from the 1660s, buying among other commodities tea, spices, sugar, fine linens, tobacco and books. Nor was it only the gentry who benefited. By the early

[14] Spufford, pp. 46–167; Wrightson and Levine, pp. 19–42, 175; J. Walter, 'A Rising of the People? The Oxfordshire Rising and the Crisis of the 1590s', *Past and Present*, CVII (1985).

[15] *Journal of Social History*, VII (1974), 399. P. Linebaugh, 'The Tyburn Riot against the Surgeons' in Hay, Linebaugh, Thompson, pp. 65–117; E.P. Thompson, 'Eighteenth-Century English Society: Class Struggle without Class?', *Social History*, III (1978), 157.

[16] e.g. A.J. Fletcher, *A County Community in Peace and War* (London, Longman, 1975), pp. 27–8.

[17] A. Clifton-Taylor, *Six English Towns* (London, BBC, 1978); C.W. Chalklin, *The Provincial Towns of Georgian England* (London, Edward Arnold, 1974); N. Pevsner, The Buildings of England series (London, Penguin).

eighteenth century the more substantial Glamorganshire farmers and tradesmen were adorning their homes with silver as well as pewter, and with clocks, maps and prints, items which had previously only been accessible to the very rich.[18] All over England by then, tea, coffee and chocolate were the drinks which denoted respectability. The consumer society was on the way.[19]

A whole range of artistic and intellectual interests also marked off the gentry of Georgian England from the people.[20] The period from 1720 to 1760, for instance, was one of the most distinguished in English sculpture, a time when artists of the quality of Michael Rysbrack and Louis Francois Roubiliac worked on busts and monuments for noble and gentry patrons.[21] There is no more forceful way of appreciating the gulf that separated the patrician and plebeian cultures than to visit one of those parish churches, such as St Martin's at Stamford, where a huge marble tomb proclaiming the confident superiority of a great aristocrat dominates an aisle or chancel. The fifth earl of Exeter died in France in 1700 having already ordered the tomb now at Stamford from Pierre Monnot in Rome.[22]

Towns became centres for leisure activities, where the gentry congregated for assemblies, balls and visiting the theatre. The town, Peter Borsay has argued, played 'a crucial role in servicing the increasing demand for status'.[23] The musical life of many towns was burgeoning: the Three Choirs Festival was founded in 1715 in connection with Worcester, Gloucester and Hereford and the Holywell Music Room at Oxford, built in the 1740s, was the first building constructed for the sole purpose of musical performances in the country.[24] This was the age of the development of the provincial press, of the multiplication of spa towns, of the discovery of landscape, of circulating libraries, of county antiquarianism, of ballooning and pleasure gardens. Many gentry became obsessed with the breeding of livestock and preoccupied with foxhunting and horse racing. The animals with which they were most closely involved – horses

[18] P. Jenkins, *The Making of a Ruling Class* (CUP, 1983), pp. 239–55.
[19] See the essays by N. McKendrick in N. McKendrick, J. Brewer and J.H. Plumb, *The Birth of a Consumer Society: The Commercialisation of Eighteenth-Century England* (London, Hutchinson, 1982).
[20] J.H. Plumb, 'The Commercialisation of Leisure', in McKendrick, Brewer, Plumb, *The Birth of a Consumer Society*, pp. 265–85; G.A. Cranfield, *The Development of the Provincial Newspaper* (OUP, 1960).
[21] M. Whinney, *Sculpture in Britain 1530–1830* (London, Penguin, 1964), pp. 67–131.
[22] N. Pevsner and J. Harris, *Lincolnshire* (London, Penguin, 1964), p. 661.
[23] P. Borsay, 'The English Urban Renaissance: the Development of Provincial Urban Culture c.1680–c.1760', *Social History*, II (1977), 581–98; P. Borsay, 'Culture, Status and the English Urban Landscape', *History*, LXVII (1983), 1–12. See also P. Clark (ed.), *Country Towns in Pre-Industrial England* (Leicester University Press, 1981), pp. 21–4, 176–84, 198–243.
[24] A. Everitt, 'Country, County and Town: Patterns of Regional Evolution in England', *TRHS*, XXIX (1979), 96–7; J. Sherwood and N. Pevsner, *Oxfordshire* (London, Penguin, 1974), p. 217.

and greyhounds for example – became privileged species worthy of an honour and praise which was denied the rest of the brute creation. 'Dogs differed in status', Keith Thomas has noted, 'because their owners did.'[25] What was common to this whole pattern of activities was a new confidence in man's mastery of the natural environment, a confidence which made possible the public pursuit of happiness. From the last quarter of the seventeenth century, J.H. Plumb argued, 'the pursuit of happiness was entangled in social emulation: it therefore became competitive . . . happiness became less private, less a state of the soul, a personal relationship with God than something visible to one's neighbours'.[26]

Popular culture, by contrast, was rooted in a view of life as hazardous and uncertain. The poorest sections of the population did not plan their careers or their marriages or their financial affairs or their purchases of land and stock or their holidays. E.P. Thompson has emphasised the plebeian lack of a 'predictive notation of time': 'hence experience or opportunity is grabbed as occasion arises, with little thought of the consequences, just as the crowd imposes its power in moments of insurgent direct action, knowing that its moment of triumph will last only a week or a day'.[27] This is not to say that the popular mentality of our period was fatalistic. It can be described in terms of the people's consolations, their defences against the tribulations of the world, their escapisms. But such an account misses the assertiveness and the toughness, the strength of belief in luck and fortune, with which many faced the world. Popular culture was certainly permeated by symbolism: in the wife sale, in the characteristic forms of economic or religious riot and protest, in the rites of passage, in the village routines of rough music and the cucking stool.[28] But such rituals were not simply defensive mechanisms clung to by those who lacked a purchase on influence and authority in the state. They were more purposeful than that and more constructive.

There is an unresolved debate about how far popular culture in our period possessed its own coherence. Before it can be resolved it seems likely that historians will have to come to terms with the recent thinking of social anthropologists and philosophers about meaning and rationality. Those anthropologists who worked in the older functionalist tradition put emphasis on the underlying psychological reasons for popular beliefs and practices rather than on any intrinsic sense they may have had. Keith Thomas's seminal *Religion and the*

---

[25] Thomas, *Man and the Natural World*, pp. 100–9.
[26] J.H. Plumb, *The Pursuit of Happiness* (New Haven, Yale Centre for British Art, 1977), p. 3; see also J.H. Plumb, *The Commercialisation of Leisure in Eighteenth-Century England* (University of Reading, 1973).   [27] *Social History*, III (1978), 157–8.
[28] For wife sales see S.P. Menefee, *Wives for Sale* (Oxford, Basil Blackwell, 1981); for rough music and cucking stools see below pp. 123–36.

Decline of Magic, published in 1971, was written, as he himself has confessed, within that tradition. It was of course at the same time informed by the wide-ranging analysis of the substratum of convictions about occult influences and sympathies, the animate universe and the symbolism of particular rituals which Thomas's reading had brought to light. His conceptual approach was challenged in 1975 by Hildred Geertz who was unconvinced by his definition of magic in pragmatic terms. She also questioned his sharp distinction between religion, which offered 'a guiding principle, relevant to every aspect of life' and magic, which he alleged was no more than 'a collection of miscellaneous recipes'. The plausibility of popular beliefs and rituals, Geertz argued, 'derives from the fact that a particular notion is set within a general pattern of cultural concepts, a conventional cognitive map in terms of which thinking and willing, being anxious and wishing, are carried out'. British historians, she suggested, should work towards 'a highly specific picture which sets off the early English popular image of reality from those of other societies and other times'.[29]

A not entirely dissimilar line of criticism was employed by E.P. Thompson in an earlier review article of *Religion and the Decline of Magic*. His research on eighteenth-century popular culture led him to conclude that 'one appears to confront a system of beliefs with its own coherence even if this is most clearly seen in relation to particular occupational groups'. E.P. Thompson called for social historians to study both dialect and old Welsh and Gaelic, repositories of 'forgotten modes of thought and habits of work'. He directed attention to poetic and symbolic meanings and to the value of literary sources, painting Thomas Hardy's Henchard in *The Mayor of Casterbridge* as the epitome of a man steeped in plebeian culture for whom magic was at the centre of all life's fortunes and accidents.[30]

These pleas for conceptual rethinking and a sustained examination of early modern popular culture on a broad front have not yet produced extensive published results. Indeed the paucity of the British output is the more remarkable when a comparison is made with the same field in France. Stuart Clark has assessed the conceptual problems raised by recent work in the French field. His conclusions can be fruitfully applied to English studies as well. Sweeping aside the whole functional tradition, he argues that the historian's initial step should be 'the acceptance of primitive "magical" and "religious" beliefs as enunciated, a literalism which recognises that the associated practices could have genuinely instrumental ends and that their rationale was a coherent system of ideas which

[29] H. Geertz and K.V. Thomas, 'An Anthropology of Religion and Magic', *Journal of Interdisciplinary History*, VIII (1975), 71–109.
[30] E.P. Thompson, 'Anthropology and the Discipline of Historical Context', *Midland History*, I (1972), 46–55.

explained the world and its workings'. But this literalism by itself, he argues, is not enough: 'if experience (material and psychological, as well as mental) is already a world of meanings, the need to explain how the latter emerge from the former disappears and is replaced by a semantic account of how practices, emotions and beliefs go together'. Literalism should be blended with 'some form of relativist account' of the rationality of the popular culture of particular societies. Historians, in this view, must escape the shackles of the old anthropology with its attendant dangers of impoverishing plebeian belief and practice by the implication that it is not reputable. They need to start their investigations with the assumption, as a simple matter of 'conceptual propriety', that the people of our period lived in a mental world that mostly made perfectly good sense to them and engaged in rituals which were seen neither as necessarily ineffective nor as merely the fragmentary cultural debris of earlier ways of thinking.[31] There is then much to be done before any kind of definitive account of early modern popular culture can be expected.

In the English village there was probably no appreciable decline of magic before 1800. Numerous folklore studies testify to the survival of magic in the Victorian countryside. James Obelkevich has found a flourishing belief in witchcraft in the South Lindsey district of Lincolnshire during the mid-nineteenth century. He documents the work of wise men who were 'public figures known over wide areas'.[32] Charles Phythian-Adams has portrayed the characteristic activities of the cunning men who plied their trade all over Victorian England.[33] Such work provides overwhelming arguments for continuity with Keith Thomas's world of seventeenth-century magic. There is also some specific evidence of lynching for witchcraft, magical healing and divination during the eighteenth century, a time when magic was no longer respectable yet the folklorists had not begun to conduct their field studies.[34]

Popular culture throughout our period remained imbued with the sense of the power of the supernatural. Keith Thomas's argument that by 1700 it is possible to draw a distinction between religion and magic is persuasive with regard to the gentry elite but not with regard to the people at large.[35] Victorian south Lincolnshire, explored by Obelkevich, provides us with an insight into an older mental world. Villagers, he writes, inhabited 'a pluralistic, polymorphous universe in which power was fluidly distributed among a multitude of beings'.

---

[31] S. Clark, 'French Historians and Early Modern Popular Culture', *Past and Present*, C (1983), 62–99.
[32] J. Obelkevich, *Religion and Rural Society: South Lindsey 1825–1875* (OUP, 1976), pp. 283–91.
[33] C. Phythian-Adams, 'Rural Culture' in G.E. Mingay (ed.), *The Victorian Countryside* (London, Routledge, 1981) vol. II, pp. 616–25.
[34] R.W. Malcolmson, *Life and Labour in England 1700–1780* (London, Hutchinson, 1981), pp. 87–91; Thomas, particularly p. 582.   [35] Thomas, p. 640.

The rural populace took from the church and its rituals what they wanted. The place of Christianity as such in their lives was only tenuous, but their reinterpretations of the church's holidays, its rites and the role of its clergy boosted the forms and structure of popular culture. Thus, while the sacramental power of the clergy failed to engage the people's imagination, ministers, churches and churchyards provided 'a vague reservoir of spiritual potency . . . which could be tapped and directed to non-Christian ends'.[36]

The evidence of the chapbooks, those small penny pamphlets sold by pedlars which fed the seventeeth- and eighteenth-century appetite for cheap literature, tells us something more about popular piety. Margaret Spufford has found that the small godly books were largely calls to repentance which deliberately evoked fear. Death was usually portrayed as 'a figure who was very well-known by and very close to' the reader.[37] Deborah Valenze has emphasised how closely eighteenth-century chapbooks were tailored to their market. Prophecies, Day of Judgement books and reports of trances were all commercially successful. Chapbook catechisms discarded the usual approach to religious education and all lessons on obedience in favour of 'a veritable dictionary of prophetic symbols and stories'. Religion emerges from this popular literature shorn of theological subtlety, at its simplest and most facile. There was clearly no market among those who patronised the roving pedlars for serious doctrine. Yet the fusion of the sacred and secular worlds, so apparent in other aspects of popular culture, is again striking: despite the corrective efforts of protestant divines and the diffusion of scientific knowledge, Valenze concludes, the 'commoner's world revolved within a universe of magic'.[38]

Plebeian identity was rooted in the sense of belonging to a local environment. John Clare's account of his feelings on leaving his village to seek work is the classic evocation of this: 'I started for Wisbech with a timid sort of pleasure and when I got to Glinton turnpike I turned back to look on the old church as if I was going into another country . . . I could not fancy England much larger than the part I knew.'[39] Local dialects were pronounced. There was only limited standardisation of vocabulary, diction or grammar. Districts had their own special kinds of drink and food and their own festivities and customs. Yet, despite this variety and heterogeneity, there were characteristic features of popular culture which were common to all regions: the relaxation from work through

[36] Obelkevich, *Religion and Rural Society*, pp. 259–312.
[37] M. Spufford, *Small Books and Pleasant Histories* (London, Methuen, 1981), pp. 194–213. See also G.A. Cranfield, *The Press and Society: from Caxton to Northcliffe* (London, Longman, 1978); V. Neuberg, *Popular Education in Eighteenth-Century England* (London, Woburn Press, 1971).
[38] D.M. Valenze, 'Prophecy and Popular Literature in Eighteenth-Century England', *Journal of Ecclesiastical History*, XXIX (1978), 75–92.
[39] Cited in Malcolmson, *Life and Labour in England*, pp. 93–4.

parish feasts, country fairs and popular sports; the socialisation and leisure activities associated with the alehouse; the fiction distributed by the pedlars; music which was so integral to a culture that remained fundamentally oral. R.W. Malcolmson has examined the huge range of sports and pastimes which fulfilled the deep human desire for fun, distraction and laughter.[40] Peter Clark and Keith Wrightson have investigated the central place of the alehouse in the village society of pre-industrial England.[41] Margaret Spufford has surveyed the art of courtship books, the slapstick and dunghill humour of the small merry books, the historical and chivalric novels. This was an essentially escapist literature, opening a world of imagination and fantasy to the unlettered reader which was always available from the chapman's bag at prices up to sixpence.[42] Music, the most accessible, public and democratic of the arts, lifted men's spirits at work and play. It has left little trace in the records, more in literature, such as John Clare's writings and Thomas Hardy's novels. The simple instruments of the poor – flageolets, tabors and pipes – are well recorded in medieval gargoyles and misericords. There must have been plenty of them in the Stuart and Hanoverian countryside, for this was the great age of dancing at weddings and festivals led by the village fiddler, of town waits and itinerant street musicians. Moreover, the eighteenth century saw the spread of church choirs and bellringing societies.[43]

We can detect then a whole series of developing polarities – of speech, dress, manners, living conditions, leisure pursuits and literary interests. What needs much closer investigation is the process by which this polarisation came into being. Essentially this was a process of withdrawal by the gentry and middling groups from a common heritage of assumptions about social integration. It did not occur in a uniform or even manner but seventeenth- and eighteenth-century records are littered with the evidence of its inexorability and dynamism.

The gentry's withdrawal from armed political demonstrations in alliance with the people had occurred by 1600. In Lincolnshire in 1536 the gentry grasped control of an outburst of discontent at the enforcement of the Henrician Reformation, mobilising their own wapentakes and preparing a set of articles to be sent to the Council in London.[44] 'It seems likely', C.S.L. Davies argues in his analysis of the Pilgrimage of Grace in this volume, 'that many gentlemen and priests were happy to allow themselves to be sworn.' Again, in 1549, in 1554 and in 1569, to a remarkable extent, the normal assumptions of society were carried

[40] R.W. Malcolmson, *Popular Recreations in English Society* (CUP, 1973).
[41] P. Clark, *The English Alehouse* (London, Longman, 1983); K. Wrightson, 'Alehouses, Order and Reformation in Rural England 1590–1660' in E. and S. Yeo, *Popular Culture and Class Conflict* (Hassocks, Harvester Press, 1981), pp. 1–27.
[42] Spufford, *Small Books and Pleasant Histories*, chapters vii, ix.
[43] Malcolmson, *Life and Labour in England*, pp. 99–101.
[44] A.J. Fletcher, *Tudor Rebellions* (London, Longman, 1983), pp. 17–19.

forward into rebellions and manifested in their leadership.[45] But John Walter's analysis of the Oxfordshire Rising in 1596 shows that not only gentry but middling men failed, at a time of dearth and enclosure, to unite with the poor: they were 'unlikely sponsors of a rising whose declared aim was to challenge the agrarian capitalism which underwrote their growing wealth and power'.[46] Yet the middling sort still had a role to play in certain kinds of armed demonstrations. In his essay on the fenland disturbances, Clive Holmes rejects the argument for gentry leadership, but shows that the leadership of the village aristocracies of middling-rich yeomen is well documented. In the few instances he has found of gentry involvement, the men concerned were barely distinguishable from their yeomen neighbours.[47]

Early Stuart elections show that the gentry had come to conceive of their political relationship with all those below them in status in terms of management. This did not preclude platforms and propaganda but there was a risk in adopting a popular stance. In the hard-fought Yorkshire election of 1625, we find shrewd manipulation of the West Riding clothworkers by one party and skilful manoeuvring to taint his opponent with the brush of social disloyalty by the other. Control of the people, who cannot safely be given their political head, had become a key issue of county politics. The issue is apparent again in late 1641 when John Pym was almost as frightened by the popular demonstrations at Westminster as the king himself.[48]

Yet the tremendous expansion of educational opportunity between the 1550s and the 1640s – through grammar schools, the universities and the Inns of Court – contributed to the growth of a homogeneous national culture.[49] If the benefits of this development fell largely upon the gentry they were not by any means confined to those of higher social status. There were many husbandmen and labourers and some servants and women who learnt to read and write.[50] The gulf between the patrician and plebeian cultures could never therefore become a simple gulf between the mental world of the literate and illiterate.[51] Literacy enriched popular culture: the fables and romances beloved by earlier generations were now disseminated by the printed word.[52] But it also broadened some

---

[45] Below, pp. 75–6. See also C.S.L. Davies, 'Peasant Revolt in France and England: a Comparison,' in *Agricultural History Review*, XXI (1973), pp. 122–34.
[46] *Past and Present*, CVII (1985).   [47] Below, pp. 179–86.
[48] A.J. Fletcher, 'Debate: Parliament and People in Seventeenth-Century England', *Past and Present*, XCVIII (1983), 152–5.
[49] L. Stone, 'The Educational Revolution in England 1560–1640', *Past and Present*, XXVIII (1964), 41–80; M.H. Curtis, *Oxford and Cambridge in Transition* (OUP, 1959); Wrightson, pp. 184–91.
[50] D. Cressy, *Literacy and the Social Order* (CUP, 1980), pp. 118–41; M. Spufford, 'First Steps in Literacy: the Reading and Writing Experiences of the Humblest Seventeenth-century Autobiographers', *Social History*, IV (1979), 407–34.
[51] Thompson in *Social History*, III (1978), 155.
[52] Spufford, *Small Books and Pleasant Histories*, pp. 258–60.

horizons and liberated some minds, fuelling the mobility which complicated the pattern of social relationships. Moreover there were some forms of literature, such as the almanacs, which bridged the gap between the high and popular cultures by bringing many people of middling rank into closer touch with new social, political and religious ideas.[53]

Social withdrawal was, in the context of these crosscurrents, more gradual than political withdrawal but in the long run just as remorseless. So far as gentry and their servants were concerned, Mark Girouard has emphasised the importance of two changes during the seventeenth century in the life of the English country house. The banishment of servants from their traditional eating place in the hall and the invention of the backstairs made servants very much less visible. The gentry's growing feeling for privacy also led to the abandonment of much of the public hospitality that had remained customary through the Tudor period.[54] Feasting and entertainment was increasingly confined to those who were clearly set apart from the rest of the community by their ownership of landed property.[55] Nicholas Assheton recorded bouts of tippling at his parish alehouse in Jacobean Lancashire that left him 'more than merry' and 'sick with drink'.[56] He was unusual, for snobbery kept most gentry away from the village alehouse.[57] They preferred to patronise the more respectable urban inns whose facilities were so much developed and improved during our period.[58]

It was the intellectual withdrawal of the gentry, hastened by a fearful reaction to the signs between 1640 and 1660 that the world might be turned upside-down, that was the most divisive aspect of this whole process and therefore the most devastating in its effects. By the end of the seventeenth century many of the gentry had thrown aside witchcraft and village magic as the delusions of the ignorant.[59] But in doing this they also rejected traditional religious ideas about anxiety and suicide. The therapeutic work of an astrological physician like Richard Napier, who treated 2000 mentally disturbed patients between 1597 and 1634, was only possible in a mental world where for most people science, religion and magic were still fused. Advances in physical science and anatomy after the Restoration prompted the ruling elite to favour secular explanations of insanity and to repudiate all magical and religious methods of healing. The secular approach

[53] B. Capp, *Astrology and the Popular Press* (London, Faber, 1979).
[54] M. Girouard, *Life in the English Country House* (London, Yale University Press, 1978), pp. 136–43.
[55] Fletcher, *A County Community*, pp. 44–53.
[56] Cited in G.E. Mingay, *The Gentry* (London, Longman, 1976), p. 147.
[57] P. Clark, *The English Alehouse*, pp. 123–5.
[58] A. Everitt, 'The English Urban Inn 1560–1760', in A. Everitt (ed.), *Perspectives in English Urban History* (London, Macmillan, 1973), pp. 91–137.
[59] Thomas, pp. 570–83, 641–7. For a caveat see P. J. Guskin, 'The Context of Witchcraft: The Case of Jane Wenham', *Eighteenth Century Studies*, xv (1981), 54–5.

was embraced the more readily because it was respectable. Medical theories about mental disorders which were contradictory and new therapies which were notoriously difficult to justify empirically were adopted, Michael Macdonald has argued, because 'they appealed to an elite sick of sectarian enthusiasm'. These theories and therapies 'lacked the subversive political implications', he suggests, 'that religious psychology and therapy had acquired during the seventeenth century'. Thus, from around 1660, numerous private madhouses were founded; from the mid-eighteenth century some municipal governments established their own asylums for pauper lunatics. Cages, chains and straw for the insane were techniques of domestication employed in a society which had identified certain groups as inferior humans.[60]

At a time when those who were wealthy and who ruled were much preoccupied by human ascendancy over animals and human control of the natural environment, the analogue of domestication sprang easily to mind. Women and children were regarded by some as nearer to the animal state than men, the former because of childbearing, the latter because they could not control their passions. Those on the margins of human society – the mad, vagrants and negro servants – were seen as the most beastlike of all people and were liable to be treated accordingly. Eighteenth-century advertisements for runaway negroes show that they often had collars round their necks. Some men only, it was assumed, should enjoy domination over the brute creation. The celebrated proverb which Denzil Holles took so much to heart nicely summarises a vital aspect of the gentry's perception of social order: 'The wisest of men saw it to be a great evil that servants should ride on horses.' It was only a short step to the further assumption that these same men should enjoy domination over lesser humans. Such thinking took men a long way from the Great Chain of Being and the old view of the body politic.[61]

Mercantilism, the most comprehensive body of economic thought available to those who ruled between 1650 and 1750, also tempted the gentry to regard the poor as inferior creatures. Its essence was the doctrine of the utility of poverty: a nation's wealth and power depended on large numbers of badly paid labourers who should be habituated to drudgery.[62] Mercantilism encouraged the gentry to suppose that, within the longstanding notion of social hierarchy, there was a basic division between rich and poor. In a defence of the charity school movement published in 1728, the dissenting minister Isaac Watts put the matter

---

[60] M. Macdonald, *Mystical Bedlam* (CUP, 1981), pp. 1–12.
[61] Thomas, *Man and the Natural World*, pp. 41–6.
[62] C. Wilson, 'The Other Face of Mercantilism', *Economic History and the Historian* (London, Weidenfeld, 1969), pp. 73–93; A.W. Coats, 'Changing Attitudes to Labour in the Mid-Eighteenth Century', *Economic History Review*, XI (1958), 35–51.

succinctly: 'Great God has wisely ordained in the course of his providence in all ages that among mankind there be some rich and some poor and the same providence hath alloted to the poor the meaner services.'[63] The poor, in other words, were a race apart to be manipulated and conditioned. Watts pleaded for humane treatment for a mass of people who were bound to be seen as despicable. Some others saw the poor as squalid in their way of life as well as ignorant and unmannerly, as beastlike in fact. 'The numerous rabble that seem to have the signatures of man in their faces are but brutes in their understanding', wrote Sir Thomas Pope Blunt in 1693, ''tis by the favour of a metaphor we call them men, for at the best they are but Descartes's automata, moving frames and figures of men, and have nothing but their outsides to justify their titles to rationality.' The vicar of Madeley in Shropshire found it hard to see how the local bargemen, 'fastened to their lines as horses to their traces,' differed from 'the laborious brutes'. 'The beasts tug in silent patience and mutual ritual harmony', he remarked, 'but the men with loud contention and horrible imprecations.'[64]

If this scathing view of the poor was the product of political economy, it was also to some extent a reflection of administrative developments. The poor law statutes of 1601 were not suddenly enforced, but they did lead to the institutionalisation of poor relief in virtually every town and village by the end of the seventeenth century. The 1662 Act of Settlement reinforced the nascent system which was to survive until 1834. Sir Dudley North's comment in the late seventeenth century, though it comes in the midst of a fierce attack on the Tudor poor law, is nevertheless instructive: 'I am certain that now late care being taken by overseers publicly chosen in every parish a great many that do have compassionate hearts do not so much in that kind as they would do otherwise . . . many people not only thinking it needless but foolish to do that which is parish business.' With the decline of private charity the face-to-face relationship between poor beggars and responsible householders was lost. Changing attitudes were expressed in the desire to set the poor apart by badging and by providing special seating in church. The disputes over pews discussed here by Susan Amussen show how seating on Sundays was becoming a weekly reminder of social hierarchy in the community.[65] Daniel Baugh has suggested that in the Hanoverian period, until Adam Smith clinched the case for rethinking the role of the poor in the national economy with *The Wealth of Nations*, policy towards this sector of society uneasily combined two attitudes which were based on different premises even if they were not mutually exclusive. The older attitude,

---

[63] Cited in D.A. Baugh, 'Poverty, Protestantism and Political Economy: English Attitudes towards the Poor 1660–1800' in S.B. Baxter (ed.), *England's Rise to Greatness* (University of California Press, 1983), p. 80.   [64] Cited in Thomas, *Man and the Natural World*, pp. 43–4.
[65] BL, Add. MS 32512, fol. 127r; below pp. 212–14.

founded on Christian ethics, emphasised 'the duty of the rich to treat the poor with kindness and compassion and to aid them in times of distress'. But since the state had relieved men's consciences in this regard, that sense of obligation was generally subordinate to the dominant attitude which 'supposed that the poor should never have misery lifted from them, nor their children be encouraged to look beyond the plough or loom'.[66]

(ii) THE RULE OF LAW

How did the gentry govern a people they were so manifestly detaching themselves from in manners and values? The starting-point for an examination of this question must be a consideration of attitudes to the law. By 1600, even more certainly by 1700, the idea of a rule of law was central to men's understanding of what gave the English political system its distinctiveness. 'It was a shibboleth', John Brewer and John Styles have remarked, 'that English law was the birthright of every citizen who, unlike many of his European counterparts, was subject not to the whim of a capricious individual but to a set of prescriptions that bound all members of the polity.'[67] How had this shibboleth come into being? The answer seems to lie in the affinity between English law and custom. The law was rooted in the productive relations of the countryside. It was backed by norms of behaviour which men at all levels of society held to tenaciously. It did not belong to one group of men. It was quite evidently not simply the instrument of a ruling class. 'The farmer or forester in his daily occupation', E.P. Thompson has noted, 'was moving within visible or invisible structures of law: this merestone which marked the division between strips; that ancient oak which marked the limits of the parish grazing; this written or unwritten customal which decided how many stints on the common land and for whom.'[68]

Those who ruled England could at any time in the seventeenth or eighteenth centuries have rejected this tradition and attempted to dispense with the rule of law. But they did no such thing. On the contrary, the gentry accepted that they, like the people, were subject to the rule of law and that they were bound to abide by its procedural rules. They based their supremacy and the legitimacy of their control on the equity and universality of England's legal forms. They understood their countrymen's expectation that the exercise of the law would be seen to be just. But it has been shown that in our period men at all levels of society felt entitled to assert their own notions of how the law represented the common good.[69] Disorder was one face of the conviction that it was proper to participate

[66] Baugh in Baxter (ed.), *England's Rise to Greatness*, p. 83.   [67] Brewer and Styles, p. 14.
[68] E.P. Thompson, *Whigs and Hunters* (London, Allen Lane, 1975), p. 261.
[69] See the case studies in Brewer and Styles.

in seeking justice; order, based on participatory assumptions which had a firm institutional basis in the English judicial system, was its other face.

The system of local government did not merely allow participation: it was dependent for its smooth working on the active involvement of men of all ranks. There were no dramatic changes in criminal process and procedure between 1500 and 1800. Its hallmarks remained its technical rigidity together with its practical flexibility and sensitivity to circumstances. The most detailed investigation that has so far been carried out of how the system worked in the earlier part of our period is Cynthia Herrup's thesis based on the quarter sessions and assize material for East Sussex between 1594 and 1640. She was concerned with the options available to wronged individuals or disturbed communities. She stresses the extent to which the initiative lay with the private citizen in detecting a crime and in the initial pursuit of a miscreant. The role of the village constable, though important in bringing an accused man before the magistrate, was usually secondary. A justice of the peace, faced with an alleged criminal in his parlour or study, had several choices and certain overriding considerations before him. It was important that he should uncover the truth and restore the local peace; he could settle the matter by arbitration; he could bind men over to a court appearance; he could send a miscreant to gaol.

Magistrates and villagers clearly differed, except in unusual cases of joint zeal for moral reform, over the desirability of strict enforcement of the laws against the common country disorders like profanity and alehouse haunting. As Keith Wrightson has put it, there were 'two concepts of order'.[70] Yet so far as theft, violence, vagrancy and bastardy, the staple items of parish government, were concerned, there were common assumptions which made for unanimity of purpose when a justice confronted a miscreant brought before him. Gentry became JPs, Anthony Fletcher argues in this volume, out of ambition as well as duty. They sought, through the exercise of office, to heighten and enhance their reputation and prestige, to offer a local leadership that would mark them out in the eyes of the community of the neighbourhood. This objective did not dictate a formal, directive approach to government, but rather suggested that JPs should be prepared to meet the populace at least half way. In any case they had little choice, for their decisions about binding over and sending to gaol depended for their enforcement on the willingness of others involved to serve as witnesses, sureties and prisoner guards. 'The most striking feature of the system used in East Sussex to identify, capture and secure criminals', Cynthia Herrup concluded, 'is its broad participatory base.'

The strong element of discretion was not removed when the focus of a case

[70] K. Wrightson, 'Two Concepts of Order: Justices, Constables and Jurymen in Seventeenth-Century England' in Brewer and Styles, pp. 21–46.

became the courtroom instead of the village and the magistrate's home. Grand juries were neither timid nor capricious. They were guided by commonsense notions of culpability. They looked for clear linkages between crimes and alleged criminals. Nor were the trial juries, who received the grand juries' indictments and proceeded to judgement, ciphers of the bench or the assize judges.[71] Trials were not so much an awesome ritual as the human centrepiece of the gossip and bustle which made up the courtroom drama. Their essence was the personal interaction of the parties who were pitted against each other. The law's business, Herrup argues, was not the achievement of a set level of results; its enforcement was 'an exercise in choices not in categorisations'. There was an acceptance and understanding of the frailty of men and women. At every stage of the criminal process there was the chance to sift the sinful from the unfortunate, to show mercy or to invoke the letter of the law.[72]

In the late eighteenth century criminal justice still rested on private prosecution: in Staffordshire between 1750 and 1800 at least 85 per cent of the cases of theft which led to recognisances to prosecute were subject to the appearance in court of the victim of the alleged offences. But nervousness about the effectiveness of a criminal code which relied too much on the occasional inculcation of terror by example and not enough on steady accusation, conviction and punishment produced efforts to encourage prosecutional activity.[73] Parliament passed a series of statutes between 1751 and 1801 for the granting of costs in felony cases which were at once put into use.[74] Another administrative expedient was the founding of associations for the prosecution of felons, whose members shared costs, agreed to curtail the practices of forgiving offenders and compounding and sometimes helped the poor to take cases to court. Douglas Hay's study of Staffordshire revealed scores of these associations springing up in the 1770s and 1780s, so that by the end of the century virtually every parish was included in the activities of one or another of them.[75]

By 1800 a system of criminal justice whose logic was based on close social relationships had come under severe strain, particularly in the new industrial cities. In the last decades of our period some began to argue that the judicial

[71] For a different view see J.S. Cockburn, *A History of English Assizes* (CUP, 1972), pp. 122–4.

[72] C. Herrup, 'The Common Peace: Legal Structure and Legal Substance in East Sussex 1594–1640', unpublished Ph.D. thesis, Northwestern University, 1982, particularly pp. 89–250, 298–313. We are grateful to Cynthia Herrup for allowing us to cite here some of the main conclusions which will be set out in her forthcoming book.   [73] Cockburn, *Assizes*, pp. 124–33.

[74] J.M. Beattie, 'Towards a Study of Crime in Eighteenth-Century England' in P. Fritz and D. Williams (eds.), *The Triumph of Culture* (Toronto, 1972), pp. 304–7; J.M. Beattie, 'Judicial Records and the Measurement of Crime in Eighteenth-Century England', in L.A. Knafla (ed.), *Crime and Criminal Justice in Europe and Canada* (Waterloo, Ontario, 1980), pp. 127, 130; J.H. Langbein, 'Albion's Fatal Flaws', *Past and Present*, XCVIII (1983), 102.

[75] D. Hay, 'War, Dearth and Theft in the Eighteenth Century', *Past and Present*, XCV (1982), 147–51.

system had failed. The movement for reform, which would eventually produce a professional police force and a revised penal code less heavily dependent on the deterrent power of the death penalty, was gathering strength. Meanwhile, however, the old forms and procedures, with their manifold opportunities for discretion, survived. Peter King's analysis of decision-making in the criminal law between 1750 and 1800 suggests that little had changed since the period that has been investigated by Cynthia Herrup. The legal process remained 'private and negotiable involving personal confrontation'. King emphasises the wide variety of participants who could influence the outcome of a case: 'it was possible for individuals and groups of widely differing social and economic status to modify or choose not to modify the severity of the law in line with their needs, beliefs and ideas of justice'. Villagers still chose whether to prosecute and, though some chose not to, many of the unpropertied labouring poor did make extensive use of the courts in relation to property crime.[76] Magistrates still chose whether to send men and women to court, though when they did commit them their anxiety about the threat that petty crime posed to local order probably persuaded them to make more use of the gaol and less of bail.[77] Nor did grand jury consideration of bills become a mere formality in the eighteenth century. John Beattie's study of people accused of crimes against property brought before the Surrey assizes and quarter sessions between 1736 and 1753 shows that 11 per cent of them were discharged. 'As the jurors assessed the value of the evidence presented before them', he suggests, 'the character of the accused (and perhaps of the prosecutor), the circumstances under which the crime was committed and the general level of crime clearly helped to shape their decisions.' Zachary Babington's comments on the independence of grand jurors, in a work written in the 1670s, suggests that little changed generally in this respect between Elizabeth's reign and George III's.[78]

Almost a third of those who were sent for trial by the Surrey grand juries between 1736 and 1753 were found not guilty. The normal reason for this, we must assume, was that the trial jury found the evidence was insufficient. But trial juries were still extremely sensitive to people's reputation. Beattie argues that 'knowledge of the character of the offender remained centrally important'. There were many cases in which favourable character witnesses predisposed juries towards a partial verdict.[79] Sentencing policies in the second half of the eighteenth century were strongly related to age, with a concentration on the group

---

[76] P. King, 'Decision-Makers and Decision-Making in the English Criminal Law 1750–1800', *Historical Journal*, XXVII (1984), 25–34; J.M. Beattie, 'The Patterns of Crime in England 1600–1800', *Past and Present*, LXII (1974), 54–5.
[77] J.M. Beattie, 'Crime and Courts in Surrey 1736–1753', in Cockburn, p. 161.
[78] Cited in Cockburn, *Assizes*, p. 127.   [79] Beattie in Cockburn, pp. 156–85.

aged from 18 to 30 in the selection of candidates for the gallows for property offences. Judges' reports were likely to be favourable where the evidence that had been given was thought to be inadequate or doubtful. Judges were particularly sympathetic to convicted criminals who had future prospects of employment or reform, who were very young or who were mentally or physically ill. Their handling of reprieves and pardons rested on a notion of degrees of guilt which was at the heart of a highly flexible system of justice which had served England well for many decades.[80]

But how far did this system as a whole retain the confidence of the poor and middling ranks throughout our period? We cannot consider this problem without confronting the argument Douglas Hay has set out that the law was used by the ruling class of the eighteenth century as an instrument of 'gross coercion' and that this coercion was merely masked by a rhetoric of 'majesty, justice and mercy'. 'The private manipulation of the law by the wealthy and powerful', he declares, 'was in truth a ruling-class conspiracy in the most exact meaning of the word . . . the common assumptions of the conspirators lay so deep that they were never questioned and rarely made explicit.'[81] We have already made clear our conviction that English society in this period cannot readily be interpreted in class terms. John Langbein has pointed out some of the difficulties about accepting Hay's thesis in this respect. He has also stressed the strengths of the alternative conventional explanation to Hay's for the explosion of capital statutes in the latter part of our period. In this line of argument, originally conceived by Leon Radzinowicz, the English gentry clung to the death penalty as a lifeline against crime. Their aversion to professional policing sprang from deeply rooted fears of centralisation and absolutism, which had been given shape by the recurrent spectre of the exercise of arbitrary state power in the 1650s, the 1680s, the 1730s and the 1760s. Langbein has also remarked upon the primitiveness of the criminal law with regard to offence definition: the English 'lacked general definitions, especially for larceny and embezzlement, with the result that they were constantly having to add particulars in order to compensate for the want of generality'.[82] In short there is no need to suppose a conspiracy in order to explain the new legislation. Moreover Peter King's account of the administration of the law relating to property theft throws much light on who used the law and for what purposes. He finds labourers and middling men, as we have seen, playing important decision-making roles within the judicial system. He describes the criminal law as 'a multi-use right within which the various groups in eighteenth-century society conflicted with, cooperated with and gained conces-

---

[80] King, *Historical Journal*, XXVII (1984), 34–51.
[81] D. Hay, 'Property, Authority and the Criminal Law' in Hay, Linebaugh, Thompson, pp. 17–63.
[82] Langbein, *Past and Present*, XLVIII (1983), 96–120.

sions from each other'. In view of his evidence it is hard to see the law at this time as the tool of a particular class.[83]

Hay's arguments have most force when they are applied to some particular aspects of the gentry's rule in the countryside. 'The game laws', he argues 'united the two great preoccupations of the landed ruling class in one knot of emotion: field sports and justice tended to merge in their minds, and often, in the end, to mean the same thing.' He has shown how, in the war between the Pagets of Beaudesert Hall on Cannock Chase and the poachers of nearby villages between 1750 and 1800, the game laws were used, with the co-operation of local gentry but largely unscrupulously, to protect the Pagets' deer, game and rabbits. Neighbouring JPs, who were avid sportsmen themselves and who kept their own parks or were sweetened by a supply of doe from the Beaudesert estate, convicted numerous men under the summary procedure which had been open to the magistracy since 1671. Few of them recorded their convictions in court, so we have no statistics of the scale of this campaign. But the correspondence of the Pagets' estate stewards indicates that the family brought at least eighty poaching prosecutions in the years 1750 to 1765 alone. That was fifteen times, Hay calculates, the number of prosecutions in those parishes at quarter sessions and assizes, by all prosecutors, for all other thefts in the same years.[84]

Severe execution of the game laws was certainly not peculiar to Staffordshire. P.B. Munsche has estimated, on the basis of the certificates that were returned to sessions in Wiltshire in comparison with the gaol calendars for the county, that there may have been approximately 1500 convictions for game offences there in the second half of the eighteenth century.[85] John Beattie has traced the steady trend away from court hearings and in favour of summary convictions in Surrey and Sussex between the 1660s and the 1780s. There is also evidence that the rural magistracy became increasingly intolerant of practices once sanctioned by custom like gleaning and wood gathering. Wiltshire conviction certificates for the period from 1740 to 1790 show that fines and even terms of imprisonment imposed for collecting fuel were becoming common.[86] This subject requires much fuller investigation. Yet at the same time the Hanoverian gentry's more blatant activities to protect their own property must be seen in the perspective of their general respect for the formalities and technicalities of the law. Such

---

[83] King, *Historical Journal*, XXVII (1984), 51–8. See also the review articles by T.C. Curtis in *Social History*, V (1977), 671–3 and J. Styles in *Historical Journal*, XX (1977), 977–81.

[84] Hay, Linebaugh, Thompson, pp. 189–253.

[85] P.B. Munsche in Cockburn, pp. 224–5; see also P.B. Munsche, *Gentlemen and Poachers: The English Game Laws 1671–1831* (CUP, 1981).

[86] Beattie, *Past and Present*, LXII (1974), 78–9: J.A. Sharpe, 'Enforcing the Law in the Seventeenth-Century English Village', in V.A.C. Gatrell, B. Lenman, G. Parker (eds.), *Crime and the Law: the Social History of Crime in Europe since 1500* (London, Europa, 1980), pp. 105–6.

activities were the unacceptable face of their guardianship of the rule of law as a whole.

A major source of the gentry's control, E.P. Thompson has argued, was 'the symbolism of their hegemony'.[87] This symbolism was most evident at the assizes, a regular visible demonstration in one county capital after another of the authority of the state. Every aspect of the visit of the assize judges was drenched with spectacle: the sheriff's procession on the judges' arrival when the town bells rang in welcome; the scarlet robes and full-bottomed wigs of the courtroom; the black cap donned for pronouncing the death sentence and the white gloves worn at the end of a 'maiden assize' when there were no prisoners for execution. The leading gentry of the shire were at the centre of all this ritual. They sat with the judge as members of the commission of the peace. They dined with him in private when the day's proceedings were over. Douglas Hay has commented on the 'tests of the rhetorical power' of the judges, which punctuated the assize. At the start there was the charge to the grand jury, which was in fact directed as much to the county's gentry; at the end there were the sentences, which were customarily given in ascending order of severity. With the death sentence the judge, the justices and the thronged courtroom experienced 'the climactic emotion point of the criminal law – the moment of terror around which the system revolved'.[88]

Neither the theatricality of the assizes, nor the other less elaborate but equally potent public demonstrations of the gentry's 'cultural hegemony' noted by eighteenth-century historians, were new to the Hanoverian period. Indeed this hegemony, in its normal social expressions, was substantially complete by the early Stuart period or even, in some districts at least, by the reign of Elizabeth. Already, before the civil war, a select group of gentry dominated the government and politics of most counties from their mansions and manor houses. Their deer parks were well stocked and well fenced; their lavish christenings, weddings and funerals were exclusive social occasions; their segregated pews in church were comfortably furnished.[89] What changed over the period from 1600 to 1800 was that the intimacy which softened the impact of gentry rule was gradually lost as they withdrew from face to face relations with their servants and the people of their village. More and more, bailiffs came between landlords and their tenants. Coachmen defended them from casual encounters with countrymen. 'The theatre of the great', Thompson has written, 'depended not upon constant, day-by-day attention to responsibilities . . . but upon occasional dramatic interventions: the roasted ox, the prizes offered for some race or sport, the liberal

[87] *Social History*, III (1978), 158.
[88] Hay, Linebaugh, Thompson, pp. 27–8.
[89] A. Everitt, *The Community of Kent and the Great Rebellion* (Leicester University Press, 1969); Jenkins, *Making of a Ruling Class*, pp. 196–216.

donation to charity in time of dearth, the application of mercy, the proclamation against forestallers.'[90]

The inherent dangers, from the gentry's point of view, in the absentee landlord's rule from afar punctuated by an annual appearance is well summarised by the remarkable events at Westonbirt in Gloucestershire in 1716. When Sir Richard Holford, London businessman and Master in Chancery, visited the village at the end of August to hold his courts and feast his tenants, in the manner to which he had accustomed himself since his purchase of the estate in 1665, all appeared to be well. Holford, David Rollinson argues, saw Westonbirt as more than just a profitable investment. He believed he had a mission to civilise a community which, through decades without a resident squire, had become highly independent and intransigent. Yet it was only three months after his visit that he first heard, from one of his correspondents there, about the capital offence which was alleged against his bailiff George Andrews. Even as he interviewed the countrymen in August, a shaming ritual was being planned. In late September Andrews' buggery of a young farm servant was re-enacted before around 180 members of the neighbourhood in the village street and churchyard. This 'groaning', which was accompanied by plentiful food, drink and music, involved the birth of a mock child, who was baptised with the words of the Anglican sacrament and named George Buggarer. To Holford the incident was a riot, an act of collective insubordination with seditious overtones, but, try as he did, he could not break the solidarity of the neighbourhood sufficiently effectively to mount a convincing case against the villagers in court.[91]

The incident at Westonbirt illustrates how the rural populace, steeped in the symbolic forms of plebeian culture, could show their antagonism to the Hanoverian state. The most shocking aspect of the villagers' behaviour, in Holford's eyes, was their 'counterfeit and ridicule' of 'the rights and ceremonies of the church and our established religion'. The blasphemous baptism turned the episode from a simple shaming ritual against an individual into a wholesale critique of gentry hegemony. Squire and parson, squire and bailiff, manor and church: the ideologies and institutions of exterior control received public mockery. The baptism expressed the collapse of Anglican control in a village where, as an agent of Holford's had put it in 1703, the people 'do not live under any government at all'. We should not assume that Westonbirt was necessarily an irreligious community but it was certainly one where people saw the ceremonies of the Church of England in terms of an alien culture. How had it come about that church and people in that Gloucestershire village were so alienated from each other?

[90] *Journal of Social History*, VII (1974), 390.
[91] D. Rollinson, 'Property, Ideology and Popular Culture in a Gloucestershire Village 1660–1740', *Past and Present*, XCIII (1981), pp. 70–97.

The church, with its clergy who were often intimate members of the village community and its apparatus of ecclesiastical discipline, had been a potent source of order in late medieval England.[92] In the century between Henry VIII's break from Rome and the civil war the close association between religion and political obligation remained a fundamental precept.[93] Yet the ultimate impact of the English Reformation was divisive rather than cohesive, fatally weakening the role the church was able to play in the defence of order. Rejecting ritual, visual imagery, even song, the reformers put all their emphasis on the printed word and its interpretation in sermons and catechisings. 'Well', says the ignorant man in Arthur Dent's *Plain Man's Pathway*, 'I cannot read and therefore I cannot tell what Christ or Saint Paul may say.'[94] The mass of the people were never persuaded to see life's travails in terms of the workings of God's providence or to accept the link between sin and misfortune that was so central to protestant theology.[95] Nor did the doctrines of election and damnation become fixed in their minds. This is not to say that all the poor were irreligious. Margaret Spufford reminds us in this volume that theological debate was sometimes very lively among the humble and she has written elsewhere about the authenticity of the religious experience of some of the poor. Yet the fact remains that the successful revivalists of the future were evangelical Arminians like John Wesley and General Booth. The critical factor in the failure of the protestant reformers was their repression of traditional culture, which hastened the intellectual polarisation which has been sketched above.[96]

The achievement of the puritan minority in the decades between 1560 and 1640, Patrick Collinson has argued, was a reinforcement of conservative social values and objectives. Recent research has made us familiar with the godly communities of Elizabethan and early Stuart England. It has brought alive the intense spiritual life of villages like Brampton Bryan, Fawsley, Ketton, Tarvin and Warbleton and towns like Cranbrook, Dorchester and Rye.[97] Yet the zeal

---

[92] P. Heath, *The English Parish Clergy on the Eve of the Reformation* (London, Routledge, 1969); C. Haigh, 'Anticlericalism and the English Reformation', *History*, LXVIII (1983), 391–407; R. Houlbrooke, *Church Courts and the People during the English Reformation* (OUP, 1979); M. Bowker, *The Secular Clergy in the Diocese of Lincoln* (CUP, 1968).

[93] C.S.R. Russell, 'Arguments for Religious Unity in England 1530–1650', *Journal of Ecclesiastical History*, XVIII (1967), 201–26.   [94] Cited in Collinson, p. 236.   [95] Thomas, pp. 78–112.

[96] Burke, *Popular Culture in Early Modern Europe*, pp. 207–86; Wrightson, pp. 166–73, 206–21; Collinson, pp. 238–9.

[97] For Brampton Bryan, Ketton and Dorchester see Collinson, pp. 164–70, 272; for Fawsley see A.J. Fletcher, *The Outbreak of the English Civil War* (London, Edward Arnold, 1981), p. 36; for Tarvin see R.C. Richardson, *Puritanism in North-West England* (Manchester University Press, 1972), pp. 122–4; for Warbleton see J.J. Goring, *Church and Dissent in Warbleton* (Warbleton and District History Group, 1980); for Cranbrook see P. Collinson, 'Cranbrook and the Fletchers: Popular and Unpopular Religion in the Kentish Weald', in P.N. Brooks (ed.), *Reformation Principle and Practice* (London, Scolar Press, 1980), pp. 173–202; for Rye see Fletcher, *A County Community*, pp. 117–20 and 'Puritanism in Seventeeth-Century Sussex', in M.J. Kitch (ed.), *Studies in Sussex Church History* (University of Sussex, 1981), pp. 145–52.

with which men conducted their search for moral reform in such places must not blind us to the tensions inherent in such a task. 'The puritans who composed the godly community were mentally and emotionally separated', writes Collinson, 'by their radical estrangement from conventional society and its mores and by the fervour and strength of their own exclusive fellowship'. Where the puritan way showed itself at its most demanding, at Sir Nathaniel Barnardiston's Ketton in Suffolk for example, the result was not so much a separation of the godly as a forcible separation of the ungodly.[98]

Collinson has suggested that, in the first phase of English protestantism, the hard way of faith and behaviour remained 'effectively voluntary, a matter of taste and choice'.[99] The majority, it seems clear, opted to reject the daunting prospect of spiritual effort and growth. Then came civil war and all the political turmoil that it produced, damning religious enthusiasm in the view of most men of substance. The Restoration church settlement, passed through parliament in the midst of a strong social reaction against sectarianism, gave Anglicanism a political connotation which it has never subsequently entirely lost.[100] With the exclusion of those who were now labelled dissenters, the lifeblood of protestant evangelisation was drained away long before the task of converting the whole nation had been completed. All that most countrymen had learnt was attendance at church on Sundays as a social duty. What was striking in the later Stuart period was the failure of the parish clergy to impose anything further in the way of religious observance. John Pruett's study of the Leicestershire clergy indicates widespread apathy towards weekday services and catechising. The parson of South Kilworth made a valiant attempt in 1718 to bridge the cultural divide: he prevailed on the village youngsters to come to his house 'under the notion of teaching them to sing' but as soon as he slipped in a doctrinal lecture they stopped attending.[101] The Toleration Act of 1689 undoubtedly encouraged neglect of Sunday worship. Bishop Secker's visitation of the diocese of Oxford in 1738 brought many reports of habitual non-attendance among the 'poorer sort'. Archbishop Herring's visitation of the diocese of York in 1743 revealed much the same picture.[102]

The pastoral resources of the church had been enhanced by the enormous improvement in the quality of the clergy between the 1580s and the 1630s. The professionalisation of the clergy, however, had removed that familiarity with local custom and tradition which was the strength of the medieval priesthood.[103]

[98] Collinson, pp. 187, 268, 273.   [99] Collinson, p. 241.
[100] R.A. Beddard, 'The Restoration Church', in J.R. Jones (ed.), *The Restored Monarch* (London, Macmillan, 1979), pp. 155–75.
[101] J.H. Pruett, *The Parish Clergy under the Later Stuarts* (University of Illinois Press, 1978), pp. 115–18.
[102] A.D. Gilbert, *Religion and Society in Industrial England* (London, Longman, 1976), pp. 8–12.
[103] R. O'Day, *The English Clergy: The Emergence of a Profession* (Leicester University Press, 1979).

The parish clergy had become outsiders. More and more blatantly, though few could boast their wealth, they adopted and proclaimed the gentry's life style.[104] They joined them as magistrates on the county benches, prompting that conception of a fusion of roles which was expressed by the contemporary term 'squarson'.[105] The Hanoverian parson was not seen, by and large, in George Herbert's ideal terms as the representative of the people before God and of God before his people, but rather as one in authority who was a provider of certain rites of passages. His rituals were taken into popular thinking in a distorted or edited form. 'The church', E.P. Thompson has commented, 'had ceased to engage with the emotional calendar of the poor'.[106] It had shorn itself first of the magical affiliations of late medieval catholicism, then of the puritan evangelical tradition which between 1560 and 1660 breathed so much life into its institutions and objectives. Thereafter it was left high and dry, unwilling to offer the discipline and moral supervision which puritan clergy had prized so highly, out of touch with the people and vulnerable to the kind of cynical mockery which we have seen was perpetrated at Westonbirt.

Viewed in this perspective, the forcefulness of Douglas Hay's argument that order in Hanoverian England necessarily rested more on an ideology of the law than on the pastoral efforts or Sunday sermons of the clergy becomes apparent.[107] The church had become an arm of the state and the strength of the state was that it rested upon an idealisation of the law which was shared between gentry and people. Several of the essays in this book illuminate this idealisation of the law. It acted as a check upon the disruptive violence which sometimes characterised the feuds and factionalism inherent in the gentry's attempt, described by Anthony Fletcher, to use office to advance their own prestige.[108] It underlay the patriarchal political theory of the seventeenth century which, Susan Amussen shows, 'provided a means to maintain order when it was most threatened'.[109] It deeply influenced the tactics and behaviour of both drainers and fenmen. The successful drainage schemes, Clive Holmes argues, were those backed by parliamentary legislation: fenmen accepted the force of statute 'and the theory of parliamentary sovereignty that sustained it'. Yet Holmes also demonstrates how, through the practical experience of service on sewers juries, many fenmen acquired a legal and political consciousness that enabled them to fight the drainers on their own ground.[110]

Some laws, particularly those concerning use rights and what were seen as customary privileges, did not have the people's respect. There were complex

---

[104] G. Holmes, *Augustan England: Professions, State and Society 1680–1730* (London, Allen and Unwin, 1982), pp. 83–114.   [105] Obelkevich, *Religion and Rural Society*, pp. 274–5.
[106] *Journal of Social History*, VII (1974), 392.   [107] Hay, Linebaugh, Thompson, pp. 29–30.
[108] Below pp. 97–109.   [109] Below pp. 196–205.   [110] Below pp. 174–95.

struggles in this period over alternative definitions of property rights and these were conducted both within and beyond the framework of the law. But attacks on specific abuses were rarely generalised into a critique of authority or the law as a whole.[111] In this respect the law bridged the divorce of cultures that ran through society. Yet, when that is said, we must be clear that the law did not provide a system that simply worked of its own accord. The crux of Stuart and Hanoverian social relations was gentry hegemony; the means of the gentry's rule was through a system of law to which they subjected themselves because they were supremely well placed to use it to protect their own interests.[112] But hegemony could only be sustained by the constant exercise of theatre and concession. There was no question of the total subordination of the people, or reaching down to dominate them at the threshold of their individual experience.[113] The vitality of popular culture precluded that. 'The fabric of authority', Hay has stressed, 'was torn and reknit constantly.' The ideology of the law did not endure because it was wholly or invariably enforced. Its strengths were its elasticity and its generality. The courts dealt in terror but also in mercy, they involved wide participation and the enforcement of common ideals of behaviour. So long as the general idea of the rule of law held firm, individual defiance and dissent could be regarded as the action of rogues and criminals. It was the reservoir of belief in the idea throughout society that made this ideology so effective.[114]

(iii) THE EXTENT OF DISORDER

An impressive array of work in recent years has broadened and deepened our understanding of the nature, sources and extent of disorder in this period. From general surveys, monographs, articles and theses, we are beginning to have a much surer sense of some of the main features of what the authorities might have termed 'disorder'. Needless to say, however, there are still some important limits to our knowledge. The records of courts, ecclesiastical and lay, present problems familiar to all historians of crime. Most notable is the question of the relationship between the recorded level of incidents and what was actually occurring. The problem of the 'dark number' of events neither reported nor proceeded against presents very considerable problems for any historian who wishes to assess the extent and frequency of disorder of particular kinds. The vagaries of the judicial system and of the procedures of arrest, prosecution and trial discussed above,

---

[111] Brewer and Styles, p. 15. See also M.J. Ingram in Cockburn, p. 116.
[112] Thompson, *Whigs and Hunters*, pp. 262–9.
[113] *Social History*, III (1978), 156–65.
[114] Hay, Linebaugh, Thompson, pp. 55–6.

and the difficulties of recognising certain kinds of disorder, such as riots, from the legal record, where they might easily be disguised as charges of theft and assault, are other well-established problems. As a recent writer has noted, 'charges of theft and assault, often brought against a few people, can hide a riot by a whole crowd'.[115]

The record of indictments is a blunt tool to gauge the level and nature of disorder within a society. John Beattie's study of crime in Sussex and Surrey has offered one attempt to examine the number and nature of riotous offences as reflected in the indictment record for the period 1660–1800. He notes, however, that in rural areas the number of indictments for these offences are 'too few in most years' to undertake any meaningful examination of levels and trends. The whole of the urban parishes of Surrey, including the Borough of Southwark, produce only a handful of indictments for riotous offences in the late seventeenth century and, in spite of some higher peaks in the 1720s and 1760s, this was to fall to an average of only about one or two indictments a year by the late eighteenth century. Such small totals – a tiny fraction of the total number of indictments – illustrates some of the problems in attempting to estimate the extent of disorder in most of the period we are considering.[116]

Other factors, too, confuse attempts at a picture of the degree of 'disorder' in a society. It is, for example, not merely that the relationship between the 'dark number' of incidents and the recorded incidence of events is difficult, if not impossible, to ascertain. The relationship between these two elements cannot be considered as constant. Changes in legal processes or their instruments; in the reactiveness of the authorities to particular concerns; in the prominence of certain categories of event through the intervention of the actors themselves, for example, through litigation, petitions or disturbances; or in the degree of enforcement attempted by those in authority – to mention only the most obvious – can all alter the balance between the two. Beattie, for example, noted that a sharp rise in the average number of indictments for riotous offences in Surrey in the early 1720s may well have been the result of the insecurity of the early Hanoverian government acting with greater severity than usual to repress any signs of discontent at a difficult time. Certainly, there is some evidence that one of the most notorious pieces of capital legislation in the eighteenth century, the 'Black Act' of 1723, was passed within the context of a Jacobite scare.[117] John Morrill and John Walter show here that the perceptions of contemporaries can

---

[115] A. Charlesworth (ed.), *An Atlas of Rural Protest in Britain* (London, Croom Helm, 1983), p. 4. See also Sharpe, ch. 3 and J. Stevenson, *Popular Disturbances in England, 1700–1870* (London, Longman, 1979), pp. 11–16.   [116] Beattie, *Past and Present*, LXII (1974), 66–7.

[117] See Beattie, *Past and Present*, LXII (1974), 72–3; for the 'Black Act' see Thompson, *Whigs and Hunters* and its review by J. Styles in *Historical Journal*, XX, 4 (1977), pp. 978–9.

easily confuse the issue of how much actual disorder was taking place.[118] The concern over vagrancy in the 1590s, over sectaries and dissenters in the mid-seventeenth century and over Jacobites in the eighteenth century were only some of the most obvious manifestations of the way in which what people thought was occurring makes it difficult to form an accurate appreciation of reality. As a result, it is not easy to assess accurately whether the amount of disorder had increased or merely the sensitivity of the authorities.

The press, including periodicals such as the *Annual Register* and the *Gentleman's Magazine* are a staple source for records of disorder in the eighteenth and nineteenth centuries, but their patchier and more spasmodic presence for the period before 1695 creates problems for an understanding of the extent of disorder in the sixteenth and seventeenth centuries. For example, the civil war and its aftermath saw a relaxation of control of the press and printing, probably unprecedented hitherto. As a result there was a flood of newsbooks, pamphlets and other printed materials which may themselves distort our perceptions of events in comparison with other, apparently more sedate, periods which were, fortuitously, less well publicised. There were inevitable regional variations in coverage. In the early eighteenth century, for example, few places outside London had more than one newspaper, and even then the chances of an incident being recorded were extremely difficult to gauge. Outside the capital, reporting was both patchy and inconsistent. The overall growth of the press itself provides a difficulty, in that it is possible to know more about events in the 1760s than, say, the 1580s. Hence one of the major difficulties, for example, in determining the changing incidence of food or enclosure disturbances over the period between 1500 and 1800 is the variation in the availability of newspaper sources. Even after they became well established, provincial newspapers bore few of the characteristics of the local newspapers that we know today. Local news, even by the end of the eighteenth century, formed a very small component of newspapers which were largely devoted to advertisements or to reprinting material from the London papers.[119]

Official and private papers are also extremely treacherous. In general terms, government records provide information only on the more serious incidents – or, more accurately, those incidents perceived to be serious by those in authority. On those occasions when we can correlate other sources to those of central government records, it is clear that only a small fraction of incidents were brought to the attention of central government. There is certainly evidence that JPs in the early modern period might refrain from reporting disturbances in their locality to the central government for fear of admitting their failure to maintain order in their

---

[118] Below, pp. 147–50.   [119] Cranfield, *The Press and Society*, especially chs. 1, 2, and 7.

own backyard and of the consequences that might ensue from the intervention of the central government or its agents.[120] After 1660 such intervention could take the form of the use of regular troops and, in the case of a serious rising or rebellion, the employment of special commissions and judicial processes, with all the potentially damaging and disruptive effects they could have upon local sensibilities and relationships.[121] This fear of the 'collateral damage' which the use of the sledgehammer of the central government involved often made local authorities wary of an overhasty or premature reporting of incidents which might elicit such a major response. Whether such feelings operated universally or continuously through this period is a difficult question to answer. Were Tudor magistrates more ready to report to central government about local disorder than their Hanoverian counterparts or not? Did the bloody suppression of successive Tudor rebellions, the experience of civil war and the notoriety surrounding the suppression of Monmouth's rebellion have an effect upon how magistrates regarded the use of the troops or a call to central government to intervene? It is difficult to be certain on all of these points, but there is little doubt that there is ample evidence of the reluctance of local authorities to seek outside assistance, and of their desire, at almost any cost, to deal with local outbreaks of disorder through their own resources.[122]

Equally, there is evidence that in seriously threatening situations, especially those with which the local authorities did not sympathise, local governors would overcome their reluctance. In some circumstances, rumour and panic could lead to the translation of fears of disorder into reports of their actuality. In the appropriate atmosphere, meetings and relatively peaceful demonstrations might be depicted as serious 'riots', 'rebellions' or 'insurrections'. As the pioneer historians of popular movements pointed out some years ago, such descriptions do not take us very far towards an understanding of often complex and sophisticated forms of popular direct action. The careful sifting of evidence about what such phrases represent has become the stock-in-trade of historians who want to form an accurate appreciation of the realities of particular events. Indeed, as John Walter has shown in his study of the Oxfordshire Rising of the 1590s, the fear of popular disorder could result in what amounted to little more than a 'clandestine gathering of less than a handful of conspirators who disbanded for lack of support' being raised into the status of a minor rebellion by the Tudor authorities as well as by subsequent historians.[123] Similarly, the events

---

[120] Charlesworth, *Atlas of Rural Protest*, p. 4
[121] See, for example, T. Hayter, *The Army and the Crowd in Mid-Georgian England* (London, Macmillan, 1978), pp. 20–34; P. Rock, 'Law, Order and Power in Late Seventeenth- and Early Eighteenth-Century England' in S. Cohen and A. Scull (eds.), *Social Control and the State* (Oxford, Martin Robertson, 1983), p. 195.
[122] Sharpe, pp. 76–7.   [123] *Past and Present*, CVII (1985).

at Westonbirt in 1716, discussed above, were blown out of all proportion by Sir Richard Holford, while a drunken undergraduate prank in the Oxford of the 1740s, because of its use of Jacobite rhetoric, could attract the attention of central government.[124] The engagement of the attention of 'great men' or powerful interests could mean that even relatively obscure incidents were recorded or could leave a legacy either in case law as fresh interpretations of offences or on the statute books as new capital crimes.

The reaction of the first tiers of local authority, constables, clergymen, JPs and even Lord-Lieutenants might be critical in determining whether 'disorderly' offences were proceeded against or recorded at all. Yet these were people subject to complex and often conflicting pressures. Keith Wrightson has vividly de-scribed the increased burden imposed upon the local officials of Elizabethan and early Stuart England. But this effort produced no regular or even pattern of enforcement. The effective implementation of the decrees of central government was conditioned by the patchy distribution of JPs, particularly in counties far from London. Moreover, Wrightson argues, 'even where magisterial activity intensified, it might be sporadic and pulsating rather than regular, distorted by local rivalries and factionalism, or highly selective in its application'.[125] The uneven character of enforcement perhaps more than anything else conditions the degree to which we can form an accurate picture of the extent of disorder in this period. While local, judicial and court records have a great deal to offer us, they can prove deceptive and misleading. The material always suffers from the defect that it is a record of processes and procedures rather than of events.[126]

Memoirs, diaries and private papers present their own problems of accuracy and bias. In many cases the only such records we have come from the educated classes. Although many were clearly well informed and sensitive to the situations around them, they often reflect characteristic prejudices which limit their value in providing evidence about people's beliefs and intentions. As a result they are frequently more useful as evidence of attitudes among the governing classes themselves than of those of the classes they seek to describe. A particular problem lies in the paucity of first-hand accounts by the participants in disturbances themselves much before the end of the eighteenth century. Moreover, to the extent that it can be sustained that there was a growing separation between the plebeian and patrician cultures, it can be argued that those most likely to be doing the recording of plebeian events were the more likely to ignore, misrepresent,

---

[124] Stevenson, *Popular Disturbances*, pp. 25–6.
[125] Wrightson, pp. 151–5; also his 'Two Concepts of Order' in Brewer and Styles, pp. 21–46 and Sharpe, pp. 74–8.
[126] Sharpe, ch. 3; R.A.E. Wells, 'Counting Riots in Eighteenth Century England', *Bulletin of the Society for the Study of Labour History'*, XXXVII (1978), pp. 68–71.

distort or completely fail to understand them and that we are already on the way to the 'opaque society' where the activities of the majority of the population were as likely to arouse incomprehension, condescension – even ridicule – as fear. Survivals of witch beliefs and occasional persecutions were to become in the eighteenth century occasions to distance the patrician from the plebeian culture. Students of eighteenth-century popular culture have suggested that much of the task of historians is to decode the actions, rituals and ceremonies of the common people. Thus the rediscovery of the 'people', often associated with the 'nativist' and 'folklorist' movements of the nineteenth century, has become a central concern of contemporary historians of popular movements in the pre-industrial period.[127] A recent study of customary society in the eighteenth and nineteenth centuries, arguing that for the common people born between the late middle ages and the advent of national teaching in the late Victorian period little had changed in terms of beliefs and outlook, has suggested that: 'much of the customary framework within which were conducted the social and economic relationships of the English rural community during Hardy's lifetime had been transmitted forward from the later Middle Ages and early modern period to the eighteenth and nineteenth centuries when, far from being a scattered collection of pictur-esque "survivals", it remained, at least for the greater part of the Hanoverian and Victorian period, an essential context for the community, informing the lives and experiences of both the labouring poor and the rural elite alike'.[128]

Amidst these discrepancies of outlook and attitude, it is remarkable how few opportunities we have to chronicle in detail or with any accuracy the incidence of disorder in particular areas or localities. The most ambitious attempts to map or itemise the extent of, for example, land or food riots have proved themselves limited by many of the constraints indicated above. Even where we have first-hand accounts through diaries and local records, it remains difficult to assess the typicality of their evidence.

(iv) THE NATURE OF ORDER

Order in this period rested on the family and household, on schooling and apprenticeship and on the formal and informal institutions of control in the parish. Relations between husbands and wives, parents and children and heads of households and their dependents and servants were deemed to be central to the

---

[127] Thompson, *Social History*, III (1978), pp. 154–65; Burke, *Popular Culture in Early Modern Europe*, pp. 23–4. In the case of witchcraft, there is the useful case study by P.J. Guskin, *Eighteenth Century Studies*, XV (1981), pp. 48–71.

[128] B. Bushaway, *By Rite: Custom, Ceremony and Community in England, 1700–1880* (London, Junction Books, 1982), p. 1.

maintenance of a well-regulated society. The supreme authority of the husband in marriage was clearly stated in law, in theology and in contemporary writing. There was considerable pressure for wives to live up to the models of modesty and obedience set out for them.[129] The assertive, quarrelsome, scolding, extravagant or immodest woman was perceived as a threat to the social order and as such was to be subject to supervision at home and, if necessary, to intervention and correction by the community in which she lived. While it was the first responsibility of the head of the household to chastise and correct wayward wives and other dependent women, public scrutiny and pressure, whether through the formal channels of the secular and ecclesiastical jurisdictions or the informal sanctions of the community, could also be employed. Although illicit sexual activities, including adultery, were traditionally subject to the ecclesiastical courts some justices, particularly in the period between 1600 and 1660, showed a considerable interest in moral reformation. In 1650 adultery temporarily became a capital offence although there is little evidence that even the lesser penalties of the statute were enforced.[130] Where formal sanctions failed, or sometimes to accompany them, popular action could publicly humiliate those in breach, or seen to be in breach, of the norms of the community. Cuckolded husbands might find themselves pointed at by neighbours, with index and little finger extended to symbolise the invisible cuckold's horns thought to grow on those whose wives were unfaithful. Ram's horns might be hung on the couple's door as a stronger deterrent or members of the village might resort to the shaming rituals of ducking or the charivari described here by David Underdown.[131]

The household was the major vehicle of discipline in the early modern period. It consisted, typically from the upper ranks of society through to the middling ones, of parents, children and servants. As head of the household, the adult male possessed, in theory, absolute power over wife, children and servants, who were enjoined to practise obedience. With late marriage as the norm, a very large proportion of the population could expect to spend a considerable period of their lives in a condition of dependency. Service – in the household, in husbandry, as an apprentice to craftsmen or tradesmen – was thus the fundamental source of

---

[129] Wrightson, pp. 90–2; L. Stone, *The Family, Sex and Marriage in England* (London, Weidenfeld, 1977), pp. 195–202; K. Davies, '"The Sacred Condition of Equality" – How Original were Puritan Doctrines of Marriage?', *Social History*, V (1977), 363–79; R. Houlbrooke, *The English Family, 1450–1700* (London, Longman, 1984), pp. 96–119.

[130] K. V. Thomas, 'The Puritans and Adultery: the Act of 1650 Re-considered' in D. Pennington and K. V. Thomas (eds.), *Puritans and Revolutionaries* (OUP, 1978), pp. 257–82; S. Roberts, 'Fornication and Bastardy in Mid-Seventeeth Century Devon: How Was the Act of 1650 Enforced?' in J. Rule, *Outside the Law: Studies in Crime and Order 1650–1850* (University of Exeter, 1982), pp. 1–20.   [131] Below, pp. 123–32.

social training.[132] Adolescents and youths were seen by many as the primary instigators of disorder. Youthful illicit sex, and other aspects of personal misbehaviour that could produce a breach of the peace, were regarded as a sign of the failure of household discipline.[133]

As Susan Amussen shows in this volume, commentators recognised the problem of the extent of a husband's authority over his wife. She was dependent on him yet she was also joined with him in the government of the household. Conjugal love, economic interdependence, mutual recreation and common religious experience in practice modified and qualified the husband's theoretical dominance. Ample evidence of quarrels, adultery, scoldings, desertion, even wives beating their husbands, reflects a much more complex set of relationships than moralistic writing leads one to expect. Yet marriage was, as Ralph Houlbrooke has reminded us, an 'unequal partnership': there was no divorce in the modern sense of the word; the law of property was stacked against wives; the common law allowed a man to beat his wife; it punished her adultery not his.[134] Personal temperament, affection and social pressure might mitigate this situation, but there is no question that the head of the household was envisaged as the linchpin of family discipline.

The evidence of diaries and autobiographies suggests that the 'power and authority over children', which William Perkins saw as the defining characteristic of parenthood, was viewed in this period in terms of care and anxiety about children's upbringing and welfare. Obedience certainly was regarded as a child's duty. It was instilled by precept and catechism but it was probably in most cases enforced more by emotional pressure than by physical punishment. References to corporal punishment of children at home are sparse and they indicate that it was only employed occasionally and reluctantly.[135] There may have been a gradual softening of attitudes towards child discipline during our period, but there is no more reason to posit a dramatic change from severity to indulgence than there is to allege a massive shift in the emotional content of parent–child relations.

It seems clear that masters felt much less inhibited about beating their servants than their children. Samuel Pepys was quite matter of fact about how he dealt with his footboy in June 1662 when his wife and the maids complained about him: 'I called him up and with my whip did whip him till I was not able to stir . . . so to bed, with my arm very weary.' He beat one of his footboys eight times in two

---

[132] P. Laslett and R. Wall (eds.), *Household and Family in Past Time* (CUP, 1972), pp. 125–203.
[133] S. R. Smith, 'The London Apprentices as Seventeenth-Century Adolescents', *Past and Present*, LXI (1973), 149–61.
[134] Houlbrooke, *The English Family*, 118–19; Wrightson, pp. 92–104; below, p. 201.
[135] Wrightson, pp. 108–18.

years.[136] Noting how infrequently they appear in the record of presentments to and orders of quarter sessions, Ann Kussmaul has suggested that by and large 'the good order of servants was effected by their masters and not by the larger state'.[137] JPs sometimes specifically referred minor offenders to the correction of their masters.[138] Employers had an enormous hold over their servants who must often have submitted to corporal punishment in the knowledge that their master held the trump card of dismissal. When a JP bound over a Hertfordshire gentleman in 1679 for 'striking his maidservant two blows with a small switch' a colleague objected to the charge in a letter to the clerk of the peace. 'If there be no more in it', he wrote, 'I conceive 'tis justifiable for a master to correct his servant with a small switch, for that is a lawful weapon in law and of this opinion is Mr. Dalton and several other lawyers.'[139]

From the early seventeenth century onwards, the rural magistracy gave much attention to enforcing the apprenticeship of poor children, a system which served the purposes of providing work, care and discipline at the same time. Some apprenticeship indentures specified that the master was to administer appropriate corporal punishment and this was certainly generally assumed. But the time and trouble that county benches gave to allegations of cruelty to apprentices shows that they appreciated how narrow the line was between effective training and brutality. Victims of cruelty and oppression were often released from their masters. Justices were not however easily persuaded to discharge masters from their responsibilities towards their charges, when they received a complaint about the failure of an apprentice to fulfil his side of the contract. They tended to assume that the onus was on the master to cajole or compel an apprentice into line without overstepping the mark and descending into ill-usage.[140]

There were probably many who would have agreed with Marchamont Needham when he declared in 1663 that the scholastic state was the 'foundation of the other three states viz economical, ecclesiastical and political . . . all persons generally behaving themselves according to those principles their childhood was first seasoned with'.[141] The rise of formal schooling, with the expansion of the grammar and petty schools in the century between the Reformation and the civil war, added an important new dimension to the control

[136] R. Latham and W. Matthews (eds.), *The Diary of Samuel Pepys* (11 vols., London, Bell and Hyman, 1970–83), vol. III, p. 116.
[137] A. Kussmaul, *Servants in Husbandry in Early Modern England* (CUP, 1981), p. 33.
[138] e.g. G. Leveson-Gower (ed.), 'Notebook of a Surrey Justice', *Surrey Archaeological Collections*, IX (1888), 178.
[139] W.J. Hardy (ed.), *Hertfordshire Sessions Rolls* (Hertford, 1905), I, 299.
[140] e.g. W. Le Hardy (ed.), *Buckinghamshire Sessions Records* (Aylesbury, 1933), I, 150, 320, 540; NRO, Aylsham MS 347, C/s2/2, C/s1/45; Fletcher, *County Community*, p. 158.
[141] Cited by K.V. Thomas, *Rule and Misrule in the Schools of Early Modern England* (University of Reading, 1976), p. 3.

and training of children. For the benefactors of Tudor and Stuart schools were just as much concerned to inculcate religion, civility, good behaviour and obedience as academic learning. They often stated such objectives quite firmly in their foundation statutes. The schoolmaster's brief at this time was wide over both boarders and day boys: he was to prevent them from robbing orchards or breaking windows, from fighting or swearing, from growing their hair too long or going about dirty or untidy.[142] The grammar school offered, as Keith Thomas has put it, 'a distinctive model of authority, governed autocratically, sustained by corporal punishment and tempered by the master's mildness, incapacity or financial dependence upon his pupils'.[143] The birch was the symbol and daily instrument of the schoolmaster's rule over his charges. There appears in this sense to have been a sharp contrast, in the earlier part of our period at least, between the severity of discipline in schools and at home. It was from the mid-seventeenth century that objections to the excessive use of the birch became increasingly common. The new charity schools placed less emphasis on it than the established grammar schools and made less of enforced punctuality and rigid clock-keeping.[144]

A much smaller proportion of the population attended the universities of Oxford and Cambridge than local schools, yet for those who did so further education continued the moral and social training of earlier years. The statutes of Brasenose College, for instance, made provision for flogging undergraduates for minor offences from the early sixteenth to the late seventeenth century.[145] In the 1630s Archbishop Laud, as Chancellor of Oxford University, issued and saw enforced new statutes which were intended to maintain order, decency and formality in all aspects of the university's life. The Chancellor's Court, sitting weekly, examined offenders charged with night walking, prostitution, slander and assault.[146] Young gentlemen, those who would have to rule in their own counties, were thus only hurried forth into the adult world after prolonged training in right attitudes and behaviour. They left their adolescence behind them when they went down from the university or the Inns of Court. Although there was a degree of tolerated misrule at set points in the educational calendar, in both moral and social terms educational attitudes were generally rigorous. Despite this pupils very rarely offered deliberate resistance to those in authority over

---

[142] Wrightson, pp. 184–91; R. O'Day, *Education and Society, 1500–1800* (London, Longman, 1982), pp. 1–8; Stone, *Past and Present* XXVIII (1953), 42, 47, 51–2; A.J. Fletcher, 'The Expansion of Education in Berkshire and Oxfordshire 1530–1670', *British Journal of Educational Studies*, XV (1967), 51–9. [143] Thomas, *Rule and Misrule*, p. 14.
[144] Thomas, *Rule and Misrule*, pp. 9–12; O'Day, *Education and Society*, p. 201.
[145] L. Stone, *The Crisis of the Aristocracy* (OUP, 1965), p. 35.
[146] K. Sharpe, 'Archbishop Laud and the University of Oxford' in H. Lloyd-Jones, V. Pearl and B. Worden, *History and the Imagination* (London, Duckworth, 1981), pp. 146–9.

them. Education outside the home, experienced by many who were above the poverty line, reinforced the softer discipline of parents and drove into men's minds the concepts of order and obedience upon which stability rested.

English society throughout our period remained predominantly rural and most men lived out their lives in the close-knit world of the village. That world came under severe stress in the decades from the 1590s to the 1640s, under the impact of dearth and plague together with the poverty and vagrancy which was accentuated by a rising population. The intensification of administrative over-sight of village life in those decades was prompted partly by central initiative and exhortation and partly by moral panic of the kind suggested by John Morrill and John Walter.[147] Sermons at assizes and quarter sessions contained vivid images of disorder and corruption. The capacity of justices of the peace, though, to impose strict control of petty theft and casual personal violence, let alone of the moral and social life of the poor, was strictly limited by the realities of how local government worked. We have seen already how much it depended upon partici-pation by villagers. Keith Wrightson has commented upon the tension that existed between 'two concepts of order': between, that is, the attempt to impose from outside higher standards of social discipline and the need to maintain neighbouring relationships. Neighbours who tried to execute the law when they held parish office were often accused of malice or of being 'too busy'. Many constables, inhibited by personal considerations, made little or no effort to pursue the agenda of matters laid before them in charges at quarter sessions and in the articles which they were sometimes expected to peruse before they made their presentments. It was hard for JPs to make parish officers understand the necessity to enforce conformity to an impersonal standard of legally defined order when the process of enforcement was itself liable to cause contention and disorder in the communities in which they lived.[148]

From 1660 quarter sessions papers for many counties become steadily less informative as local government settled into a routine that required only nominal magisterial oversight and the arbitration of disputes between parishes and individuals. The tempo of regulation had always depended to a great extent on the initiative of justices living in a particular neighbourhood. With the formalisation of petty sessions in many counties this became even more the case. But how far this meant that the battle to improve and reform the behaviour of the poor had been lost or abandoned has yet to be established. It seems likely that in closed parishes, where a select vestry of village notables were responsible for poor law administration, a more regular and effective form of control was

---

[147] Below, pp. 147–52.
[148] Wrightson in Brewer and Styles, pp. 21–46; Wrightson, pp. 157–9; Sharpe in Gatrell, Lenman and Parker (eds.), *Crime and the Law*, pp. 97–119; Sharpe, pp. 183–4, 223 n. 54.

achieved in the late seventeenth and eighteenth centuries than had been possible previously.[149]

Between 1500 and 1800 there was an unprecedented growth in the population of English towns. In the first two centuries of our period, Peter Clark and Paul Slack have argued, towns underwent major economic and political changes 'which transformed and to some extent vitiated traditional urban life'.[150] Charles Phythian-Adams's analysis of crisis in Coventry between 1518 and 1525 indicates one possible pattern of consequences when long-term economic decline was followed by the sudden coincidence of a local slump, high food prices and a national trade depression: an insurrectionary riot and radical criticism of misgovernance.[151] Paul Slack's examination of poverty in early Stuart Salisbury shows how intractable the problem could prove to be. But, while the rulers of early modern towns failed to have any decisive impact on the basic problem of poverty, they did become more skilled in dealing with its consequences. From the seventeenth century, greater expenditure on poor relief, new and better-supervised institutions and a slackening of population growth permitted a containment of some of the tensions and pressures of the Tudor period.[152] One of the main reasons for this may have been the strength and cohesiveness of the middling groups whose growing affluence enabled them both to operate as an effective governing sector and support the burden of poor relief.[153] It has been suggested that by the eighteenth century, in terms of their social order and general viability, towns were 'much less violent, criminal, and anarchic than their critics feared'. Although crime remained a serious cause of concern during the eighteenth century, per capita rates of indictments for crime appear to have been relatively low in towns. They do not reveal an intrinsic urban criminality.[154]

None the less, towns became from the mid-sixteenth century the most frequent locations for popular disturbances, particularly those associated with religious and political conflict, prices and labour disputes. J.A. Sharpe has shown that Colchester, for instance, witnessed at least half a dozen major disturbances between 1550 and 1750 and a number of other incidents of communal violence.[155] Neither there, nor elsewhere, however, does it appear that there was anything

---

[149] Wrightson and Levine, pp. 175–83.
[150] Clark and Slack (eds.), *Crisis and Order in English Towns*, p. 30.
[151] Phythian-Adams, *Desolation of a City*, pp. 51–67, 249–68.
[152] P. Slack, 'Poverty and Politics in Salisbury 1597–1666' in Clark and Slack (eds.), *Crisis and Order in English Towns*, pp. 164–203; P. Clark and P. Slack, *English Towns in Transition, 1500–1700* (OUP, 1976), pp. 124–5.
[153] P.J. Corfield, *The Impact of English Towns 1700–1800* (OUP, 1982), pp. 130–5; Clark and Slack, *English Towns in Transition*, pp. 121–3.
[154] Corfield, *Impact of English Towns*, pp. 144–5; J.M. Beattie, 'Crime and the Courts in Surrey, 1736–1753' in Cockburn, pp. 155–86.
[155] Sharpe, pp. 135–9; for other disturbances see Stevenson, *Popular Disturbances*, pp. 17–53.

approaching a breakdown of urban society. Most so-called 'riots' indeed reflected a process of negotiation and reciprocity in which demonstration, ritual and theatre were intermingled. There was a sense in which such riots confirmed the social order of urban England rather than offered a fundamental challenge to it.[156]

Nor does it appear that London was a complete exception. Certainly, it represented urban problems on a scale far larger than elsewhere. Living there was living in a world apart from the experience of the villages and small towns. London's growth and size was phenomenal, with a population rising from around 60,000 in the early sixteenth century to almost 750,000 by the middle of the eighteenth. By 1750 it was the largest city in western Europe and it contained 11 per cent of the total population of the country.[157] The capital was flooded each year by several thousand fresh, and often young, immigrants. E.A. Wrigley has characterised them as 'household servants of both sexes, apprentices and labourers . . . together with girls in trouble, younger sons without local prospects, fugitives from justice, those unable to find work, the restless and those attracted by the scale and consequence of city life'.[158] Large numbers of 'masterless men', together with the very scale of London's urban problems, meant that it repeatedly became the focus of anxiety about crime and disorder.[159] From the Tudor period through into the eighteenth century London was seen quintessentially as the haven of the professional criminal, its 'mob' a force to be feared for its interventions on issues of the day. Even London, however, did not witness a breakdown of urban society. Its crime and disorder remained within bounds which allowed the capital to continue to grow and expand.[160]

We are left with a powerful impression of a surprisingly stable society considering the fragility of the means of control. Neither patriarchalism nor the ideology of the rule of law rested in the end on anything more than persuasion and propaganda. Justice and good government in the village depended on the active co-operation of unpaid, annually appointed, amateurs who were always men looking in two directions. Magistrates faced many temptations to abuse their authority. The militia never became a formidable or arbitrary force. The central government lacked effective means of coercing local officeholders into

[156] See Thompson, *Social History*, III, (1978), pp. 158–65; Corfield, *Impact of English Towns*, pp. 160–5; Brewer and Styles, pp. 17–20.
[157] Clark and Slack, *English Towns in Transition*, pp. 62–81.
[158] Cited by G. Rudé, *Hanoverian London, 1714–1808* (London, Secker and Warburg, 1971), pp. 6–7.
[159] C. Hill, *The World Turned Upside Down*, (London, Temple Smith, 1972, pp. 32–4; Sharpe, pp. 111–14; G. Salgado, *The Elizabethan Underworld*, (London, Dent, 1977).
[160] Clark and Slack, *English Towns in Transition*, pp. 62–81; Corfield, *Impact of English Towns*, pp. 144–5; G. Rudé, *The Crowd in History, 1730–1848* (New York, John Wiley, 1964), pp. 47–65; V. Pearl, 'Change and Stability in Seventeenth-Century London', *London Journal*, V (1979), 3–34.

the enforcement of policies with which they were unsympathetic. In view of all this it may seem predictable that historians are coming to lay so much emphasis on the negotiations and cajolery which were always at the heart of early modern government. Further research is likely to refine our view of this pattern and perhaps reveal more fully the regional variations in obedience and orderliness that undoubtedly existed. There were pockets of persistent disorder: the Scottish borders at least until the middle of the seventeenth century; isolated stretches and parts of the coast in Sussex, at Portland and in Cornwall; the proto-industrial 'frontier', such as the mining areas of Kingswood and the Forest of Dean. Some such districts have begun to be explored but others still await their investigators.[161]

The contributors to this volume were given no editorial line. Our aim was to invite participation on aspects of the general theme from active historians who would bring to bear upon it a diversity of experience in the political, religious, social and economic history of the period. Without seeking to tie any of the contributors to any of the arguments contained in this introduction, which is solely the responsibility of the editors, we would venture to suggest that a degree of consensus does emerge on some central issues. A sense of the desire for order, despite the passions and quarrels that undermined it, of men's search for it and the anxiety with which they clung to it, runs through these essays.

Several of the essays emphasise the many facets of the propaganda of order, a theme that has been much explored elsewhere.[162] David Underdown suggests that the fascination with rebellious women in Elizabethan and early Stuart literature reflects uneasy feelings that too many existed. Susan Amussen considers the use by political theorists of the familial analogy to bind society together from top to bottom. John Morrill and John Walter, scrutinising the alarmist literature and hyperbolic language of the 1640s and 50s, show how the appeal to a basic fear of social and political breakdown was generally adopted in a period when the times were seen to be out of joint. Clive Holmes, reviewing the complaints of drainers and pleas of fenmen to a succession of regimes, shows how both are marked by an appreciation of changing assumptions and sensitivities at the centre. He indicates a local political consciousness which enabled both

---

161   See R.W. Malcolmson, 'A Set of Ungovernable People: the Kingswood Colliers in the Eighteenth Century' in Brewer and Styles, pp. 85–127; B. Sharp, *In Contempt of An Authority* (Berkeley, University of California, 1980) pp. 125–219; Hay, Linebaugh, Thompson, pp. 119–25, 167–81; G.J. Davies, 'Wreck and Plunder in 18th Century Portland', *Dorset Natural History and Archaeological Society Proceedings*, CIII (1981), pp. 1–4; R. Newton, 'The Decay of the Borders: Tudor Northumberland in Transition' in C.W. Chalkin and M.A. Havinden (eds.), *Rural Change and Urban Growth, 1500–1800* (London, Longman, 1974).

162   G.J. Schochet, *Patriarchalism in Political Thought* (OUP, 1975); W.H. Greenleaf, *Order, Empiricism and Politics, 1500–1700* (OUP, 1964); M.A. Judson, *The Crisis of the Constitution* (New Brunswick, Rutgers University Press, 1947).

sides in the fenland disputes to play tunes which time and again chimed nicely with current conceptions of order in London. C.S.L. Davies's reassessment of the Pilgrimage of Grace probes deeply into the puzzle of how, in a society so imbued with deference, such a huge number of people managed in the autumn of 1536 to rebel. His stress on its ideology – 'a fusion of religious values and a sense of communal property set against destructive spoliation' – enhances our understanding of the solidarity of the rising. What he has to say about imagery and rituals – the oath, the badge and banners, the Pilgrim's song – indicates some of the ways in which it was possible to inculcate a sense of order in the midst of disorder. Davies's vignette of the mob at Kendal insisting upon their priest praying for the pope during the weeks following the king's pardon, 'a reaffirmation and reinforcement of a rapidly disappearing cohesion', is an evocative instance of the anxious human responses that so often underlay the search for order.

One of the marks distinguishing early modern from industrialised and urbanised society is the lack of a concept of privacy. This striking finding of recent research, reaffirmed at several points in this volume, seems to be crucial to the enforcement of authority in our period. Taking a long perspective, Margaret Spufford argues that the attempt to control the more private aspects of people's behaviour was not specifically a puritan response but was rather a spontaneous reaction by those in a position to exert such control in times of demographic and economic stress. The essays by Susan Amussen and David Underdown indicate some of the forms that the assertion of a rigid system of gender and family relations took in the decades of greatest tension within the period with which we are concerned. Some women were seen as a visible threat to effective patriarchalism. Neighbours thought it proper to intervene in cases of domestic violence. Verbal insult was a currency of village life that could not be treated lightly. Anthony Fletcher's analysis of the checks imposed on casual talk about justices of the peace exposes the same attitudes and the same anxiety about the disruption that could begin with caustic language. People were never entirely safe from prying and reporting either at the alehouse bench or in their own homes at this time. But there was a rationale to this intrusiveness which we can perhaps appreciate by concluding, however tentatively, that the English people in the early modern period were not an ungovernable people. This is not to say of course that they were never intransigent or invariably docile.

1

Puritanism and Social Control?

M. SPUFFORD

One of the current received suppositions appears to be, put very crudely, that from the 1580s the group of more prosperous men who had always provided the officials to run village society, now labelled 'village puritan elites', were imposing a stricter moral code of behaviour, particularly on the poorer villagers. It is sometimes implied that this imposition was new. This tightening-up is reflected in the escalating number of cases of fornication, adultery, incontinence and, above all, illegitimacy, presented in the ecclesiastical courts. This essay is intended to examine this supposition and the assumptions about religious belief on which it rests for the late sixteenth and early seventeenth centuries and to compare this early modern period with the late thirteenth and early fourteenth centuries, which was in some ways demographically similar. The comparison should show whether the imposition of a stricter moral code of behaviour was indeed 'new'.

The main evidence for the escalating number of moral cases presented in the courts has been given by Keith Wrightson, who shows that nearly one-third of the cases of bastardy presented between 1570–1699 for Terling in Essex were brought between 1597 and 1607, and another notable group between 1613 and 1616. He calls this dramatic upswing 'an astonishing and, until recently, unsuspected aspect of the history of the period'.[1] Bastardy was very much an offence of the poor and obscure and even bridal pregnancy was increasingly presented for the poor. Martin Ingram, in his thesis on 'Ecclesiastical Justice in

---

[1] Wrightson and Levine, pp. 127–8. See also pp. 113–19, 132–3. This upswing was found elsewhere. P. Laslett and K. Oosterveen, 'Long Term Trends in Bastardy in England', reprinted and amended in P. Laslett, *Family Life and Illicit Love in Earlier Generations* (CUP, 1977), pp. 102 ff. See also D. Levine and K. Wrightson, 'The Nadir of English Illegitimacy in the Seventeenth Century' in P. Laslett, K. Oosterveen, R.M. Smith (eds.), *Bastardy and its Comparative History* (London, Edward Arnold, 1980), especially pp. 172–5.

Wiltshire, 1600–1640',[2] has done a very subtle analysis of presentments in the ecclesiastical courts. He shows that, in two parishes in the increasingly impoverished, populous and partly industrialised area of the county, 60 per cent and 75 per cent of the cases in which pre-nuptial pregnancy can be firmly deduced from the parish registers ended up by being presented in the ecclesiastical courts.

But in another pair of parishes where population pressure was far less great, on the sheep–corn uplands, either no cases or only 7 per cent of cases of pre-nuptial pregnancy were presented. He, too, demonstrates that presentment for fornication or conception out of wedlock was far more likely if the sinners were poor. The suggestion, very reasonably, is that at a time of increasing population pressure, immediately after the introduction of the new poor law, the village officials were afraid of the cost of bastards falling on the rates. This financial lever added, as it always so wonderfully does, an additional impetus to the moral fervour of these officials. This fervour stemmed naturally from their puritan beliefs, and their desire to impose godly discipline upon the unruly bottom of rural society, that mass of servants, vagrants and late Elizabethan poor which Peter Clark has christened the 'Third World' of the 1590s.[3] Peter Clark's 'Third World' appears to be approximately the same group as Peter Laslett's 'sub-society of the bastardy-prone'.[4] In the case of Terling, this moral fervour extended itself from the suppression of promiscuity into the suppression of alehouse keeping, always the recourse of the poor in times of great stress. The increase in alehouse cases there also ran between 1607 and 1625; again the initiative was taken by parish officers against the village poor, and the suppression was described as 'the very foundation of reformation'.[5]

Keith Wrightson suggests that we are witnessing a very important social change in the late sixteenth and early seventeenth centuries in which the increasing economic differentiation of village society was 'accompanied by a significant differentiation of attitudes and behaviour'. The manifestation of this was the willingness of the 'rich', the officeholders, of whom a high proportion happened also in Terling village to be the 'elect and chosen' of God, to present their lesser, and possibly also less regenerate, brethren in the courts. 'Custom', he writes, 'was on the retreat in Terling before changes in social attitudes which were to play a significant part in remoulding the pattern of social relationships in the village.'[6] This thesis is worrying for several reasons. The most important are

[2] M. Ingram, 'Ecclesiastical Justice in Wiltshire, 1600–1640, with Special Reference to Cases Concerning Sex and Marriage' (unpublished D.Phil. thesis, University of Oxford, 1976), particularly ch. 5 on 'Sexual Offences'.
[3] P. Clark, *English Provincial Society from the Reformation to the Revolution: Religion, Politics and Society in Kent, 1500–1640* (Hassocks, Harvester Press, 1977), pp. 155–7, 175–7, 235–44.
[4] Laslett, *Family Life and Illicit Love*, p. 107.   [5] Wrightson and Levine, pp. 134–6.
[6] Wrightson and Levine, pp. 140–1. See also pp. 115–16, 133–6, 156, 161–3.

these. The unwary student draws from it the implications, which are not necessarily in the protagonists' minds, first, that puritanism always, or normally, spreads from above through the village, that is, that it is imposed by the group of yeomanry, 'the elite', who fill village office as bailiffs, reeves, churchwardens and so on. So religious belief becomes, to the student, a by-product of social and economic position. It then follows logically that it is either forced on, or foisted off onto, the poorer members of village society, who are not themselves interested in religious belief, or concerned with doctrinal change. If they do take an interest they are assumed, without much hard evidence, like Peter Clark's 'Third World', to be interested in magic, and probably reactionary catholics.[7] Secondly, the emphasis on 'puritanism' as an instrument of social control leads in no time at all into a simplified equation of puritanism with social control.[8] Too many students of social history asked to discuss religion in the later sixteenth and early seventeenth centuries produce a discussion of 'the mechanics of social control' in the period instead. This essay is both an attempt to discuss the distortions involved in this approach and also an attack on the central theses from which these distortions stem.

It sometimes appears that many social historians think that religious belief is primarily about moral behaviour and social attitudes, rather than the relationship of the individual with the being he thought to be exterior, whom he described as 'God'. From this relationship, of course, his relationship with his group of co-'believers' and his moral attitudes stemmed, so there is indeed a strong connection. But this is different from not comprehending the centrality to the believer of his or her relationship with 'God'. In other words, the first great commandment comes before the second.[9] Secondly, I do not believe that we know enough about the diffusion of puritan or 'the hotter sort of Protestant'[10] or indeed, separatist, beliefs socially, to state or even suggest as a maxim that puritan beliefs were the prerogative of the yeomanry, enforced on a reluctant and

---

[7] Clark, *English Provincial Society*, pp. 155–7.

[8] It is interesting to note that although 'this mounting initiative in the prosecuting of religious offences was undoubtedly aimed at persons low in the social scale for the most part', such persons naturally predominated numerically in the village of Terling. Therefore it is not significant that 53 per cent of those presented for failure to attend church were overwhelmingly drawn from Category IV, which in Wrightson and Levine's analysis is made up of those charged on, or excused, duty on one hearth in 1671, since 51 per cent of Terling people fell into that category in any case: Wrightson and Levine, pp. 156 and 35. Other figures which the authors quote of proportions of obdurates, excommunicates, evil-livers and so on are indeed significant, but these figures should always be checked against the proportion in the group on the key tables on pp. 34 and 35.

[9] 'Jesus said, "the first commandment is this: Hear, O Israel: the Lord our God is the only Lord. Love the Lord your God with all your heart, with all your soul, with all your mind, and with all your strength. The second is this: Love your neighbour as yourself. There is no other commandment greater than these" ' (St Mark, 12, vv. 29–31).

[10] P. Collinson, 'A Comment: Concerning the Name Puritan', *Journal of Ecclesiastical History*, XXXI (1980), 484.

possibly promiscuous mass of humbler villagers. Thirdly, I do not believe that
the attempt to enforce 'godly discipline' was in any sense new, or unfamiliar, in
the late sixteenth century.

I do not propose to discuss the first issue, about the nature of religious belief
and the social attitudes flowing out of it, at all in this essay, although it is my most
fundamental point. Evans-Pritchard, in his conclusion to *Theories of Primitive
Religion*, wrote of anthropologists in a way that is not inapplicable to social
historians.

As far as a study of religion as a factor in social life is concerned, it may make little
difference whether the anthropologist is a theist or an atheist, since in either case he can
only take into account what he can observe. But if either attempts to go further than this,
each must pursue a different path. The non-believer seeks for some theory – biological,
psychological, or sociological – which will explain the illusion; the believer seeks rather to
understand the manner in which a people conceives of a reality and their relations to it.
For both, religion is part of social life, but for the believer it has also another dimension.
On this point I find myself in agreement with Schmidt in his confutation of Renan: 'If
religion is essentially of the inner life, it follows that it can be truly grasped only from
within. But beyond a doubt, this can be better done by one in whose inward consciousness
an experience of religion plays a part. There is but too much danger that the other (the
non-believer) will talk of religion as a blind man might of colours, or one totally devoid of
ear, of a beautiful musical composition.'[11]

The social historian also can, and should, take into account only what he can
deduce from ascertainable fact. But after that point, the non-believer's interpretations will vary from the believer's. Some current writing, ostensibly about
religion, sometimes does indeed seem to talk of religion as a blind man might of
colours.

My second point is that we need to know more about the social distribution of
puritan, or separatist, beliefs at the parish level to state that they were the
prerogative of one group of villagers over another. One or two, or even three or
four, case studies will not do to establish the norm, if indeed there was such a
thing. There are several types of argument to suggest that the 'poorer sort' may
have had their own religious convictions. Much the most general evidence is to
point out that in the sixteenth and early seventeenth centuries religion was 'news'
at the alehouse level, as well as in the inn, and, as such, hotly discussed amongst
mixed social groups. The earliest such case I have so far found is the delightful
one in 1538 when a former friar was accused of heresy. He had been at a
discussion at the 'Sign of the Bell' in Northampton at which the nature of the
sacrament of the altar was hotly debated. A certain 'Sir' Thomas was there, who
said it was 'only god his bodye', and when the ex-friar refuted this, a butcher of

---

[11] E.E. Evans-Pritchard, *Theories of Primitive Religion* (OUP, 1965) p. 121.

Northampton who was present said 'I saw this day the body of god present between a pristes hands.'[12]

Rather later, in 1553, an opposing line was taken by a lesser villager in Orwell in Cambridgeshire, who not only made an extremely rude gesture to explain his feelings about the reintroduction of the Mass, but also offered to hand round a ballad called 'maistres mass' in the alehouse.[13] Only a couple of years after that, in 1555, a half-yardlander, a 15-acre man of Willingham, walked to Colchester to refresh his soul with 'spiritual exercises'. In the inn overnight the husbandman of Willingham and a friend from St Ives tangled in debate on the divinity of Christ with a 'serving man' to a gentleman, two 'women gospellers' and a heretical joiner. The Willingham husbandman was so upset by his inability to argue his case in favour of Christ's divinity satisfactorily that he fully intended to walk to Oxford to seek council of Bishop Ridley and Mr Latimer, but, fortunately for his feet, met someone who satisfied his conscience in the 'mean season'. In the mid-seventeenth century, it was the regular habit of a group of men who marketed in Royston, and formed the seed-bed of a later congregationalist conventicle, to meet together and 'spend their penny in a private room, where without interruption, they might talk freely of the things of God'.[14] This was probably a more select and less argumentative group; but a whole range of cases has been found in which the alehouse formed a meeting-place at which anti-puritan songs could be sung, and anti-puritan feelings expressed or, alternatively, conventicles could be held. Some of the protagonists were very poor, like the Kentish tiler who rejoiced at the suspension of local puritan preachers.[15] So theological debate was very lively amongst the humble, not only the village oligarchs, in the sixteenth century. Women, tilers and husbandmen were involved. And cheap print was addressed to them, right from the opening of the *Stationers' Company Registers* in 1557.[16]

A much less general and more convincing proof is a monetary one. If humble people are prepared to put cash down in support of their beliefs, it seems likely that these beliefs mattered to them. And there is ample proof that the humble were indeed willing to put cash down. The involvement of individual smallholders, husbandmen, shopkeepers, craftsmen, artisans and their wives who all contributed in the 1470s to the building of the splendid new church at Walberswick in Suffolk has recently been demonstrated. At nearby Blythburgh, the contributors to the building of the church included both a small shopkeeper

[12] M. Bowker, *The Henrician Reformation: the Diocese of Lincoln under John Longland, 1521–1547* (CUP, 1981), p. 166.   [13] Spufford, p. 245.   [14] Spufford, pp. 244–5, 246–7.
[15] P. Clark, *The English Alehouse* (London, Longman, 1983), pp. 156–8. I am grateful to Mr Clark for letting me have access to this in page proof.
[16] M. Spufford, *Small Books and Pleasant Histories* (London, Methuen, 1981), p. 10.

and the madam of the brothel.[17] At Eye, the whole congregation passed the hat round in the early sixteenth century to make up the required sum for the foundation of a chantry.[18] Just as the people of the 1470s were willing to contribute substantial sums, in many cases worth a year's rent to them, so also two centuries later the Quakers were willing to pay the £20 fines originally designed to control Elizabethan recusants rather than to conform. In many cases, they faced total financial ruin. The case histories of individuals who were initially poor anyway can be traced through the Volumes of Sufferings, and the gradual distraint of their goods can be demonstrated until, as in one example, the final blow was struck and one man had two cows distrained, 'being all he then had'.[19]

The ultimate proof of religious involvement is surely the willingness to suffer martyrdom. No amount of external social pressure can account for a willingness to be burnt for one's beliefs. Therefore, the most striking piece of evidence in favour of the involvement of the humblest of the laity in the Reformation is the fact that over half the martyrs listed by Foxe whose social status was given were said to be agricultural labourers.[20] Of course these were the people most defenceless, and least likely to be able to retreat into exile.[21] In view of their martyrdoms, however, reformed beliefs do not appear to have been the preroga-tive of 'village elites'. Indeed, the distribution of reformed beliefs has not yet been adequately studied at the village level. No one, to my knowledge, has looked properly at the social backgrounds of the later Lollards, and this could be done with precision.[22] Meanwhile, it seems likely that Dr Bowker was right to characterise them as 'weavers and threshers'.[23] Nor have other, later groups of the 'hotter sort of protestant' been investigated sufficiently. I have found protestants of conviction throughout the strata of village structure in Cambridgeshire in the late sixteenth and early seventeenth centuries, but I have only worked in detail on five places.[24] This is not enough. I have also looked at the social distribution of post-Restoration dissent and have found that it certainly did not necessarily spread downwards. The deaf old fenwoman, a day-labourer

---

[17] C. Richmond, *John Hopton: a Fifteenth Century Suffolk Gentleman* (CUP, 1981), pp. 174–7.

[18] M. Cook, 'Eye (Suffolk) in the Years of Uncertainty, 1520–1590' (unpublished Ph.D. thesis, University of Keele, 1982), pp. 57–8.   [19] Spufford, p. 289.

[20] A.G. Dickens, *The English Reformation* (London, Batsford, 1964), pp. 266–7. The cases of a Suffolk agricultural labourer who would not receive the sacrament, and those of a husbandman and a linen-weaver who refused to hear Mass, all of whom were burnt, are discussed by Cook, 'Eye in the Years of Uncertainty', pp. 162–6.

[21] 'Nearly all of the 350 people known to have found refuge on the continent were gentlemen, merchants or clerics.' D.M. Palliser, 'Popular Reactions to the Reformation during the Years of Uncertainty, 1530–1570' in F. Heal and R. O'Day (eds.), *Church and Society in England: Henry VIII to James I* (London, Macmillan, 1977), pp. 43–4.

[22] J.A.F. Thomson, *The Later Lollards 1414–1520* (OUP, 1965), does not attempt this. Derek Plumb is doing so in a Cambridge Ph.D. now in progress.

[23] M. Bowker, *Henrician Reformation*, p, 146.

[24] Spufford, chs. 12 and 13, especially pp. 298–306, 320–44.

who was converted to Quakerism by the written word, was one proof of that. So also were the villages where dissent concentrated at the bottom of the social structure, or spread evenly through it. But there were other communities where dissent did make more appeal to the more prosperous. We simply do not know enough yet, and it would be unwise to generalise on the basis of less than a full examination of all the varieties of dissent across the whole of two contrasted counties of England. This has not yet been done.[25]

Individual case studies have, of course, been offered us. Terling, in Essex, with a living in the hands of the Mildmay family, provides one example of a village society which had an elite group of puritan officeholders in the 1620s.[26] On the other hand, the officeholders in the sixteenth century in the little Suffolk borough of Eye were divided between crypto-catholics, and those who tended towards protestantism.[27] Here are two conflicting examples; we will not know which is more 'normal' for different regions of the country until much more work has been done. Meanwhile, restraint seems highly necessary before religious belief of a particular bent is equated with any particular social or economic status at the top, or indeed, the bottom, of village society.

The hypothesis that the attempt to enforce 'godly discipline', particularly sexual discipline, on the poor was an innovation of the late sixteenth century suggests, reduced to the crudest possible form, that puritanism in the most practical terms equalled the greater enforcement of moral behaviour on the poorer villagers by the richer. It is demonstrated by an escalation of cases brought against the more humble in the ecclesiastical courts.

One way to test such a hypothesis is by removing one of the variables of the equation. Was puritanism a necessary condition for a greater enforcement of moral behaviour on the poor? The evidence for a catholic, post-Tridentine country would show whether there were similar developments in 'social control' at the end of the sixteenth century.[28] On the other hand, late thirteenth- and early

---

[25] Except by Vann, for the Quakers of Buckinghamshire and Norfolk, and for the initial leaders of the movement, 'the valiant sixty'. Amongst the latter, there were relatively large numbers of 'gentlemen' (11%) but over two-thirds (67%) were employed in agriculture and a quarter (24%) were 'husbandmen' as opposed to 'yeomen'. Amongst Quakers in general, the core of support seems to have been the yeoman and the wholesale traders, but, even so, early Quakers 'drew adherents from all classes of society except the very highest and the very lowest, ranging from the lesser gentry down to a few totally unskilled labourers'. R.H. Vann, *The Social Development of English Quakerism, 1655–1755* (Cambridge, Mass., Harvard University Press, 1969), pp. 47–87, especially pp. 55, 73, 74–5.

[26] Wrightson and Levine, pp. 154, 177–8.

[27] Cook, 'Eye in the Years of Uncertainty', pp. 275–6, and appendix E, pp. 290–1. The religious affiliation of about three-quarters of the officeholders is reasonably certain, and the occupational status of about half of them is known. 'Gentlemen' and 'yeomen', who were officeholders, tended to be catholic, whereas craftsmen who were officeholders tended to be protestant.

[28] F. Lebrun, *Histoire des Catholiques en France* (Toulouse, Privat, 1980), pp. 135–40, and bibliography, pp. 143–5, seems to provide an excellent point of departure for such an exercise.

fourteenth-century England is, in many ways, a period so parallel to sixteenth- and early seventeenth-century England that the inducement to see what happened then is high. This seems a much more possible exercise to an English economic historian. I have therefore chosen to look at English case studies for the late thirteenth and early fourteenth centuries.

Let me begin by underlining just how alike, in many ways, the sixteenth century and the thirteenth century were. Between 1550, when enough parish registers became usable, and 1650, the population of England rises very steeply indeed: it almost doubles, from a little over 3 million in 1550, to nearly 5.5 million in 1650, when it stabilises, or even sags. The very bad period of starvation in northern Europe from 1595–7 brought mortality crises in north and north-western England also.[29] The smaller farmers in the open, arable areas disappeared. The wage-labourers at the bottom of society saw a particularly disastrous fall in the purchasing power of their wages during the sixteenth century inflation: the wage-labourer's wages bought him less food in 1597 than at any other point recorded between the 1260s, when the records open, and 1950.[30] The distress was immense: this is the background to Peter Clark's 'Third World' of the 1590s and its vagrants. It is also, incidentally, the background to the boom in alehouse licensing that Wrightson observed, and that Peter Clark has worked on. To set up an alehouse one only needed a bench or two, and some ale. It was one of the additional ways for the very poor to try and make a living without taking to the roads. This is also the background to the wealthy yeomen of Terling and their puritanism, for it was the wealthy yeomen who made a profit out of scarcity, since the small surplus they did have for the market earned them much more. Moreover, and it is not a minor point, they could afford to marry off their daughters: a dowry for them was conceivable, whereas for the small husbandman and for the labourer, it was not. Wrightson, Levine and Martin Ingram are all scrupulous in pointing out the connection between the dowryless state of, for instance, daughters of the poor, girls in service and the greater sexual licence allowed them. So, indeed, are the sub-literary 'chapbooks' dealing with courtship in the 1680s, which treat the lack of dowry, and the greater freedom of individual choice it allowed servants, as a known fact of life.

Why is the thirteenth century so demographically like the sixteenth century? Between 1086 and 1377, dates for which we have information which will yield estimates of inhabitants, the population of England rose even more steeply than

---

[29] R.M. Smith, 'Population and its Geography in England, 1550–1730' in R.A. Dodgshon and R.A. Butlin (eds.), *An Historical Geography of England and Wales* (London, Academic Press, 1978), pp. 204, 207, 213–14.

[30] E.H. Phelps-Brown and S.V. Hopkins, 'Seven Centuries of the Prices of Consumables, Compared with Builders' Wage-Rates' in E. Carus Wilson (ed.), *Essays in Economic History* (London, Edward Arnold, 1962), vol. II, p. 186.

between the mid-sixteenth and the mid-seventeenth centuries. It tripled, and possibly quadrupled, between the end of the eleventh century and the second quarter of the fourteenth century.[31] The peak then was between 4 and 6 millions. In fact, population then was certainly as high as it was in the mid-seventeenth century, and was possibly even higher than at any time until the mid-eighteenth century.[32] This dramatic rise in population inevitably had its effect on the size of holdings: between 1275 and 1400, 85 per cent of the holdings of recorded size being conveyed in the manor of Hakeford Hall at Coltishall in Norfolk were of less than 5 acres, and the median was only 1 acre.[33] It is sinister, but not in the least surprising, that in, or after, the years of bad harvests between 1248 and 1309–19 on five manors of the Abbey of Winchester in counties as widespread as Somerset, South Hampshire and Berkshire, it was the poorer villagers, with fewest beasts and, by inference, little or no land, whose heirs paid the fines due on death.[34] So people were starving to death in the south of England, and not just the north-west, in the thirteenth century, even before the great series of harvest failures of 1315–22 which checked the population explosion, and have been described as 'a dividing line in the history of the medieval countryside'.[35] The landless, the wage-labourers, of course, suffered worse: the wage-labourer's wages bought him less food in 1316–17 than at any other date, except 1597, between the 1270s and 1950. The manor courts of the period were run by a village oligarchy. Dr Smith has convincingly demonstrated this for the two Suffolk manors of Rickinghall and Redgrave in the thirteenth century.[36] The tenants who then filled the local government and administration jobs, that is, the chief pledges, reeves, jurors, constables, bailiffs and ale-tasters, came from families with over ten acres. These do not sound large holdings, but they were, in terms of the sort of size of holdings in the east of England which the thirteenth-century population explosion had created. In fact, these officeholders were the exact equivalent of their sixteenth-century counterparts.

On the very extensive estate of the Abbey of Halesowen, in Worcestershire, recent investigation has again shown that the composition of the village oligarchy was exactly the same as on Dr Smith's Suffolk manors. Men from

[31] M.S. Campbell, 'Population Pressure, Inheritance and the Landmarket in a Fourteenth Century Peasant Community' in R.M. Smith (ed.), *Land, Kinship and Life-Cycle* (CUP, 1985), pp. 87–134, and E. Miller and J. Hatcher, *Medieval England: Rural Society and Economic Change, 1086–1348* (London, Longman, 1978), pp. 28–33, 57–8, 60–1.

[32] Smith in Dodgshon and Butlin (eds.), *An Historical Geography*, p. 207.

[33] M.S. Campbell in Smith (ed.), *Land, Kinship and Life-Cycle*, p. 106.

[34] Miller and Hatcher, *Medieval England*, pp. 57–8.

[35] Miller and Hatcher, *Medieval England*, pp. 60 ff.

[36] R.M. Smith, 'English Peasant Life-Cycles and Socio-Economic Networks: A Quantitative Geographical Case Study' (University of Cambridge Ph.D. thesis, 1974), pp. 9, 392. See also Edward Miller, *The Abbey and Bishopric of Ely* (CUP, 1951), pp. 252–5, for a description of the election and responsibility of reeves, bailiffs, haywards and beadles in the thirteenth century.

poor families were never elected to public office between 1270 and 1400: the yardlanders, men with 25 to 30 acres, dominated the community, and Dr Zvi Razi writes, 'the major public offices in Halesowen were filled by members of a small group of families which dominated and led the village community for generations'.[37] So we may, I think, take it as firmly established that village officials in the sixteenth and seventeenth centuries, and in the thirteenth and fourteenth centuries also, were drawn from exactly the same groups of the more prosperous landholders and craftsmen in village society. This variable did not change over time.

On the two Suffolk manors of Rickinghall and Redgrave, between 1259 and 1319, or in a period economically comparable with the 1550s and 1620s, the manor courts were extending their interest to more and more people who had not previously come within their orbit. There was a dramatic increase in the volume of court business, presented, of course, by the village oligarchy.[38] But the motive was not financial. Although the number of cases increased over threefold, the level of fines sank with people's inability to pay, and more and more tiny fines reflected the poorest tenants attempt to make a living by baking bread and, just as in the late sixteenth century, by brewing ale. Exactly the same phenomena are found on yet three more Winchester manors in Wiltshire and Hampshire at the end of the thirteenth century.[39] So at the end of the thirteenth century, as at the end of the sixteenth century, running an alehouse was the way out for the poorest. Meanwhile, available land was increasingly concentrating in the hands of fewer people, just as in the late sixteenth century.[40] Also just as in the late sixteenth century, the thirteenth-century 'yeoman' could afford to give his daughter a dowry, so she could marry. The lesser man could not.

So when does religion, and the morality that should flow from it, come into this comparative picture? The thirteenth century, following the fourth Lateran Council of 1215 was, in some ways like the sixteenth century, a century of moral reform, although this is not a parallel I would want to push too far. Not only the morals and good behaviour of the parish clergy, but also those of the laity, were being tightened up. Indeed, in the diocese of Lincoln from 1253 onwards, there was considerable ecclesiastical pressure to see that Sunday was properly observed. By the mid-fourteenth century, Sabbatarianism was even extended

---

[37] Z. Razi, *Life, Marriage and Death in a Medieval Parish: Economy, Society and Demography in Halesowen, 1270–1400* (CUP, 1980), pp. 77–9, 122–3.
[38] R.M. Smith, 'English Peasant Life-Cycles', pp. 19, 43, 53. Dr Smith shows, for instance, that 66 fines worth 155/4d were paid in 1262, but that 213 and 273 fines worth 158/4d and 162/8d were paid in 1307 and 1309 at Rickinghall.
[39] A.N. May, 'An Index of Thirteenth Century Peasant Impoverishment? Manor Court Fines', *ECHR*, XXVI (1973), 389–402.
[40] R.M. Smith, 'English Peasant Life-Cycles', p. 175.

backwards into Saturday.[41] At the parish of Bardney in 1246, the nature of the faults enquired into on visitation were Sabbath and festival-breaking, wrestling and dancing, attendance at church – ales and playing at dice.[42] These all have a very familiar ring about them to the early modern historian.

The great difficulty in pursuing the parallels between the thirteenth century and the sixteenth century in a scholarly way is the absence of English archidiaconal records for exactly the period 1280–1320 which we need for a proper comparison with 1580–1620. The earliest surviving archidiaconal records are early fourteenth century.[43] There is indirect evidence on the effects of the archidiaconal courts and, indeed, the public dislike in which archdeacons were held. In 1215, one of the decrees of Lateran IV bothered to lay down the number of horses by which the archdeacon might suitably be accompanied on visitations.[44] In 1237, archdeacons were made responsible for 'overseeing the holy vessels and vestments' in the parishes.[45] A public debate was actually held in the University of Paris on the tricky, and obviously highly emotive, subject of whether an archdeacon could be saved. A metrical English satire of the late thirteenth century is a satire on the consistory courts. Its chief complaint is the particular severity shown towards poor men in the church courts. The only sins which are even mentioned in it are sexual ones, and the subject of grievance is the concentration by the courts on sexual behaviour. Furthermore, the author resented what he felt to be the way the clergy always took the part of women against men. He described the setting and personnel of the court, and wrote:

No ordinary man can lead his life [untroubled], however skilful a workman he may be, the clergy so lead us astray. If I happen to go with a girl, I must be brought up before them and learn their law, and I shall regret their advice . . . I wish to escape injury, and flee from my companion; they did not care what the offence was so long as they had it . . . If I am accused in their document, then I am slandered; for they make many men to blame for the misfortune of women . . . Moreover six or seven summoners sit there, misjudging men according to their natural ability, and bring out their register. Herdsmen and all men's servants hate them, for they put every parish in pain . . . A beadle rises, and proceeds with his rod, and shouts out loudly so that the whole court should hear, and calls Maggie and Moll. And they come, as covered with dirt as a moorhen, and shrink for shame, and are ashamed in men's presence, those unbeautiful ladies.[46] One of them begins to shriek, and soon screams out, 'if my lies have anything to do with it, it shall not happen so, everyone

[41] M. Gibbs and J. Lang, *Bishops and Reform, 1215–1272* (OUP, 1934), pp. 95–130, 143, 158–73.
[42] D. Owen, *Church and Society in Medieval Lincolnshire* (Lincoln, History of Lincolnshire Committee, 1971), pp. 110, 120.
[43] See Lincolnshire Archives Office, D. and C. A/2/24, *passim.* I am very grateful to Mrs Owen for this reference.   [44] Gibbs and Lang, *Bishops and Reform,* p. 99.
[45] Owen, *Church and Society in Medieval Lincolnshire,* p. 117. The parishioners were to provide the holy vessels and vestments required.
[46] This phrase is a comic inversion of a formula meaning 'lovely ladies'.

shall bear witness that you must marry me and have me as your wife'. . . I am chased like a dog at church and through market, so that I would rather be dead than live like this, to the sorrow of all my relations. In the consistory court they teach us trouble and wish that things should go from bad to worse for us. Then a priest as proud as a peacock marries us both; they bring trouble to us far and wide because of women's doings.[47]

The archdeacon described by Chaucer at the beginning of the *Friar's Tale* seems to have shared the same preoccupations.

> there was dwelling in my contree
> An erchedekene, a man of heigh degree,
> That boldely dide execucioun
> In punishing of fornicacioun,
> Of wicchecraft, and eke of bawderye,
> of diffamacioun, and avoutrye,
> Of chirche-reves, and of testaments,
> Of contracts, and of lakke of sacraments,
> Of usure, and of symonye also,
> But certes, lechours dide he grettest wo;
> They sholde singen if that they were hent . . .[48]

At the end of the fourteenth century, the Dominican John Bromyard (fl. 1390) picked up the theme, and complained that even when wealthy fornicators and adulterers had been sentenced to bodily punishment in the ecclesiastical courts, they would come in and offer bribes to bishops, archdeacons and court officials, and get off without pain whereas, he wrote, 'the "simple" on the other hand, may be seen doing their penance naked in church and market-place, with other humiliations'.[49] From the beginning of medieval homiletics in English, meanwhile, preachers waxed as eloquent as any Nicholas Bownde against 'wowynges', 'kyssynges' (secret), 'syngnges', gay array, 'nice chere' and all such 'thynges that beth forbode as dawnsynge of women and other open syztes that draweth man to synne'.[50] 'Lechery' and 'taverns' form two of the biggest index

[47] Attributed to the reign of Edward I (d. 1307), although the manuscript from which it is taken, MS Harl. 2253, fol. 70v. is of the reign of Edward II. Thomas Wright (ed.), *The Political Songs of England* (Camden Society, vol. VI, 1839), pp. 156–9. The text of this poem has been re-edited in R.H. Robbins (ed.), *Historical Poems of the XIV and XV Centuries* (New York, Columbia University Press, 1959), pp. 25–7. The editor dated it very precisely to 1307. He did not retranslate it. Since the translation made in 1839 was unsatisfactory, Mr A.C. Spearing has very kindly spent time to make the present translation. He tells me that some phrases (which I have queried) are very obscure. He would also date the poem to the early fourteenth century, but says alliterated poetry of this kind is 'notoriously hard to date accurately'. MS Harl. 2253 is usually dated 1330–40, but most of the poems in it could have been written at any time in the previous eighty years. I am much indebted to Mr Spearing for his help.

[48] N.R. Haveley (ed.), *The Friar's, Summoner's and Pardoner's Tales* (University of London, 1975), pp. 57–8: 'avoutrye' is adultery. Again, I am very grateful to Mrs Owen for this reference.

[49] G.R. Owst, *Literature and Pulpit in Medieval England* (CUP, 1933), pp. 247, 251–4.

[50] Owst, *Literature and Pulpit*, p. 384.

entries in G.R. Owst's book on *Literature and Pulpit in Medieval England*, just as the harlot's door and the alehouse bench filled the thunderous warnings of the 'godly' chapbooks of the 1680s.

But all this, though suggestive, is not the kind of quantifiable proof we need of a parallel situation of escalating moral presentments in the late thirteenth and early fourteenth centuries with the late sixteenth and early seventeenth centuries, although we do have evidence of escalating presentments for all types of offence bringing in more and more people to the manor courts. The surviving ecclesiasti-cal presentments of faults amongst the records of the Dean and Chapter of Lincoln for the 1330s and 1340s heavily emphasise, in a way most familiar to all sixteenth-century ecclesiastical historians, presentments for adultery and forni-cation, and even for harvest working on Sundays.[51] The dating is still too late for this purpose, however.

Yet even if the ecclesiastical records do not survive except in very small groups, there is still a possible way out. The manorial lord had a customary right to a fine on the marriage of a villein's daughter or, in lieu of this, a fine called 'leyrwite' or 'childwite' for her fornication or for her bearing of a bastard.[52] Whereas the ecclesiastical records do not survive, manorial records do. The relationship between the two sets of record is obscure. One suggestion is that when an active manorial lord was exacting fines for incontinence and bastardy, the local archdeacon might well concentrate on other villages, and vice versa. Certainly in an ecclesiastical peculiar, this jurisdiction seems to have been left to the lord of the manor. Occasionally, an unfortunate villein might fall into the, presumably inevitable, confusion between two jurisdictions and be fined twice for the same sin, as was the Cottenham man Henry Waveneys fined for wasting his lord's substance in the 'court Christian' in the manor court, after he had been presented for adultery with women in Dry Drayton and Cambridge in the archdeacon's court.[53]

Whatever the relationships between the two jurisdictions were, and presum-ably they may have varied from diocese to diocese, archdeaconry to archdeaconry and even manor to manor, it does not seem very likely that

---

[51] Owen, *Church and Society in Medieval Lincolnshire*, p. 121.

[52] There is a difference of opinion amongst medievalists about whether a leyrwite fine indicates the bearing of a bastard outside marriage, possibly even outside 'troth plight' or betrothal, or whether it is a fine on fornication only. For my purposes, this distinction does not matter, since early modernists are drawing attention to increasing prosecution of bridal pregnancy, bastardy and fornication. A count of leyrwite fines together with childwite, if they were separately taken, therefore gives a comparable figure of presentations for sexual misdemeanour, whether or not it resulted in the bearing of a child.

[53] J.R. Ravensdale, 'Deaths and Entries: the Reliability of the Figures of Mortality in the Black Death' in F.M. Page (ed.), *Estates of Crowland Abbey* (CUP, 1934), and 'Population Changes and the Transfer of Customary Land on a Cambridgeshire Manor in the Fourteenth Century', in R. M. Smith (ed.), *Land, Kinship and Life-Cycle*, pp. 197–226.

manorial lords were less exacting, when they had a right to dues, than ecclesiastical courts, since the rent-roll may be possibly as powerful an incentive as moral
fervour. It therefore seems to me valid to look at the studies that have been made
of fines taken for leyrwite and childwite in the late thirteenth and early
fourteenth centuries, and see how these compare with the rising number of
presentations for fornication, bastardy and pre-marital pregnancy[54] in the late
sixteenth and early seventeenth century.

Richard Smith has analysed in detail the marriage patterns, and also the
presentations for childwite of unmarried girls, on the manor of Rickinghall and
Redgrave, but unfortunately only for the short period from 1260–93.[55] We know
already that these girls were presented by jurors from the richest quarter of
village society. Smith found thirty-five girls fined at Rickinghall in this period,
and fifty-one at Redgrave. In both communities, the girls concerned commonly
came from families who were landless or deficient in land. They also frequently
came either from families presented for illegal brewing and baking, or were
themselves illegal brewers or bakers. Both of these activities were also signs of
poverty. The strongest link between these girls, however, was the number of
them who came from much larger families than normal. That is, they came from
families in which it was impossible, or nearly impossible, in a time of great
economic pressure, to find a dowry. Furthermore, few of them were able to
marry later.[56] At Redgrave, only a third of them eventually married; at
Rickinghall, only a sixth did so, and they usually only married some years after
their pregnancies. So we are entitled to say that in Suffolk in the thirteenth
century, the richest amongst the villagers were not inhibited from presenting the
poorest among the villagers for bearing illegitimate children, and that the
pressures which led to these illegitimacies were economic ones. The 'sub-society
of the bastardy-prone in English history' was not new to the sixteenth century.[57]
And the age of marriage of the very poor was late, or non-existent. The jurors
who presented these thirteenth-century girls were certainly aware that fornication was a sin, and one heavily punished by the ecclesiastical authorities, but
they cannot have been motivated by any spirit of 'election'.

The fullest case study that has been made of medieval marriage and illegitimacy is the recent one by Zvi Razi of Halesowen on the border of Worcestershire

[54] Wrightson and Levine, p. 127.
[55] R.M. Smith, 'English Peasant Life-Cycles', appendix H, pp. 454ff, and ch. 4.
[56] See however, the caveat entered by Dr Smith in his unpublished paper 'Some Thoughts on the
Social and Economic Content of Illegitimacy in English Rural Communities, in the Thirteenth and
Fourteenth Centuries', p. 16, where he suggests that merchets, or marriage fines, may only be taken
for girls with dowries, and therefore the marriage of dowerless girls may have gone unrecorded. I
am grateful to Dr Smith for lending me the typescript of this paper.
[57] R.M. Smith, 'Some Thoughts on the Social and Economic Content of Illegitimacy in English Rural
Communities', p. 20

and Shropshire.[58] Dr Razi shows that, on this huge manor of the Abbey of Halesowen, in the period from 1270 to 1348, before the Black Death, the numbers of women who paid leyrwite was very high indeed. For every two who married, almost one woman fornicated, or bore a child out of wedlock.[59] Again, there was an absolutely definitive connection between bastardy, or fornication, and poverty; 42 per cent of daughters from poor families were fined for fornication or conceiving out of wedlock, but only 10 per cent of daughters of rich families were fined for fornication or bearing bastards.[60] The reasons for fornication and the bearing of bastards were, as in Suffolk, not licentiousness, but poverty. Girls in Halesowen born to the families of yardlanders, 25- to 30-acre men, had dowries, married young and were at risk for only a short time. Girls born to poor families were often presented for stealing, gleaning and gathering firewood. They were dowryless, for fewer poor girls presented for sexual sins married than did the daughters of the better-off.[61] Some poor girls were even declared *persona non grata* and not allowed to stay in the village. Their families, in any case, were usually only there for one generation, unlike those of the landed.[62] A detailed breakdown of the figures for leyrwites for 1271 to 1348 shows that no significant attention was paid to the collection of leyrwites in the 1270s. From 1280 on, there was a general rise in the leyrwite rates up to the Great Famine, and then a decline and a rise again in the late 1320s and in the 1330s.[63]

But, as soon as the population pressure ended, and it became possible for girls with small, or no, dowries to marry in the second half of the fourteenth century, the number of leyrwites recorded in the court rolls fell sharply.[64] Truly, the medieval sermon writer was right in his analysis. In view of man's frailty, he says, God has permitted marriage, 'to lyve in Goddes law'

But mony wedd hem wyvys for her wordly goodes, for her grete kynne, other for ther fleschely lust: as, be a woman a pore wenche, and ther-wyth well condiciond, *abell of person, and have no wordly goodes and be come of sympell kynne the whiche may not avaunce here,* full fewe men covetyn suche on. Som had lever to take an old wedow, though sche be ful lothelyche and never schall have cheldren. And, fro the tyme that he hathe the mocke that he wedded her for, and felethe her breth foule stynkynge and her

---

[58] Razi, *Life, Marriage and Death*.

[59] See n. 52, above, on the dispute over the meaning of leyrwite fines. Dr Razi takes the leyrwite figures as indicating illegitimate births, p. 65.

[60] I have put together the figures for fornication and illegitimate births from Razi, *Life, Marriage and Death*, p. 66, in view of the doubt on terminology expressed in n. 52 above.

[61] See Razi's own reservation on figures for marriage drawn from merchet, p. 66, and n. 56 above.

[62] Razi, *Life, Marriage and Death*, pp. 66–9.

[63] Private communication from Dr Razi, breaking down the contents of his table 12, p. 67, by date.

[64] In the late 1340s, the collection of leyrwites again became insignificant. There was probably a high local rise in mortality amongst marriageable women in Halesowen in the period 1343–5, before the general mortality of 1348. This would have accounted for the fall in leyrwites before the Black Death. Razi, *Life, Marriage and Death*, pp. 41–2.

eyen blered, scabbed and febyll, as old wommen buthe, then they spend a-pon strompettes that evyll-getyn goodes. And sche shall sytt at home wyth sorowe, hungry and thrusty. And thus levythe they in a-vowtry, peraventure all her lif tyme. If a mayde be to wedde, the furste thynge that a man woll aske-what her frendes woll yeve to mary here wyth: and but they acorde ther in, . . . they kepe not of here. *It semeth, then, they wedden the goodes more than the womman. For, had not the goodes be, sche schuld goo un-wedded, as all day is seyne.*[65]

Although I cannot demonstrate with precision for more than one place that in the late thirteenth and early fourteenth centuries the number of presentations for sins of incontinence rose in the same pattern as the late sixteenth and early seventeenth centuries, these initial figures from Halesowen are suggestive. It would be highly unwise to suggest a strong correlation between population pressure, poverty and leyrwite prosecutions on the basis of this one place. But it certainly looks as if the topic, and its early modern parallels, deserves a further search for evidence.

What can certainly be established is that there was no new social division in the villages of late sixteenth-century England between officeholders and the poor they were willing to present. Medieval evidence from several places has shown that presentations for sexual immorality, whether to church or to manor court, were traditionally made by the richest villagers who filled local offices. They were presentations of the poorest families in village society, whose daughters were not just an incontinent and lecherous group, but simply a dowryless group. Late thirteenth- and early fourteenth-century society was affected by the same stringent economic pressures as late sixteenth- and early seventeenth-century society. Under them, the young behaved in the same way, with the same results. But we are not dealing with a 'third world' of the immoral poor, with the exception of girls who repeatedly bore bastards; nor are we necessarily dealing with a 'subculture' untouched by religious scruple or moral conviction. We are dealing with the poor and the dowryless girls, whose luckier peers became pregnant too, but whose fathers were in a position to pay a portion. The willingness of the 'rich', the officeholders, to present their poorer neighbours for sexual offences in the courts was not, as Keith Wrightson thought, new to the late sixteenth and early seventeenth centuries. Their 'ancestors' had done it all before. In both societies, sins of the flesh were thought of as sins: but the fact that the officeholders of Terling in the early seventeenth century also happened to think of themselves as the 'elect and chosen of God' was probably not fundamental to their actions, although their actions may have been lent extra fervour by their particular beliefs. I suggest that religion and religious belief are, in this

---

[65] My italics. This example is not dated by Owst, *Literature and Pulpit*, pp. 381–2, but it apparently echoes a sermon as early as the first half of the thirteenth century, and Bromyard echoes it in his *Matrimonium* of the late fourteenth century.

particular interpretation, a gigantic red herring. Puritanism was not necessary in the thirteenth century to bring about presentments like this: nor need it have been in the late sixteenth and early seventeenth centuries. The term 'puritan' has been removed from my hypothesis and yet without it, the rest of the equation does not collapse. May we not then question whether 'puritan' is a necessary term in the hypothesis?[66] I do not for one instant dispute that in any period, people of strong religious convictions will express these in rigidly held moral attitudes and actions, unless they happen to be antinomians. I do dispute that this situation was in any way peculiar to puritanism.

I have been arguing, in part, that there is a serious current danger of religious belief being equated with the practice of puritan 'godly discipline', and that it is very necessary to separate puritan beliefs, or the beliefs of the 'hotter sort of protestant' and, indeed, any other type of religious belief, from their moral application to everyday living. Religion cannot only, and solely, be equated with 'social control'. On the other hand, some social historians do not conceive of religion as primarily the recognition on man's part of an external and unseen power with whom he is in relationship, and who is entitled to obedience, reverence and worship, and secondarily with the moral attitudes stemming from this belief, and their effect on the community. I am, of course, perfectly prepared to agree that the moral attitudes of the believer have a profound effect on the community, and that they did so, in the late sixteenth century, in a way Wrightson and Ingram have demonstrated in the ecclesiastical courts. I would not be prepared to admit that this effect was in any way new, although we may, of course, be talking about one of those waves of reform and tightening-up that happen from time to time in both reformed and non-reformed countries in the history of the Christian church.

I have attempted to demonstrate that the lives of very humble people were affected in the late thirteenth century and that they were fined for adultery and fornication then, as in the late sixteenth century, more often if they were poorer. Finally may I extend the principle to its logical and possibly even risible conclusion. The Ten Commandments were themselves, regarded in this light, a prime instrument of social control. From the dating of the earliest version of them, possibly in the thirteenth century BC,[67] even the poorest Jews were liable, judging from *Deuteronomy*, to considerable and possibly unwanted interference in their lives if they coveted their neighbours' wives, or maidservants or actually committed adultery. To regard puritanism as exclusively to do with social control is to do it a gross injustice and to underestimate it. Further, to think or to imply that such social control was new shows a certain shortness of historical perspective on the part of the historians concerned.

[66] See above, pp. 42–3.   [67] J. Bright, *A History of Israel* (London, SCM, 1972), pp. 121–3.

2

Popular Religion and the Pilgrimage of Grace

C.S.L. DAVIES

In October 1536 an army of some 20,000 men drawn from the six northern counties of England confronted King Henry VIII's forces across the River Don. In form at least this was a popular rising: its 'grand captain', a hitherto unheard-of lawyer, Robert Aske; its members bound together not by feudal loyalties but by an elaborate oath. Its imagery was religious; the rebels called themselves 'Pilgrims', they carried banners of the Five Wounds of Christ and invoked God's grace and defence of Holy Church in their marching song. They demanded the rooting out of heresy, the restoration of recently dispossessed monks and nuns to their convents, an end to the despoliation, and even the renunciation of the recently asserted royal headship of the church. With the immediately preceding (and quickly suppressed) rising in Lincolnshire, the Pilgrimage of Grace constituted the only major armed challenge to the Henrician Reformation, that series of revolutionary changes otherwise implemented with the apparent acquiescence if not the outright approval of the English people.

Naturally a movement drawn from a vast tract of country from the Lincolnshire wolds to the Cumberland fells, and embracing all ranks of society, contained within it a number of contradictions. Nobles and gentlemen were prominent in the leadership, even though disclaiming any part in initiating proceedings and deferring to the nominal command of Aske. Secular concerns figured among the demands, and still more were hinted at in the various proceedings on a local level. Nobles and gentry were concerned about changes in the land-law represented by the recent Statute of Uses. Many of them resented the loss of ancient franchisal jurisdiction, and more distrusted the thorough rationalisation of the system of government being undertaken by the king's minister Thomas Cromwell. All groups protested, predictably, at taxation, many of the commons took the occasion to attack tithe-barns, demolish enclosures and demand lower rents. Historians have argued at length about the 'real' causes of the Pilgrimage: how far it was spontaneous, how far it was instigated from above, by nobles, gentlemen or clergy; whether the apparent emphasis on religion was merely a mask for more mundane interests; in short, whether the movement really can be seen in terms of a repudiation of the king's proceedings by a substantial part of his subjects.

I have myself argued on an earlier occasion that it is wrong to ignore the 'religious' dimension, to treat it merely as a 'cloak' for earthier aims.[1] Historians, I suggested, pull apart the various factors involved in a complex movement in the course of their analysis and set them in rank order; in the process they are inclined to forget that it is precisely the interaction and fusion of several grievances which make revolt possible. Dr Rachel Reid's remark, 'even if there had been no Reformation, there must have been a rising in the North about this time', is merely the exaggeration of a fairly common implicit assumption.[2] I contended that it was the historian's business to explain 'why the Pilgrims, whatever their other grievances, marched behind the Banner of the Five Wounds and, ostensibly at least, were prepared to fight for the defence of the church as they knew it', without, in so doing, underestimating or 'explaining away' the other factors involved. An understanding of the total situation was required, rather than skirmishing about the relative importance of various factors, none in themselves providing a sufficient explanation.

I stand by that article, though not by its every detail or shade of emphasis.[3] And I make no apology for returning to the subject. There has been a mass of work since that time which has emphasised especially the part played by nobles, gentlemen and clergy in stirring the revolt.[4] It has rather taken for granted the

[1] C.S.L. Davies, 'The Pilgrimage of Grace Reconsidered', *Past and Present*, XLI (1968), 54–76; reprinted in P. Slack (ed.), *Popular Protest and the Social Order in Early Modern England* (CUP, 1984), pp. 16–38.

[2] R.R. Reid, *The King's Council in the North* (London, Longman, 1921), p. 126.

[3] My main retraction would be on the question of harvests and economic conditions. I argued that while the harvest of 1535 had been bad, that of 1536 was less bad; and suggested therefore that had economic factors been sufficient explanation revolt would have happened a year earlier. I stand by the point that bad harvests do not generally produce revolt. Nevertheless the phrasing of the argument is too mechanical, and underestimates the cumulative effects of a 'less bad' harvest after a year of crisis for those who had to suffer them.

[4] A.J. Fletcher, *Tudor Rebellions* (London, Longman, 1968). M.E. James, 'Obedience and Dissent in Henrician England: the Lincolnshire Rebellion of 1536', *Past and Present*, XLVIII (1970), 3–78, esp. 45–9, and his many suggestive papers, reprinted in *Society, Politics and Culture, 1485–1640: Essays and Studies* (CUP, forthcoming). M. Bowker, 'Lincolnshire 1536: Heresy, Schism and Religious Discontent?', in D. Baker (ed.), *Studies in Church History*, (1972), vol. IX, pp. 195–212. See also her *The Henrician Reformation* (CUP, 1981), esp. pp. 147–56. R.B. Smith, *Land and Politics in the England of Henry VIII: the West Riding of Yorkshire, 1530–46* (OUP, 1970), ch. 5. C.A. Haigh, *The Last Days of the Lancashire Monasteries and the Pilgrimage of Grace* (Chetham Soc., 3rd Ser, XVII, 1969) and his *Reformation and Resistance in Tudor Lancashire* (CUP, 1975), ch, 9. S.M. Harrison, *The Pilgrimage of Grace in the Lake Counties, 1536–7* (Royal Historical Society Studies in History,

participation of the commons; or at least implied that their activation is a
relatively minor problem, that a judicious use of the normal muster mechanism
supplemented by cash and carefully sown rumour was enough to produce a
somewhat inchoate armed assembly which found itself rather surprisingly facing
a (somewhat similarly recruited) royal army. In doing so, it has obscured the
immediate impact of the revolutionary changes brought about, or apparently
threatened, by the implementation of the Royal Supremacy in the church, and the
massive distrust of the crown's motives which they engendered over a wide and
geographically, socially, and culturally, very diversified area of England.

Thanks to the thorough investigation conducted by the government after its
suppression, the Pilgrimage is by far the best documented of any sixteenth-
century English revolt. It would, indeed, make possible a number of 'in-depth'
(or 'thick description') studies of particular events on the level of Le Roy Ladurie's
Romans, if not of his *Montaillou*.[5] This is not the place for such an investigation.
But I would wish to press further the question of just what was involved in the
'religious' issue in 1536; and in doing so to throw some light on what is the key
question of the English Reformation, the apparent disparity between widespread
conservative religious commitment; and, in the event, the paucity of forceful
resistance to far-reaching change.[6]

The successful mobilisation of the commons, then, is the theme of this essay;
and not merely the initial mobilisation but the forging of a rather suprising and
often underestimated degree of solidarity. What might have been expected was
the sort of thing which actually happened in Lincolnshire.[7] There the initial
rioting, which began at Louth on 2 October 1536, spread rapidly in a fairly

---

XXVII, 1981). D.M. Palliser, *The Reformation in York, 1534–53* (Borthwick Papers, University of
York, 40, 1971), and *Tudor York* (OUP, 1979). G.R. Elton, 'Politics and the Pilgrimage of Grace' in
B. Malament (ed.) *After the Reformation: Essays in Honor of J.H. Hexter* (University of
Pennsylvania Press, 1980), pp. 25–56, reprinted in his *Studies in Tudor and Stuart Politics and
Government* (CUP, vol. III, 1983, pp. 183–215); my references are to the *Studies* version, G.W.
Bernard, *The Power of the Early Tudor Nobility: a Study of the Fourth and Fifth Earls of
Shrewsbury* (Brighton, Harvester Press, 1985). All of these authors and other friends have endured
discussions on the Pilgrimage. Dr Susan Brigden let me read her Manchester BA thesis (1973) on
'The Northern Clergy in the Pilgrimage of Grace: A Study in Resistance', and discussed Vicar
Kendall's London connections.

[5] E. Le Roy Ladurie, *Carnival in Romans: A People's Uprising at Romans 1579–80* (Eng. transl.,
London, Scolar, 1979), and *Montaillou* (Eng. transl., London, Scolar, 1978). This essay disregards
local variations; for which I plead in mitigation limitations of space and time. The general point I
am arguing does, I believe, hold true, with different degrees of emphasis, for Lincolnshire, all those
parts of Yorkshire so far studied, North Lancashire and the Lake Counties, in spite of the contrasts
in geography, economy, political and social structure between those areas. Durham and Northumberland remain shrouded in obscurity.

[6] I am aware of fighting a running battle through this essay with, especially, M.E. James, 'Obedience'
and G.R. Elton, 'Politics'. This is the more difficult because, as with the other authors cited in n. 4,
these interpretations differ from mine primarily in emphasis.

[7] For good succinct summary of these confusing events (with map), see Fletcher, *Tudor Rebellions*.
Dodds remains indispensable for detailed narrative.

restricted area. There was a lynching, the swearing-in of various gentlemen (willingly or otherwise), the march on the county capital, followed by a collapse on 11–12 October with the reading of a royal proclamation and the approach of a royal army under the Duke of Suffolk. No military confrontation took place, although Suffolk reported on 18 October that the country was still unsettled and hostile.

The main Pilgrimage presents an entirely different picture. The Yorkshire and Durham rebels not only occupied York itself (16 October 1536) and captured the royal castle at Pontefract (19 October), almost certainly with the connivance of its commander, Lord Darcy; they also proceeded to confront the Duke of Norfolk's and the Earl of Shrewsbury's troops across the River Don at Doncaster. They comprised a very substantial force, possibly a majority of the able-bodied men from the areas concerned.[8] Norfolk and Shrewsbury preferred to parley rather than risk what could have been a very unequal confrontation.[9] A truce was concluded on 27 October; Sir Ralph Ellerker and Robert Bowes were dispatched to present the Pilgrims' petition to the king. Under the terms of the truce both armies were to disperse. Clearly Norfolk hoped that the rebel forces

---

[8] For estimates of numbers see Dodds, vol. I, pp. 261–2. Norfolk described the army as the 'flower of the north' (*ibid*, p. 269). Estimates range from 20 000 to 40 000; the lower figure is as large as any army raised by the English against the Scots in the sixteenth century, the higher the equivalent of the biggest English military exploit of the period, the Boulogne expedition of 1544. (See C.S.L. Davies, 'Provisions for Armies, 1509–50', *ECHR*, NS, XVII (1964), 234–48). Some 5000 men appear to be involved in the attack on Carlisle in February 1537, from the Lake Counties; while in November 1536 some 3000–5000 men, mostly Lakelanders, faced Derby at Bentham Moor, near Lancaster (Harrison, *Lake Counties*, p. 97; Haigh, *Reformation and Resistance*, p. 131). Julian Cornwall suggests, on the basis of the Rutland returns of 1522, that only 10 per cent of the total population were militarily serviceable adult males (*Revolt of the Peasantry 1549*, London, Routledge, 1977), p. 95; I confess to finding it difficult to extract this figure from his 'The People of Rutland in 1522', *Transactions of the Leicestershire Archaeological Society*, XXXVII (1963), 7–28, or his *The County Community under Henry VIII* (Rutland Record Series, I, 1980), where he projects a total Rutland population of about 7000 from a muster return of 1400. If 10 per cent is the real proportion of serviceable males, then 5000 must represent a large turnout of a Lakeland population of under 70 000. Even taking a more likely 20 per cent, the rebels represent a substantial proportion of the available manpower; assuming 56 per cent of the population were men and women aged from 15 to 60, as in E.A. Wrigley and R.S. Schofield, *The Population History of England 1541–1871: a reconstruction* (London: Edward Arnold, 1981), table A3.1, pp. 528 and 565–8. The six northern counties could muster some 60 000 fighting men in 1573; on that basis figures like 20 000 or 30 000 in arms at Doncaster and 5000 in the Lake Counties represent an impressive turnout, especially as, as Professor Elton notes ('Politics', p. 189) not all areas were equally involved, while South Yorkshire was firmly under the control of the loyal Earl of Shrewsbury. (For 1573 figures see E.E. Rich, 'The Population of Elizabethan England', *ECHR*, NS, II (1950), 247–65, esp, 254).

[9] Norfolk and Shrewsbury had between them about 15 000 troops (Dodds, vol. I, pp. 244–5, 257). The official line was that Norfolk was prevented from fighting by a rain-storm which either swelled the River Don to dangerous proportions or made it impossible for archers to draw their bow-strings! (Edward Hall, *Chronicle* (1809 edn), p. 823; Charles Wriothesley, *Chronicle* (ed. W.D. Hamilton, Camden Series, 2 vols., 1875–7), vol. I, pp. 57–8.) Norfolk himself blamed foul weather, lack of provisions, pestilence, inferior numbers and bad morale for his decision not to fight (see his letter in Dodds, vol. I, pp. 268–9). The first three points presumably applied equally to the Pilgrims.

would fall apart while they waited for the king's decision; reckoning no doubt that once the Pilgrim army had dissolved it would be impossible to reassemble it.[10]

These hopes were disappointed. The Pilgrim forces were for the most part sent home. But the command structure remained in being; indeed it exercised reasonably effective government through most of the northern counties. Watches were kept, garrisons installed in strategic centres like Wressle and Hull and money levied for the cause. Robert Aske as 'Grand Captain' issued orders for the restoration of the dispossessed religious to their houses, and decreed a *modus vivendi* between the monks and the new occupants of their lands. When Ellerker and Bowes reported to the rebel leaders on their return from Windsor on 18 November, the king's reply was referred to a meeting of the Great Council at York. No fewer than 800 men, including commons, as well as gentry, as representatives of parishes and wapentakes, assembled from 21 to 25 November. The Council, with further reinforcements, reassembled at Pontefract from 2 to 4 December to draw up a detailed statement of demands, and on 4 and 5 December, a meeting of clergy debated the spiritual points at issue. A substantial armed force (complete with mobile bridge) had by this time reassembled.[11] Norfolk could do nothing but concede (with the king's reluctant consent) a free pardon, without exemptions, and the king's promise to have the grievances debated at a free parliament. Only then, and even so with some difficulty, did Aske get the rebels to disperse; tearing off his Five Wounds badge and proclaiming 'we will wear no badge nor sign but the badge of our sovereign Lord'.[12]

After this apparent victory the Pilgrimage gradually disintegrated during the extended truce until the promised parliament. Latent suspicions by the commons that they were being betrayed by their leaders came to the fore, culminating in the renewed rebellion in the East Riding in January 1537 led by Sir Francis Bigod and John Hallom, and in the separate outburst in the Lake Counties with the attempt to seize Carlisle in February 1537. Many of the gentry who had been involved in the main Pilgrimage now sought to clear themselves by taking up arms against the rebels – Sir Ralph Ellerker, Sir Thomas Hilton, Sir Thomas

[10] See Norfolk's letter of 25 October to the king, printed in Dodds, vol. I, pp. 259–60, in which he asks to be excused for any oath or promise made to the rebels 'for polecy'. There is, of course, a distinct possibility that Norfolk was pulling his punches in the hopes that negotiations with the rebels might produce desirable changes of government policy; his eagerness to explain his actions shows his vulnerability to suspicion on this score. The under-estimation of the rebels' cohesion is nicely shown in Lancaster Herald's report, at the end of October, that once the royal proclamation was read 'the plough commonalty would go home . . . for they say they be weary of that life they lead, and if they say to the contrary to the captains will, he shall die immediately' (*State Papers*, vol. I, 487: *LP*, II, no. 826).   [11] Dodds, vol. I, p. 344, for the proto-Bailey Bridge.

[12] Aske's 'Narrative', ed. M. Bateson, *EHR*, V (1890), 331–43, 341–2; cp. Elton, 'Politics', p. 194, for Aske's quasi-governmental behaviour.

Tempest, Lord Latimer, Sir Christopher Danby and Sir William Babthorpe, among many others.[13] Norfolk had the excuse to move in his forces. After Sir Christopher Dacre's victory at Carlisle, he began the work of repression, using martial law in the north-west, then proceeding to the trial of those who had put themselves outside the reach of the pardon by renewed rebellion after 9 December. The principal leaders were arrested and sent to London for examination, trial and punishment. Aske himself was executed at York on 12 July 1537. The promise of a 'free parliament' and the discussion of grievances was ignored.

The narrative is familiar; but its full implications have not been properly appreciated.[14] The size of the movement, or series of movements, is impressive. It may reasonably be claimed as the largest 'popular revolt' in English history, up to that time, or indeed ever, in terms of numbers and geographical range. ('Popular' at least in its organisation, with nobles and gentry sheltering behind the ostensible leadership of Aske, with the invocation of the commons and of the Common Wealth, the inclusion of representatives of the commons in the councils, the paraphernalia of oath-taking and so on.) Its solidarity during the waiting days of November, with the Pilgrim leadership exercising what seems to have been reasonably effective authority as a provisional government, is striking. So, above all, is Norfolk's still being faced in December with a formidable military force and having to pledge his own and his master's honour to far-reaching and damaging concessions.

The degree of organisation obviously suggests the active connivance, to put it no more strongly, of numerous noblemen and gentlemen. Indeed, the contrast between the events of autumn 1536, and those of the renewed rebellions of 1537, when most nobles and gentlemen conspicuously disassociated themselves, helps to make the point; so too does the contrast between Lincolnshire, where upper-class participation was less open, and Yorkshire. Certainly, many of the great northern lords were involved, either directly or by proxy. Lords Lumley, Latimer (John Neville), Scrope of Bolton and Conyers were all involved in the first rebellion and attended the Pontefract Council; Lumley's son was also involved in the Hallom–Bigod rising for which he was executed.[15] The Earl of Westmorland

---

[13] See under their names in S.T. Bindoff (ed.), *The History of Parliament: the House of Commons 1509–1588* (History of Parliament Trust, 3 vols., 1982). (For Latimer see his entry as Sir John Neville.)

[14] Elton, however, cites the raising of troops as a mark of organisation, and uses it as an argument for prior planning and conspiracy ('Politics', p. 194).

[15] See *Complete Peerage; DNB; Dodds, passim;* E. Milner and E. Benham (eds.), *The Records of the Lumleys of Lumley Castle* (London, 1904); Bindoff (ed.), *History of Parliament* (for Latimer, under Sir John Neville); A.G. Dickens, *The Clifford Letters of the Sixteenth Century* (Surtees Society, CLXXII, 1962) (for Scrope); and M.E. James, *Family, Lineage and Civil Society: a Study of Society, Politics, and Mentality in the Durham Region, 1500–1640* (OUP, 1974), pp. 46–7 (for Latimer and Lumley: James misnames Lumley's son George, 'Roger').

shut himself out of the way at Brancepeth, but convinced Aske of his sympathy; his teenage heir Lord Neville was a leader of the Durham contingent and attended the Pontefract Council.[16] On the other hand, the Earl of Cumberland, whether from loyalty or because of the hatred of his tenants, suffered siege by the rebels in his castle at Skipton.[17] Lord Dacre of Gilsland, fresh from the unusual experience of acquittal in a treason trial, lay low. Richard Dacre, a kinsman apparently of Lord Dacre, was very actively involved as 'Grand Captain' of the Cumberland rebels. Lord Dacre's uncle Sir Christopher played a moderating role in the first rising, and wiped out the suspicion which attached to him by his defence of Carlisle in February 1537.[18] Lord Ogle, in Northumberland, as a member of the 'Carnaby group' was not involved and, indeed, was a prime target for supporters of Thomas and Ingram Percy.[19] Most important of all was the loyalty of the Earls of Shrewsbury and Derby (even if in Derby's case it was not unambiguous), and Derby's kinsman Lord Mounteagle, who were placed in command of royal forces which effectively bottled up the rebellion by holding South Yorkshire and Lancashire against the Pilgrims.[20]

The most striking example of family charisma attached itself to Thomas and Ingram Percy, the younger brothers of the sixth Earl of Northumberland (who lay on his sickbed at Wressle throughout the troubles). Indeed, their aim of preventing their brother effectively ending Percy influence by leaving his lands to the crown was taken by Rachel Reid to be the key to the whole rebellion.[21] Percy influence was powerful in the main rebellion, when Thomas Percy rode 'gorgeously' into York at the head of a powerful troop to be greeted with cries of 'Lord Percy'. Aske himself stirred up the commons at Wressle and Howden with the traditional cry, 'Thousands for a Percy'. George Lumley accused Thomas Percy of being the 'lock, key and ward' of the second Yorkshire rebellion (the Bigod-Hallom rising) and certainly the belief that he was involved encouraged

---

[16] Dodds, vol. I, pp. 204, 345; vol. II, p. 78; James, *Lineage*, pp. 45–6. *Complete Peerage*, 12, I, pp. 553–4. *LP*, 12, i, no. 29. It is generally assumed that 'Lord Neville' was Henry, who succeeded his father as Earl of Westmorland in 1549. Henry, however, was born in 1524 or 1525; his parents had been married in 1520. No remark is made about 'Lord Neville's' extreme youth in 1536; it may be that this was in fact an elder brother who subsequently died. *LP* 11, no. 945 for Henry Eure's report to Aske of Westmorland's secret sympathy and service for the cause.

[17] M.E. James, 'The First Earl of Cumberland (1493–1542) and the Decline of Northern Feudalism', *Northern History*, I (1966), 43–69.

[18] Harrison, *Lake Counties*, pp. 81, 118, 123. *LP*, 11, no. 1331. Harrison assumes that Richard Dacre was Lord Dacre's son, but I know no indication of the actual relationship. Bindoff (ed.), *History of Parliament*, vol. II, p. 1.

[19] Dodds, vol. I, pp. 32, 197; vol. II, p. 81. *Complete Peerage*, 10, p. 34. *LP* 12, i, nos. 220, 1086 ii, 1090 pp. 505–6.

[20] Though for Derby's ambivalence, see Haigh, *Lancashire Monasteries*, pp. 72–4, and *Reformation and Resistance*, pp. 129–36; and B. Coward, *The Stanleys, Lords Stanley and Earls of Derby, 1385–1672* (Chetham Society, 3rd ser., xxx, 1983), pp. 96–8, 152–3, 164.

[21] Reid, *Council of the North*, pp. 133–5.

many to join.[22] But equally the Pilgrimage was not led only by great lords. As Professor Elton stresses, two of the key figures, Lords Hussey and Darcy, were not great magnates, but first-generation peers who had risen through service to the monarchy.[23] Below the peerage level a large number of gentlemen were involved; what proportion of the total gentry in the north is not easy to calculate. But the number of prominent gentlemen whose careers prospered subsequently in spite of their participation, suggests the difficulty of finding enough men of influence to carry on local government without them. The great abbeys had considerable military power over their tenants, and some of them tried to use it; the abbot of Holme Cultram mustered his tenants in February 1537 to induce them to take part in the Carlisle rising.[24] Nevertheless landlords, large or small, ecclesiastical or secular, could not just turn out their tenants on command. Even the monks of Furness had to provide cash and general exhortation, as well as threaten life and property, to get a response from their tenants.[25] Quite often rebels defied their lords; the rebel party in Beverley were those opposed to their lord, the archbishop of York; John Hallom opposed the prior of Watton, Robert Holgate; and Peter Middleton's tenants besieged him for fifteen weeks on an island in Derwentwater.[26] Professor Elton argues that the main method of raising troops was not through the 'feudal' landlord–tenant relationship, but through the machinery of the parish muster system; although in real terms, the two overlap, Elton himself talking of the gentry 'calling out the *tenantry* [my italics]

---

[22] Dodds, vol. I, p. 232. Milner and Benham (eds.), *Lumleys*, pp. 32–45. (*LP*, 12, i, no. 369). Presumably the designation of 'Lord Percy' (courtesy title for the heir to the earldom) was to underline Thomas Percy's claim to the inheritance; 'the best of the Percys that is left next to my lord of Northumberland' (*LP*, 12, i, no. 393: full version in E.B. de Fonblanque, *Annals of the House of Percy* (2 vols., London, 1887) vol. I, pp. 447–52, 462–3). For Aske's Percy connections see Reid, *Council of the North*, p. 133.

    I fail to follow Professor Elton's argument ('Politics', p. 208) that, since the Percy brothers were fighting 'for their inheritance, lost to them by the earl's bequest of his possessions to the Crown' they were therefore 'trying not to recreate the Percy lordship but to keep the Percy lands, in a very unfeudal and totally gentlemanlike way'; nor do I see that 'when the cry of Percy was raised, as it was at York, feudalism effectively against the earl, feudalism seems a long way off'. Traditional loyalties, surely, need not attach to the head of the house, if that head has betrayed his trust. Thomas and Ingram Percy represented, or seemed to represent, the interests of the family and its clients far more than the childless and sick sixth earl. Elton has equally mistaken form for substance in arguing that the involvement of Lord Latimer somehow tells against the 'feudal' interpretation because of his being 'the offspring of a cadet-branch, and a member of that anti-feudal institution the Council of the North'. 'Feudalism' is of course a dangerously imprecise term. But there is surely little doubt that both Latimer and the Percy brothers represented an assertion of family loyalties of a traditional kind which awoke a response among the commons; and which was in opposition to the policies being pursued by the central government.

[23] Elton, 'Politics', pp. 209–10.   [24] Coward, *Stanleys*, p. 96. VCH *Cumberland*, vol. II, p. 171.

[25] *LP*, 12, i, no. 841(3).

[26] For Beverley, Reid, *Council of the North*, pp. 121–2. For Hallom and Holgate, A.G. Dickens, 'Robert Holgate' in his *Reformation Studies*, (London, Hambledon Press, 1982), pp. 323–52, esp. 328–9. For Middleton, Harrison, *Lake Counties*, pp. 110–1.

in formal musters'.[27] But even mustering could not in itself produce an army or keep it together. We need to look more closely at the influence brought to bear on the commons.

A very vivid picture is given by George Lumley of what happened during the Bigod–Hallom rising near his seat at Thwing; the constable, seeing a beacon fired and consulting with the constable of the next township, calling out the musters; the arrival of Bigod with a hundred horse; his haranguing the commons on how they had been betrayed and the pardon's being of no effect ('the King hath sent us the fawcet and keepeth the spigot himself'); the swearing-in of the assembled multitude; and Bigod's departure with an augmented band.[28] Those holding out were naturally threatened: 'I came out of fear of loss of all my goods and I came forth for fear of burning of my house and defacing of my wife and children', as Norfolk sardonically reported the excuse offered him by those involved.[29] At Chorley in Lancashire Hugh Parker 'clapped a book to [Percival Saunders's] mouth and said "Thou must be sworn to God, the King, and the Commons" ' as he lay in bed; when Percival refused and made to get his shirt, Parker and his friends knocked him to the ground, and said 'if he should not be sworn he should see his own blood before his own eyes'. Parker (aged 16) afterwards pleaded that this was just a drunken teenage prank.[30] Intimidation was obviously rife. Drink flowed pretty freely, especially where the Beverley leader John Hallom was involved.[31] Money was distributed; Mervyn James has emphasised this for Lincolnshire and Professor Elton talks of 'organised agitators who even paid to rent their crowd'.[32] Hopes of spoil must have bulked large. William Breyar reported talk at Beverley about the riches of Cheapside. William Aclom, gentleman, of Moresby in Yorkshire accused the prior of York Holy Trinity of appropriating beds that Aclom himself had looted; behaviour hypocritical in a religious.[33]

An eye on the main chance of this sort was important. (It probably also explains the apparent ease with which armies for foreign service were raised.) But the significance can be exaggerated. Any armed force depends on pay and supplies. The Pilgrims were supported by contributions levied on the clergy (the appropriation of lands of absentee incumbents, a tax on the beneficed clergy and on religious houses); contributions on townships and the appropriated goods of opponents; the capture of a royal ship in which Edward Waters was carrying

[27] Elton, 'Politics', p. 194.
[28] Milner and Benham (eds.), *Lumleys*, pp. 32–45. Cp. similar examples in Harrison, *Lake Counties*, p. 96.   [29] Quoted in Harrison, *Lake Counties*, p. 125 (*LP*, 12, i, no. 498).
[30] In T. Northcote Toller (ed.), *Correspondence of Edward, Third Earl of Derby* (Chetham Society, NS, XIX, 1890), pp. 70ff, esp. 71–2; (*LP*, 11, no. 1230).   [31] *LP*, 12, i, no. 201.
[32] James, 'Obedience', p. 12; Elton, 'Politics', p. 194; Harrison, *Lake Counties*, p. 106.
[33] *LP*, 11, no. 841; 12, i, no. 536.

£100 for the loyalist garrison at Scarborough.[34] A good deal was no doubt unofficially 'liberated', but although the interrogation of the ringleaders fastened on the question of spoil, misappropriation for private ends never seems to have been made part of a formal charge or of government propaganda.[35] Even rebels had to live. The abbot of Jervaulx boasted that the Pilgrims could raise men for 8d a day, while the king had to pay (so the abbot thought) 18d.[36] On the other side the Earl of Derby wrote that it would not be possible to prevent his troops joining the enemy if pay were not sent them soon.[37]

Pay and the hope of spoil, then, are not a sufficient explanation of rebellion. The government blamed rumour-mongers for inciting the people. The theme was taken up by contemporary commentators and is well supported by the evidence gathered after the Pilgrimage. The Trinitarian canons of St Robert's at Knaresborough, especially one Robert Esche of Ashton, were busy spreading rumours about new taxes (6s 8d on every plough and for every baptism, 4d on each beast) before the first rising. Esche was again involved in the Bigod–Hallom rising.[38] The diffusion of the chalice-confiscation and church-closure rumours in Lincolnshire seems to have been due to a lawyer in ecclesiastical service, Peter Effard, registrar to the archdeacon's official, and an ex-mayor of Lincoln.[39] The rumour gained credence from Hull's having sold off some corporation plate, apparently fearing royal confiscation, and applying the proceeds to necessary repairs, including the town streets; rumour quickly changed this to the sale of church goods.[40] Several witnesses under interrogation, asked when the rumours began, said about a month or six weeks before the outbreak of the rebellion.

[34] Dodds, vol. i, pp. 288, 314. Harrison, *Lake Counties*, pp. 76, 96. Milner and Benham (eds.), *Lumleys*, pp. 32, 38. (*LP*, 12, i, no. 369).

[35] *LP*, 12, i, no. 201, p. 90 (Hallom's interrogation); Milner and Benham (eds.), *Lumleys*, pp. 32, 38.

[36] Milner and Benham (eds.), *Lumleys*, pp. 34–5.

[37] Northcote Toller (ed.), *Derby Correspondence*, p. 33 (*LP*, 11, no. 857); cp. Haigh, *Lancashire Monasteries*, p. 72.

[38] *LP*, 11, no. 1047, 12, i, no. 392; Dodds, vol. i, pp. 151, 153, 163; vol. ii, p. 266. (Esche and his fellows were referred to as friars but were in fact Trinitarian canons; A. Hamilton Thompson, *The English Clergy and their Organization in the Later Middle Ages* (OUP, 1947), p. 121.) That particular rumour seems perennial. See, e.g. B.L. Beer, *Rebellion and Riot; Popular Disorder in England in the Reign of Edward VI* (Kent State University Press, 1982), p. 72; G.R. Elton, *Policy and Police: the Enforcement of the Reformation in the Age of Thomas Cromwell* (CUP, 1972), pp. 67–70. See Y.-M. Bercé, *Histoire des Croquants* (2 vols., Geneva, 1974), vol. ii, pp. 622–4, for persistent fears in seventeenth-century France of taxes on baptisms, marriages and burials; Bercé comments (p. 624), 'Il paraissait sacrilège d'attacher un impot à des sacraments religieux. Il paraissait dénaturé d'obliger les assujettis à acheter leur droit à l'existence. La révolte devenait ici la défense d'une dignité essentielle.'

[39] Bowker, 'Lincolnshire, 1536', p. 198.

[40] *VCH Yorkshire (East Riding)*, vol. i, p. 91. The vicar of Louth held that Hull's action (which seems unexplained except in terms of a general distrust of the government's designs in 1536) lay behind the belief in imminent confiscation; *LP*, 11, no. 970 and 12, i, no. 70 i. A Hull shipman advised the men of Grimsby to follow their example, and sell *church* plate and jewels to pave the town; *LP*, 12, i, no. 481, p. 228.

William Breyar (a suspicious character, an ex-sanctuary man travelling the disaffected regions in the queen's livery, perhaps a government spy, perhaps a tool of the conspirators) reported the belief in Dent, apparently in mid-September, that churches were to be pulled down.[41]

Rumours, if they are to result in action, need to be related, in however distorted a form, to the experience of their audience. The seed-bed of the rumours produced in 1536 was the sheer state of crisis produced by the action of Tudor government at its most 'revolutionary', in conditions of economic distress (the bad harvest of 1535, to be followed by the disappointing one of 1536); the levy of peacetime taxation (the subsidy voted in 1534 and levied in 1535 and 1536);[42] the attack on traditional land-owning practices involved in the Statute of Uses and the Act of Liberties and Franchises, both passed in the final session of the Reformation parliament (February to April 1536); the visitation of the monasteries (June 1535 to February 1536), followed by the suppression of the smaller ones during the summer of 1536; the apparent threat to traditional religious practices in the Ten Articles (July 1536) and Cromwell's injunctions (August), and the suppression of superfluous saints' days (decreed in August); followed in September–October, in Lincolnshire, by the despatch of diocesan officials to see to their implementation.[43] The Ten Articles mentioned only three of the sacraments as scripturally based; the preaching of sermons against purgatory posed a direct threat to the elaborately funded apparatus of prayers and masses for the dead; the general attack on superstition could easily develop from an attack on abuses to an attack on catholic practice as such.[44] Since most of these changes would have been inconceivable a few years before, there seemed every reason to believe even the more far-fetched of the current crop of rumours.

The clergy in particular had suffered heavy blows to their material position, their self-esteem and their theological presuppositions in the last few years; not

---

[41] E.g. *LP*, 12, i. nos. 70, 380, 700, 1011. For Breyar, see *LP*, 11, no. 841, and Harrison, *Lake Counties*, p. 90.

[42] Although the subsidy was the lowest assessed since the beginning of the reign and affected only those with £20 p.a. (and of course nobody in Northumberland, Durham, Cumberland and Westmorland) it was unusual in being levied in peacetime, and in advancing reasons additional to those of defence in justification. See Elton, *Studies*, vol. III, pp. 193, 220, G.L. Harriss, 'Thomas Cromwell's "New Principle" of Taxation', *EHR*, XCIII (1978), 721–38, esp. 727–8, and J.D. Alsop, 'The Theory and Practice of Tudor Taxation', *EHR*, XCVII (1982), 1–30, esp. 5–7, for discussion of just how novel the 1534 subsidy was. Alsop notes (p. 3) that a collector was threatened with hanging. The subsidy commissioners were of course at work in Lincolnshire when the rebellion broke out, and in Yorkshire (Elton, 'Politics', p. 197). The events of 1497 and 1525 underline the potential of taxation to inflame rebellion.

[43] James, 'Obedience', p. 14; Bowker, 'Lincolnshire 1536', pp. 196–7; *Henrician Reformation*, pp. 149–50.

[44] A. Kreider, *English Chantries: the Road to Dissolution* (Harvard Historical Studies, XCVII, Cambridge, Mass., 1979), pp. 105–17, 129. Archbishop Lee reported in October 1535 that the people objected to anti-purgatory preaching (*LP*, 9, no. 704).

only the imposition of a layman as their Supreme Head, but of another, Thomas Cromwell, as a very active Vice-Gerent, suspending the jurisdiction of bishops, and regulating forms of worship (the injunctions were in his name); the promotion of notorious heretics (Latimer and Shaxton) to the episcopal bench; a huge increase in taxation, with the likelihood of yet worse to come since the compilation of the Valor Ecclesiasticus had provided the government with a realistic assessment of clerical income;[45] the suspicion that the suppression of the smaller monasteries was only the prelude to the general confiscation of ecclesiastical property; or that the issue of royal orders was an excuse for the crown to examine the competence of priests and remove them from their benefices.[46] One monk of Sawley expressed what many if not most clergy must have felt: that it was never a merry world since 'secular men and knaves rule upon us' and that 'there should be no lay knave head of the Church'.[47] Heresy was associated with the recent changes; hence no doubt the venom of the clergy in the Louth area instigating book-burning.[48] The clergy were in the best position to spread rumours, and to incite the people, and they had excellent reasons of their own for doing so.[49]

Of course, the ecclesiastical patronage system meant that beneficed clergy were almost all under obligation to lay patrons, or to ecclesiastical corporations

[45] F. Heal, 'Clerical Tax Collection under the Tudors: the Influence of the Reformation' in R. O'Day and F. Heal (eds.), *Continuity and Change: Personnel and Administration of the Church of England 1500–1642* (Leicester University Press, 1976), pp. 97–122, and J.J. Scarisbrick, 'Clerical Taxation in England, 1485–1547', *Journal of Ecclesiastical History*, XI (1960), 41–54. Scarisbrick reckons that the clergy paid some £46 000 to the crown in 1535 and nearly £52 000 in 1536; compared with an average of about £4800 to Rome and £12 500 to the crown before the Reformation; and smaller clerical incomes were disproportionately hit, (pp. 50, 52–3). For Wolsey's use of the 1522 muster returns to levy more realistic taxes, see J.J. Goring, 'The General Prescription of 1522', *EHR*, LXXXVI (1971), 681–705.

[46] Bowker, 'Lincolnshire 1536', p. 204.   [47] Haigh, *Lancashire Monasteries*, p. 96.

[48] *LP*, 11, no. 968, 12, i, no. 380 (p. 174).

[49] Cp. the allegation that they misrepresented the introduction of parish registers in 1538 by mumbling confusedly when they read the royal injunctions and inserting a misleading commentary: *LP*, 13, ii, no. 1171. The confessional was also important; cp. Sir William Bulmer sending his chaplain to the neighbouring priests 'to enquire if the commons would rise again, which they should know by men's confessions' at Easter 1537 (Dodds, vol. II, p. 159). Materialistic motives here are obvious; but it would be wrong to dismiss here an element of what could be categorised variously as theological principle and as personal pride in the defence of clerical status. No doubt the two were as intimately interlinked as in, one might guess, those clergy today opposing the ordination of women. I would suggest that acceptance of Henry as Supreme Head was very much a reluctant acquiescence in the apparently inevitable; again, an analogy with the ordination of women may be relevant. Not all the clergy involved were ignorant, even were it true that the theologically uninformed are likely to be merely self-seeking. Thomas Kendall, Vicar of Louth, where the Lincolnshire revolt originated, was not only an Oxford theologian, but had been employed as a heresy hunter by the Bishop of London (A.B. Emden, *A Biographical Register of the University of Oxford, A.D. 1501 to 1540* (OUP, 1974), pp. 327–8). Kendall preached the inflammatory sermon at Louth which instigated the Lincolnshire rising (see nn. 43 and 45). Longland granted away the advowson of Louth to the king in 1535, so that Kendall would no doubt expect to be succeeded by one of 'Cromwell's chaplains'; Bowker, *Henrician Reformation*, p. 100.

(especially monasteries). But this does not make them puppets, incapable of acting on their own behalf. Of course some clergy acted on behalf of the patrons: Thomas Maunsell, vicar of Brayton, and a servant of Darcy's, was very active in his master's interest in the early stages of the revolt.[50] But there seems very little evidence of this on a wide scale.[51] Nor is the argument that the Pilgrimage can be explained primarily in terms of conspiracy by Lords Hussey and Darcy convincing.[52] The evidence that rumours were spread by the agents of upper-class conspiracy, whether the Darcy-Hussey court group, or the Percy family or even an 'anti-court' country party of gentry, seems thin; Edward Hall's account is probably just in putting the main blame on the priests, even though 'many even of the nobility did not a little countenance and stir up the ignorant and rude people'.[53] Rather than large-scale prompting, whether from disgruntled heads of ancient families or factionalist conspirators, it does look as if there was a rapid spread of disaffection in the summer, instigated for the most part by the clergy and evoking a real response from the commons; nobles, gentlemen and ecclesiastical dignitaries then hurried to turn the situation to their own advantage.[54] Mrs Bowker remarked of the commissions at work simultaneously in Louth that 'too

[50] Smith, *Land and Politics*, pp. 183–4. Maunsell was specifically exempted the pardon of November 1536, nonetheless was included in the July 1537 pardon, and held his living until his death in 1555, in spite of being arrested in 1541 on suspicion of trying to stir another rising.

[51] Bowker, 'Lincolnshire 1536', pp. 204–5, notes that five of the thirty-two beneficed clergy said to be involved in the Lincolnshire rising owed their livings to gentlemen who were themselves implicated. This seems hardly to justify Professor Elton's gloss ('the clergy most active in the business would seem to have been the clients of the disaffected gentry', 'Politics', p. 194). In any case one should not necessarily assume that influence in the patron–client relationship always flowed downwards. Much more significant in the Lincolnshire case would surely be the twenty priests appointed by suppressed and rebellious religious houses.

[52] See appendix, pp. 89–91.

[53] Hall, *Chronicle*, pp. 819–25, esp. 820.

[54] Conspiracy theory is always seductive; and the multiplication of biographical works of reference and of investigation of local history increasingly produces connections which *may* be meaningful. The danger, however, is that of necessarily ascribing guilt (or credit) by association. For instance, Bernard Towneley, Rector of Caldbeck and Chancellor of the Bishropic of Carlisle, hanged in 1537 for his involvement in the Lake Counties rebellion, was probably close kin to the brothers Sir John and John Towneley, the latter of whom played a role in the Lancashire revolt (*LP*, 12, i, no. 687, Harrison, *Lake Counties*, pp. 103, 126; Haigh, *Lancashire Monasteries*, pp. 71, 75). To discover, therefore, that until 1531 Towneley had been Vicar of Horncastle, one of the centres of the Lincolnshire revolt (Emden, *Oxford 1501 to 1540*, p. 572) seems at first highly significant; Towneley, one would guess, must have been instrumental in co-ordinating action in Lincolnshire and Cumberland, and possibly Lancashire. Horncastle, however, was a vicarage in the gift of the Bishop of Carlisle, who was rector of the parish, and also had a manor-house there (A. Hamilton Thompson, *Lincoln Diocesan Visitations*, vol. II (Lincs. Record Society XXXV, 1944) pp. xii–xiii, 21; P. Hembry, 'Episcopal Palaces, 1535 to 1660' in E.W. Ives, R.J. Knecht, and J.J. Scarisbrick (eds.), *Wealth and Power in Tudor England: Essays Presented to S.T. Bindoff* (London, Athlone Press, 1978, p. 146–66, 150). This makes the coincidence of Towneley's career less surprising and to that extent diminishes the suspicion that the connection must be significant in terms of conspiracy, though of course leaving open the possibility. Kinship networks and patronage networks within and between the gentry and clergy were close-knit; discovery of connection, although providing a possible line of investigation, cannot be taken as significant without further investigation.

much innovatory action was taking place in so small an area'.[55] Louth represented in concentrated form the situation over much of the north, indeed over much of the country.

The stories which rumour-mongers spread tell us something of popular attitudes, hopes and fears.[56] There was fear of an ever-encroaching and demanding state; the almost universal belief in a radical extension of the taxation system, with taxes on oxen, on the poor eating white bread or white meats (cheese and other dairy products), levies on churching, marriages, funerals and so on; a compulsory reminting of gold coins. Coupled with this was the perceived threat to the parish church; the belief that church treasure was to be confiscated, gold and silver chalices replaced by copper and tin, non-parochial churches torn down, even parochial churches rationalised, leaving only one in every 5 to 10 miles.[57] The trouble at Louth began with an emotive sermon by the vicar, Thomas Kendall, followed by an outburst by a singing-man at the carrying of the crosses in procession ('Our Lord speed you, for I think ye shall be taken away shortly, so that we shall never follow you more'),[58] whereupon the poor (instigated by various of their superiors) demanded the keys of the church treasury to protect it from the threatened visitation. The church issue was the focus of the general fear of spoliation by the government.

Another emotive issue was the recent rationalisation (and drastic diminution, especially in August and September) of saints' days or holidays; economically sensible, no doubt, even from the point of view of the wage-earner, but nonetheless we might expect exponents of leisure preference to be amongst the more vocal of protestors. Bound up with the holiday issue was that of local pride, touched off by the particularly tactless decree that in future all patronal festivals were to be celebrated on 1 October, except when the church was lucky enough to have a major festival for its feast. Trouble broke out at Watton and at Kirkby Stephen where the priest did not announce the patronal festival.[59] In the north-

---

[55] Bowker, *Henrician Reformation*, p. 149.

[56] See Dodds, vol. I, ch. 4. Rumours, of course, were not confined to the north. See Elton, *Policy and Police*, pp. 67–71. (The orders for parish registers of 1538 were especially productive of rumours.)

[57] *LP*, 11, nos. 534, 968, 970; 12, i, nos. 70, 380 (for Lincolnshire); 11, no. 768, ii (general rumours in the north); 12, i, no. 200 (Aske distributing bills in Holderness); 12, i, no. 392 (East Riding); 12, i, no. 1011 (Richmond); 11, no. 841 (Dent).   [58] *LP*, 11, nos. 828 (iii) (i) and 968 (p. 389).

[59] *LP*, 12, i, no. 201, pp. 89–90, no. 687 (2). The decrees are in Wilkins, *Concilia*, 3, 823–4. For their impact (and especially the dramatic reduction of holidays in the harvest season) see B. Harvey, 'Work and Festa Ferianda in Medieval England', *Journal of Ecclesiastical History*, XXIII (1972), 289–308, and Bowker, *Henrician Reformation*, pp. 150–2. Bowker notes that Louth itself was not affected by the 1 October date; but the combination of 29 September as a permitted festival, followed by 1 October for most churches, brought together potentially dangerous crowds in, presumably, somewhat relaxed mood with their harvest work done. For Kirkby Stephen, see Harrison, *Lake Counties*, pp. 78–9. The impact of the change seems to depend on the initiative of the bishop: in Cornwall it was believed that patronal festivals had been spared by Cromwell's intercession; A.L. Rowse, *Tudor Cornwall*, (London, Cape, 1941), p. 189. A.N. Galpern, *The Religions of the People in Sixteenth-Century Champagne* (Cambridge, Mass., Harvard University Press, 1976), pp. 47–54, on the importance of patronal festivals.

west there was similar trouble about the public prayers ('bead bidding').[60] All this points to a good deal of manipulation of the situation by the clergy, especially in the one-sided interpretation of the teaching of the Ten Articles and the injunctions. (The clergy had every reason to distrust the king's intentions; they themselves had been instructed not to publicise the royal order to reduce holy days, 'whereby the people might take occasion either to murmur, or to contemn the order taken therein', but merely to let them fall into disuse.)[61] But it also says something about the investment, emotional and monetary, in the parish church and its furnishings. The pockets of the poor, and community investment, community pride, seemed to be under attack simultaneously by a rapacious king misled by a scheming minister; the combination was an explosive one.

In a tense situation issues simplify and polarise; at each pole a number of disparate matters fuse into a single undifferentiated whole, at least for those immediately involved. Defence of the church and defence of the poor against the crown became a single issue.[62] 'Cromwell' becomes a convenient bogey for the various ills of 1536; the evil genius of the government, extorting taxation, suppressing monasteries, threatening apparently both the traditional form of parochial worship and its very fabric. He was 'that heretic and all his sect which made the King put down praying and fasting'.[63] 'Their especial great grudge is against the Lord Cromwell, being reputed the destroyer of the commonwealth', said Aske.[64] Of low birth (easily exaggerated into 'villein blood') and therefore stirring the traditional distrust of the commons for their fellows in high office, Cromwell was the subject of fantastic rumours that he was aiming for the throne.[65] 'Cromwell's chaplain' seems to have been a general term of abuse.[66] His

---

[60] Harrison, *Lake Counties*, p. 77. A new form for bead bidding was issued in June 1535, naturally omitting pope and cardinals and inserting the king as Supreme Head; a shorter and more definite form was issued in July 1536. See W.H. Frere, *Visitation Articles and Injunctions of the Period of the Reformation* (3 vols., *Alcuin Club Collections*, nos. 14–16, 1916), vol. II, p. 17.

[61] Wilkins, *Concilia*, 3, 824.

[62] *LP*, 8, no. 626 for a popular belief that Becket had died to prevent a tax on children being sent to school and of poor men eating meat; and the invocation of Becket against parish registers in 1538 (*LP*, 13, ii, no. 1171).

[63] *LP*, 12, i, no. 163. William Breyar's report of conversation at Dent, before the revolt ('if we had him here we would crum him . . . that he was never so Crumwed') is the classic expression of anti-Cromwell gossip (*LP*, 11, no. 841).

[64] *EHR*, V (1890), 342–3.

[65] *LP*, 12, i, no. 532; Dodds, vol. I, pp. 317–18. 28 Henry VIII c 7, passed in the parliament of June–July, had allowed Henry to determine the succession to the crown by will in default of legitimate offspring, and gave a tinge of plausibility to the allegation. The belief that Henry might marry Cromwell to Princess Mary originated in Catherine of Aragon's circle, though disbelieved by Chapuys (*LP*, 11, no. 41). Possibly 'Vice-Gerent' was seen as a suggestive title.

[66] Harrison, *Lake Counties*, p. 138. William Hallom, challenged on why he believed Bigod's accusation that the Prior of Watton, Robert Holgate, was one of Cromwell's chaplains, instanced his harsh treatment of his tenants (and of Hallom in particular) PRO E 36/119 f. 30 (*LP*, 12, i, no.

servants became a by-word for arrogance. A serving-man who said that a silver dish in Louth church was 'meeter for the King than for them' was significantly assumed to be Cromwell's servant; two of them were lucky to escape lynching in the Lincolnshire revolt.[67] When George Dakyn, servant to Cromwell's nephew, was indicted for being involved in the murder of one of Sir Ralph Eure's men, Cromwell intervened in his favour; Eure obeyed, though protesting.[68] It may be, as Professor Elton suggests, that a particular virulence emanated from the More circle in the London legal world, and this may be reflected in Aske's personal hostility to Cromwell.[69] But Cromwell's prominence in government, as the normal recipient of letters begging favours or providing excuses for dereliction of duty, his role on the Council before which offenders of various sorts were brought to explain themselves, as well as the apparent arrogance of his servants, make it natural that he should become the target of general opprobrium and bear the responsibility for the mass of revolutionary changes introduced in the last three years. After all, as the king's Vicar-General and Vice-Gerent in ecclesiastical affairs his name was on the various commissions to investigate the state of the monasteries, and to compile the Valor Ecclesiasticus: 'I, Thomas Cromwell, knight, Lord Cromwell, keeper of the privy seal . . . and vicegerent . . .' issued the 1536 injunctions.[70] His personal responsibility seemed undeniable, and it seems unnecessary to invoke the special machinations of a court party or of an affronted gentry interest to explain it.[71] Given the usual, and useful, tacit assumption that the king personally should not be held to blame, not only would

20/iv). The origin of the phrase may lie in the licensed preachers sent to propagate the Supreme Headship in the north: Archbishop Lee had protested, and was to do so again, against their disruptive influence (*LP*, 9, nos. 704, 742; 10, no. 172; 13, i, nos. 1247, 1317; see Dodds, vol. I, p. 71; J. Block, 'Thomas Cromwell's Patronage of Preaching', *Sixteenth Century Journal*, VIII (1977), 37–50).

[67] *LP*, 11, nos. 828 (i) (vii), 968; Bindoff (ed.), *History of Parliament* (under John Bellow and John Millicent). Presumably it was one of these who made the remark at Louth – possibly the spark which set off the entire explosion.

[68] *LP*, 11, no. 237. Reid, *Council of the North*, p. 131. This was referred to in the general indictment of Cromwell usually ascribed to Sir Thomas Tempest, *LP*, 11, no. 1244. See Bindoff (ed.), *History of Parliament* vol. III, p. 433, for doubts about Tempest's authorship; cp. Elton, 'Politics', p. 207. The memorandum also accuses one of Cromwell's servants called 'Brabazon' of interfering in justice: I have found no trace of this incident. George Brabazon was army treasurer in Ireland; the offender may have been his kinsman John, who had joined George in Ireland by November 1536 (*LP*, 11 nos. 527, 1157, p. 467).

[69] Elton, 'Politics', pp. 204–5, a convincing explanation of the mention of Rastel and St German among the heretics.

[70] H. Gee and W. J. Hardy (eds.), *Documents Illustrative of English Church History* (London, 1896), p. 269.

[71] Elton, 'Politics', pp. 206–7, 213, doubts whether Cromwell and Rich 'were so universally hated as has been alleged' and that 'the crucial significance of the court factions . . . help to explain the concentrated attack' on them.

complaint focus on Cromwell, and his protégés,[72] but 'heresy' would seem to be at the heart of their offending. Heresy becomes in these circumstances a generalised term of abuse.

The lists of actual 'heretics' produced at various times by the Pilgrims abound in absurdities; on the one hand, 'Anabaptist' seems to have been taken for a person, on the other names such as Oecolampadius and Bucer can hardly have been on the tip of every tongue in Yorkshire alehouses. Therefore, it is suggested, anti-heretical feeling was not a popular demand.[73] Clearly the specific names were suggested by interested parties, presumably in this case very largely by the clergy. ('Programmes' of rebellions tend to heap together various disparate demands and to reflect disproportionately the influence of leaders. It is therefore misleading to read too much into them, either as expressing the views of the 'people', or, by reaction, as minimising the importance of the popular feeling. Examining how people behaved during the rebellion, the incidents which provoked them, the cries to which they responded, the form which actions took, provides a closer insight into motives than does an analysis of programmes which reflect their interest at second or third hand; nor is the irrationality of a demand proof of its unimportance.) Ill-informed, theologically unsophisticated and indecisive as even their leaders may have been, the Pilgrims were surely right in perceiving that recent changes of all sorts were due to the new influence at court of men of advanced religious opinions, of 'heretics'. The groundswell of opinion was more than 'vague discontent concerning the reform';[74] rather it was a general reaction against a whole mass of innovation imposed by commissioners on orders from Westminster. On a village level 'heresy' was no term of exact theological scholarship, but the expression of a, no doubt unthinking, prejudice against deviants and disturbers of the peace. Dislike of change imposed from outside, dislike of challenge to accepted religious ideas, could only be mutually reinforcing.[75]

Circumstances produce unexpected bed-fellows. Fellow victims of a rapacious

---

[72] An incautious smith accused the king of being a thief because he was pulling down the churches, when Breyar was at Dent. But he was quickly rebuked and conversation rapidly diverted against Cromwell (*LP*, 11, no. 841).

[73] Elton, 'Politics', p. 204. 'Anabaptist' and 'Pelagian' presumably crept in from the condemnation in the Ten Articles, cp. Hardwick, *A History of the Articles of Religion*, (3rd edn, London 1876), p. 243. Canterbury Convocation presented in June 1536 a list of 'Mala Dogmata', heretical or ribald opinion unfortunately popularised since the break with Rome; R. W. Dixon, *History of the Church of England* (6 vols., OUP, 1878–1902), vol. 1, 389–409.

[74] Elton, 'Politics', p. 205.

[75] Heresy featured prominently among the sins denounced in the 'Great Curse' periodically pronounced with great solemnity in parish churches; H. Maynard Smith, *Pre-Reformation England* (London, Macmillan, 1938), p. 129; J. Mirk, *Instructions for Parish Priests* (ed. G. Kristensson, Lund Studies in England 49, 1974), pp. 104–6. See below, n. 77 for the Craven commons.

government, like the dispossessed religious, become allies to be defended (often against their will), their fate taken as an augury of what was more generally in store: 'the people saw many abbeys pulled down in deed, they believed all the rest [of the rumours] to be true', remarked John Hallom.[76] Several times between Christmas 1536 and February 1537 mobs at Kendal insisted that their priest pray for the pope when bidding the beads, threatening him with a ducking if he refused.[77] There is no need to postulate deep-seated papalism in Kendal. The point is surely that in the uneasy conditions following the pardon, with suspicion growing of betrayal, insistence on one of the more extreme and unequivocally radical points of the programme could be a test of continuing solidarity, a reaffirmation and reinforcement of a rapidly disappearing cohesion, a sign of anxiety, not of confidence.

Religious imagery was important in the rebellion; the use of the banner of the Five Wounds, the Pilgrim marching song, the very use of the term 'Pilgrimage'. So too were religious sanctions, above all the Pilgrim oath. Most people, as we saw from George Lumley's account of what happened at Thwing, took the oath hastily, under moral pressure and often physical threat, with little opportunity to consider the implications.[78] Oath-taking seems to have been done with due ceremony, the oath being sworn on a book. Hugh Parker, the Chorley teenage prankster (if that is what he was) produced any old book apparently; none of them, after all, was learned or lettered, though presumably the book purported to be the gospels or a missal from the church.[79] That oath-taking had about it an element of magic, that people may have been trapped into something they did not understand, does not, however, mean that it was therefore ineffective or irrelevant; mystery may have worked to strengthen the binding character of an oath imposed 'under pain of deadly sin'.[80] The sanctity of the oath was advanced as an excuse by many of the gentry and clergy accused of involvement; they had tried to avoid taking the oath, but, once it was forced upon them, under threat to themselves or their dependants, they had no choice but to go along with the rebels. The government, of course, regarded such excuses with scepticism, arguing that oaths taken under duress were not binding,[81] and it seems likely that many gentlemen and priests were happy to allow themselves to be sworn. Nevertheless, some gentlemen who had little sympathy for the cause also

---

[76] PRO E36/119 f. 54 (*LP*, 12, i, no. 201 iv).
[77] *LP*, 12, I, nos. 384, 914. The commons of Craven similarly demanded that the vicar of Arncliffe should 'bid beads and rehearse the points of cursing in the parish church' and pray for the pope (*LP*, 11, no. 655 and p. 717). More unexpectedly, a Lincolnshire priest 'bid the beads' for pope and cardinals; Bowker, 'Lincolnshire 1536', p. 210.   [78] Above, n. 28.
[79] Northcote Toller (ed.), *Derby Correspondence*, p. 74 (*LP*, 11, no. 1230).
[80] Thomas, p. 64.
[81] E.g. the question put to Darcy, *EHR*, v (1890), 554, Qs 65–72.

behaved in this way.[82] They at least seem to have thought that the oath had some objective validity, as did the Pilgrims who went to great pains to impose it, especially on potentially dangerous opponents; while the government's own imposition of a loyalist counter-oath shows that oaths were thought to be more than mere words.[83]

Oaths and religious symbolism were necessary because the Pilgrims were, after all, directly challenging the royal authority, in challenging the policies on which the king had staked his authority in the last two or three years. Of course, that did not mean that they were proposing the king's deposition. Few rebels, after all, ever did.[84] It makes more sense to accuse the king's advisors, so giving the king himself a chance to retreat without totally losing face. Opprobrium was therefore better directed at Cromwell and his low-born heretical associates. Few direct challenges were posed even to the king's ecclesiastical authority (though the Lancashire rebels pointedly referred to the king as Defender of the Faith, not Supreme Head, deplored the spoliation of the church, and blasphemy against the Virgin and saints and prayed for God to send the king good counsel).[85] The

[82] E.g. Sir William Fairfax, author of a violent memorandum to Cromwell in January 1537 denouncing the clergy of all levels for 'wagging' the people, himself farming from the king the suppressed priory at Ferriby, tried to avoid the oath, but once taken sat on the Pontefract Council (LP, 12, i, no. 192; Dodds, vol. I, pp. 162, 237, 345). Sir James Layburn, an extremely unpopular landlord, and a correspondent of Cromwell's, avoided taking the oath between 15 and 27 October, but then went along with the Westmorland army into Lancashire; Harrison, Lake Counties, p. 108; LP, 12, I, no. 914; Bindoff (ed.), History of Parliament, vol. II, p. 531. Sir Francis Bigod, whose strange metamorphosis from Cromwellian reformer to rebel leader has been so well analysed by Professor Dickens, is a striking, if perhaps eccentric or even neurotic, example; A.G. Dickens, 'Sir Francis Bigod and his Circle' in Lollards and Protestants in the Diocese of York, 1509–1558 (OUP, 1959), pp. 53–113. Sir Ralph Ellerker won the approval of Cromwell's nephew, Richard, and a commendary letter from the king, for his defence of Hull, before joining the Pilgrims and representing their case to the king; he was active against the Bigod rebellion and was appointed to the reconstituted Council of the North in 1537; Bindoff (ed.), History of Parliament, vol. II, p. 90; Dodds, vol. I, pp. 165–6; LP, 11, no. 820, VCH Yorkshire (East Riding) I, p. 91. Some of those who tried to prove conspicuous loyalty in 1537 and won their way back to favour had been sympathisers with the original Pilgrims. It seems difficult, however, to see any of the above as other than trapped into acquiescence by the oath.

[83] Dodds, vol. II, pp. 99–101; LP, 12, i, no. 520.

[84] I am puzzled by Professor Elton's remark about the 'truly feudal attitude of defiance leading to the overthrow of the dynasty which had characterised the fifteenth-century civil wars' ('Politics', p. 212). Fifteenth-century nobles seem almost as reluctant to challenge the crown directly as sixteenth-century ones, when they were faced with a settled dynasty; what is surely striking about Henry VI's reign is how long it took in the face of disaster before any noble party challenged the king's right to the throne. Nor is the tactic, used by the nobles in 1536, of sheltering behind a commons revolt and an upstart 'great captain', without fifteenth-century precedent. The kingmaker Earl of Warwick encouraged a rebellion headed by his proxy 'Robin of Redesdale' in the north, and another in Lincolnshire headed by Sir Robert Welles as 'Great Captain of the Commons', presumably so that either could be disclaimed if it went wrong; Charles Ross, Edward IV (London, Methuen, 1974), pp. 126–30, 138–41; James, 'Obedience', pp. 69–71.

[85] LP, 11, no. 892 (i) (Harrison, Lake Counties, p. 75); full version in Northcote Toller (ed.), Derby Correspondence, pp. 47–9.

Pilgrims would obviously prefer not to oppose the king, provided he would give way: Aske tore off the Pilgrimage badge when the king apparently granted the substance of the demands. But in the circumstances real concessions were unlikely. Even the pretended concessions of December were extorted by the November stalemate, the result of the cohesion and determination of the Pilgrims. To achieve their ends peacefully, the Pilgrims had to be prepared to fight: it was this which distinguished the main Pilgrimage from events in Lincolnshire, which Mr James can describe (with, I believe, some exaggeration), as an expression of 'dissidence' played according to a well-understood set of conventions on each side.[86] The Pilgrims needed an ideology of resistance; challenged directly on this point in his interrogation, Aske admitted that 'if his grace had refused their petitions, then their cause had been just'.[87]

The various oaths exemplify the dilemma neatly; the Pilgrims swore to be true to God, the faith, church, king and Common Wealth.[88] True religion and to a lesser extent the Common Wealth were necessary to legitimise a movement against the king. Philip Trotter at Horncastle produced first the Dymoke banner, but then abandoned it because he thought this would be treason. It was replaced by a banner with plough, chalice and host, the Five Wounds and a horn (for Horncastle).[89] Nicholas Sanderson provided a banner with the Trinity. The

---

[86] James, 'Obedience', pp. 69–78.

[87] *EHR*, v (1890), 553, 571 (Q 53). Cp. also 559 (Q 21) – originally the Pilgrims hoped to have their griefs remedied by petition, 'if they could not so obtain, to get them reformed by sword and battle'. Aske also agreed in response to questioning (555 and 573, Q 74) that the oath was designed 'for the animating of the soldiers that they might think that they had a just cause to fight in pretending their rebellion to be for the defence of the faith of Christ'. Hugh Latimer, recalling his conversation with Darcy in the Tower in 1537, reported Darcy's statement that if 'I had seen my sovereign lord in the field, and I had seen his grace come towards us, I would have lighted from my horse, and taken my sword by its point, and yielded it unto his grace's hands'. (Significantly Darcy was not prepared to act in this way towards Norfolk, the king's commissioner.) Latimer commented, 'It hath been the cast of all traitors to pretend nothing against the king's person; they never pretend the matter to the king, but to the other'; G.E. Corrie (ed.), *The Works of Hugh Latimer* (Parker Society, 2 vols., 1844–5), vol. I, p. 163. M. James makes the case in his *English Politics and the Concept of Honour 1485–1642* (*Past and Present* Supplement, III, 1978), pp. 37–9, for a division between those eager to fight (Lords Lumley and Latimer and Sir Robert Constable, among others) and those who, like Darcy and Aske, hoped that the king, faced with a show of strength and through the mediation of conservatives at court, would give way. The latter tactic needs, of course, even more elaborate organisation; to arouse a protest might be easy, to keep it in being without the stimulus of a fight much more difficult; in the circumstances the conspiracy theory becomes an even less sufficient explanation.

[88] The Lincolnshire version was the simplest (God, church, king, and commons), Aske's very elaborate. Dodds, vol. I, pp. 109, 182. The Lake Counties version was very close to the Lincolnshire one; Harrison, *Lake Counties*, p. 106. Aske's version no doubt reflected his personal motivation in emphasising the religious element, disclaiming both private ends and any 'Commonwealth' motivation – 'for the love that ye do bear unto Almighty God his faith, and to his Holy Church militant and the maintenance thereof, to the preservation of the King's person and his issue'; it nevertheless went on to demand 'the purifying of the nobility' and the expulsion of 'villein blood and evil councillors against the commonwealth' from the Council.

[89] *LP*, 11, no. 828, p. 323, 975, p. 401, 12, i, no. 70, p. 39.

Durham contingent marched under the venerated banner of St Cuthbert, but also wore badges with black crosses and the Five Wounds. The accidental death of one of Bowes's contingent suggested the need for a distinguishing badge, and conveniently Darcy remembered a set of Five Wounds badges left over from his crusade against the Moors in 1511.[90] However sceptically one regards this story, the point remains that the Five Wounds was a potent and meaningful symbol.[91] So too was the sustained religious imagery of the Pilgrim Song. Sir Marmaduke Neville repeated the saying 'if they call us traitors, we will call them heretics'.[92]

Religious imagery went furthest in the Lake Counties (contrary to the usual view about the essentially 'secular' nature of the north-western rebellion),[93] with the elaborate rituals of captains and secretaries of poverty. At Penrith there was a daily 'captain's Mass', with the four captains processing daily into church with drawn swords; during the Mass, Robert Thompson, Vicar of Brough (and 'Secretary of Poverty') would read one of the commandments, while, on the captains' command, five aves, five paternosters and the creed were said daily.[94] These rituals helped create a scene of solidarity in a movement always, by its nature, liable to fall apart.

I am not trying to argue the case for a 'spontaneous' commons revolt. I accept that rumours were deliberately spread, though I suggest that the clergy rather than the aristocracy were behind them. I accept, too, that the adhesion of

[90] *EHR*, v, 571–2; James, *Lineage*, p. 48; Elton, 'Politics', pp. 196–7. (Elton misidentifies the expedition as the attack on Gascony in 1512.) It is interesting that the Pilgrims invoke Christ rather than the saints, or even the Virgin. Popular religion may have been more Christocentric than is often implied.

[91] The devotion to the Five Wounds had spread rapidly in fifteenth-century England; they were habitually depicted in the missals of both Sarum and York uses; R.W. Pfaff, *New Liturgical Feasts in Later Medieval England* (OUP, 1970), pp. 83–91. The devotion was associated with that of the Holy Name of Jesus; indeed the preserved Pilgrim banner includes the IHS symbol as well as the Wounds; F. Rose-Troup, *The Western Rebellion of 1549* (London, 1913), frontispiece, and appendix A: and see the cover of Fletcher, *Tudor Rebellions*. The potency of the vivid depiction of Christ's sufferings was appreciated by those organising revolt in Cornwall in 1537 and Hampshire in 1549: Rowse, *Tudor Cornwall*, p. 230; Beer, *Rebellion and Riot*, p. 156. Oddly the image was retained in the purged 1541 breviary; Pfaff, *Liturgical Feasts*, p. 91. The image of the suffering Christ was, of course, dominant in church, in the rood; G. Williams, *The Welsh Church from Conquest to Reformation* (Cardiff, University of Wales Press, 1962), p. 476. Passion plays emphasised the point; so did the popular devotion of the sorrows of the Virgin.

[92] *LP*, 11, no. 1319; 12, 1, no. 29.

[93] Elton, 'Politics', p. 189, talks of 'a peasant protest against exploiting landlords' which 'had little more than chronological coincidence with the Pilgrimage'. The north-west (the Lake Counties, and the Dent–Sedbergh area of the West Riding) certainly saw more intense anti-landlord feeling than elsewhere, but it does not follow that this excludes the religious element; on the contrary, the religious factor seems actually stronger there than elsewhere. See Harrison, *Lake Counties*, *passim.*, but esp. pp. 135–7. The issue has been muddied by anti-clericalism; see n. 100 below. For the survivalist catholicism of the area, which only a lack of missionary priests prevented becoming an important recusant area, see C. Haigh, 'The Continuity of Catholicism in the English Reformation', *Past and Present*, XCIII (1981), 37–69, 60–4.

[94] Harrison, *Lake Counties*, p. 72. *LP*, 12, 1, nos. 384, 687(2), 914.

noblemen or gentlemen, whether open or covert, once the Pilgrimage was under way, gave it a cohesion it would otherwise have lacked. Rumours, however, to be effective needed both to be credible, in the sense of having some connection with verifiable events (hence the importance of the various commissions in 1536), and to appeal to authentic sentiments among the commons. Fear of draconian taxation was one of these; alongside were a variety of 'religious' issues, of which fear of a wholesale attack on the practices, furnishing and even the fabric of the parish church seems to be the core. Images and church furnishings were the flashpoints of confrontation in Europe generally through the Reformation: the most tangible manifestation of popular catholicism, emotive symbols for both sides. For traditionalists they represented the sense of the holy, represented too their own participation, individual and communal, in the *opus Dei*, the continuous process of worship, whether on the level of the widow's mite or of ostentatious self-advertisement. For their opponents, they were a symbol of pollution, a blasphemous distraction from the centrality of Christ, a reminder of the church's skill at financial extortion. In both cases the combination of the spiritual and the material is a powerful one. Symbols stand vividly for what might be only dimly perceived on an intellectual level.[95]

In a sense what we have here is a concern for existing investment. To describe that, however, as a 'money' matter (with the implication 'only a money matter') is misleading.[96] Parishioners had, after all, little direct material interest in the state of the church; the use of tin chalices would not hurt their pocket, although it might offend their sense of propriety and their communal pride. What they were defending was the result of free-will offerings, for the foundation of chantries, the improvement of the fabric, the upkeep of decoration, the gilding of images or the maintenance of lights. No doubt simple piety is not sufficient explanation; bequests, especially testamentary ones, were inspired by fear, by individual or family pride or by unthinking conformity. The church, in the countryside at least, was the only tangible manifestation of the community, the centre of secular as well as religious activity; its splendours, however meagre, some alleviation of the austerity and utilitarianism of everyday life. It was not something 'other', separate from or opposed to the interests of the laity. Laymen were heavily

[95] Cp. D.J. Nicholls, 'The Nature of Popular Heresy in France, 1520–42', *Historical Journal*, XXVI (1983), 261–75, esp. 273; A. Duke, 'The Face of Popular Religious Dissent in the Low Countries 1520–1536', *Journal of Ecclesiastical History* XXVI (1975), 41–67; N.Z. Davis, 'The Rites of Violence: Religious Riot in Sixteenth Century France', *Past and Present*, LIX (1973), 51–91. M. James, 'Ritual, Drama and Social Body in the Late Medieval English Town', *Past and Present*, XCVIII (1983), 3–29. Cp. S.E. Ozment's comment, *The Reformation in the Cities* (Yale University Press, 1975), p. 44, 'the outburst of iconoclasm . . . may . . . indicate the reaction of people who felt themselves fooled by something that they had not taken lightly at all but had in fact believed all too deeply and in spite of the personal shortcomings of its representatives'.

[96] Elton, 'Politics', p. 193. 'Money, not the faith, caused the people to stir.'

involved in the administration of the church at the local level; in their membership of gilds and fraternities, in the administration of bequests, as churchwardens
in the care of the fabric. A sense of communal proprietorship is central to this
question of church furnishings, indeed of church building; a matter of 'honour',
perhaps, or at least of self-respect, rather than of 'money' in a crude sense.[97]

Recent writing on the German Reformation has made the point that lay
involvement in the affairs of the church, and the development of a fervent lay
piety, might well be, from a traditionalist clerical point of view, a mixed blessing;
that that very sense of lay proprietorship might evoke a generally more critical
attitude to the performance of their duty by the clergy, could lead through a
demand for higher standards, through 'anti-clericalism' to, ultimately, protestant rejection of a sacerdotalist–sacramental religion.[98] On a theological spectrum this may seem a world apart from a traditionalist reaction like that of 1536.
In practice the leap from one to the other may not be so very great. The Pilgrims
were not merely unthinking, ignorant traditionalists, easily roused by unscrupulous priests. Rather they were involved in a rational defence of their own interests
against what they saw as a policy of spoliation. To try and gauge the situation in
terms of 'catholic traditionalism' as opposed to incipient protestantism is to ask
the wrong question; a question which was not in practice posed in 1536, when the
Henrician changes plainly appeared in purely destructive guise. What was
involved was rather a fusion of religious values and a sense of communal
property set against destructive spoliation; a fusion which in the particular
circumstances could only take the form of a defence of traditional and hence of
'catholic' values against innovations.

The situation in the Lake Counties illustrates this well. The rebels at Penrith
went in for much more explicit religious imagery than those elsewhere, and it was
at Kendal that the mob noisily insisted on prayers for the pope.[99] But tithe-barns
were a prime focus of attack in early 1537, and from this historians have argued
for the essentially 'non-religious' element of the north-western revolt.[100] Resent-

[97] J. J. Scarisbrick, *The Reformation and the English People* (Oxford, Basil Blackwell, 1984) which I
was lucky to hear as the Ford Lectures in 1982; James's expression of this concept in an urban
context in his 'Ritual, Drama and Social Body', esp. p. 13. Villages did not have the formal
corporate existence of towns, and their churches might have been less sumptuously furnished, but
there is no reason to deny a spirit of local pride. Scarisbrick stresses particularly the importance of
lay involvement through confraternities; see Galpern, *The Religions of the People in Sixteenth-
Century Champagne, passim.*, on confraternities and for community feeling in villages.

[98] B. Moeller, 'Religious Life in Germany on the Eve of the Reformation' in G. Strauss (ed.), *Pre-
Reformation Germany* (London, Macmillan, 1972), pp. 13–42; and see the discussion in Ozment,
The Reformation in the Cities, ch. 2. In Spain the bishops were concerned to control the
dangerous enthusiasm of lay brotherhoods which were inclined to throw off clerical tutelage;
W. A. Christian, *Local Religion in Sixteenth-Century Spain* (Princeton University Press, 1981), p.
168. For a reconsideration of 'anti-clericalism' in England, see Haigh, 'Anti-clericalism and the
English Reformation', *History*, LXVIII (1983), 391–407.   [99] See above nn. 77 and 94.

[100] Dodds, vol. I, p. 225. Reid, *Council of the North*, pp. 124–5; Elton, 'Politics', p. 190.

ment, however, was directed not against the local clergy, but against absentees who failed to provide hospitality and against monastic appropriators of tithe; the tithe-barns of St Mary's Abbey, York, to which a large number of north-western rectories were appropriated, were a special target.[101] The Penrith rebels demanded instruction in the faith.[102] The Westmorland manifesto appears to envisage a system of purely voluntary tithes;[103] not surprising, in fact, when we notice that the rectory of Kendal was appropriated to St Mary's, while the vicarage (worth an astonishing £99) was held by a well-known clerical bureaucrat and careerist, Thomas Magnus, archdeacon of the East Riding and formerly Wolsey's right-hand man in the north.[104] Yet the general tenor of these demands is not very different from the demands of the Norfolk rebels in 1549: clerical residence, the clergy to provide for education, the ejection of non-preachers (and a suggestion of popular election of their successors), an equitable and simple solution to the problem of tithe.[105] In 1549, such demands were associated with the ostentatious use of the new protestant Prayer Book. In 1536 circumstances dictated that they be set in traditionalist mould, directed against outsiders associated with the government, 'Cromwell's chaplains'. 'Anti-clericalism', in the sense of hostility to ostentatious clerical wealth, a potentially 'protestant' trait, could also reinforce traditionalist religion against an outside threat.

Kendal church was particularly large, well equipped and provided with a large number of gilds and chantries.[106] So, too, was that other focus of rebellion, Louth, the birthplace of the Lincolnshire revolt. The magnificence of Louth church, with its recently completed steeple, paid for by donations and built under the direction of the churchwardens is well known; in Professor Dickens's words, its 'three hundred feet of soaring grace still bear witness to the devotion and pride of a little town standing apart from the mainstream of Tudor England'.[107] The churchwardens also supported a semi-professional choir, one of whose members took a conspicuous part in stirring up trouble. (Historians are prone to ignore the importance of music, less tangible than that of the visual arts.) There were a large number of gilds, which, amongst their other functions, contributed jointly to the

[101] Harrison, *Lake Counties*, pp. 57, 59, 120, 135, 138. Other targets were the barns of lay farmers of the tithe.   [102] *LP*, 12, i, no. 687(2), p. 303.
[103] Harrison, *Lake Counties*, p. 138. Similarly Bigod, in his usual confused way, promised that his followers should be supported by the 'fat priests' benefices of the south that were not resident upon the same, and money of the suppressed abbeys'; Milner and Benham (eds.), *Lumleys*, p. 38, and Dickens, *Lollards and Protestants*, p. 100.
[104] *Valor Ecclesiasticus*, vol. v, p. 268. For Magnus see *DNB*.
[105] Fletcher, *Tudor Rebellions*, pp. 120–3, or in Beer, *Rebellion and Riot*, pp. 105–7.
[106] J.F. Curwen, 'The Parish Church of Kendal' in *Transactions in the Cumberland and Westmorland Antiquarian Society*, XVI (1900), 157–220; R.I. Whitwell 'Chantries in Kendal and Lonsdale Wards, 1546', *ibid.*, NS, 8 (1908), 124–35; C.M.L. Bouch and G.P. Jones, *A Short Economic and Social History of the Lake Counties 1500–1830* (Manchester University Press, 1961), p. 18.
[107] Dickens, *The English Reformation* (London, Batsford, 1964), p. 10.

upkeep of a schoolmaster: in 1536 one John Goodall. With the eventual suppression of the gilds under the 1547 Chantries Act, a grammar school was founded, with Goodall as its first master. Before April 1547 large amounts of plate had been sold 'for the relief of the poor people' and other necessaries. A 'new hospital' was founded in 1560, again presumably to replace the gilds in this role. Louth had rapidly become a town of conspicuous and purposive good works. It had made the transition from a 'sixteenth-century Chartres' (Margaret Bowker's phrase) to proud 'protestant', even 'puritan' municipality.[108] The apparently paradoxical transition seems in fact a perfectly natural one, an example of continuity, rather than dramatic change.

Of course, many towns took the opportunity of the Reformation to convert religious endowments to utilitarian secular purposes. Some, no doubt, did so gladly, others more reluctantly, to prevent local funds being swallowed by the state; York as much as Hull, in spite of the very different religious complexion the two towns were to take on in the Elizabethan period.[109] In spite of some well-known examples (e.g. the buying off of the opposition of Lynn and Coventry to the passing of the 1547 Chantries Act), there is mounting evidence that towns lost out in the process of secularisation, and that the fears expressed in 1536 were justified in the long run.[110] Nevertheless, once secularisation had taken place, towns, like owners of monastic lands, had acquired a vested interest in the new

---

[108] Bowker, *Henrician Reformation*, p. 149. R.C. Dudding (ed.), *The First Churchwardens' Book of Louth* (OUP, 1941). *LP*, 11, no. 828 (1) for Thomas Foster, the rebel singing man. G.A.J. Hodgett, *Tudor Lincolnshire* (Lincoln, History of Lincolnshire Committee, 1975), pp. 142–3. A.F. Leach in *VCH Lincs*, vol. 11, pp. 460–6, and R.B. Walker, 'Reformation and Reaction in the County of Lincoln, 1547–1558' in *Reports and Papers of the Lincolnshire Architectural and Archaeological Society*, IX (1962), pp. 49–62, esp. 55. R.W. Goulding (ed.), *Louth Old Corporation Records*. This Goodall has to be distinguished from the protestant agitator at Salisbury of the same name; Elton, *Policy and Police*, pp. 103–7, and Bindoff (ed.), *History of Parliament*, vol. 11, pp. 228–30. Which, if either, was the Etonian and Fellow of King's (see W. Sterry (ed.), *Eton College Register 1441–1698* (London, Spottiswode, Ballantyne, 1943)) is unclear. Scarisbrick, *Reformation and English People*, pp. 95–6. In 1604 the vicar of Louth was one of the only two ministers in the county deprived for nonconformity; C. Holmes, *Seventeenth-Century Lincolnshire* (Lincoln, History of Lincolnshire Committee, 1980), p. 93.

[109] For Hull, see n. 40 above. Cp. the city of York which, as early as 1527, was agitating for the suppression of certain chantries to benefit ailing municipal finances; and which in Edward's reign closed fifteen of the city's forty churches; yet in terms of its religious orientation York, at both aldermanic and popular level, remained notoriously traditionalist until well into Elizabeth's reign. See D.M. Palliser, *Tudor York* (OUP, 1979), pp. 49–51; Kreider, *Chantries*, pp. 159–60. Kreider (p. 158) notes the elaborate scheme at Richmond to cheat the king while continuing the chantries. For the contrasting religious history of York and Hull, see Claire Cross, 'Parochial Structure and the Dissemination of Protestantism', in D. Baker (ed.), *The Church in Town and Countryside* (Studies in Church History, XVI, 1979), pp. 269–78.

[110] See A.L. Beier, 'The Social Problems of an Elizabethan Country Town; Warwick 1580–90' in P. Clark (ed.), *Country Towns in Pre-Industrial England* (Leicester University Press, 1981), pp. 45–85; further references in Clark's introduction, p. 14. For Lynn and Coventry, see Kreider, *Chantries*, pp. 193–5.

order. The change from catholic piety to protestant public spirit is a perfectly natural one; neither attitude had much in common with the negative confiscatory policies which seemed to be the hallmark of the changes of the 1530s.

Basically similar reaction could produce politically very different results. It would be natural, for instance, for urban opposition to a powerful ecclesiastical corporation to lead to a protestant, or at least 'anti-traditionalist' stance. Yet in Beverley, as we have seen, the leaders of the rebellion seem to have been the leaders of the party opposed to the archbishop; they were assisted by the notoriously active Trinitarian canons of Knaresborough, and by the Franciscan Observant Father Bonaventure.[111] Enmeshed here was also the vexed matter of the election of Robert Holgate as Prior of Watton; Holgate's enemies, especially John Hallom, were leaders of the revolt.[112] As at Kendal, 'anti-clericalism' took on traditionalist, not radical, forms. Something similar happened at Salisbury, where the traditional jealousy of the ecclesiastical establishment on the part of the civic authorities took on, when the protestant Nicholas Shaxton was bishop, a decidedly 'catholic' flavour.[113] By contrast, in Norwich, a long-established jealousy of the cathedral establishment was worked on from a protestant angle by Cromwell's protégé Robert Watson. Watson was influential in the 1549 rebellion, and it is tempting to see his influence behind the anti-clerical demands of the Norfolk rebels and, perhaps, of their ostentatious use of the new protestant Prayer Book on Mousehold Heath.[114] 'Anti-clericalism' is a catch-all phrase. Hostility to clerical privilege could take the form of support for poorer vicars and curates, rather than outright opposition to the clerical estate as a whole. The poorer clergy might castigate their superiors as traitors to their own calling and to traditional belief; alternatively as the embodiment of catholic corruption and as living arguments for Lollardy or protestantism. In the particular circumstances of 1536 in the north the former was the dominant attitude.[115]

This sense of lay proprietorship which lay at the heart of the commitment to traditional religion contained the seeds of a very different religious orientation. Whether those seeds would ever germinate depended, however, on circumstances; on the force of protestant evangelisation, on the gradual effects of vested interest in the new order or on sheer lack of the resources to sustain the catholic

---

[111] Reid, *Council of the North*, pp. 127–8. Dodds, vol. I, pp. 144–8.
[112] Dickens, *Reformation Studies*, pp. 328–9. *LP*, 12, i, nos. 201, 202, 392.
[113] Elton, *Policy and Police*, pp. 100–7.
[114] Elton, *Policy and Police*, pp. 138–9. Bindoff (ed.), *History of Parliament*, vol. II, pp. 560–1. Nicholas Sotherton, 'The Commoyson in Norfolk, 1549' in B.L. Beer (ed.), *Journal of Medieval and Renaissance Studies*, VI (1976), 73–99, esp. 82. Watson's influence, deployed in 1549 in the cause of moderation, no doubt owed a good deal to his demagogic past.
[115] For the co-existence of traditional and of civic humanist, potentially protestant, tendencies, and for an attempt to relate these to different political and social circumstances, see James, 'Ritual, Drama and Social Body'.

tradition.[116] Patently in 1536 the crown had not yet succeeded in enlisting to its side a significant degree of lay feeling against the church, at least in the north of England; clerical abuses were associated with entanglement with the state machine, whether under the aegis of a Wolsey or of a Cromwell and the crown was the enemy, the despoiler, to be fought in the name of the true old religion. But to try to explain religious emotion in 1536 is not to explain it away. I am not suggesting that a commitment to traditionalist religion was somehow a 'cover' for communal self-interest; quite the contrary, the sense of communal proprietorship strengthened the natural conservative commitment to familiar forms, and was in fact an integral part of it.

And yet the Pilgrimage was and remained an extraordinary event. The north was to endure further provocations but not produce another major revolt until 1569. In the rest of the country, the only large-scale religious revolt was that of the West Country against the protestant Prayer Book in 1549. More generally, as Dr Robert Whiting has pointed out, there is a paradox at the heart of Tudor popular religion; on the one hand the continuation at a high level of traditional devotional practices (the provision of images, prayers and Masses for the dead etc.), well attested in cash payments and bequests; on the other, the apparent ease with which those practices were abolished by government fiat, with a surprising lack of overt resistance.[117]

The problem Dr Whiting has so neatly posed is fundamental for the interpretation of the English Reformation. For the narrower question, at least, some answers are possible. The very defeat of the Pilgrimage was obviously a disincentive to renewed resistance; attempts to stir up further rebellion in 1541 and 1549 were fiascos.[118] The manner in which the Pilgrimage eventually disintegrated was clearly an important factor here. Defence of a clergy apparently unwilling to be defended could easily turn into 'anti-clericalism' of a different sort. When two leading priests, Bernard Towneley and Richard Dalton, demurred at negotiating with the Carlisle authorities on behalf of the rebels, Percy Simpson called out 'things would never be well until they had stricken off all priests heads, saying they would but deceive them'.[119] There was an ugly scene

---

[116] Haigh, *Past and Present*, XCIII (1981), for Wales and north-west England, and his 'From Monopoly to Minority: Catholicism in Early Modern England' in *TRHS*, 5th ser., XXXI (1981), 129–47.

[117] R. Whiting, 'Abominable Idols: Images and Image-breaking under Henry VIII', *Journal of Ecclesiastical History*, XXXIII (1982), 30–47, esp. 46–7. 'For the Health of my Soul: Prayers for the Dead in the Tudor South-West', *Southern History*, V (1983), 68–94. See also his unpublished Ph.D. thesis (Exeter University, 1977), 'The Reformation in the South-West of England'. I am grateful to Dr Whiting for letting me see his work before publication.

[118] A.G. Dickens, 'Sedition and Conspiracy in Yorkshire during the Later Years of Henry VIII', and 'Some Popular Reactions to the Edwardian Reformation in Yorkshire', repr. in his *Reformation Studies*, pp. 1–40.   [119] *LP*, 12, I, no. 687(2). Harrison, *Lake Counties*, p. 135.

at Pontefract when, with the arrival of Lancaster Herald, Archbishop Lee thought it prudent to preach a sermon on obedience.[120] John Dakyn, Vicar-General to the powerful but absentee archdeacon of Richmond, William Knight, was attacked (he claimed) preaching against the pope shortly after Christmas 1536. Many of the clergy (again like the gentry) got off and indeed prospered after the Pilgrimage, in spite of having played a leading role in it; Dakyn himself, for instance, or even more surprisingly Thomas Maunsell, although he had been originally exempted from the pardon as an active agent of Darcy's in stirring up the rebellion.[121] The end result of the Pilgrimage may have been to sow such distrust between clergy and commons, and between gentry and commons, as to prevent any repetition for a generation.

It is tempting, then, to accept Professor Elton's verdict that 'the religious purposes of the Pilgrimage had shallow roots, except amongst the few who dominated its ideology, eloquence and propaganda'.[122] Tempting, perhaps, but I believe this formulation is narrowly but crucially off target. Rachel Reid's categorisation, catholicism 'by use and wont rather than by reasoned conviction' is perhaps nearer the mark.[123] The indictment is a familiar one and, as far as it goes, justified. The church's rites were accepted with little questioning. There was implicit belief in their efficacy, and a somewhat mechanistic, perhaps quasi-magical, understanding of their operation. Images were superstitiously venerated, and their favour invoked for selfish or materialistic purposes; as indeed was the Mass itself on occasion.[124] The crudity of such criticism as there was, whether Lollard, or what one might call 'ale-house cynical', mirrors the materialism of popular devotion.[125] In spite of the requirements for a regular, systematic, elementary exposition of the essentials of the faith, it is unlikely that priests put much effort into this duty, or that their congregations took much notice if they did.[126] Attacks on the church were either ignored, or countered by persecution and anathema rather than by polemic. Indeed, polemic would have been beyond the capabilities of most priests. The cry of 'foul' was clearly heard in the famous article of the Devon and Cornwall rebels in 1549. 'We will have the Bible and all

---

[120] Dodds, vol. I, pp. 379–80.
[121] *LP*, 12, i, nos. 786–9. *Valor Ecclesiasticus*, vol. v, p. 235. Knight was a pluralist on a large scale, diplomat, later (1541) Bishop of Bath and Wells, *DNB*. For Maunsell, see n. 50 above. For Dakyn's subsequent career, see J. and S.A. Venn, *Alumni Cantabrigienses* (4 vols., CUP, 1922–7), vol. II, p. 3, and Dickens, *Lollards and Protestants* (numerous references – see index). His kinship to George Dakyn (see n. 68 and LP, 12 i, no. 788) may have helped him survive.
[122] Elton, 'Politics', p. 203.   [123] Reid, *Council of the North*, p. 122.
[124] J. Bossy, 'The Mass as a Social Institution, 1200–1700', *Past and Present*, c (1983), 28–61. Thomas, ch. 2.
[125] Dickens, *Lollards and Protestants*, pp. 16–52. Bowker, *Henrician Reformation*, pp. 57–64.
[126] P. Heath, *English Parish Clergy on the Eve of the Reformation* (London, Routledge, 1969), pp. 92–103.

books of scripture in English to be called in again, for we be informed that otherwise the clergy shall not of long time confound the heretics.'[127]

But this picture is overdrawn and one-sided. That religion was heavily symbolic, even materialistic or 'magical', does not imply that it was somehow unauthentic, still less that it was lacking strength; indeed, the opposite may well be the case, that the more unthinking and accepting a religious tradition, the stronger it is. Reason, after all, opens the way to uncertainty. Those who have castigated late medieval popular religion as being unchristian, even pagan in essence, are applying unattainably high standards to what was, and had to be, a mass religion, and underestimating the capacity for 'real' devotion among the inarticulate and ill-instructed.[128] Protestant clergy of the next century, university degrees notwithstanding, seem not to have been much more successful at expounding the elements of the faith, to judge by the general failure to grasp the crucial protestant teaching on justification.[129] The application of real rather than ideal points of comparison presents the late medieval church in a much better light.

Recent studies have underlined the toughness, the capacity for survival of traditional religion, even in unpropitious circumstances. Images, holy water, a literalistic belief in the sacrament of the altar, a veneration for shrines and wells, persisted as folk-religion in puritan England, even in areas more 'advanced', more exposed to protestant preaching than the counties involved in the main Pilgrimage.[130] (Lincolnshire was not to feature, in protestant eyes, as one of the 'dark corners of the realm'.)[131] Catholic recusancy did not, it is argued, involve a new beginning, a peculiarly 'Counter-Reformation' spirituality which repudiated the legacy of medieval popular religion as worthless superstition; rather recusancy evolved naturally from traditional English catholicism, and the contribution of the foreign seminaries was not so much a new catholicism, as an indispensable (and in the event inadequate and badly distributed) supply of priests to replace those Henrician and Marian survivors who kept the torch burning in Elizabethan England.[132]

---

[127] Rose-Troup, *Western Rebellion*, p. 493, or Beer, *Rebellion and Riot*, p. 64.

[128] E.g. J. Toussaert, *Le Sentiment Religieux en Flandre à la fin du Moyen-Age* (Paris, Librairie Plan 1960); Jean Delumeau, *Catholicism between Luther and Voltaire* (Eng. transl. 1977 London, Burns & Oates).

[129] Collinson, ch. 5, esp. pp. 202–3.

[130] See the survey by C. Haigh, 'The Recent Historiography of the English Reformation', *Historical Journal*, XXV (1982), 995–1007.

[131] C. Hill, 'Puritans and the "Dark Corners of the Land"', in his *Change and Continuity in Seventeenth-Century England*, (London, Weidenfeld, 1974), pp. 3–47. Hodgett, *Tudor Lincolnshire*, pp. 168–88.

[132] Haigh, *Past and Present*, XCIII (1981), 37–69 and *TRHS*, XXXI (1981), 129–47. Compare Benedict's argument that in Rouen, and indeed in France generally, the shift from a 'negative' to a positive response to protestantism (denunciation giving way to renewal), which took place in the 1580s

It is not, then, a matter of shallow roots. To pursue the metaphor, traditional religion was well-rooted but had not yet developed resistance to two wholly new dangers; that posed by an aggressive state, and, in the longer term, that of evangelical protestantism. (Dr Haigh's 'survivalists' seem to be successful not so much in beating off a positive protestant challenge but in keeping catholicism going in conditions of official proscription.) A religion which paid so much regard to externals, which had a rather naive understanding of providence, reward and punishment, would seem particularly open to be discredited. The particular fears of 1536 were shown to be false, at least in Henry VIII's reign. The drift towards doctrinal protestantism was first checked and then reversed and the attack on the parish church did not materialise. That the Henrician Reformation did not incur manifestations of divine disapproval; that the country was not · invaded, or afflicted with exceptional dearths or epidemics, the king himself not struck down for sacrilege, may have played its part in reconciling Henry's subjects once the immediate crisis of 1536 had passed away. The government's carefully staged campaign against superstitious images in 1538 makes the same point; consigning famous images to the flames in an elaborate public ceremony, complete with edifying sermon and if possible a demonstration of any trickery used in producing 'miracles'. What had been the disregarded or derided scepticism of a few eccentrics now acquired official sanction.[133] The banner of St Cuthbert, which the Durham contingent had taken with them to York in 1536, was reputed to give certain victory in battle, and to be indestructible by fire. The wife of the Elizabethan dean, William Whittingham, had it ceremonially burnt.[134] Mockery was a potent weapon, especially when authority countenanced or encouraged derision of the sacred. To the young, especially, where they were exposed to government propaganda and to effective protestant preaching, the sense of liberation from previous taboos is palpable; in turn, the strength of that reaction testifies to the reality of the sense of the sacred, in

was a cause, not a consequence, of counter-Reformation measures, was internally generated in response to political crisis rather than the result of Roman-inspired reform or the advent of new religious orders; *Rouen During the Wars of Religion* (CUP, 1981), esp. pp. 190–208, 244–8. There can be little doubt, for instance, of the strength of catholic conviction of Robert Parkyn, who nonetheless remained curate of Adwick-le-Street, near Doncaster, from about 1542 until his death in 1569. See A.G. Dickens, 'The Last Medieval Englishman' and 'Robert Parkyn's Narrative of the Reformation', *Reformation Studies*, pp. 245–85 and 287–312.

[133] J. Phillips, *The Reformation of Images; Destruction of Art in England 1536–1660* (University of California, 1973), ch. 3, esp. pp. 73–81. Thomas, pp. 74–7. I. Luxton, 'The Reformation and Popular Change' in F. Heal and R. O'Day (eds.), *Church and Society in England: Henry VIII to James I* (London, Macmillan, 1977), pp. 70–1.

[134] James, *Lineage*, pp. 48, 56, 58; *Rites of Durham* (Surtees Society, xv, 1842), p. 23. The gesture may have had a feminist as well as an iconoclastic point, since traditionally 'no woman was to enter into any Church that belonged to St Cuthbert', R. Hegg, *Legend of St Cuthbert* (1626), printed G. Allan, *Collectanea Dunelmensis* (1977, p. 27). This was presumably before 1569, since the banner does not seem to have been used in that rebellion.

churches, in images, in the priesthood, above all in the sacrament of the Mass, now being defied.[135]

Lack of resistance was not, then, a mark of tepidity, of lack of fervour among the commons, or among the lower clergy. It was due in large part to political circumstances, to the marked reluctance of nobility and gentry to hazard rebellion (so that, even on a 'conspiracy' theory of the Pilgrimage, they preferred to instigate a rebellion by the commons rather than come out in direct opposition), above all to the narrow avoidance of a succession struggle which would have polarised and inflamed religious passions. (I hope my stress on the 'commons' factor in 1536 is not taken as minimising the importance of upper-class involvement; both elements were indispensable in the situation.) Similarly the lower clergy were held back by the reluctance of their superiors, well illustrated by the dithering of the clerical dignitaries, from Archbishop Lee downwards, at Pontefract, to give a lead in resistance or even to encourage it.[136] Medieval catholicism had not, after all, developed an ethic of popular resistance; and such an ethic was slow to develop in protestant circles, let alone catholic ones, in the sixteenth century. Catholicism, so long the religion of the status quo, was caught wrong-footed by the assault mounted by the Henrician state. What is remarkable about the Pilgrimage was not so much that resistance crumbled, but that it existed at all, on an unprecedented scale in numbers and different social groups involved. It measures both the impact of the Henrician Reformation, and the degree to which that revolution in its early years presented itself in an almost totally destructive guise.

[135] S. Brigden, 'Youth and the English Reformation', *Past and Present*, xcv (1982), 37–67.
[136] Dodds, vol. I, pp. 382–7.

Appendix

This essay's argument is compatible with the 'political' interpretation advanced for Lincolnshire by Mr Mervyn James and developed more generally by Professor Elton;[1] namely, that a 'conspiracy' on the part of Lords Hussey and Darcy as representatives of a defeated 'Aragonese' court-faction is the prime cause of the Pilgrimage. As I have argued, such a conspiracy could only work by manipulating the prejudices of the commons, and the means used would therefore still provide a valuable insight into popular attitudes. But I would suggest that 'conspiracy' is a far from adequate explanation of the 'stirring' of the revolt.

Certainly Darcy and Hussey had treasonable dealings with the Imperial ambassador Chapuys in 1534 in which they appear to be outlining what actually happened in 1536; they would 'animate the people', the rebellion would then be joined (and financed) by the nobility and clergy, they would march behind the banners of the crucifix and of Charles V; in return they asked for a small force from Charles V and his encouraging the King of Scots to invade.[2] As Dr James argues, Hussey may have encouraged the Lincolnshire rebellion until he lost his nerve, and there can be little doubt that Darcy surrendered Pontefract deliberately, and played a major role thereafter in the Pilgrim leadership. I find, too, the emphasis on the London legal connection (and through conservative lawyers back to the More circle) of men like Thomas Moigne, George Stones and of Robert Aske himself, convincing and enlightening on their own motivation and on the drawing up of the various demands.[3]

Nevertheless, although it is clear that Hussey, Darcy and Aske hoped for a rising like that which eventually happened and, at least in Darcy's and Aske's

[1] James, 'Obedience', and Elton, 'Politics'.
[2] *LP*, 7, no. 1206. Chapuys's contacts with Darcy continued through the first half of 1535.
[3] James, 'Obedience', pp. 24, 26. Elton, 'Politics', pp. 199–200.

cases, played a leading part in shaping the Pilgrimage once it had broken out, the evidence for the outbreak itself being the result of their planning is unconvincing. There is some evidence to suggest pre-planning. The Duke of Norfolk reported in October on rumours circulating in East Anglia in September, promising a good living at diking and fowling for anybody who cared to make their way to Lincolnshire by Michaelmas; intriguing certainly in view of what happened, but Norfolk was erring on the side of caution in having the matter investigated, and there seems no further report on the matter.[4] Darcy, on 1 October, partly in his own hand, drew up a list of 'knights, squires and gentlemen and their numbers of household servants promised to serve the King's grace' in the honour of Pontefract, of which he was steward; those named (many of whom signed their own names) promised to be ready at an hour's warning to serve under Darcy or his deputy.[5] There is the leading role taken by Darcy's agent Thomas Maunsell, the vicar of Brayton, in raising men and general organisation even before Darcy himself had surrendered Pontefract.[6] And of course there are the suspicious circumstances of the stock of Five Wounds badges at Pontefract, allegedly left over from Darcy's crusade against the Moors in 1511;[7] and of Aske's immediate and ostensibly improbable acceptance as leader in the East Riding, indicating that preparations had been made beforehand.[8]

On the other hand there is also evidence that the actual sequence of events was not that planned by the 'conspirators'. Hussey and Aske both seem to have been unprepared for the actual outbreak in Lincolnshire.[9] If Darcy really was drawing up a list of potential supporters for a rebellion on 1 October, he was leaving things rather late (and at least one of those marked, Sir William Gascoyne, who promised a hundred men, eventually opposed the Pilgrimage); while another memorandum of the same day, about provision of wine, a new saddle and some cloth, betrays no sense of urgency.[10] Vicar Kendall's sermon at Louth on 1 October evidently fired the gun too soon. The speed with which the rebellion spread suggests that popular and clerical grievances were more autonomous than Professor Elton allows, and that they distorted any initial plans or, at least, that the quantity of explosive material was such that it needed very little to set it off.[11]

---

[4] *LP*, 11, no. 543.

[5] *LP*, 11, no. 522. See the discussion of this document in Smith, *Land and Politics*, pp. 191–4.

[6] *LP*, 11, no. 1402 (his confession). See Smith, *Land and Politics*, pp. 183–4, 191.

[7] *EHR*, v, 554–5, 571–2.   [8] Elton, 'Politics', p. 197.

[9] James, 'Obedience', pp. 57–65. Elton, 'Politics', p. 214.

[10] Smith, *Land and Politics*, p. 193: *LP*, 11, no. 522 (2).

[11] As I indicated above, n. 49, Kendall had a militant conservative background in a London diocese and could conceivably be himself connected with the More circle. (Dr Susan Brigden tells me she has not discovered one in her studies of Reformation London.) But there is, again, no evidence of direct connection with Hussey or the other 'conspirators'. The polarisation of provincial spontaneity and metropolitan conspiracy is too simple. There seem in fact to be a multiplicity of lines

If there was large-scale and intensive plotting, covering key figures over a large area of the north, it is odd that the government's interrogation did not unearth hard evidence for it in 1537. However much Hussey, Darcy and Aske were conspiring, both the actual outbreak and its outcome seem to have surprised them.[12] 'Conspiracy' undoubtedly shaped the form the Pilgrimage took; it is far from providing a complete explanation of how it broke out, let alone its subsequent extent and force.

connecting the rebels with London conservatives, lines which may well have got crossed, rather than a single ramifying conspiracy.

[12] I am unhappy at the use of the term 'faction' with its implications of profit and place as ends in themselves. It is difficult to see a reason for two septuagenarians like Hussey and Darcy, who had risen in court service, dabbling in treason unless there were reasons of principle at stake. Elton suggests, for instance, 'Politics', p. 209, that Hussey supported Mary's cause because he was her chamberlain. But presumably his appointment as chamberlain in 1533 indicates that he was then considered a reliable servant of the crown, and had since been converted to the cause. James, 'Obedience', pp. 52–5, shows Hussey's commitment to militant catholicism. If religious motives mattered anywhere, they surely mattered to Hussey and Darcy – and presumably to Aske.

3

Honour, Reputation and Local Officeholding in Elizabethan and Stuart England

A.J. FLETCHER

In Elizabethan and Stuart England, as in almost all settled states, order depended in the last resort less on courts and procedures than on officeholders and personal relationships. At the county level, government drew its strength from unity of purpose among groups of gentry who sat together on the bench and debated policy in their favourite hostelries. In the neighbourhoods, it drew its strength from the partnerships of able and vigorous JPs who were willing to be often in the saddle and constantly receiving constables and petitioners at their door.[1] But officeholding was a public act which made men peculiarly vulnerable to defamation. Recent work on this period has established that men and women at all levels of society showed extreme sensitivity over slights against their good name.[2] Office in county government – as a JP, a subsidy commissioner or a deputy-lieutenant – exposed a man on two fronts. While his credit among his peers might be elevated by their appreciation of his concern for justice, it could also be blotted if it became known or was believed that he abused his authority. His standing among the people could sink if gossip about his conduct, whether malicious or well founded, was allowed to spread unchecked. The theme of honour and reputation therefore provides an entry to the social world of Elizabethan and Stuart government, a world of ambition and assertiveness, sometimes of feud and personal conflict. Prestige not wealth was the principal reward of office. One

---

[1] I hope to elaborate these points in *Reform in the Provinces* (forthcoming).
[2] J.A. Sharpe, *Defamation and Sexual Slander in Early Modern England: the Church Courts at York* (Borthwick Papers, no. 58, St Anthony's Hall, York, 1980); J.A. Sharpe, 'Such Disagreement Betwyx Neighbours: Litigation and Human Relations in Early Modern England' in J. Bossy (ed.), *Disputes and Settlements: Law and Human Relations in the West* (CUP, 1983), pp. 167–88. M.J. Ingram, 'Ecclesiastical Justice in Wiltshire, 1600–1640, with Special Reference to Cases Involving Sex and Marriage', unpublished D.Phil. thesis, University of Oxford, 1976.

of the most crucial foundations of order was the sense among the gentry that office was worth undertaking for the reputation it brought. Another was the respect of the people for the integrity of those who ruled over them.

A man's reputation is a composition of various elements which can be more easily separated in description than they are in life. A man's honour, in this period, was the essence of his reputation in the eyes of his social equals: it gave him his sense of worth and his claim to pride in his own community and it contributed to his sense of identity with that community. By the seventeenth century a gradual modification of the chivalric code of honour was taking place. The sources of honour were still seen to be lineage and virtue. 'To traduce my actions, stain my blood and dishonour my father, which is long since dead, are three mortal wounds to my soul which can never be cured', wrote Sir Anthony Drury to his Norfolk kinsman Sir William de Grey, describing the speeches of a 'malicious adversary' in the 1620s. The Tudor and Stuart preoccupation with genealogy and the registering of coats of arms testifies to the gentry's continuing care to create lineage even where its foundations were flimsy.[3] But the warlike emphasis of the honour code in the late medieval period had become transmuted into a stress on self-assertiveness.[4]

Since social climbing was endemic in this society, there were many gentry to whom competitiveness came easily. Reputation was best advanced by activity and involvement, by the humiliation of rivals that was part and parcel of the desire for rule. Where could this be more conveniently pursued than on the bench or in the lieutenancy, with the unparalleled opportunities that both offered for the exercise of influence, mercy and arbitration? The prizes, in terms of fame and acclaim, were glittering but the risks could be unnerving. Most of the time the routines of good manners and courtesy, the traditional politesse of gentry society, veiled the rank competitiveness which drove men to be activist administrators in their own districts or in the wider circles of the shire. Officeholders nevertheless brought their honour with them onto the stage. They had no choice. For it was a public quality, an absolute, a condition of integrity which had to be zealously protected against insult or betrayal.[5] 'Honour is not in his hand who is honoured', wrote John Cleland in *The Institution of a Young Nobleman*, published in 1607, 'but in the hearts and opinions of other men.'[6] Public opinion within a particular social circle was the tribunal before which the claims to

---

[3] Norfolk RO, Walsingham MSS xvii/2, 410 × 5, fol 33r. For a useful brief introduction see Sir A. Wagner, *Heralds and Ancestors* (London, British Museum Publications, 1978). See also L. Stone, *The Crisis of the Aristocracy* (OUP, 1965), pp. 23–7.
[4] M. James, *English Politics and the Concept of Honour* (*Past and Present* Supplements, III, 1978), pp. 2–6.
[5] J.K. Campbell, *Honour, Family and Patronage* (Oxford, Clarendon Press, 1964), p. 269.
[6] Cited in James, *English Politics and the Concept of Honour*, p. 4.

honour were brought, the 'court of reputation' as it has been called, against whose judgements there was no redress.[7] Vindication, through withdrawal in face of the challenge of the aggrieved party or if necessary through the duel, could restore honour that had been called in question. Otherwise public ridicule, which kills reputation, would follow. Yet, although plenty of duelling went on in this period, most of the quarrels that will be discussed in this essay did not lead to a duel.[8] This appears to be because, although men thought about their honour incessantly and talked about it as well, the call for satisfaction was only seen to be appropriate on the evidence of blatant slander or following an open challenge before witnesses. Specific provocation, in other words, was an essential prelimi-nary to that call. There was plenty of provocation of rivals in the administrative dealings of this period, as we shall see, yet the ambiguities of the code of honour it seems played into the hands of those most adept at underhand behaviour and at sailing close to the wind. Competitive relationships in the government of the shires were not usually swiftly resolved but rather were kept in persistent tension for periods of months or sometimes years. Pursuit of office created personal rivalries but men's conduct of office, it will be argued, because it absorbed their energies, served to strengthen rather than weaken local government. An ultimate respect for the law and the concern to preserve gentry hegemony were strong inducements against behaviour that disrupted order for any length of time.

Since the language of honour was the common possession of a whole social class, whether courtiers in London or aspirants for office in the localities, arguments based upon the concept were ones that an ambitious man was foolish to neglect. Lord Hunsdon no doubt did seriously consider that family pride was at stake when he wrote to Sir Robert Cecil in 1596 about the succession to the office of justice *en oyer* in the Isle of Wight. But it made sense to make vigorous use of a language he knew Cecil would understand. He always 'esteemed an ounce of honour more than a pound of profit', he insisted: it would be 'honour for Her Majesty to give and disgrace for me not to receive, being so with a general allowance named to it that none . . . stand competitors with me'. His fifty years and long experience in local administration, he added, qualified him to follow in his father's footsteps.[9] A letter of 25 September 1625 from the Earl of Warwick to the Duke of Buckingham shows how far special pleading on the basis of an individual's need to preserve his honour could go. Only a fortnight before he had joined the Earl of Sussex, who had held the office on his own for the previous

---

[7] J. Pitt-Rivers, 'Honour and Social Status' in J.G. Peristiany (ed.), *Honour and Shame* (London, Weidenfeld, 1965), p. 27.

[8] For duelling see Stone, *Crisis of the Aristocracy*, pp. 242–50; P. Jenkins, *The Making of a Ruling Class: The Glamorgan Gentry 1640–1790* (CUP, 1983), pp. 199–201.

[9] *HMC Salisbury MSS*, IV, 488.

twenty-two years, in the lieutenancy of Essex. Warwick was in his late thirties, on close terms with Buckingham and ambitious for local advantage.[10] He was already a considerable territorial magnate with a strong commitment to the patronage of puritan ministers in the livings he controlled.[11] His mind was on supremacy in the county and he saw a chance to elbow Sussex aside. His partner, he told Buckingham, was willing to retire, 'besides mine own honour is suddenly disparaged, so that if this voluntary commission of my Lord should not receive His Majesty's allowance and be pursued with his grant accordingly it would not a little lessen the opinion of His Majesty's grace towards me and make me less able to do him service'.[12] This plausible account of the matter failed to move Buckingham, with whom Warwick shortly fell out. The next year he and four of his leading supporters in Essex were excluded from the government of the shire.[13]

Dismissal was always a disgrace, the more so when a single person was picked out from the throng. Offended by his sponsorship of a petition of puritan ministers in Northamptonshire, James I deprived Sir Francis Hastings of his places on the bench and in the deputy-lieutenancy. Hastings was devastated. He was the epitome of the godly magistrate, a man, as Claire Cross has written, who 'did not see service in the locality solely as a natural outlet for one of his birth and talent but as an obligation placed upon him by God'. He had recently established himself in Somerset after a long period of labour in Leicestershire. His newly found eminence in his adopted community suddenly blasted, he pleaded in April 1605 with Sir Robert Cecil to speak on his behalf: 'I might justly think myself a most unhappy man, if after thirty-seven years painful and faithful service . . . I should shut up my last days with disgrace, when his kingly countenance to regard and kingly hand to reward is stretched out to so many to their no small comfort.' He clung to the remnants of his local prestige. But in August, when he begged the Earl of Hertford, the lieutenant of Somerset, that he should be allowed to retain his colonelship of one of the militia bands, Hertford replied that this was a matter for the Privy Council and in the meanwhile he had appointed a deputy to perform Hastings's duties. With the musters about to begin this was a new blow. He feared that his being denied the right to appoint his own deputy, he told Hertford, would 'raise great doubts of me in the thoughts of the vulgar sort in my county'. Rivals exploited his discomfiture: 'there are some who make themselves merry at my disgrace and will be found forward enough in willingness to trample upon me if they find even so small stepping stone to lift them up'. When court favour

---

[10] R. Lockyer, *Buckingham* (London, Longman, 1981), pp. 196, 271, 277–8.
[11] C. Holmes, *The Eastern Association in the English Civil War* (CUP, 1974), p. 19.
[12] Bodleian, Firth MS c.4, p. 176.
[13] J.C. Sainty, *Lieutenants of Counties 1585–1642* (BIHR Special Supplement, no. 8, 1980), p. 20; R.P. Cust, 'The Forced Loan and English Politics 1626–1628', unpublished Ph.D. thesis, London University, 1984, pp. 309–10.

was so decisively removed, this incident shows, the friendship of the great men of the shire like Sir Edward Phellips, the builder of Montacute, counted for little. Hastings's sense of vulnerability was suddenly acute. His letters provide unusual insight into the state of mind of a public man shorn of his public platform. Reputation, his sense of identity even, was slipping away from him.[14]

The bitterest pill was dismissal in public. When Sir Thomas Wentworth was delivered a note informing him that he had been removed from the bench in the presence of his colleagues at the West Riding sessions in 1626, he protested his loyalty to the king, expressed his desire to serve his county and denounced his enemies. 'I could wish', he declared, 'they who succeed me had forborn this time for this service, a place in sooth ill chosen, a stage ill prepared for venting such poor, vain, insulting humours'.[15]

From the 1670s, with the growth of party political manipulation of the lieutenancy and the commissions of the peace, dismissals from office that had nothing whatever to do with administrative efficiency became more common. Two instances relating to the Harley family illustrate possible reactions and repercussions. Sir Edward Harley's reply in 1682 to repeated letters from the Marquess of Worcester, lieutenant in the marches of Wales, seeking the return of his deputy-lieutenancy commission is a classic expression of personal mortification. He began with excuses for having ignored Worcester's missives, mentioning illness in the family and the death of a near relation from smallpox. 'I do with all humility', he continued, 'submit to your Lordship's superseding me.' But on reflection this draft would not do. Harley changed 'all humility' to 'humble readiness'. And why should he actually part with his commission? 'I do conceive it a justice due to those who have had the honour to be your lordship's deputies', he wrote, 'to permit unto them the custody of those commissions, though vacated, as warrants for their acting therein.' In a recent case two constables who had carried an offender to gaol by his warrant were sued. But the fear of being questioned for past actions, one suspects, was only part of the story. Grieved at his dismissal, Sir Edward Harley maintained the courtesy on paper expected of one of his rank with great difficulty. His wish to let his commission rest in the family archive was a very human response to his predicament.[16]

Sir Edward's son Robert, the future Earl of Oxford, was on the other side of the fence in the quarrel with Thomas Lewis of New Radnor, which led to a dastardly attack on him in the street there on 2 October 1693. Lewis was a protégé of Harley's. The family's influence in the borough was well established and Harley

---

[14] C. Cross (ed.), *The Letters of Sir Francis Hastings* (Somerset Record Society, LXIX, 1969), pp. xxv, 92–7.
[15] W. Knowler (ed.), *The Earl of Strafford's Letters* (1729), I, 36; Cust, Forced Loan and English Politics, pp. 293–4, 297–300.   [16] BL, Loan MS 29/49.

was responsible for his advancement in town and county government. He assumed, quite wrongly, that Harley's influence at court also accounted for his removal from the bench in the Welsh reshuffle that took place in 1692. That regulation had produced considerable discontent in Radnorshire, though, as Harley explained in a letter to one of those who felt aggrieved, it was unavoidable in view of the need for active justices and the permanent limitation of the Welsh commissions to eight members.[17] Lewis felt betrayed by his patron and was not prepared to let the matter rest. When Harley came down to witness the swearing in of a new bailiff the next year his plans were laid. With his brother Nourse and some cronies hiding nearby, Lewis greeted him in the street. He proceeded to accuse him of having 'said somewhat ill of me in London'. When Harley gently denied the charge, Lewis spelt out the gossip he had heard: 'You said I was a man of desperate fortune and that Mr. Lewis of Nantguilt was fitter to be a justice of peace than I.' Nothing Harley said was likely to deter Lewis at this stage. He had manoeuvred his adversary so that his back was turned towards his brother, who ran at him with his sword outstretched. Harley managed to save his life by parrying two thrusts with his cane and by some deft swordplay. None of the crowd which quickly gathered intervened until it was clear that the attack had failed.[18] It was obviously unusual for a man to respond so violently to loss of office, but the New Radnor incident does confirm the potency of disgrace.

The payment of honour in the daily life of this society was offered through marks of respect such as the doffing of caps. The Suffolk JP Edmund Bohun, in his tract on the office in 1693, was scathing about those who 'look to nothing but the credit, honour and reputation they shall gain by it and if they can gain the title of Right Worshipful and have their neighbours stand bare-headed to them they have their designs'.[19] Most gentry were highly sensitive to such transactions of honour, symbolic representations of the differences in social rank and quality on which order rested. When the mayor of Nottingham omitted civilities that he believed were his due in 1676, the Duke of Newcastle wanted to go to law with him, but was warned off doing so by Secretary Coventry: 'I am told that of what temper so ever the mayor is there are some that have power of him that do almost undertake to bring him to make those public acknowledgements and submissions to your Grace as he may deserve your forgiveness.'[20]

There were numerous opportunities for battles over precedence. In Elizabethan Norfolk factional politics became so fraught that several gentlemen

---

[17] L.K.J. Glassey, *Politics and the Appointment of Justices of the Peace* (OUP, 1979), p. 110.
[18] J.A. Downie, 'The Attack on Robert Harley MP by the Lewis Brothers of Hampton Court in the Streets of New Radnor, 2 October 1693', *National Library of Wales Journal*, XX (1977), 40–5.
[19] E. Bohun, *The Justice of the Peace, his Calling and Qualifications* (London, 1693), p. 135.
[20] BL, Add. MS 25124, fols 87–90, 101–2; J.R. Western, *Monarchy and Revolution* (London, Blandford, 1972), p. 51.

intrigued at court to have their name placed above a local rival at the next renewal of the commission of the peace.[21] One Hertfordshire JP in the early Stuart period regularly signed his name with the addition of the number in a ring which represented his place in order of seniority.[22] Deeply entrenched quarrels could splutter into violence when the tensions of appearance in the public arena focused men's minds on questions of pre-eminence. At the Norwich sessions in 1582, Sir Arthur Heveningham, faced with charges of misconduct by Edward Flowerdew, 'burst out into a great and vehement kind of railing speech' against him.[23] A brawl with their fists between Sir Thomas Reresby and William Wentworth at the Rotherham quarter sessions in the 1590s turned into a scuffle with swords involving the two men's followers.[24] Arguments over seating arrangements on the bench were not uncommon. When the Tory Lord Cheyne and the Whig Lord Wharton appeared together on the Buckinghamshire bench in 1699, Cheyne objected to his rival sitting on the chairman's right hand and after the business they retired to duel.[25] Militia business raised similar issues. Captain Dillington's claim that his colours should take pride of place because he was the most senior trained band captain, on the occasion of Charles I's visit to the Isle of Wight to inspect the troops for the Rhe expedition in 1627, began a long wrangle. Another captain, Captain Urry, subsequently refused to muster his company believing that his seniority was being flouted. But he found himself publicly reprimanded by one of the deputies as a 'base clown, base jack and puppy'. It seems that Urry's social pretensions were not too securely founded: his family was of little account in the island until his father married into the highly respectable Oglander family. Rather than suffer ridicule, Urry hurried to see one of the heralds 'who found out his coat for him'.[26]

Serious clashes about precedence could also occur at election times. When a contest for the knightships of the shire was avoided, there was still the possibility of contention about which of the knights should be named first in the sheriff's return. Some correspondence between Sir Robert Harley and Sir Walter Pye about the Herefordshire election in 1626 is particularly interesting in this respect. Harley related to Pye in a letter of 12 January that at the quarter sessions in Hereford Sir John Scudamore had proposed they should be the knights:

I asked him in his ear whether it were his meaning that you should be first returned. To which he answered, aye. Then I spoke to the hearing of the rest that were present, that I

[21] A. Hassell Smith, *County and Court* (OUP, 1974), pp. 183, 190.
[22] J.B. Calnan, 'County Society and Local Government in the County of Hertford c.1580–c.1630', unpublished Ph.D. thesis, University of Cambridge, 1979, p. 150.
[23] Hassell Smith, *County and Court*, p. 195.
[24] D. Robinson, 'The Local Officeholders of Elizabethan Yorkshire', unpublished Ph.D. thesis, University of Leeds, 1980, pp. 102–3.
[25] Glassey, *Justices of the Peace*, p. 30.
[26] L.O.J. Boynton, *The Elizabethan Militia* (London, Routledge, 1961), pp. 281–2.

being a Knight of the Bath and Sir Walter Pye a Knight Bachelor, I understood it would point at my dishonour in this service to have second place, and wished the gentlemen to nominate some other to stand with you unless I might have first.

After some debate, he explained, during which a cousin of Harley's suggested that 'he thought you would not contend with me for the first place', it was resolved that Harley should be named first. But it was left to him to request his partner to stand down. In his reply on 14 January Pye protested that he had all along been willing to give way, but went on to assert his position:

I do really and freely desire that you may be first returned and this is done for the love I bear Sir Robert Harley and his house . . . But that it is his right, I acknowledge it not, nor that he should be first placed in the love of my particular obliged friends. I am well assured he will not expect it. If there be anything in my power to do Sir Robert Harley any real courtesy, I will be ever ready to observe him.

This icy letter provoked an equally icy response on 28 January. After thanking him for 'so large an expression of real respects', Harley continued:

And I hope you do not suspect me to be of so left handed a judgment as to think that it is either your or my right to be knights for the parliament or to have precedency in that troublesome honour, both depending on a public suffrage of our country. But if you please not to acknowledge the right precedency to belong to my knighthood before yours, you will then give me leave to justify it in such a way as shall maintain my honour and not impair yours.

Harley and Pye were left with a gnawing sense that their colleagues in county government had not so much adjudicated between them as knocked their heads together. Their first consideration had been to choose two men they could trust. They then expected them to work together and to put 'the quiet of the country' before private sensibilities. Both men were proud, but both were aware of the 'public suffrage' which brought them to the most prestigious role in county politics and both shared the general consensus that their task was to do the county service and 'maintain the peace of it'.[27]

Once in office a JP had manifold opportunities for favouritism and vindictiveness. The Star Chamber papers of the reigns of James I and Charles I, hardly yet exploited, contain much evidence about the methods by which men played out their local rivalries through their conduct of business. It is often hard to separate truth from scurrility in these cases, but it is quite clear that allegations of misuse of judicial powers were often a pretext to undermine the credit of other justices. Ambitious and aggressive magistrates easily found themselves caught up in a vicious circle of dubious practice, charge and counter-charge. Once involved it was hard to escape or withdraw. Sir Henry Cocke's letter seeking the support of

[27] BL, Loan MS 29/202. I am grateful to Myra Rifkin for making available a typescript of these letters.

Lord Burghley against his neighbour William Purvey in 1588 nicely makes the point. He was wearied by the continual slander and backbiting of his rival on the bench: 'I have lived (I thank God) many years amongst men of sundry humours and strange affections yet never found I (amongst them all) anyone so full fraught with disdainful pride and malice as my overthwart neighbour Mr. Purvey.' Cocke was enraged by Purvey's recent words to the bailiff of Hertford and others when they visited him on some official business. 'He knew them not', Purvey declared, 'nor would know them, but he would make them to know him, and to come to him with their empty baskets as well as they did go to others with their full baskets.'[28] Cocke believed this barb was aimed at him, but, whatever provocation he had given, he was hardly going to mention it to Burghley. He protested his innocence: 'I am sure that neither he nor any other shall be able to prove that I received any one as a gift of bribery for wresting or neglecting justice.'[29]

What forms then did the struggle for reputation take? In the first place a particular enmity often led to the division of a district or a whole shire: feud was more than likely to turn into factionalism. A mutual antagonism sent ripples across the pool, so that constables, overseers, stewards of manors, jurymen, plaintiffs and defendants came to be manipulated and involved. The more diffused a quarrel became the more difficult it was for either party to resolve the matter by bringing it to the point of honour. The rewards went to the man who kept cool under provocation, who could take scorn and insult and find his revenge in due time. Ambushed by his inveterate enemy Sir Arthur Heveningham as he rode along the Wymondham to Norwich highway in 1583, Edward Flowerdew refused to duel, pleading that he was about the queen's business and unarmed. Heveningham spurred his horse after him and struck him on the head, giving him a grievous wound, the proof of which was showed in court shortly afterwards when one of Flowerdew's servants appeared with his master's bloodstained hat. But such was Heveningham's backing among the gentry that it was only with difficulty that Flowerdew's supporters got him and his men bound to keep the peace. Eventually though Heveningham did settle a Star Chamber case with Flowerdew out of court, agreeing to pay six hundred pounds in damages.[30] Sir Thomas Posthumous Hoby, that most overbearing, touchy and resentful of Yorkshire magistrates, alleged against Sir Richard Cholmley in Star Chamber in 1609 that Cholmley had twice spoken to him contemptuously at musters in the hope of provoking an open quarrel or even a duel and that he had also publicly denounced the validity of his magisterial warrants. Hoby triumphed in the long run in the North Riding through sheer persistence. He kept

[28] Calnan, 'Local Government in Hertfordshire', pp. 151–2.   [29] HMC Salisbury MSS, XII, 44.
[30] Hassell Smith, County and Court, pp. 197–8, 233–4.

up his disputatious career with one rival after another for more than thirty years and eventually, in the 1630s, became Custos Rotulorum.[31]

There were a few exceptionally prolonged struggles for supremacy, such as that between Sir Robert Phellips and Lord Poulett in Somerset which lasted from 1614 to 1638.[32] By and large though the death or exhaustion of one of the parties closed disputes more quickly. Sir Richard Cholmley, at odds with Hoby since 1601, withdrew from the bench in 1609 to avoid further trouble with him. If an opponent's abuse of authority had been blatant, victory could come swiftly. Sir Henry Winston was prosecuted in Star Chamber in 1602 by a neighbouring JP, Sir Thomas Throckmorton, for attacking a bailiff who had arrested one of his servants. He was also alleged to have shown mercy to two or three offenders who were his dependents. Acknowledging the court's censure, he pleaded with Sir Robert Cecil for remittance of the punishment of public confession of his offence at Gloucester assizes. 'I desire rather to remain in prison', he wrote, 'than to receive open disgrace in my country.' Sir Robert Monson, who had been removed from the West Riding bench through the machinations of Henry Grice, fought back and had Grice dismissed, after he had admitted striking a poor taylor sent to the house of correction on suspicion of theft. Sir Thomas Wentworth later refused to countenance his reinstatement because he was convinced that Grice was unworthy of office.[33]

Open violence between gentry antagonists was comparatively rare. Duelling was checked by royal disapproval as well as by the diffraction of the gentry's power struggles. The Norfolk gentleman Thomas Lovell got short shrift when he tried to call Sir Nicholas Bacon to the point of honour in 1586. His letter to Bacon, following an accusation that he had suborned and corrupted witnesses, offered three alternative kinds of duel. It is a masterpiece of invective:

I tell thee thou liest, thou liest and liest in thy throat . . . and I do by this my letter challenge thee as a lying knight . . . who doth first endamage the enemy, let the other be accounted recreant, a dastard, and a discredited person in all honourable and honest company . . . But if thou shall refuse the performance of the one of these three, then I will secretly repute thee and openly blast thee as a dunghell spirited man, as one that did nothing participate in thy generation with the silver mould of thy honourable father.

Bacon forwarded the letter to the Council, which wasted no time in summoning Lovell and committing him to the Marshalsea prison. He remained there until a friend at court secured his release and turned the tables by getting Bacon reprimanded for his vindictiveness.[34]

[31] G.C.F. Forster, 'Faction and County Government in Stuart Yorkshire', *Northern History*, XI (1975), 74–86.

[32] T.G. Barnes, *Somerset 1625–1640* (OUP, 1961), pp. 281–98.

[33] *Northern History*, XI (1975), 71–2, 79, 82.   [34] Hassell Smith, *County and Court*, p. 184.

In so far as violence did occur, it was just as likely to take the form of an undignified scrap such as occurred in the Norwich highway in 1583, at the Rotherham sessions in the 1590s or at New Radnor in 1693 as the controlled combat allowed by the rules of the duel. In certain counties gentry rivalry also kept alive, within the context of local government, the intimidation and armed assertiveness characteristic of fifteenth-century bastard feudalism. Herefordshire in the Elizabethan period is an outstanding case. The boastful and swaggering gentleman Thomas Coningsby used his offices as a justice and deputy-lieutenant to raise his family to one of the foremost in the county during the 1580s. He was followed around by a band of liveried retainers known locally as the 'redcoats'. His feud with the anciently established Croft family reached a climax in the fierce night-time battle that occurred in Hereford during the 1588 assizes. Coningsby himself was wounded and Thomas Wigmore, a gentleman who supported Croft, was slain. Herbert Croft, the heir to the family estates newly appointed to the bench, attended the Lent assizes in the following year with fifty armed followers. His first appearance at sessions that Easter was a critical moment. He came in with 300 of his grandfather's tenants and appeared himself at the court house wearing a pistol. Having avoided the rest of the company at the preliminary dinner, he insisted on taking his place above Coningsby on the bench. Coningsby retired with his followers in face of Croft's show of strength and turned to Star Chamber where he subsequently wore down his opponent by attrition. By 1590 the violent phase of this struggle was over. Whereas, on his appointment as a JP, Herbert Croft undoubtedly used his power as a faction leader to the detriment of law and order, R.E. Ham has shown how during the 1590s, seeking county leadership, he became one of the crown's most trusted agents in Herefordshire. If in the short run the Croft and Coningsby feud weakened local government in the shire, in the longer run it probably did something to bolster its effectiveness.[35]

The Star Chamber depositions of the Monmouthshire gentry Edward and Sir William Morgan in 1606 provide another example of the use of force and numbers. Sir William Morgan, we are told, 'being a justice of peace and a great man in his country, upon former malice and quarrel with Edward Morgan, had caused a challenge to be sent to him and his sons'. The challenge was not a call to single combat but a declaration that he would disgrace his opponent by a show of force at the Usk quarter sessions. Sir William

had sent and spoken to divers of his friends and kinsmen to come strong to meet at the sessions, and thereupon he himself came accompanied with forty men, some with swords,

[35] R.E. Ham, 'The Career of Sir Herbert Croft: A Study in Local Government and Society', unpublished Ph.D. thesis, University of California 1974, pp. 44–73, 137.

rapiers and daggers, steel caps, privy coats, javelins and swords and bucklers and bills and long staves, in so much as the town was full of weapons and there came 140 to assist.

Edward Morgan replied in kind, bringing a strong band of his own

some armed with privy coats, quilted caps, swords and bucklers, halberts, javelins and pike staves and trooped up and down the town with their weapons after proclamation made by the sheriff for keeping the peace.

This balance of terror was effective: there was only a single minor injury to one of Sir William Morgan's kinsmen who suffered 'a great blow in the face'. But three of the judges declared that 'this seeking to be great and bear a side, in those countries especially, is very dangerous'.[36]

The indivisibility of government and politics in this period does much to account for the ease with which quarrels over credit and reputation flourished. They received much of their impetus from the urgent public issues which offered a convenient front for the pursuit of private rivalries. Intermixture of personal hostilities and issues of principle was of their essence. Loyalty to church and state or to the locality and county community were beguiling concepts, ready to hand for clever and ambitious men to brandish in their own interests. Men like Sir Edward Dering in Kent, Sir Robert Phellips in Somerset and Sir Thomas Wentworth in Yorkshire opportunistically exploited the differences between court and country viewpoints on matters of religion and government.[37] Malice could be concealed under a display of dutifulness which distracted attention from the sheer egocentricity that so often lay behind the devotion men gave to local affairs. At the same time the increasingly sophisticated standards of gentry society forced antagonists to conduct their relationships with at least a modicum of decency and courtesy. So everything pointed to intrigues and whispering campaigns rather than to duels or affrays.

As Hassell Smith's study of Elizabethan Norfolk shows, the range of issues that could be brought into play was immense. Bassingbourne Gawdy used Thomas Lovell's recusant connections as a means of humbling him. The Flowerdew and Heveningham conflict was one of personalities but also one of values. Flowerdew was the precise common lawyer, working for his own advancement within the context of shire administration, whereas Heveningham saw himself as the agent of the court. 'Energetic, flamboyant, irascible, quarrelsome', writes Hassell Smith, 'he displayed supreme contempt for those cumbersome administrative processes which depended upon agreement among justices

[36] J. Hawarde (ed.), *Les Reportes del Cases in Camera Stellata*, pp. 312–15.

[37] I have examined the impact of these men's ambitions on county politics in my essay, 'National and Local Awareness in the County Communities' in H. Tomlinson (ed.), *Before the English Civil War* (London, Macmillan, 1983), pp. 154–61.

meeting in quarter sessions.' Heveningham's procurement of a patent to repair the Cambridge to Southwold highway in the Suffolk parish of Metfield in 1581 concentrated the misgivings of his puritan colleagues with a firm training in the common law about intrusions upon local autonomy. They were suspicious about licences which could produce subordination of the community's well-being to the ambition of an individual. The ambush attempt on Flowerdew, mentioned above, arose directly from Heveningham's hotheaded anger when he discovered he had been out-manoeuvred at court and kept off the bench at a crucial moment in this local contest.[38]

Sir Thomas Hoby's campaigns of aggrandisement in the East and North Ridings were based on policy as well as personal assertiveness. He came to Yorkshire as an agent of the regime of Sir Robert Cecil, set upon probing the immunities from the law enjoyed by a group of closely connected recusant gentry and catholic sympathisers. His Star Chamber case against four colleagues on the East Riding bench in 1615 was based on the charge that they had conspired to prevent the due indictment and conviction of certain catholics. He told a story of lobbying, procedural tricks and acrimony in public as the men concerned fought to outwit him. Disagreements about prosecution of recusants also figured largely in Hoby's struggle with the Cholmley family, known for their catholic connections, in the North Riding.[39]

It would be a mistake if, through preoccupation with men seeking reputation for its own sake, we were to suppose that selfish motives were always predominant in the exercise of office. In his examination of 'magistracy and ministry' in the period from 1559 to 1625, Patrick Collinson has pointed to the idealism and deep concern for social reform of justices like Sir Anthony Cope in Oxfordshire, Sir Nathaniel Barnardiston in Suffolk and Sir Robert Harley in Herefordshire.[40] Godliness was the core of these men's sense of reputation. In their analysis of the public career of the Cheshire baronet Sir Richard Grosvenor, Richard Cust and Peter Lake argue that he was a man intent upon 'forging important ideological links between the arena of national politics and local society'. They see him as a reformer moved by 'some concept of the common good that transcended pure localism'. In his charges to the grand jury at Chester in 1625 and 1626, Grosvenor lectured his countrymen on the ills of the commonwealth.[41] Many a puritan JP did the same in the Elizabethan and early Stuart decades. There were plenty of

[38] Hassell Smith, *County and Court*, pp. 183, 193–5, 228–34.
[39] G.C.F. Forster, *The East Riding Justices of the Peace in the Seventeenth Century* (East Yorkshire Local History Series, XXX, 1973), pp. 37–9; *Northern History*, XI (1975), 74–7, 85.
[40] Collinson, pp. 145, 164–70. For Barnardiston see also A. Everitt, *Suffolk and the Great Rebellion 1640–1660* (Suffolk Records Society, vol. III, 1960), pp. 12, 16.
[41] R. Cust and P.G. Lake, 'Sir Richard Grosvenor and the Rhetoric of Magistracy', *BIHR*, LIV (1981), 40–53.

unscrupulous men at one end of the spectrum of magistracy, but these men were at the other. Altruism, however, did not make men immune from the criticism or rivalry of their colleagues. It could of course provoke them.

The fate of Thomas Milward, who set his mind on reforming the subsidy administration first of Worcestershire then of Hampshire, indicates the hazards of interference in a field which offered maximum opportunities for patronage and favouritism. His account of his public disagreements with Sir Richard Grevis makes hilarious reading. He was a most unusual subsidy commissioner, a man who was naive and literal-minded enough to take his office seriously and believe he should do the job properly.[42] Yet the letter and memorandum he sent to his friend Sir Thomas Jervoise in 1626 is so ingenuous that it can be taken at face value. By then he was at the end of his tether, having been removed from the bench through Grevis's machinations. Petulant and humiliated at having been painted in London as 'the veryest rascal in the country and the basest companion and unfittest for such an engagement', he wanted support from Jervoise in an appeal to the Lord Keeper. In brief, Milward's case against Grevis was that he systematically used subsidy administration to extend his own credit. They had first tangled in Worcestershire, where Milward discovered Grevis working through a recusant dependent of his who he had appointed as an assessor. It was not through 'ambitious motives of my own' he became a commissioner in Hampshire, Milward told Jervoise, but to check Grevis's 'conceited greatness'. Grevis, he explained, sought, 'out of his ambition to be reputed the ruler of the roost in his country', to manage the whole business himself. He had failed to hold a preliminary meeting of the assessors to instruct them in their duty as the statute directed. He excused friends and kept down the books to their old level, ignoring many chances to increase the burden on men who escaped ridiculously lightly and to bring in newcomers who escaped altogether. Milward's vehement conclusion to his letter sprang from a mixture of pique at his own exclusion from the bench and frustrated zeal for reform of the most notoriously corrupt aspect of the fiscal system. Grevis, he avowed, was a 'shallow pated knight', as suited to the offices of magistrate, deputy-lieutenant and subsidy commissioner

as a knighthood garnished with store of money bags may be conceived to enable a man base in his original (as the son of a wheelwright), never bred either in university or inn of court, no not so much able as to write good English to explain himself in his places with sensible and significant terms and so free from all material goodness as that his daily actions manifest him to be composed of these four elements as rather bad conditions and qualities: malice, ignorance, untruth and avarice.[43]

---

[42] For the gentry's sabotage of the subsidy see my *A County Community in Peace and War: Sussex 1600–1660* (London, Longman, 1975), pp. 202–5, 360–3.
[43] Hampshire RO, Herriard MSS, Box F9.

Whereas the magistracy was the sphere of the gentry, the militia brought the aristocracy onto the public stage. Many of the noblemen appointed as lieutenants of the counties were conscientious about their obligations: they gave attentive concern to the implementation of the Council's orders and took pride in the performance of their county at musters. Their reputations at the centre depended in part on the evidence of their ability to bring their subordinates into line. Thus the Earl of Northampton, requesting information from his Norfolk deputies about training at musters in 1608, revealed his fear of loss of face. 'I desire to know from yourselves what course you take herein', he wrote, 'least hereafter just exceptions to defects or errors light upon myself, who desire in causes that concern public chiefly to be blameless.'[44] The Earl of Dorset, affronted at hearing that there was open resistance to the forced loan of 1626, reminded his Sussex deputies of the need to inculcate in the people 'faith to their sovereigns word'. 'Believe I am one', he added, 'on whom no such disgrace shall be laid as to be made the instrument of deception.'[45]

Occasionally a lieutenant actually found himself in the front line. The Duke of Beaufort, terrified by the approach of William of Orange's army in November 1688, panicked about the impact of an ignominious surrender on his credit at court. 'I know the King does not expect a man should undertake a thing wherein he sees an impossibility of coming off with honour', he wrote to the Earl of Middleton, 'which the defence of this place would be with a small, slighted, disaffected and (at best) inexperienced militia.' A day or two later, when it seemed the danger of a siege was past, Beaufort thought better of this letter, sent as he put it to Middleton in a further missive, 'out of an apprehension of dishonour to myself'. The charge of cowardice before the enemy, he now realised, could ruin the esteem in which he was held more certainly than a token defiance of the invader.[46]

The deputy-lieutenancy gave a select group from within the county benches special powers in the military sphere. When these powers rested solely on the prerogative, which was the case between 1604 and 1642, there was a fruitful source of tension between deputies and gentry called upon to assist them as militia captains or justices. Incidents in Sussex and Norfolk show how the insertion of a rather artificial kind of hierarchy into gentry administration could make for awkwardness. The Sussex deputies were angry in August 1615 at the defiance, as they saw it, of the justices in Chichester rape who refused to carry out their instructions without copies of the Council's letters. The justices' hesitancy was very likely due as much to doubts about their ability to impose obligations that were not already customary as to any quarrelsomeness, but the deputies

[44] BL, Kings MS 265, fols. 314v, 315r.
[45] Fletcher, *A County Community*, p. 196.   [46] BL, Add MS 41805, fols. 157r, 178.

detected a question of trust. 'They prevailing over us in this case', they told the lieutenants, 'we fear it will be an impairing of our estimation and so hereby made less able to execute your lordship's designs.'[47] The trouble in Norfolk the following year arose from the intemperate behaviour of Sir Arthur Heveningham, that veteran East Anglian campaigner for local glory and power, who was still up to his old tricks. He altered the form of some warrants to militia captains, after his fellow deputies had agreed them, in such a way that at least two of them, Sir William de Grey and Sir Thomas Holland, felt bound to protest publicly that they took exception to the disparaging tone Heveningham had adopted. De Grey attempted to make Heveningham see that there were issues involved of respect between social equals. Some of the phraseology, he told him, was 'more proper to be directed to chief constables than one gentleman to another, between whom too much courtesy as I thought could not be used'. Heveningham would hear none of this, bitterly declaring that he had previously used such terms to better men who held militia captaincies in the past. At this point De Grey as good as offered his resignation and retired in pique to seek support by writing round to his friends. Sir Thomas Holland also stood his ground, telling Heveningham he believed the captains were 'as worthy to do that service belonging to them as himself was in his, how meanly soever he accounted of them'. He was not so 'rash-pated', he told De Grey in a letter, as to apologise before the deputy-lieutenant's bluster. 'I meddle not with his better parts', he concluded, 'but will defend my reputation in the performance of my service without fear of his contestations or giving leave to write his errors upon my forehead.' Heveningham's reaction to the captains' obstinacy was at one point to threaten resignation. But no resignations took place and the quarrel was patched up.[48]

The exceptional demands placed upon deputies during the years of Charles I's exact militia programme imposed strains upon local relationships. Gentry were even more touchy than usual about how their good name might suffer as a result of public duties. It is perhaps predictable that it was in Norfolk, one of the most politically precocious of the English counties, that the whole programme came closest to collapse. The tension over militia burdens there is evident from a letter sent by Sir Charles Cornwallis, Sir William de Grey and Sir John Hare to Sir John Hobart in September 1627. Hobart was a hot-tempered man who probably sought the leadership of the band of eight deputies acting under the Earl of Arundel.[49] His colleagues had heard that he was responsible for spreading a story

---

[47] Clwyd RO, D/HE/505, p. 33. I am grateful to Richard Cust for drawing my attention to the deputy-lieutenancy book in which this reference occurs.
[48] Norfolk RO, Walsingham MSS, XVII/2, 410 × 5, fols. 15v–17r.
[49] R.W. Ketton Cremer, *Norfolk in the Civil War* (London, Faber, 1969), pp. 38–40.

at the King's Head in Norwich that they had condoned bribery and corruption in the management of the recent impressment of soldiers at Kings Lynn. They felt accused of baseness and infidelity to the lieutenant's commands. They could not accept that Hobart, 'such do we know to be your own birth and breeding and such your knowledge of the true terms of honour and reputation', could have been 'either the publisher or pronouncer of such an aspersion upon us, except some proof or testimony (without all exceptions) had been made and given unto you of the same'. Well aware that their 'faith and sincerity' would be widely called in question, the three deputies insisted that the whole matter should be fully investigated at the next quarter sessions, where they would answer their accusers face to face.[50] Whether it was in the end necessary for them to do so is uncertain. Within months it was necessary for the deputies to rally together against a general tide of opposition. Norfolk's restiveness reached its climax in 1628. After a disastrous muster, six deputies gathered at Norwich, including Hobart, Cornwallis, De Grey and Hare, wrote in despair to the Earl of Arundel on 20 August. Their letter provides a unique insight into the fragility of the early Stuart militia, an institution of local government that rested entirely on the ability of influential men in the provinces to command respect and obedience. There was 'no hope of reducing this service to any better terms', declared the deputies, because the people of Norfolk were fully convinced, and of course correctly informed, that the militia lacked a basis in statute.[51] Whereas previously they and their predecessors could rely on the directions of the monarch and his Council – directions which had in themselves provided the deputies 'with much security' – these no longer carried weight. The militia had always drawn authority from at least the tacit backing of the entire gentry community, but men of the deputies own kind now led the revolt in Norfolk. At the Kings Lynn sessions in July a JP who was a serjeant-at-law had publicly questioned a tax to pay the costs of billeting some Irish soldiers sent to Norfolk by the Council. Moreover

he moved the other justices his associates to join with him in sending up our warrants to the parliament, but did also in a contemptuous manner openly put into his pocket one of the warrants directed to the chief constables for that purpose, saying that he would answer the same and that much more money had been levied than was needful for the service or words to like effect.

This lead had a catastrophic effect. Several of the captains had already, by late

[50] W. Rye (ed.), *State Papers relating to the Musters, Beacons, Ship Money in Norfolk* (Norwich, 1907), pp. 102–3.

[51] Fletcher, *A County Community*, pp. 187–8; A. Hassell Smith, 'Militia Rates and Militia Statutes 1558–1663' in P. Clark, A.G.R. Smith and N.R.N. Tyacke (eds.), *The English Commonwealth 1547–1640* (Leicester University Press, 1979), pp. 93–110.

August, resigned and others pleaded to be allowed to do so. Such was the general mood, it would be 'exceeding difficult if not impossible' to find replacements. The deputies felt bitterness and intense humiliation. They unanimously decided to ask Arundel to beseech the king to discharge them from their offices

wherein in the meantime we continue to our own infinite discontentments, in regard that we find neither means nor hope to perform for His Majesty's service either what doth agree with his honour, the safety and good of this county or with our own poor credits, which we more value than what else in this world we possess or look for.

For the next year the Norfolk militia hardly existed. Then Arundel, who had remained deaf to all pleas for resignation, sent down his son Lord Maltravers to inject encouragement and vigour into the musters. The normal assumptions of patronage and deference began once more to oil the wheels and the deputies went back to work.[52]

The 1662 Militia Act gave deputy-lieutenants the confidence they had previously lacked: they could bring the force of law to sustain their demands instead of having to rely far more heavily than they wished on personal standing and persuasion. Yet concern for public face was undiminished. A letter from John Milward to the Earl of Devonshire in 1665 nicely illustrates a Derbyshire deputy's anxieties on this source. He had just suffered the indignity of being served with a subpoena by the earl's steward of his manorial court of Hartington in the presence of the gentry of the High Peak at the Bakewell musters. Milward, who was very much a protégé of the lieutenant's, explained his readiness to give satisfaction in the matter under dispute but expressed his dislike of the steward's manner of proceeding. His action, had not Milward been 'more private in the business than such an affront deserved', might have produced an unseemly disturbance. 'I hope your lordship will give me leave', he continued, 'to regard my honour and reputation, especially when I am discharging your honour's commands in His Majesty's service.' Devonshire sought to mollify him, in his reply, with an assurance that, had he known about it, he would never have let the steward deliver the subpoena without acquainting him of the matter.[53]

So far we have been considering the dealings of the nobility and gentry with each other. In their dealings with inferior officers JPs just as frequently showed touchiness about their credit and standing. The clerk of the peace was a key figure in the smooth running of shire administration and an intermediary between individual JPs and the bench.[54] There was mostly considerable trust between the clerks and justices but, as an incident in Somerset in 1615 indicates, when a JP suspected that a clerk had shown partiality rancour could develop.

---

[52] Rye (ed.), *Musters, Beacons and Ship Money*, pp. 141–7, 152–7, 163–72.
[53] BL, Add MS 34306, fol. 49.   [54] Fletcher, *A County Community*, p. 145.

Barnaby Lewes was determined that an alehouse at Midsomer Norton should be closed, because he was convinced the publican was unfit to hold a licence. The publican went behind his back to other justices and to the clerk in order to reverse his decision. Lewes was furious when he found that the clerk had drawn an order referring the whole matter to three of his colleagues, allowing him to join 'if he will'. 'I must tell you', he wrote to the clerk, 'that I have been deeply abused by him and have complained and will prove it without exception or else I will not sit on the bench again, for I will never be braved or opposed against by an audacious alehousekeeper and shameless as he is.'[55] Roger Shoyswell, newly appointed to the Sussex bench in 1665, was deeply offended when a bailiff arrested him for not being legally sworn. His first reaction was to demand that the bailiff should be indicted but the matter was subsequently composed, he reported to the clerk of the peace, the bailiff having 'acknowledged his folly and promised never to commit any more such an absurdity as to arrest a JP without a writ of privilege be first sent out'.[56]

Constables could equally as well as clerks or bailiffs fall foul of a JP's wrath. Although most JPs were quite prepared to go along with informal mechanisms of arbitration, they were sometimes sensitive about the way these were used once they had involved themselves by issuing a warrant. Ambrose Barcroft records in the register that he kept as high constable of Blackburn hundred in Lancashire in 1681 that he received Thomas Braddyll's warrant to bring a yeoman and two husbandmen who were in dispute with Anthony Bauldwine before him at his home in Portfield on 9 June. On the way there with the men concerned he managed to end the quarrel so the parties saw no need to appear on Braddyll's summons. But the justice, concerned at gossip that had reached him about his intervention, looked upon the matter differently. He was 'displeased that they were not brought before him to satisfy the law for the misdemeanours so far as they were criminal and for false reports some of them had cast upon him as to his business'.[57]

Honour was only at stake between equals; reputation was at stake with everyone. Disrespect and defamation by countrymen were constant threats to the effective exercise of local government. There were always a few ready to ignore the norms of deference and fly in the face of authority. Not content with refusal to pay his poor rate in 1665, a Sussex man disputed the assessment of the parish over his ale in the Swan at Southover. 'Sir Thomas Nutt and Mr. Rivers', he declared, 'were no gents if they confirmed the book and that if Mr. Rivers had

---

[55] E.H. Bates Harbin (ed.), *Somerset Quarter Sessions Records* (Somerset Record Society, XXIII, 1907), vol. I, pp. xxvi, 141.   [56] East Sussex RO, QR/E 147/60.

[57] R. Sharpe France (ed.), 'A High Constable's Register 1681', *Transactions of the Historic Society of Lancashire and Cheshire*, vol. CVII (1956), pp. 68–9.

done it he would spit in his face'. In 1675 Roger Shoyswell presented a Ticehurst labourer 'for giving approbrious language to him'; in 1683 his colleague John Apsley had a man arrested for his 'ill carriage and demeanour towards him'.[58] Such cases were common enough. Sometimes men acted out of a general sense of rebelliousness. 'Have not the justices yet shown all their tyranny and spite against me?', declared a Manchester gentleman in 1621, struggling with the churchwardens to rescue a black gelding which they had attempted to distrain.[59] Christopher Goddier of Bagginton in Warwickshire, having lived with his family at the expense of the village for six months in 1651, threw away his claim to maintenance when he appeared in court by his insolency before the bench, which caused the justices present to send him to gaol.[60] Sometimes there was a particular quarrel which became bound up with the exercise of justice. A yeoman of Sutton-upon-Trent in Nottinghamshire, appearing on a charge of spending a Sunday morning in the alehouse rather than at church, burst out with an accusation against one of the magistrates present. 'Mr. Cartwright had a bond of his', he announced, 'and he would worm it out of his nest and that he would get him to be thrust off the bench.'[61]

Countrymen's taunts were meant to hurt and annoy. The kinds of abuse justices suffered give a fair indication of the qualities and standards that were expected of those put in authority. Social prestige, wisdom and probity were clearly assumed to be the requisites for magisterial office. The Cheshire justice Henry Bradshaw took offence in 1651 when he heard it reported that Joshua Gerard had said that 'a stranger would not think he was a man of that eminency in the country, he going so plain in apparel'. A Manchester grocer insisted that a JP who had him bound to good behaviour in 1669 'never had been worth a groat': he himself was a better man because 'he could show two coats of arms'.[62] The Norfolk bench was informed in 1682 that a particularly recalcitrant criminal then in the Norwich goal frequently spoke evil of the magistracy, especially of John Shadwell, whom he decried as 'a bankrupt and beggarly rogue and runaway'.[63] The Sussex labourer Thomas Pettite made his views about the local magistrate absolutely clear during the discussion at Heathfield in 1608 about why an alehouse which Sir Edward Culpepper had suppressed was still open. Culpepper's warrant, he insisted, 'is not regarded this much for other justices will not allow of it'. Culpepper was an 'old dotish who in some actions was as wise as one's arse'.[64] Parvenu Devon justices who came in for abuse during the 1650s had

[58] East Sussex RO, QR/E 146/64, E 187/4; QO/EW 8, fol 135r.
[59] E. Axon (ed.), *Manchester Sessions* (Record Society of Lancashire and Cheshire, vol. XLII, 1901), p. 138.   [60] S.C. Ratcliff and H.C. Johnson (eds.), *Warwick County Records*, III (1937), 91–2.
[61] H.H. Copnall (ed.), *Nottinghamshire County Records* (1915), p. 53.
[62] J.S. Morrill, *Cheshire 1630–1660* (OUP, 1974), p. 227; Manchester Central Library, MS F347, p. 221.   [63] Norfolk RO, C s3, box 54 A.   [64] Fletcher, *A County Community*, p. 226.

their social and intellectual disabilities summarised in similarly colourful language: Richard Cockram 'had no more wit to be a justice than his breach'; William Fry 'was no more justice than his arse'. Fortunately for him, declared a Devon man about Justice Wollocomb, who, he alleged, he had bribed without difficulty, he was not on the bench when he was called, otherwise he would have publicly accused the JP and 'it should have sounded badly to his credit'. Wollocomb had been at a sermon instead, he added, 'he is one of the new set and his clerk is fitter to be a justice than he is'.[65] A Whitby innkeeper was presented in 1685 for calling Sir Hugh Cholmley 'a thick, idle, sapheaded, sleepy drone'.[66]

The attacks on JPs' probity took various forms. Some were generalised. For example a Yorkshire man was alleged in 1616 to have called one of the most senior magistrates William Mauleverer 'a knave and a bad justice of peace'; a Sussex gentleman declared in 1642 that Thomas Middleton was 'no honest man but a knave'; a baker of Atherston in Warwickshire in 1680 disparaged Edward Hinton in similar terms.[67] Occasionally a justice was accused of sexual misbehaviour. Before the home of a JP in the residential district of Westminster one day in January 1687, for example, Thomas Pride made a verbal attack on the justice in the hearing of others which began 'Justice Lawrence by God is a pimp.' There were charges of excessively ardent behaviour, busybodying and interference. Sir Thomas Hoby, predictably enough, encountered a good deal of this sort of criticism. He was variously decribed as a 'scurvy urchin', 'a spindle-shanked ape', 'the busiest saucy little jack in all the country' and 'a busy and giddy-headed justice'.[68] The monopolist and Worcestershire magistrate Sir Henry Spiller had something of the same reputation. He was 'so fiery', one man avowed in 1625, 'one must not speak to him'. His critic added, in an interesting reference to the practice of duelling abroad, 'that if he were on Calais Sands and if he would fight there might be an end of the matter'.[69] There were also direct charges of favouritism and corruption. The Somerset JP George Poulett was publicly rumoured in the years before the civil war to be willing to take bribes, 'half a crown for himself and so much more for his man'.[70] The day after he appeared before Samuel Harsnett in 1667 a dissatisfied Norfolk woolcomber told a villager

[65] S.K. Roberts, 'Participation and Performance in Devon Local Administration 1649–1670,' unpublished Ph.D. thesis, Exeter University, 1980, p. 63; A.H.A. Hamilton, *Quarter Sessions from Queen Elizabeth to Queen Anne* (London, 1878), p. 159.
[66] J.S. Cockburn, 'The North Riding Justices 1690–1750: A Study in Local Administration', *Yorkshire Archaeological Journal*, XLI (1935–6), 483n.
[67] J.C. Atkinson (ed.), *North Riding Quarter Sessions Records*, II (1885), 135; B.C. Redwood (ed.), *Quarter Sessions Order Book 1642–1649* (Sussex Record Society, LIV, 1954), 22; Ratcliff and Johnson (eds.), *Warwick County Records*, VII (1946), 189.
[68] J.C. Jeaffreson, *Middlesex County Records* (London, 1892), IV, 313–14; *Northern History*, XI (1975), 74.
[69] J. Willis-Bund (ed.), *Worcestershire Quarter Sessions Papers 1591–1643*, pp. 394–5.
[70] Bates Harbin (ed.), *Somerset Quarter Sessions Records*, II, xxv.

that he had a warrant from another justice who would show him as much favour as Harsnett showed her.[71] Benjamin Banner of Birmingham slandered Sir Charles Holt in 1682 with a story that he would give ten pounds for a false witness against his master who had been bound over to assizes.[72]

A thorough search of quarter sessions files would doubtless reveal more sporadic cases of the kind cited above. Magisterial policy towards such loose talk, it is quite clear, was firm. Fines were often imposed; men were sometimes sent to goal. Where the slander was heinous, a JP could reasonably expect his name to be cleared by a public submission. Thus Benjamin Banner was made to read out a paper confessing his crime at the Birmingham market cross. It included this passage:

I do here publicly declare myself to be deeply sensible of my great offence . . . against the just honour and worthiness of Sir Charles Holt, for which high offence I have deserved and had undergone greater punishment, unless the said Sir Charles Holt had in his clemency and goodness interceded for me to have this my humble submission and testimony of repentance to be accepted of.

Nothing reinforced a gentleman's credit like a display of magnanimity.[73]

The problem of open defiance and disaffection to the justices and their sessions became rather more serious than usual in some counties between 1645 and 1660 when, for political reasons, there was a marked decline in the social standing of the commission of the peace.[74] John Morrill found cases of disrespect and disobedience at almost every sessions in Cheshire.[75] In Wiltshire a gentleman abused two of the JPs as 'journeymen justices'.[76] In Devon, Stephen Roberts has noted a marked loss of confidence among the JPs, though he suggests that this 'reflected insecurity in the collective consciousness of the governing class as much as it mirrored the objective reality of popular scorn'.[77] But the extent of the problem, even in this disrupted period, should not be exaggerated. Honour and reputation have been explored in this essay not because the theme points to the instability of Stuart government but because it illuminates its strength.

Yet we are left with questions. Why did social deference bring so much force to the implementation of the law? Why did people challenge JPs and deputy-lieutenants so seldom? It is certainly not the case that the behaviour of officeholders was universally impeccable or that they were all men whose sheer charisma brought them respect. The answer must lie partly in Englishmen's attitude to the law. For the gentry the law became, more certainly than ever

---

[71] Norfolk RO, C/51/47A. I am grateful for this reference to Mr Timothy Wales.
[72] Ratcliff and Johnson (eds.), *Warwick County Records*, vol. VII (1946), pp. liii, 242.
[73] Ratcliff and Johnson (eds.), *Warwick County Records*, vol. VII (1946), p. 249.
[74] G.E. Aylmer (ed.), *The Interregnum* (London, Macmillan, 1972), p. 26.
[75] Morrill, *Cheshire*, p. 227.   [76] J. Birch (ed.), *Thurloe State Papers*, III, 155–6.
[77] Roberts, 'Devon Local Administration', pp. 64–6.

before during the Stuart period, the means of their purchase upon power and upon the facilities of social life. Inhibitions were imposed upon monarchical power; control was confirmed, through the panoply of the law, on the people. The rest of English society accepted this process because the law was already deeply embedded in the productive relations and the social patterns of people's lives. The regulation of village life often involved a high degree of autonomy from institutional processes. But the same general mores underlay informal arbitration and the conduct of quarter sessions. There were ways in which law and custom clashed, but for the most part they coincided. So men respected and obeyed the local officeholders because, though individuals sometimes chafed, the community as a whole respected the law.

Moreover the actual exercise of the law was becoming the most forceful expression of what E.P. Thompson has called the gentry's 'cultural hegemony'.[78] His work, which can be applied as fruitfully to the seventeenth century as to the eighteenth, directs our attention to 'the images of power and authority, the popular mentalities of subordination'. 'The hegemony of the gentry and aristocracy', he has written, 'was expressed, above all, not in military force, not in the mystifications of a priesthood or of the press, not even in economic coercion, but in the rituals of the study of the justices of the peace, in the quarter sessions, in the pomp of assizes and in the theatre of Tyburn.'[79] It may be that in the eighteenth century open challenges to the authority of justices became rarer than they had been previously. Relations between governors and the governed in that period require much fuller investigation than they have yet received. Meanwhile we can note a ritualistic incident in 1768 designed to discredit an unpopular magistrate in Somerset, which suggests that, however heavy the hand of justice had become, the people still found ways of expressing their displeasure with individuals. James Woodforde, dining at the parsonage in Castle Cary on 5 November, heard that the effigy of Justice Creed was being paraded through the streets on the town's fire engine, before being ceremoniously burnt in front of his house on the Guy Fawkes bonfire. The town had fallen out with him because he had indicted its churchwardens for not presenting one of their number 'for making a riot in the gallery at Cary Church some few Sundays back'.[80]

Despite the stress put on competitiveness and self-assertion, it has not been the intention of this essay to argue that men took office, by and large, more out of pride and ambition than out of duty and a sense of obligation to their communities. The history of personal motivation is always fraught with difficulties

[78] E.P. Thompson, 'Patrician Society, Plebeian Culture', *Journal of Social History*, VII (1974), 387.
[79] E.P. Thompson, *Whigs and Hunters: The Origin of the Black Act* (London, Allen Lane, 1975), p. 262.
[80] J. Woodforde, *The Diary of a Country Parson 1758–1802*, ed. J. Beresford, (OUP, 1978), p. 53. I am grateful to Lynn Blacoe for this reference.

because motivation is usually in itself so complex. In the last resort gentlemen served as deputies or justices because they knew it was expected of them. There is scope for much more work on the concept of the public man in the Stuart period, but the epitaph of just one of the hundreds who dispensed local justice will serve to indicate something of the mixture of virtues that made up reputation. At the death of Sir Robert Atkyns of Pinbury Park in Gloucestershire in 1711 his wife erected a monument in Sapperton church recording the 'obliging virtues' which 'endeared him to his country':

He was always loyal to his Prince, loving to his wife, faithful to his friends, charitable to the poor, kind and courteous to his neighbours, just to all, sober and serious in his conversation and a peacemaker to the uttermost of his power.[81]

This essay has concentrated on some of the more contentious figures in Elizabethan and Stuart government, but it is suggested that they, like their more passive colleagues, shared a sense of the limits to the disruption of good government that personal antagonisms could be allowed to inflict. The gentry knew that they could not afford to let quarrels over their good name threaten the social unity on which government rested, any more than they could afford to let those outside their charmed circle get away with so much as pricking their façade of honour and reputation. Every nuance of daily life and activity – clothes, speech, modes of address, assumptions about social intercourse – helped to confirm gentry control of Stuart society. The gentry's code of honour, something beyond credit or renown, something which was more sacred and precious, set them apart from other men. Their reputation was the very essence of their ability to govern.

[81] J. Simmons (ed.), *English County Historians* (Wakefield, EP Publishing, 1978), p. 63.

4

The Taming of the Scold: the Enforcement of Patriarchal Authority in Early Modern England

D.E. UNDERDOWN

Fears of an impending breakdown of the social order have been common in many periods of history. At no time were they more widespread, or more intense, than in early modern England: the 'crisis of order' detected by modern historians in the sixty years before the civil war[1] accords with the perceptions of many people in that period. Among the causes and symptoms of the apparently growing instability were those now familiar problems of excessive population growth, inflation, land shortage, poverty and vagrancy, all of which have attracted the attention of recent scholars. There are those who, like Peter Laslett, stress the stability of English society throughout the entire pre-modern period, and dismiss the signs of tension as the minor conflicts that exist in even the most smoothly functioning social system.[2] Few contemporaries would have agreed with them. It could no longer be safely assumed that all Englishmen and women were bound together in that interlocking network of households and communities on which, according to the prevailing orthodoxy, stability depended. 'Was there ever seen less obedience in youth of all sorts, both menkind and womenkind, towards their superiors, parents, masters and governors?' the puritan Philip Stubbes demanded in the 1580s, echoing a common preoccupation.[3] Even the patriarchal family, the linch-pin of the whole structure of order, appeared to be threatened.

These anxieties were not confined to puritan moralists. The flood of Jacobean anti-feminist literature and the concurrent public obsession with scolding

[1] For example, Wrightson, esp. chs. 5–6; W. Hunt, *The Puritan Moment: The Coming of Revolution in an English County* (Cambridge, Mass., Harvard University Press, 1983), chs. 2, 3.
[2] P. Laslett, *The World We Have Lost* (London, Methuen, 1965).
[3] Philip Stubbes, *The Anatomie of Abuses*, 4th edn (London, 1595), Epis. Ded. For the fear of disorder, see C. Hill, *Change and Continuity in Seventeenth-Century England* (London, Weidenfeld, 1974), ch. 8.

women, domineering and unfaithful wives, clearly suggest that patriarchy could no longer be taken for granted. By itself the literary evidence is not conclusive. The misogynist tradition in literature is a long one, the battle of the sexes an eternally popular theme. But late Elizabethan and Jacobean writers do seem to have been uncommonly preoccupied by themes of female independence and revolt.[4] They were particular favourites of dramatists: men, of course, so it is not strange that the plays usually reflect the patriarchal consensus. Juliet Dusinberre and other literary scholars have shown, to be sure, that female independence is sometimes portrayed sympathetically, but most of this literature rests on conventional assumptions. Beatrice and Rosalind are given their brief hour of freedom, but both Shakespeare and his audience know that in the end they must submit to their proper wifely roles. On the stage, as in carnival, gender inversion temporarily turns the world upside-down – but to reinforce, not subvert, the traditional order.[5]

In *The Taming of the Shrew*, Shakespeare provides the classic caricature of the assertive woman. The play contains some ambiguities, for Kate's creator well knew how to handle the tension between ideal and reality. Kate's belated submission to patriarchal authority is witnessed by the ne'er-do-well Christopher Sly, who, as Dusinberre points out, is going to have to go home 'to face the music from his harridan wife': to face reality, in other words. But although it is tempting for a modern audience to take Kate's final speech ironically – 'Thy husband is thy lord, thy life, thy keeper / Thy head, thy sovereign', and so on – the fact is that it expresses fairly accurately the ideal of husband–wife relations propounded by countless Elizabethan sermons and conduct books. It also includes the crucial political analogy: 'Such duty as the subject owes the prince, / Even such a woman oweth to her husband.' Patriarchal authority within the family was the cornerstone of Elizabethan and Jacobean political theory, the ultimate, 'natural', justification for obedience to the state: to reject either was to threaten the entire social and political order. Ian Donaldson rightly points out that Shakespeare's play, like the many other seventeenth-century shrew comedies, was a product of a society with 'formalized ideas about the relative rights, dignities, and duties pertaining to the roles of husband and wife' – though also

[4] I. Donaldson, *The World Upside Down: Comedy from Jonson to Fielding* (OUP, 1970), p. 10; J.S. Dusinberre, *Shakespeare and the Nature of Women* (London, Macmillan, 1975), pp. 6–7; J.E. Gagen, *The New Woman: Her Emergence in English Drama 1600–1730* (New York, Twayne Publishers, 1954), pp. 18–20 (I am indebted to Ruth Silberstein for this reference). S. Shepherd, *Amazons and Warrior Women: Varieties of Feminism in Seventeenth-Century Drama* (Hassocks, Harvester, 1981), pp. 32–3, and chs. 4–8, 10, 14. For the misogynist tradition, see K. Rogers, *The Troublesome Helpmate: A History of Misogynist Literature* (Seattle, University of Washington Press, 1966).

[5] Donaldson, *World Upside Down*, pp. 12–20. But see the argument in Dusinberre, *Shakespeare and the Nature of Women*, pp. 5–8.

one, to be sure, that was more than a little worried about whether those ideal roles were being performed in practice.[6]

Seventeenth-century assumptions about the connection between household and other kinds of order are particularly explicit in Thomas Heywood and Richard Brome's *The Lancashire Witches*, dating from 1634, just after some sensational witchcraft trials in that county. At the start of the play a local community is thrown into chaos by the inversion of social and familial norms: wives rule their husbands, children their parents, servants their employers. 'This is quite upside-down', a scandalised character exclaims, '. . . sure they are all bewitched.' He is right, of course: witchcraft has satanically inverted the natural order. When the virtuous wife of Mr Generous starts behaving independently, riding abroad alone and concealing it from her husband, we know it is the first step on the road to ruin. Eventually the witches are brought to justice, the natural lines of marital and social obedience restored, and the world turned right side up again. The social and political implications could not be clearer.[7]

The fascination with rebellious women is equally evident in popular literature. Titles like *The Cruell Shrew* and *Hic Mulier, or, the Man-Woman* show what was on people's minds, or at least what Grub Street thought was on their minds. There seems to have been a steady demand for such reading-matter among the urban, middle-class public. Joseph Swetnam's *Arraignment of Lewd, Idle, Froward and Inconstant Women* went through ten editions between 1615 and 1634, and other hack writers exploited the theme. Always one with a good sense of the market, the 'Water Poet' John Taylor provoked a lively exchange over the 'woman question' in the late 1630s in works with such titles as *Divers Crabtree Lectures*, and *The Womens Sharpe Revenge*, this last under the pseudonym Mary Tattlewell. One of the Crabtree Lectures summarises the conventional message:

> Ill fares the hapless family that shows
> A cock that's silent, and a Hen that crows.
> I know not which live more unnatural lives,
> Obedient husbands, or commanding wives.[8]

The endless reiteration of such commonplaces would surely have been unnecessary had there not been uneasy feelings that too many such families existed. An

---

[6] Donaldson, *World Upside Down*, p. 10. Dusinberre, *Shakespeare and the Nature of Women*, pp. 105–8. For the political uses of patriarchy, see G. J. Schochet, *Patriarchalism in Political Thought* (OUP, 1975).

[7] Thomas Heywood, *Dramatic Works* (6 vols., London, 1874), vol. IV, pp. 178–83.

[8] [John Taylor], *Divers Crabtree Lectures, Expressing the Severall Languages that Shrews read to their Husbands* (London, 1639), pp. 73–4. The literature is reviewed in C. Camden, *The Elizabethan Woman* (London, Cleaver House Press, 1952), pp. 255–71; L.B. Wright, *Middle-Class Culture in Elizabethan England* (Chapel Hill, University of North Carolina, 1935), ch. 13: and R. Masek, 'Women in the an Age of Transition, 1485–1714' in B. Kanner (ed.), *The Women of England From Anglo-Saxon Times to the Present: Interpretative Bibliographical Essays* (Hamden, Conn., Shoestring Press, 1979), pp. 146–50.

unquiet woman was 'the misery of man', declared Nicholas Breton: 'she looks at no law and thinks of no lord, admits no command and keeps no good order'.[9] Masculine worries about sexually aggressive women were compounded by fears of the subversive notions they might pick up in their probably excessive leisure time. 'Do you come from an alehouse bench', bawls one of Taylor's henpecked husbands, 'from amongst the rest of your talking gossips, to tell me what I have to do?'[10]

Did this anxiety about patriarchal order have any solid basis or was it a merely literary phenomenon, a matter of perception, not reality? One way of approaching the question is through local court records. Between about 1560 and 1640 – precisely the period of greatest concern about other kinds of disorder – such records disclose an intense preoccupation with women who are a visible threat to the patriarchal system. Women scolding and brawling with their neighbours, single women refusing to enter service, wives dominating or even beating their husbands: all seem to surface more frequently than in the periods immediately before and afterwards. It will not go unnoticed that this is also the period during which witchcraft accusations reach their peak. All this provides the context necessary for an understanding of the literary and sub-literary works previously surveyed, and it needs further exploration.

Let us begin with the scold: the person (usually a woman) who disturbs the peace by publicly abusing family members or neighbours. Such people had always existed, of course, but before the middle of the sixteenth century the authorities do not seem to have been particularly concerned about them, and they were dealt with by the routine processes of presentment to the ecclesiastical or manor court, with penance or small fines as the customary punishments.[11] From the 1560s, however, many places began to show increasing concern about the problem. At Southampton, for example, it reached a climax in James I's reign. In 1603 the leet jury noted 'the manifold number of scolding women that be in this town'; a year later they complained of their constant 'misdemeanours and scolding', lamenting that the mayor was 'daily troubled with such brawls'.[12] A country parish, Langridge, near Bath, provides a typical example: Anne Weeks, presented in 1620 as 'a common scold, a raiser of idle reports and fames, and a common sewer and breeder of discord between her neighbours'.[13]

---

[9] Breton, 'The Good and the Badde' (1616), p. 12 in A.B. Grosart (ed.), *The Works in Verse and Prose of Nicholas Breton* (2 vols., New York, 1966), vol. II.
[10] [Taylor], *Divers Crabtree Lectures*, p. 71.
[11] Examples in C.H. Mayo (ed.), *Municipal Records of the Borough of Shaftesbury* (Sherborne, 1889), p. 21; G.P. Scrope, *History of the Manor and Ancient Barony of Castle Combe* (1852), p. 326.
[12] F.J.C. and D.M. Hearnshaw (eds.), *Southampton Court Leet Records* (Southampton Record Series, 1905–8), vol. I, pp. 381, 401.
[13] Somerset RO, D/D/Ca, 220: Langridge presentment, 20 Sept. 1620.

Men were occasionally presented for scolding, but it was overwhelmingly a female offence, and equally overwhelmingly one committed by women of low status against equals or superiors. Prosecutions of women of high rank are rare indeed: one of the alleged misdeeds of the foreman of a leet jury at Tettenhall, Staffordshire, in 1621, was his presentment of Judith Grosvenor, wife of an esquire and daughter of a knight, as a scold.[14] Women who were poor, social outcasts, widows or otherwise lacking in the protection of a family, or newcomers to their communities, were the most common offenders. Such women were likely to vent their frustration against the nearest symbols of authority, the village notables. Alice Harper was accused of abusing 'the best men and women in the town' (Steeple Ashton, Wiltshire) including the tithingman and his wife, people of 'good repute and estate', the husband having 'divers times served in other offices in the town'.[15]

This epidemic of scolding, violating the ideal of neighbourliness and 'living in quiet', coincided with a marked increase in the incidence of other typically female offences against good order. One of them was witchcraft. The social context of English witchcraft has been thoroughly explored by Alan Macfarlane and Keith Thomas and therefore need not detain us.[16] At first sight it may seem odd to set the witch in the category of independent women, for the typical suspect was usually old and powerless. But that of course is precisely the point. Witchcraft was one response (or imagined response) of the powerless to alienation from the community, and, in a period when the old bonds of 'good neighbourhood' were breaking down, to oppression that was both social and sexual in nature. The scold who cursed her more fortunate neighbour and the witch who cast a spell on him (or her) were both rebelling against the place assigned them in the social and gender hierarchies. The chief fault of witches, Reginald Scot observed, 'is that they are scolds', and occasionally the two crimes are explicitly connected. Elizabeth Busher of Henton, Somerset, was accused of living in 'woods and obscure places without obedience to the laws of God and this land', and of being

of lewd life and conversation, as namely the mother of divers base children, the suspected maintainer of incontinency in her own house, the continual disturber of her neighbours'

---

[14] PRO, STAC 8/151/12 (Grosvenor v. Anson, 1622). For presentments of men, see C.Z. Wiener, 'Sex Roles and Crime in Late Elizabethan Hertfordshire', *Journal of Social History*, VIII (1975), 59, n. 64. When women of higher status were convicted, they were sometimes given the option of a fine rather than a ducking: see e.g., J.W. Horrocks (ed.), *Assembly Books of Southampton* (Southampton Record Series, 4 vols., 1917–25), vol. II, p. 94. A later case in Antigua suggests how deep-rooted was the assumption that propertied women ought not to be ducked: *Calendar State Papers Colonial, America and West Indies, 1708–9*, p. 391.

[15] B.H. Cunnington (ed.), *Records of the County of Wilts . . . of the Seventeenth Century* (Devizes, 1932), p. 217.

[16] A. Macfarlane, *Witchcraft in Tudor and Stuart England* (London, Routledge, 1970). Thomas, esp. ch. 17.

quietness and threatening mischief against them, and lastly both reputed and feared to be a dangerous witch through the untimely death of men, women and children.[17]

The chronology of public anxiety about scolds and witches is roughly similar, and is paralleled by the chronology of a third category of rebellious woman, the domineering wife, or, as Natalie Davis describes her, the 'woman on top'. All over Europe festive processions – charivari – had for centuries been employed, with or without official sanction, as shaming rituals against people who violated their community's sexual norms. In France they were most commonly directed against marriages between mismatched couples – usually elderly husbands marrying young wives – and this definition of charivari is the one given in Cotgrove's French–English dictionary, dating from 1611.[18] However, in England the more elaborate forms of charivari – as distinct from simple rough-music processions accompanying the carting or 'riding' of a whore – were nearly always directed against couples of whom the wife had beaten or otherwise abused the husband. Recorded instances of this form of charivari nearly all date from the later sixteenth and seventeenth centuries. There are a few examples after the Restoration, but, by the eighteenth century, as E.P. Thompson has shown, the targets began to change towards mismatched couples, sexual offenders, and eventually, in a reversal of earlier custom, husbands who beat their wives.[19] The 'woman on top', like the scold and the witch, seems to be primarily a phenomenon of the century between 1560 and 1660.

How are we to explain all this? There is, of course, much excellent recent historical work with which we can connect it: by Keith Thomas and Alan Macfarlane on witchcraft, E.P. Thompson and Martin Ingram on charivari, Keith Wrightson and numerous other scholars on various manifestations of social disorder.[20] Neither these nor historians of the family, however, have

---

[17] E.H. Bates (ed.), *Quarter Sessions Records for the County of Somerset*, I, *James I* (Somerset Record Society, XXIII, 1907), 96–7. The two phenomena occasionally ran in families: W.S. Weeks, *Clitheroe in the Seventeenth Century* (Clitheroe, n.d.) pp. 89, 94. Scot is quoted by Thomas, p. 530.

[18] R. Cotgrove, *A Dictionarie of the French and English Tongues* (London, 1611). On the whole subject, see N.Z. Davis, *Society and Culture in Early Modern France* (Stanford, Stanford University Press, 1975), chs. 4, 5; P. Burke, *Popular Culture in Early Modern Europe* (London, Temple Smith, 1978), pp. 198–204; E.P. Thompson, '"Rough Music": Le Charivari Anglais', *Annales ESC*, XXVII (1972), 285–312; Martin Ingram, 'Le charivari dans L'Angleterre du XVIe et du XVIIe siècle', and E.P. Thompson, '"Rough Music" et charivari: quelques réflexions complémentaires' in J. le Goff and J.-C. Schmitt (eds.), *Le Charivari* (Paris, 1981), pp. 251–64, 273–83.   [19] Thompson, *Annales ESC*, 294–5.

[20] Citations of the first four authors listed are in notes 16 and 18 above. On the general subject of order, see also the chapters by Wrightson and Walter in Brewer and Styles; their article, 'Dearth and the Social Order in Early Modern England', *Past and Present*, LXXI (1976), 22–42; the chapters by J.A. Sharpe and M.J. Ingram in Cockburn; and P. Slack, 'Vagrants and Vagrancy in England, 1598–1664', *ECHR*, 2nd ser., XXVII (1974), 360–79.

systematically considered the possibility of a crisis in gender relations in the years around 1600. The Cambridge Group's formidable researchers have generated copious statistical data on quantifiable aspects of the household, but their methodology rules out the pursuit of qualitative questions about how the institution actually operated at the human level.[21] We can, to be sure, turn to studies of the puritan family, and for the elite household to Lawrence Stone's important book.[22] But for family and gender relations within the wider population we are less well served. There are a few recent works that bear on the subject, but none that provide the sort of guidance that we need.[23] In fact we have to go back to a book published over sixty years ago, Alice Clark's *Working Life of Women in the Seventeenth Century*, for a detailed treatment of the family as a social and economic unit, and for serious discussion of the impact of early modern developments on the lives of non-elite women. Clark deals mainly with the urban and industrial populations, but her chronology has been generally accepted by later historians – a more or less linear decline in the status of women from the medieval period, when they enjoyed a good deal of economic independence, to the eighteenth century, when they had virtually lost it. In that process the onslaught of capitalism was, in Clark's view, the crucial causal element.[24]

For all the magnitude of Clark's achievement, some questions remain. In the long run, by separating home from work, by disrupting the traditional family economy, capitalism did indeed help to bind women even more completely into a redefined patriarchal order. But great social processes rarely operate simply and in one direction; there are often phases in which contradictory developments produce conflict. As Clark's recent editors point out, the advance of capitalist market relations did not proceed at an even pace in all parts of England. In some places, and at certain times, they may indeed temporarily have encouraged a greater sense of independence and self-sufficiency on the part of some women. The evidence surveyed earlier in this paper suggests that the century between 1560 and 1660 may have been such a period. If we turn from the chronology to the regional distribution of the various forms of female assertiveness already identified we may perhaps encounter some significant patterns on which firmer conclusions may be based.

[21] See especially, P. Laslett and R. Wall (eds.), *Household and Family in Past Time* (CUP, 1972).
[22] L. Stone, *The Family, Sex and Marriage in England 1500–1800* (London, Weidenfeld, 1977). Much of the literature on the puritan family is surveyed in R. Hamilton, *The Liberation of Women: A Study of Patriarchy and Capitalism* (London, Allen and Unwin, 1978), ch. 3.
[23] R. Thompson, *Women in Stuart England and America* (London: Routledge 1974), is stronger on America than on England. G.R. Quaife, *Wanton Wenches and Wayward Wives: Peasants and Illicit Sex in Seventeenth Century England* (London, Croom Helm, 1979), presents much important material, but with no adequate conceptual framework.
[24] A. Clark, *Working Life of Women in the Seventeenth Century*, rev. edn by M. Chaytor and J. Lewis (London, Routledge, 1982).

We should first note that scolds were originally an urban problem: in medieval times there are few signs of rural anxiety about them. When concern began to intensify during Elizabeth's reign it was again most evident in the towns. The usual mechanism for punishing scolds was the ducking-stool, or cucking-stool as it was usually called: the see-saw-like contraption on which the victim was seated in order to be ducked in pond or river. By the sixteenth century ducking was regarded as a punishment only for women, but in medieval times this had not been the case. It was used for a variety of offences against the common weal: inappropriate dress on a feast day, for example, but particularly for violations of the laws of weights and measures. Such violations were, to be sure, often committed by women because of their prominence in the brewing and baking trades, but they could also lead to a ritual ducking if men were the offenders.[25] The association between the cucking-stool and gender-related offences – sexual incontinence as well as scolding – began to appear in the fifteenth century and became even clearer in the sixteenth. As early as 1401 a cucking-stool was built at Colerne, Wiltshire, and it was soon put to use against scolds. There was one at Bedford by 1507, and they are mentioned in the records of a few other places, most of them urban, during the next fifty years. It may be significant that the 1547 'Homily Against Contention' associates the use of the cucking-stool against scolds only with 'well-ordered cities'.[26] It was not, however, the only instrument available. In the north of England the barbaric 'scold's bridle', or brank – an iron collar with a bit to prevent the victim from talking – was more commonly employed.[27]

But the cucking-stool was usually the preferred solution. After 1560 evidence for its adoption begins to multiply, and again that evidence is mainly urban.

[25] F.J.C. Hearnshaw, *Leet Jurisdiction in England* (Southampton Record Series, V, 1908), pp. 43–62. J.W. Spargo, *Juridical Folklore In England Illustrated by the Cucking Stool* (Durham, N.C., Duke University Press, 1944), pp. 34–5, 39, 144–8. E.K. Chambers, *The Mediaeval Stage* (2 vols., Oxford, 1903), vol. I, p. 122. F.A. Carrington, 'On Certain Ancient Wiltshire Customs', *Wiltshire Archaeological Magazine*, I (1854), 70, 77–8. W.M. Bowman, *England in Ashton-Under-Lyne* (Altrincham, Sherratt, 1960), p. 307. An apparently transitional stage had been reached at Chester by 1499: G.L. Fenwick, *History of the Ancient City of Chester* (Chester, 1896), pp. 387–8. John Taylor makes no explicit mention of a cucking-stool; however, a baker's wife says that her husband deserves to be 'ducked in St. Clement's Well' for his unkindness, and then accuses him of violating weights and measures and having lost his ears in the pillory for making 'light bread': [Taylor], *Divers Crabtree Lectures*, pp. 103–5.

[26] *VCH Wiltshire*, vol. V, p. 65. J. Godber, *History of Bedfordshire 1066–1688* (Bedfordshire County Council, 1969), p. 157. *Certain Sermons Appointed by the Queen's Majesty*, ed. G.E. Corrie (CUP, 1850), p. 147. Spargo, *Juridical Folklore*, pp. 34–5, gives other early examples. The cucking-stool was also used against women convicted of taking part in enclosure riots: J. Hawarde, *Les Reportes del Cases in Camera Stellata 1593–1609*, ed. W.P. Baildon (London, 1894), pp. 103–4.

[27] Weeks, *Clitheroe*, p. 90. Bowman, *England in Ashton-Under-Lyne*, p. 585. Carrington, 'Facts and Observations as to the Ancient State of Marlborough', *Wiltshire Archaeological Magazine*, VII (1862), 32–42.

Norwich had acquired one by 1562, Bridport by 1566; Shrewsbury and Kingston-upon-Thames built them in 1572, Marlborough got one in 1578, Devizes five years later. They existed at Clitheroe, Thornbury and Great Yarmouth by 1600, and were in active use in such Dorset towns at Dorchester, Lyme Regis and Weymouth soon after that date.[28] When the Southampton jury first proposed the renovation of an older, now abandoned cucking-stool in 1576 they mentioned its use only 'for the punishment of harlots', but in subsequent presentments scolds became the primary targets. By 1601 the stool had stood at the town ditch long enough to need repairs; the jury helpfully suggested 'something to be devised to be kept dry and to be used at the crane at full sea . . . half a hogshead will serve as well as anything'.[29]

So much for the towns: what of the rural areas? Here we run into problems, for rural records tend to survive less well than urban ones. Cucking-stools are frequently mentioned in manor court books, but not always in ways that prove that the village actually used or even possessed one. A presentment by a leet jury that a village lacks such a device is no proof that one was ever built. The increasing frequency of such presentments may indeed simply reflect the growing standardisation of court procedures in the sixteenth and seventeenth centuries, as manorial stewards came to rely on printed handbooks like John Kitchin's *Le Court Leete*, in which the proper maintenance of pillory, stocks and cucking-stool was routinely listed. Indeed if the presentment is repeated, with no evidence of actual use in the meantime, it is probably an indication that the place never had a cucking-stool at all.[30]

Still, evidence for the actual use of cucking-stools does exist in rural parishes,

[28] J. Glyde, *The Norfolk Garland* (London, 1872), p. 124. T. Wainwright, 'Bridport Corporation Records', *Dorset Natural History and Antiquarian Field Club Proceedings*, XI (1890), 103. W. Carew Hazlitt, *Faiths and Folklore of the British Isles: A Descriptive and Historical Dictionary*, rev. edn (2 vols., New York, Benjamin Blom, 1965) vol. I, p. 158. J.C. Cox, *Churchwardens Accounts from the Fourteenth Century to the Close of the Seventeenth Century* (London, Methuen, 1913), p. 337. B.H. Cunnington (ed.), *Historical Records of Marlborough* (1928–30), pp. 4–11. Cunnington, *Some Annals of the Borough of Devizes . . . 1555–1791* (Devizes, 1925), pt 1, p. 80. Weeks, *Clitheroe*, pp. 88–9. PRO, STAC 8/128/1 (Eddis v. Baker, 1604). BL, Cotton MS Aug. I.i.74 (view of Great Yarmouth, *c*.1585). H.J. Moule, 'Notes on a Minute Book belonging to the Corporation of Dorchester', *Dorset Natural History and Antiquarian Field Club Proceedings*, X (1889), 75–6. C.H. Mayo (ed.), *Municipal Records of the Borough of Dorchester* (Exeter, W. Pollard, 1908), pp. 654–64. Dorset RO, B7/1/8 (Lyme Court Book, 1613–27), p. 465. Wilts. RO, Dean's Pec. Presentments, 1635, no. 73. H.J. Moule (ed.), *Descriptive Catalogue of . . . Documents of the Borough of Weymouth and Melcombe Regis* (Weymouth, 1883), pp. 63–4, 73.

[29] F. and D. Hearnshaw (eds.), *Southampton Court Leet Records*, vol. I, pp. 141, 162, 174, 345.

[30] J. Kitchin, *Le Court Leete, et Court Baron* (London, 1580 and later edns). See also Hearnshaw, *Leet Jurisdiction*, pp. 35–42, and J.P. Dawson, *A History of Lay Judges* (Cambridge, Mass., Harvard University Press, 1960), p. 212. A Clitheroe charge of 1678 appears to have been lifted straight from Kitchin: Weeks, *Clitheroe*, p. 14. For examples of repetition of presentments, see Cunnington (ed.), *Records of Wiltshire*, pp. 24, 121; and W. Symonds, 'Sherston Manor Rolls', *Wiltshire Notes & Queries*, VII (1911–13), 248, 299, 371, 404, 539.

and it suggests some distinctly regional characteristics. The familiar typology of English rural communities proposed by Joan Thirsk and other agricultural historians divides them into arable and woodland or pasture types: cucking-stools were more likely to be employed in the latter than in the former. The Gloucestershire clothing village of Minchinhampton acquired one in 1567, the forest villages of Gillingham in Dorset and Henley-in-Arden in Warwickshire were regularly ducking scolds in the 1620s and 30s, and there is scattered evidence of the same sort for several parishes in the Dorset pasturelands and the wood–pasture region of north Somerset.[31] Cucking-stools were not unknown in the arable regions of the western counties – the principal focus of my research – but they were distinctly less common, and scolding women who did not respond to the informal mediation of parson or neighbours were liable to be prosecuted in the ecclesiastical rather than the secular courts.[32] An example of what may have been a typical situation in arable villages comes from Nettleton in Wiltshire. In 1612 two village women were presented at the court leet for scolding. The parson was asked to persuade them to reform themselves, but two years later they were again in trouble and were sentenced to be ducked. It was then realised that Nettleton did not have a cucking-stool and one had to be hastily improvised. But it almost immediately fell into disrepair, the court was never willing to spend any money on it, and when one of the same women was again accused of scolding in 1621 she had to be presented to the ecclesiastical court, presumably because the manor court was powerless to deal with her.[33] In a similar case at West Horsley in Surrey in 1629 two scolding women had to be fined, there being no other form of coercion available, and the inhabitants were ordered to set up a cucking-stool without delay.[34] The evidence is admittedly imperfect, but it does seem to suggest that cucking-stools were more common in wood–pasture villages than in arable ones, and women correspondingly more likely to be punished as scolds in those places.

What conclusions can we draw from all this? Let us return to the arable/

---

[31] J. Bruce (ed.), 'Extracts from Accounts of the Churchwardens of Minchinhampton', *Archaeologia*, XXXV (1853), 428. F.C. Wellstead (ed.), *Records of the Manor of Henley in Arden* (Stratford-upon-Avon, 1919), pp. 87–8, 94, 107. J.H. Bettey, 'Revolts over the Enclosure of the Royal Forest at Gillingham, 1626–1630', *Dorset Natural History and Archaeological Society Proceedings*, XCVII (1975), 23. Dorset RO, QSOB, 1625–37, fol. 229 (Epiph., 1629/30). Quaife, *Wanton Wenches*, pp. 198, 201. E.H. Bates Harbin (ed.), *Somerset Quarter Sessions Records*, vol. III: *Commonwealth* (Somerset Record Society, XXVIII, 1912), pp. 295–6.

[32] For cucking-stools in arable villages: Dorset RO, P9/CW 1 (Charlton Marshall churchwardens accounts, 1583–1656), fols. 31, 55, 85; P 22/CW 1 (Cerne Abbas churchwardens accs., 1628–85). For presentments to ecclesiastical courts: Wiltshire RO, AS/ABO, 11 (1612–16), fol. 24v (Laverstock, 1612); B/ABO, 7 (1613–15), fol. 15 (Figheldean, 1613).

[33] PRO, STAC 8/123/16 (Davis v. Bishop, 1615). BL, Add. MS 23, 151 (Nettleton Court Book, 1600–62), fols. 48v, 50, 52, 73, 77. Wilts. RO, AW/ABO, 5 (1616–22), fol. 106v.

[34] BL, Egerton MS 2559 (Nicholas MSS), fol. 126.

pasture typology. Arable parishes tended to be small in area, with compact, nucleated village centres, often with resident squires and strong manorial institutions – effective mechanisms for social control. Especially where open-field farming survived – as it did longer in western arable regions than in more capitalist areas like East Anglia – they also tended to retain strong habits of neighbourliness and co-operation. Wood–pasture parishes, on the other hand, were often larger in area, with scattered settlement patterns rather than nucleated centres. Manorial institutions were weaker or non-existent, they were less likely to have resident squires, and their mode of agriculture – dairy farming or cattle-raising – involved individually owned, enclosed farms rather than the more co-operative systems of farming that prevailed in open-field villages. Some wood–pasture regions, like the Wiltshire 'cheese country', were also industrial areas devoted to clothmaking as well as dairying, thus attracting in-migration in times of population growth, migration which their weaker manorial institutions made it harder for them to control. They were therefore liable to experience more serious problems of poverty than their arable neighbours, especially during periods of depression – and, as already suggested, scolding was a natural psychological outlet for the frustrations of the poor and the alienated. Wood–pasture villages had less effective mechanisms for informal mediation of disputes, and their parish elites were more likely to be puritan and thus to have a more rigorous concept of order than their counterparts in the sheep–corn regions.[35] The Wiltshire antiquary John Aubrey was right in thinking that the inhabitants of the clothing region were both more litigious and more puritan than those of the sheep–corn country.[36] There probably were more scolds in the pasturelands than in the arable regions, but even if there were not, the lack of adequate mechanisms of social control made those that existed a more visible threat to order. *Mutatis mutandis*, much the same conditions apply to the towns: more poor people, less social cohesion, more individualistic attitudes on the part of the governing elite.

The preoccupation with scolding women during the century 1560–1660 can therefore be seen as a by-product of the social and economic transformation that was occurring in England during that period – of the decline in the habits of good neighbourhood and social harmony that accompanied the spread of capitalism. This is of course much the same conclusion that was reached by Thomas and Macfarlane in their studies of witchcraft. Unfortunately the sources for the

[35] Wrightson, 'Two Concepts of Order', in Brewer and Styles, ch. 1. For the arable–pasture typology, see J. Thirsk (ed.), *Agrarian History of England and Wales*, vol. IV (CUP, 1967), ch. 1.
[36] John Aubrey, *Natural History of Wiltshire*, ed. J. Britton (London, 1847), pp. 11–12. J.E. Jackson (ed.), *Topographical Collections of John Aubrey* (Devizes, 1862), p. 266.

western counties do not permit the elaborate study of witchcraft that Macfarlane was able to undertake in Essex. An impressionistic survey of the cases that survive provides some support for John Aubrey's contention that witches were most common in woodlands and pasture regions like the 'wet clayey parts' of north Wiltshire.[37] But this aspect of the subject clearly awaits further investigation.

Firmer conclusions can be drawn from the evidence about other kinds of unruly women. Like scolds and witches, women who defied the authority of their husbands, whether in sexual behaviour or household governance, and the even more culpable husbands who feebly tolerated this, threatened the entire patriarchal order. Scolds and witches could be prosecuted in the courts; unruly women who beat their husbands usually could not, so they had to be dealt with by unofficial community action, by shaming rituals like charivari. How frequent such incidents were it is impossible to tell – they come to our notice only when something went wrong and the law was broken. But the apparent familiarity of English villagers with the customary rituals suggests that they may have been quite common. Unfaithful wives and their cuckolded husbands – like their henpecked counterparts automatic targets of ridicule – are in an intermediate situation so far as the record is concerned. Adulterous married people were often presented in the ecclesiastical courts, but evidence of infidelity was usually less obvious than in the case of pre-marital liaisons, and the arguments for doing nothing and avoiding scandal much greater. But local gossip often brought unprosecuted cases to light and led neighbours to seek retribution in their own way. The two kinds of offence were often linked: the dominated husband, it was generally assumed, was almost certainly being cuckolded, and vice versa. The rituals employed in each case were correspondingly similar.

Processional rituals of the charivari type were often an officially sanctioned component in punishments ordered by the magistrates for violations of sexual or gender norms. A procession making 'rough music' – to quote Cotgrove's dictionary, 'the harmony of tinging kettles and frying-pan music' – was a routine accompaniment to the 'carting' or 'riding' of a whore, the placarding or ducking of a scold. At Devizes in Elizabeth's reign couples convicted of extra-marital sexual relations were sentenced to be 'led about the town with basins', and this practice was common in all areas.[38] The popularity of terms of abuse like 'ridden

---

[37] Aubrey, *Natural History of Wiltshire*, p. 11. In an unsystematically collected sample of about thirty cases, 1600–70, in Dorset, Somerset and Wiltshire, only five are from arable villages.

[38] Cotgrove, *Dictionarie*. Cunnington, *Annals of Devizes*, pt 1, p. 35; pt 2, p. 3. For other instances, see Carrington, *Wiltshire Archaeological Magazine* VII (1862), 37; J. Lister (ed.), *West Riding Sessions Records*, Yorkshire Archaeological Society Record Series, vol. II (1915), p. 18; C.L. Kingsford (ed.), *A Survey of London by John Snow* (2 vols., OUP, 1908), vol. I, 190; Glyde, *Norfolk Garland*, p. 124. See also Thompson in le Goff and Schmitt (eds.), *Le Charivari*, n. 17.

whore' or 'carted whore' suggests its familiarity. During a quarrel between two Hertfordshire women, one of them clapped her hands and called for 'a cart, a cart, and a cucking stool'. The ritual provided cathartic release for community tensions, gave its participants a virtuous sense of enforcing moral standards and was for all but the victims an enjoyable, festive occasion. 'If you beat poor cuckold your husband about the horns again', a woman at Cawston, Norfolk, told a neighbour in 1615, the village would have an even better riding than they had had before.[39]

If the magistrates failed, or were not required, to act, individuals or groups were usually available to uphold public morality and patriarchy. The cuckolded husband might be confronted by ritual repetition of the words 'thou art a cuckold', or written libels might be circulated, recited in taverns or attached to the church door.[40] Even more effectively, the horns of rams or other beasts might be displayed outside the cuckold's house or in some equally public place.

Horns were of course the universal symbol of cuckoldry. 'Take that for the key to your bedchamber door', a Norwich man shouted as he threw a pair of ox horns into a shop in 1609. The mere mention of them was enough to start a lawsuit. 'Fulbrooke hath longer horns than my cow, dost thou know what I mean by it?' a countryman leered in the market place at Abingdon – and William Fulbrooke duly took him to court when he heard about it.[41] Great ingenuity might be used in their display. In one case we find them made out of the branches used to decorate the church and attached to the target's pew, in another tied to the necks of a neighbour's geese.[42] At Berkley in north Somerset in 1611, William Swarfe's mare was led around the village amid 'great laughter and derision, with great clamours, shouts and outcries'; the mare was wearing horns and a paper attached to her tail summoned Swarfe to a 'court of cuckolds'.[43] Rams' horns hung on the churchyard gate during the marriage of a couple at Charminster, Dorset, 'caused people to laugh and deride them in very uncharitable manner, and to the great grief and scandalizing of them and their credits'.[44]

These examples are too few in number to permit anything more than

[39] Wiener, *Journal of Social History* VIII (1975), p. 47. Norfolk RO, ANW/7/3 (Docking v. Kemp, 1615). Ecclesiastical court records contain many other such allusions.
[40] For example at Wiveton, Norfolk, 1600: Norfolk RO, Bishop's Deposition Book, 31, fol. 114; at Bremhill, Wilts., 1618: PRO, STAC 8/164/18 (Harrys v. Rawlins); at Compton Abbas, Dorset, 1603: STAC 8/190/7 (King v. Lawrence).
[41] Norfolk RO, Bps. Dep. Bk., 35, fol. 31v. Bodleian, MS Oxf. Archd. papers: Berks, c.155 (Dep. Bk., 1594–1600), fols. 171–2.
[42] Norfolk RO, Bps. Dep. Bk. 26, fol. 315 (Westwick, 1591). PRO, STAC 8/79/1 (Boyse v. Jenkinson, 1620).
[43] PRO, STAC 8/92/10 (Graye and Swarfe v. Hoskins, 1611). For other Somerset cases, see Quaife, *Wanton Wenches*, p. 199, and Somerset RO, D/D/Cd 65 (Depositions, 1628–30), Lidford v. Long, 20 Jan. 1628/9.   [44] Wilts. RO, Dean's Pec. Presentmts., 1609, no. 18.

impressionistic conclusions. Yet they appear to be significantly more common in urban or wood–pasture communities than in arable ones: out of sixteen recorded incidents involving horn rituals or similar libels in the three western counties of Dorset, Somerset and Wiltshire, twelve occurred in places of the former type. Such communities appear to have been especially concerned about the threat of patriarchal authority by female sexual offenders, as we have already noted they were about unruly women who disturbed their neighbours by scolding. They were more inclined to resort to public shaming rituals. And their rituals, including those against domineering wives (about whom, again, they seem to have been more worried than arable villages were), were more elaborate and involved the playing of more clearly marked theatrical roles than were the undifferentiated rough-music processions of the arable regions. In France, Davis shows, charivari against 'women on top' tended to occur in towns rather than country villages (the preferred targets in the latter were more likely to be mismatched couples), and the richer, more literate culture of the cities was reflected in their correspondingly more colourful, theatrical charivari.[45] The situation in England was not very different, except that to the towns can be added wood–pasture regions.

The charivari against violent wives, like other riding forms, was a ritual deeply rooted in custom – 'an antique show', to quote the well-known description in Samuel Butler's *Hudibras*. Andrew Marvell also provides a description in 'Last instructions to a painter', and comments approvingly:[46]

> Prudent Antiquity, that knew by Shame,
> Better than Law, Domestic Crimes to tame.

Between them, Butler and Marvell describe the standard ingredients of the ritual: a rough-music procession headed by a drummer and a man wearing horns; the enlisting of the next-door neighbours as surrogates for the offending couple; the acting-out of the proscribed behaviour by the 'husband' riding backwards on horse or donkey and holding a distaff, the symbol of female subjection, while the 'wife' (usually a man in woman's clothes) beats him with a ladle. The husband, it should again be stressed, is as much the subject of disapproval – for tolerating the offence – as the wife.

The close association of charivari against rebellious wives with wood–pasture

[45] The absence of elaborate ritual in arable regions is clear from later examples in E. Porter, *Cambridgeshire Customs and Folklore* (London, Routledge, 1969), pp. 8–9; and D. Jones-Baker, *The Folklore of Hertfordshire* (London, Batsford, 1977), pp. 69–71. For France, see Davis, *Society and Culture*, pp. 100, 109–10, 116–17.

[46] Samuel Butler, *Hudibras*, ed. John Wilders (Oxford, 1967), pp. 143–4, esp. line 592. Marvell, 'Last Instructions to a Painter', lines 387–9, in H.M. Margoliouth (ed.), *Poems and Letters of Andrew Marvell*, 3rd edn (2 vols., OUP, 1971), vol. I, pp. 156–7.

regions is clear in the west-country version of the ritual, the 'skimmington'. Although the term and its variants – 'skimmity' for example – were later to spread over much of southern England and into the American colonies, in the late sixteenth and early seventeenth centuries the skimmington was a localised ritual centred in Somerset and north Wiltshire. Both the word and the ritual come from the pastoral dairy country, for the implement used in the beating, from which the custom and its principal character get their names, is the skimming ladle – used in the making of butter and cheese.[47] The skimmington's relative complexity accords with other evidence that the wood–pasture regions contained communities in which people had a stronger sense of individual identity, and whose rituals therefore demanded the performance of more distinctly defined roles than the ordinary rough-music processions of the arable regions required. But however individualistic, these were still communities with norms and values to uphold – and in the case of gender relations, very traditional ones.

West Country skimmingtons were of several different kinds, but almost all of them were located either in towns or in wood–pasture villages. One obvious distinction is between those directed at unfaithful wives, and those directed at women who had beaten their husbands. The former kind have much in common with what in later times was known as the 'Hooset hunt', or in Dorset, the 'Ooser'. In this case the rough-music procession to the offender's house was led as usual by the masked figure wearing horns, but there was no acting-out of the offending incident – seventeenth-century street theatre was not *that* permissive. Instead poles or other implements sometimes draped with a chemise and surmounted by a horse's head or skull with horns attached were held up and shaken in front of the windows. An 'Ooser', a terrifying horned devil-mask, still existed at Melbury Osmond in Dorset in the nineteenth century. It, or something like it, was in use in that same village in 1623.[48] The skimmington at Quemerford, near Calne, in 1618, was of the 'Hooset hunt' type. There was the masked figure heading the procession – a man on a red horse 'having a white night cap upon his head, two shining horns hanging by his ears, and counterfeit beard upon his chin made of a deer's tail, a smock upon the top of his garments'. There was the ritual

---

[47] G.E. Dartnell and E.H. Goddard, *A Glossary of Words used in the County of Wiltshire* (London, 1893), pp. 145–6. J. Wright, *English Dialect Dictionary* (6 vols., London, 1898–1905), vol. V, p. 475. C.R.B. Barrett, 'Riding Skimmington and Riding the Stang', *Journal of the British Archaeological Association*, NS, I. (1895), 58–9. V. Alford, 'Rough Music or Charivari', *Folklore*, LXX (1959), 508. Thompson, *Annales ESC*, XXVII (1972), 288.

[48] Dartnell and Goddard, *Glossary*, p. 82. Wright, *Dialect Dictionary*, vol. III, pp. 227, 353. B. Lowsley, *Glossary of Berkshire Words and Phrases* (London, 1888), p. 92. Carrington, *Wiltshire Archaeological Magazine*, I (1854), 88–9. H.S.L. Dewar, 'The Dorset Ooser', *Dorset Natural History Archaeological Society Proceedings*, LXXXIV (1962), 178–80. PRO, STAC 8/153/29 (Gordon and Francis v. Anncell *et al.*, 1623).

shaking of horns in front of the house while rough music was played: 'rams horns and bucks horns carried upon forks' were 'lifted up and shown'. But there was no mock husband-beating, and the intention was to take the victim to Calne and 'wash her in the cucking-stool' – a further indication that infidelity rather than physical violence was her main offence. At Ditcheat in Somerset in 1653 the target was again an unfaithful wife and the ritual was the same. The leader was a man with 'a great pair of horns', followed by others with 'buck's horns, manikins, long staves', all of them 'whooping and hallooeing' and threatening to throw the woman in the pond.[49]

We have noted the assumed connection between female dominance and infidelity. Still, when the primary offence was husband-beating the ritual was somewhat different. Not all the recorded instances of skimmingtons of this second type took place in western wood–pasture villages. Some of them were urban. The one described by Marvell soon after the Restoration took place in the more or less urban setting of Greenwich, near London, and there was also one at Barking in Essex in 1683.[50] There was at least the threat of another urban outbreak (it is not clear whether it actually materialised) at Dorchester in 1630: two men went to borrow a horse 'for the next neighbour to ride' after hearing that a townsman had been beaten by his wife.[51] Recorded rural episodes, however, occurred mostly in wood–pasture villages. A particularly well-documented one took place at Wetherden, Suffolk, on Plough Monday, 1604. A drunken tanner staggered home from the alehouse, was greeted by his wife with 'Out drunken dog, drunken pisspot' and the advice to 'get him to his whores again', and was beaten out of the house. The result was a re-enactment of 'an old country ceremony used in merriment upon such accidents', as the participants described it. They did not use the term skimmington, and it was a bit less elaborate than the west-country version – a cowlstaff was used instead of a horse, for example. But other ingredients were present – the acting-out of the beating with a man in woman's clothing playing the wife, the next-door neighbours as surrogates, the rough-music procession to the offenders' house. It served its purpose – the shamed couple soon left the village – and it took place in a wood–pasture area.[52]

West Country examples of this, as of the other kind of domestic skimmington,

---

[49] B.H. Cunnington, ' "A Skimmington" in 1618', *Folk-Lore*, XLI (1930), 287–90; also in Cunnington (ed.), *Records of Wiltshire*, pp. 65–6. Somerset RO, CQ 3, 1/86, 2 (Sessions Rolls, 1653), fol. 154; see also Quaife, *Wanton Wenches*, p. 200.

[50] The Greenwich incident is also noted by Pepys: R. Latham and W. Matthews (eds.), *Diary of Samuel Pepys* (11 vols., London, Bell, 1970–83), vol. VIII, p. 257. I am indebted to Joyce Malcolm for information on the Barking case.

[51] Mayo (ed.), *Dorchester Records*, p. 655; further details in Dorset RO, B2/8/1 (Dorchester Court Book, 1629–37), fol. 48v.   [52] PRO, STAC 8/249/19 (Rosyer v. Hamond, 1604).

are all from the dairy region or close by. The 'Skymmety' panels in the great hall at Montacute illustrate a fairly primitive form of the ritual, with only the 'husband' being carried on the pole, and no acting-out of the beating. But this is of rather early date – before 1600 – and Montacute is in south Somerset, outside the area in which the ritual attained its most developed form.[53] An elaborate skimmington of this type occurred in 1626 at Marden in the Vale of Pewsey – not a typical pasture parish, but not a typical arable one either, lying in the valley and close to the main dairying region. It included the usual disorderly procession behind a horse carrying 'two young fellows, one of them arrayed . . . in women's apparel', and the usual drumming and firing of guns outside the offending couple's house.[54]

Before we draw further conclusions from this evidence, a few miscellaneous points should be made. First we should note that the term 'skimmington' was applied to demonstrations against violators of other kinds of community norms besides gender and sexual ones: people who enclosed common land or otherwise threatened customary rights, for example. Large-scale riots against enclosures in the Forest of Dean and the Wiltshire forests in 1630–1 were led by mythic leaders who adopted the names 'Skimmington' or 'Lady Skimmington'.[55] Making 'skimmington' a positive term is a classic instance of inversion: it usually referred to something or someone undesirable. In the Quemerford incident the rioters came to the village looking for 'a Skimmington dwelling there'; in 1625 there were some semi-festive brawls between the neighbouring villages of Burbage and Wilton in Wiltshire, each attempting to 'bring skimmington' into each other's parish and being forcibly resisted; and on one occasion during the Forest of Dean riots a 'skimmington' – an effigy of one of the enclosers, the unpopular Sir Giles Mompesson – was ceremonially buried.[56] Even some of the 'domestic' skimmingtons were provoked by a combination of offensive sexual or marital behaviour with other kinds of misconduct. The woman who was threatened with one at Dorchester was alleged to have been slandering a neighbour, while the target at Marden had not only beaten her husband, but had threatened to murder him and her step-daughter. In a later case from Warwickshire (1691) the presence of other issues is very clear. A crowd led by a man wearing horns and another in woman's clothes paraded around the offenders' house shouting, 'Pay for the

---

[53] The Montacute panels are reproduced by Ingram in le Goff and Schmitt (eds.), *Le Charivari*, pp. 256–7. For descriptions, see Barrett, *Journal of the British Archaeological Association*, NS, I (1895), p. 64; and *Notes and Queries*, 4th ser., IV (1869), 105.

[54] Cunnington (ed.), *Records of Wiltshire*, pp. 79–80. For Marden, see *VCH Wilts.*, vol. X (1975), pp. 119–25. For less well-documented cases at Cameley and Leigh-on-Mendip, see Bates Harbin (ed.), *Somerset Quarter Sessions Records* vol. I, Intro., p. xlix; vol. III, Intro., p. 1.

[55] The fullest account of the riots is in Sharp.

[56] Ingram in le Goff and Schmitt (eds.), *Le Charivari*, p. 255. Sharp, pp. 95–6, 129.

timber, you rogue, you cuckoldly dog, which you stole', and 'Pay for the chickens and ducks, you whore.'[57]

Secondly, we should note the festive elements. They are obvious in the Burbage–Wilton brawls (in other parts of the country football might have been the pretext for the violence), but they are also present in some of the 'domestic' incidents. The Suffolk people, it will be recalled, spoke of the custom being used 'in merriment', while the incident at Ditcheat took place during the Whitsun week – the normal time for village revels – people being induced to come 'to make merry with Skimmington' by the promise of plentiful supplies of beer. At Cameley, Somerset, in 1616 there was a skimmington on the day of the revel feast; just a bit of innocent fun, the participants assured the JPs, 'without any hurt done or misdemeanours otherwise at all'.[58] So perhaps we should simply dismiss these incidents as mere youthful pranks? Before we do so, however, we should consider that we only know anything about them because the victims were sufficiently concerned about their reputations to take their tormentors to court. The Rosyers – the targets in Suffolk – did not think it was particularly funny: they had to leave the village and they made a Star Chamber matter out of it. There was some ugly violence in the Quemerford incident; 'Come, Ran, we will have he, we must have he', one of the crowd bellowed as the door was forced.[59] As for the jovial glee of the participants, it is of course a familiar theory of comedy that we laugh loudest at the things that trouble us most, particularly when sexual matters are involved.

Next a few words about the composition of the participating crowds. Most of the people mentioned in court proceedings were, not surprisingly, men (though women participants are depicted in the Montacute panel). In a few cases there is evidence of elite involvement, but statements that local JPs were believed to have given their approval – as at Ditcheat and in the later Barking case – cannot be taken at face value. At Marden the evidence that people were encouraged to take part by substantial, propertied villagers is rather more convincing, and in a Derbyshire case cited by Joan Kent it was the constable who organised the rough-music procession. But Dr Ingram's analysis of participants in Wiltshire skimmingtons confirms that the crowds were drawn from the middling and lower elements of village society, with a fair sprinkling of people who had been in trouble with the law for other reasons.[60] People of higher rank, and especially puritans, disliked such demonstrations as expressions of the worst, most disorderly features of the old festive culture they were trying to suppress. This, it

---

[57] H.C. Johnson and N.J. Williams (eds.), *Warwick County Records, 9: Quarter Sessions Records 1690–1696* (Warwick, Warwickshire County Council, 1964), Intro., pp. xiii-xiv.

[58] Somerset RO, CQ, 3, 1/25 (Sessions Rolls, 1616), no. 23.

[59] See above, n. 49.

[60] J. Kent, 'The English Village Constable, 1580–1642', *Journal of British Studies*, xx, no. 2 (1981), 38–9. Ingram in le Goff and Schmitt (eds.), *Le Charivari*, p. 256.

might be thought, casts some doubt on the argument for the regional distribution of skimmingtons, for were not these wood–pasture areas in which they occurred the strongest centres of rural puritanism? The difficulty is more apparent than real. Puritanism was the religion of the middling sort – the yeomen and better-off craftsmen – and such people certainly had more success in imposing their conceptions of social discipline in these areas than their counterparts in the arable regions. But there always remained a sort of underclass, resistant and potentially hostile to puritan reformation, and these were the people from whom participants in skimmingtons and other horn rituals tended to be drawn.

One other possible objection remains. I have argued that capitalism and dispersed settlement made wood–pasture villages more individualistic than open-field arable ones. Yet these supposedly individualistic villagers seem more inclined to use collective methods of enforcing community norms than their more co-operative neighbours in the arable areas. Again the contradiction can be resolved if we remember two things. First, the individualism and legalism were most characteristic of the middling sort, who did not participate in skimmingtons. Secondly, even if the wood–pasture village was more dispersed and individualistic, it was still a community. Its inhabitants shared many elements of a common stock of culture, many assumptions about familial and gender roles and appropriate community behaviour. But the wood–pasture village enforced its social norms in its own way, by rituals which expressed the greater sense of individual identity which even many of the poorer inhabitants were likely to possess. And lacking the cohesiveness of the arable community, lacking the resources of informal mediation available through squire, parson, and more closely bonded neighbours, its residents were more likely to have occasion to take direct action in this way.

Which brings us to that old problem, the argument from silence. Once again we should recognise that evidence of charivari survives only when the victims were sufficiently angry (and wealthy) to go to court, or when something went wrong and there was violence to persons or property. A degree of caution is advisable before we make too much of the absence of recorded charivaris in more traditional areas. It may be that 'women on top' were just as common there as in the pasturelands, but that like scolds they were more easily controlled by informal means; or that even if they were not, the resulting charivaris were more likely to receive official tolerance, less likely to be presented to the courts. Definitive proof is impossible, but even if it could be found we should still be confronting important differences between the societies of the arable and pasture regions. However, in the light of all the evidence we have surveyed, the impression that female assertiveness and consequent strains in gender relations were more frequently perceived as problems in towns and wood–pasture villages seems inescapable.

Towns and pasture or clothing districts appear to have been more troubled in the early modern period by scolds and rebellious women, and to have more commonly resorted to public shaming rituals – official and unofficial – to deal with them. Now these were the communities most subject to the destabilising effects of economic change, and to the decline of old habits of neighbourliness. There were more poor and disorderly – even masterless – poor in these places than there had previously been, or than there were in the more 'closed' arable parishes; and there were less effective means of pacifying them. The local elites were more preoccupied with order not just because they were puritan, but also because their communities were in fact more disorderly. The preachers, publicists and playwrights did not invent it: there *was* a real threat to order in both social and familial relations in the century after 1560.

This might be an adequate explanation for the obsession with scolds – women who were venting their frustrations upon their neighbours. But it does not explain why married women were rebelling against patriarchal authority, or were thought to have been doing so. Were Englishwomen really attempting to assert an unusual degree of independence in this period? Playwrights were not the only ones to think so: England, ran the proverbial saying, was 'a women's paradise'.[61] This may seem a curious statement to anyone acquainted with the grim realities of the patriarchal system, yet it may be that for some women in some places there had been a slight enlargement of their roles in the household economy, leading to a greater sense of independence which men found threatening. A possible clue may lie in the skimmington. The geographical location, the name and the form of the ritual all seem to have some connection with dairy farming. Now household manuals of the period, like Gervase Markham's *English Housewife*, naturally stress that the wife's duty is always to obey her husband. But they also show that not only did the dairy farm wife make the butter and cheese, she was also responsible for marketing it. So she always had been, to be sure. But in areas like north Wiltshire the market economy was rapidly expanding, and an increasing proportion of land was being devoted to dairy farming, in the sixteenth century.[62] There were more women with direct access to the market than ever before; certainly more than in the arable regions, where the husbandsman's wife had no such responsibilities. Women in the wood-pasture villages were also more likely to be involved in clothmaking, usually through spinning, but sometimes with larger responsibilities which might include run-

[61] C. Williams (ed.), *Thomas Platter's Travels in England 1599* (London, Cape, 1937), p. 182. Similar opinions are cited by R.L. Greaves, *Society and Religion in Elizabethan England* (Minneapolis, University of Minnesota Press, 1981), p. 257.
[62] Gervase Markham, *The English Housewife* (Bk. 2 of *Country Contentments*, 1615 and later edns). On Wiltshire agriculture, see E. Kerridge, 'Agriculture *c.*1500–*c.*1793', *VCH Wilts.*, vol. IV (1959), pp. 64–75.

ning the family business when the husband was away. The growth of a market economy may thus have given more women a greater sense of independence, making men liable to retaliate when they encountered instances of flagrant defiance of accustomed patriarchal order.

This does not mean that there was a direct connection in individual cases. The couples against whom charivaris were directed were not usually prosperous dairy farmers – they were more likely to be quite marginal landholders. But the increased independence of some women may have made men touchy about the behaviour of all women, producing a change in the general mood. And there were undoubtedly other reasons for it. One, surely was the impact of protestant, and especially puritan, teaching on marriage and the family. Puritanism was scarcely an ideology of women's liberation, and in the long run its mainstream varieties reinforced rather than weakened patriarchal authority. Still, puritan teaching always stressed the partnership aspect of marriage, and gave the wife a responsible role in the moral ordering of the household.[63] The popularity of advice manuals and conduct books in this period suggests that people were having to work out a new relationship between spouses, one that could no longer be taken for granted. Among the more extreme separatists women often had a much greater degree of equality in church membership. The dairying and cloth-making region of north Somerset and Wiltshire were distinctly puritan, and contained more separatists than most other parts of the country. Here, then, is another possible source of female independence, whose implications may have been exaggerated and extended to all women by men who were consciously or subconsciously worried about it.

The region from which much of the evidence used in this paper is drawn has its own peculiarities. Other English counties were at different stages of economic development: in Norfolk, for example, capitalist agriculture was more advanced in arable as well as pasture regions, and the cloth industry existed in arable parishes, as it rarely did in the western counties. One might expect these and other related differences in social structure to be reflected in local variations in the patterns of gender relations. Eventually it may be possible to incorporate such regional differences in a general theory, and perhaps to modify, more convincingly than the current state of research permits, Alice Clark's picture of a steady decline in the independence of women. That decline obviously happened in the long run. But the process may have been more complicated than her book suggests. At present we are entitled to conclude that the anxieties of Jacobean authors had some basis in fact: that there really was a period of strained gender relations in early modern England, and that it lay at the heart of the 'crisis of order'.

[63] Hamilton, *Liberation of Women*, pp. 56–63, provides a recent survey of literature on this subject.

5

Order and Disorder in the English Revolution

J.S. MORRILL and J.D. WALTER

Despite the hopes of a few (like the Somerset man who declared that there was now no law in force) and the fears of many more, Charles I's execution was not to be the signal for the collapse of that social order whose keystone he had claimed to be. Previous 'interregnums' had seen an outbreak of rioting prompted by the belief that the law died with the monarch, but the 'year of intended parity' saw no popular rising emerge to take advantage of such beliefs; the intention remained unrealised.[1] Indeed, an examination of disorder in the 1640s and 50s might suggest that the possibilities of an 'intended parity' were greater in the fantasies projected by the fears of the propertied classes than in the reality of popular disorder in the period. There exists a notable discrepancy between both the character and level of disorder generated by the 'moral panic' that gripped propertied contemporaries and the evidence recoverable in the historical record. While the Revolution imposed new sources of conflict on pre-existing social and economic tensions, it failed to produce that popular explosion, fear of which ran like a red thread through the political history of the period.

Measuring disorder is at the best of times a difficult (and even questionable) exercise. To the familiar problems of the under-reporting of riot and patchy record survival, the Revolution added its own obstacles. That what the people said and did continued to be less often witnessed to by themselves, than reported by men of property who 'talked of the danger of a popular uprising in order to discourage each other from taking up arms',[2] makes even harder the Solomon-like task of disentangling reality from rumour and the paranoia of the propertied.

[1] Somerset RO Q/SR 81/47; *The Souldiers Demand Shewing the Present Misery, And Prescribing a Perfect Remedy, Printed at Bristoil in the yeare of intended Parity*, BL, Thomason Tract E555 (29), a reference we owe to the kindness of Margaret Sampson.
[2] L. Stone, *The Causes of the English Revolution 1529–1642* (London, Routledge, 1972), p. 77.

The cessation of judicial activity for a time in some areas and at the centre the collapse of those prerogative courts preoccupied with the punishment of riot compounds the problem.[3] While this might have had the effect of understating the level of disorder, the switch to other courts, and notably parliament, probably had the opposite effect. Both as the focus of contemporary concern with civil conflict and as an institution that has left full documentation, parliament's assumption of the prosecution of various forms of riot may have served to inflate both contemporary and historical perceptions of the scale of disorder in the Revolution.[4] At the same time, the collapse of censorship and the emergence of unprecedented forms of communication reporting riot – pamphlet, broadsheet and newspaper – would have had the same effect.[5] The immediacy of this reporting was in stark contrast to the muffled, delayed and confused reports by which one region had heard of disturbances in other regions in preceding decades. Furthermore, there was an extensive correspondence between MPs and others in London and their families and friends in the provinces in which reports and rumours of disorder featured prominently.[6] Even if there had not been an actual increase in the incidence of disorder, these changes in the manner of reporting and recording riot would have inflated contemporaries' perceptions.

All this, we would wish to argue, has contributed to a tendency by some historians to misread the trajectory of disorder in the 1640s and 1650s. While this period witnessed an undoubted increase in disorder, it also registered important discontinuities with an earlier pattern of disorder and in the forms and levels of riot within the Revolution itself. The potential for some important forms of popular disorder (enclosure and grain riots) had been removed from some areas

[3] J. Mather, 'Parliamentary Committees and the Justices of the Peace, 1642–60', *American Journal of Legal History*, XXIII (1979), 122–3, 133n.

[4] That the House of Lords assumed the judicial business of Star Chamber (whose records exist mainly in manuscript and are largely missing, reports excepted, for the reign of Charles I) not only assured that evidence of disorder would be easier to recover by historians, but also that MPs would be made continuously aware of riots in the provinces and reflect this awareness in letters to friends and family.

[5] J. Frank, *The Beginnings of the English Newspaper* (Cambridge, Mass., Harvard University Press, 1961), pp. 19–31. For general comments on the astonishing growth of publications at this time, see P. Zagorin, *The Court and the Country* (London, Routledge, 1969), pp. 203–5; G.K. Fortescue, *Catalogue of the Pamphlets of George Thomason* (2 vols., London, 1908), vol. I, pp. xx–xxiv. The total number of known publications between 1640 and 1660 exceeded the total number from 1485 to 1640. Thomason collected 721 items in 1641 and 2104 in 1642. S. Lambert, 'The Beginnings of Printing for the House of Commons', *The Library*, 6th ser., III (1981), p. 45n., suggests that in these years, Thomason may have collected less than half the items actually published. We know that these publications were distributed very widely and passed from hand to hand: R. Cust, 'Perceptions of Politics and the Dissemination of News in Early Seventeenth Century England' (forthcoming); Morrill, *Cheshire 1630–1660* (OUP, 1974), pp. 39–42.

[6] For some examples, see D. Hirst, 'The Defection of Sir Edward Dering 1640–41', *Historical Journal* XV (1972), pp. 193–208; D. Gardiner (ed.), *The Oxinden Letters, 1607–1642* (London, Constable, 1933).

before 1640; within the Revolution there were two separate peaks of disorder, the early and late 1640s, with little continuity, and some surprising breaks, in the forms of riot. These discontinuities challenge the accepted wisdom of an interpretation that sees popular disorder growing throughout the period.

Disturbances were undoubtedly at their greatest in the first peak of disorder in the early 1640s. Enclosures were thrown down, altar rails torn out. Elections, both municipal and parliamentary, had seen the unwelcome and sometimes tumultuous intrusion of 'fellowes without shirts'. In the provinces, crowds attacked and pillaged the houses of recusants and malignants; in London, they pressed round parliament. And all this took place against a clamour of unemployed clothworkers and multiplying evidence of a breakdown of the traditional bulwarks of church and state.[7] Aggregating the various disturbances thus catches contemporaries' uneasy perception of what seemed to them a social order in dissolution. But to disaggregate these various disturbances is to question the accuracy of that contemporary perception upon which historians have sometimes placed overmuch reliance as evidence of the *actuality* of disorder.

As MPs nervously debated and argued, it could indeed appear that their disagreement with the king might let loose a popular movement for 'Lex Graria', the confiscation and redistribution of their estates.[8] There was a notable increase in the number of agrarian riots in the early 1640s. To see these as the culmination of a *rising* trend of agrarian protest is to ignore the contradictory evidence of the changing geography of disorder. The classic locus of earlier enclosure riot and rebellion, the fielden Midlands, remained remarkably still. For the most part, enclosure riots were restricted to areas where the radical challenge of enclosure to local economies prompted, and local social and economic structures permitted, the persistence of active, collective resistance. It was in the western forests and eastern fens and the larger estates whose royal, aristocratic and episcopal owners were associated with a discredited regime that most riots were to be found.[9]

In the charged political atmosphere of the 1640s, the tendency to equate the levelling of enclosures with the threat of levelling in society became more

---

[7] B. Manning, *The English People and the English Revolution 1640–1649* (London, Heinemann, 1976) gives a vivid sense of these years.

[8] Manning, *English People*, p. 58.

[9] The discussion of agrarian disorder is based on systematic research on a wide variety of sources, including *State Papers; Journals of the Lords and Commons*; Main Papers, House of Lords RO; PRO, King's Bench; *Historical Manuscripts Commission* and Quarter Sessions Records for a large number of counties. Further discussion of, and further references for, the points raised in the following discussion will be found in J. Walter, 'The Poor Man's Friend and the Gentleman's Plague: Agrarian Disorder in Early Modern England' (forthcoming paper). A. Charlesworth (ed.), *An Atlas of Rural Protest in Britain, 1548–1900* (London, Croom Helm, 1983), pp. 16–22, 39–42, provides a good, concise discussion. See also Sharp; Lindley.

pronounced. As a description of the politics of agrarian disorder this reveals more about the propertied classes' fears than the rioters' intent. While recent assessments of agrarian disorder as non-ideological or apolitical are too cut and dried (it is possible to reconstruct the politics of enclosure rioters in contexts other than those of class or party allegiance),[10] it remains the case that agrarian crowds were intent on a recovery of rights that involved the righting, not the transformation, of a world turned upside-down. The not unsurprising decision of the House of Commons (whose earlier attack on enclosure in the Grand Remonstrance had raised popular hopes) to throw their weight behind enclosers after 1643 ensured that enclosure rioters did not form a radical agrarian wing of the parliamentarian cause. Land and liberty was not to be the cry of the English Revolution. But this failure to meet popular expectations did not lead to a radicalisation of agrarian disorder. At its greatest in the early 1640s, agrarian disorder became progressively restricted. It remained a problem in forest and fen or flared up when new owners of confiscated estates attempted to enclose. There was, however, to be no revolution in the countryside. The passivity of the Midlands (outside of its forests) suggests that the possibilities of a revolt of the fields may already have been undermined by the very changes in social and economic relationships which provoked popular discontent, an important point to which we later return.

What made agrarian disorder more threatening was the simultaneous occurrence of other disturbances. Popular iconoclasm was probably more common than the destruction of hedges; in Essex, for example, the authorities needed to hold a special court to deal with those who broke down altar rails.[11] A reaction to Laud's 'beauty of holiness', such riots nevertheless could seem to presage a more general toppling of traditional structures. Some contemporaries saw iconoclasm as 'abolishing superstition with sedition'.[12] It might involve the riotous destruction of altar rails and images, but iconoclasm had its own sources of legitimacy (parliamentary declarations and preaching) and discipline. Not infrequently, it involved the tacit co-operation of local elites.[13] Events like those at Chelmsford in

---

[10] Some preliminary comments on the politics of riot in early modern England are to be found in J. Walter, 'Reconstructing Popular Political Culture in Early Modern England' (forthcoming).

[11] J.R. Phillips, *The Reformation of Images* (Berkeley, University of California, 1973); J. Morrill, 'The Church in England, 1642–9' in J. Morrill (ed.), *Reactions to the English Civil War 1642–1649* (London, Macmillan, 1982), pp. 94–5, 231–2 nn.16–17; Morrill, *Cheshire*, pp. 36–7; D. Underdown, *Somerset in the Civil War and Interregnum* (Newton Abbot, David and Charles, 1973), p. 27, 38, 44, 78; W. Hunt, *The Puritan Moment: The Coming of Revolution in an English County* (Cambridge, Mass., Harvard University Press, 1983), pp. 285–6; Sharpe, pp. 84–6; [Bruno Ryves], *Mercurius Rusticus, or the Countries Complaint of the Sacriledges Prophanations and Plunderings.*   [12] Manning, *English People*, pp. 32–45.

[13] See, for example, J.T. Evans, *Seventeenth-Century Norwich: Politics, Religion, and Government, 1620–1690* (OUP, 1979), pp. 128–9; House of Lords RO, Main Papers, 30 June 1641; HMC *Buccleuch Mss.*, III, pp. 415–16; PRO, SP 16/460/31.

which the royalist clergyman and polemicist, Bruno Ryves, drew a direct link between religious and social radicalism were, if true, an exception.[14] Popular iconoclasm was at its height in the early 1640s; after 1643 it became the prerogative of reforming parliamentary troops at whose hands many cathedrals suffered.[15]

More alarming were the attacks on recusants and malignants. Here could be seen more direct evidence of the people taking advantage of the times to challenge their 'betters'. According to Clarendon, malignants' goods were seized 'by the fury and license of the common people, who were in all places grown to that barbarity and rage against the nobility and gentry (under the style of *Cavaliers*) that it was not safe for any to live at their houses who were taken notice of as no votaries to the parliament'.[16] The focus on the riots in the Stour Valley in 1642 (on whose example Clarendon drew) in which crowds looted gentry households has, however, obscured the more general point that only a tiny minority of recusants were attacked. Even in the Stour Valley riots local evidence suggests that some victims owed their selection to a previous history of conflict with their local community; at Colchester, Sir John Lucas was in conflict with the corporation and popularly detested for his enclosures.[17] Attacks were concentrated in the period before the onset of armed conflict when official licence, rather than the collapse of political authority, made catholic and 'malignant' gentry legitimate targets. With the exception of those catholic officers murdered by troops raised to fight the Scots, violence when it did occur was directed against property and not persons. The outbreak of war saw a decline in this form of disorder which coincided with an end to the panics and alarums over supposed 'Popish plots'.[18] Where such attacks persisted it was the work of parliamentary troops who had been often at the heart of earlier crowds. But the English Revolution was not to be stained by the bloody violence that marked religious conflict on the continent.

What gave these generally distinct forms of disorder in the early 1640s their

[14] [B. Ryves], *Mercurius Rusticus* no. 3, pp. 17–21.

[15] Morrill in *Reactions to the English Civil War*, p. 95; I. Gentles, 'Conflict between Soldiers and Civilians in the English Revolution, 1640–1655'. We are grateful to Professor Gentles for allowing us to read this valuable unpublished paper.

[16] Clarendon, *The History of the Rebellion and Civil Wars in England*, ed. W.D. Macray (6 vols., OUP, 1888), II, pp. 318–19.

[17] C. Holmes, *The Eastern Association in the English Civil War* (CUP, 1974), pp. 35–6, 43–4; CUL, Add. MS 33, fols. 19–21; *HMC Braye Mss.*, pp. 147–8; PRO, SP 16/458/12 and 13; House of Lords RO Main Papers, 5 August 1641; R. Clifton, 'The Popular Fear of Catholics during the English Revolution', *Past and Present*, LII (1971), 23–55, reprinted in P. Slack (ed.), *Rebellion, Popular Protest and the Social Order in Early Modern England*, (CUP, 1984), pp. 129–61.

[18] Clifton, *Past and Present*, LII (1971), 32ff. A Hughes, 'Politics, Society and Civil War in Warwickshire 1620–50', unpublished Ph.D. thesis, University of Liverpool 1979, p. 265; Manning, *English People*, pp. 165–6; PRO, SP 16/491/119, 133, 138; 492/2, 11; *Lord's Journal*, v, 294–5; N.Z. Davies, 'The Rites of Violence: Religious Riot in Sixteenth-Century France', *Past and Present*, LIX (1973), 51–91.

menace was the political context in which they took place. In London, sullen crowds jostled members of both Houses and prevented them from taking their seats in parliament, while the lord mayor found his authority flouted.[19] The worst actual violence occurred in May 1640 when rioters swarmed around the archbishop's palace at Westminster but failed to carry out their threat to burn it down. When some of the leaders were seized and imprisoned, rioters broke open the gaol and delivered the prisoners, for which they were tried for treason.[20] Thereafter the London crowd demonstrated against and intimidated church-men, politicians and the royal family.[21] These examples in the capital of crowds who showed scant regard for established authority and of the coercive petition-ing of parliament gave provincial disorders a threatening and unfolding unity they perhaps did not merit seen in isolation and in their local context. In the provinces, exaggerated reports of events in London had the same effect.

In reality, however, there was a failure to link radical ideas with popular grievances in the collective action of the early 1640s. Even in London the crowds often embraced substantial citizens and were well disciplined; there were few attacks on property or persons. As Valerie Pearl has written of events in the capital, here was 'a striking phenomenon . . . unknown in the rest of Europe: the rise of mass political activity of a new kind, accompanied by demonstrations in the streets and petitions . . . the absence of attacks on private property contrasts sharply with the behaviour of eighteenth-century city mobs . . . London re-mained without a popular uprising, even without significant bloodshed, during some of the most disturbed years in English history . . . The point was not lost on the French ambassador: blood would certainly have flowed in the streets of Paris, he wrote in 1642, if similar events had happened there.'[22] A third, popular force did not emerge from the widespread disorders of the early 1640s. There was, in fact, discontinuity in the patterns of disorder carried into the civil war. Much of the force of this earlier popular political initiative had been dissipated. It had been alienated by the failure of parliament, a body of landowners, to respond to their appeals, sublimated in the wider military conflict between crown and parliament or ultimately turned against both by the costs of the war.

It was the strains of the civil war and the politico-religious conflicts accom-panying it that explain the second peak of disturbances in the later 1640s. The armies became the major direct and indirect source of disorder. Plundering troops prompted conflicts between civilians and the military that culminated in

[19] V. Pearl, *London and the Outbreak of the Puritan Revolution* (OUP, 1962), pp. 212–16 and *passim*.
[20] S.R. Gardiner, *History of England from the Accession of King James I to the Outbreak of the Civil War* (10 vols., London, 1884), vol. IX, pp. 133–5.
[21] Manning, *English People*, pp. 71–98.
[22] V. Pearl, 'Change and Stability in Seventeenth Century London', *London Journal*, IV (1979), 5.

the Club risings in south and south-west England.[23] Ill-paid troops became themselves a source of disorder, staging mutinies in at least thirty-four English counties and in most of Wales in the years 1645 to 1647.[24] The excise, a new form of indirect taxation introduced to meet the costs of the war, occasioned riots in both the larger cities (London, Norwich) and smaller communities. Though we lack a full study of excise riots, this form of disorder seems to have been at its height when the harvest failures of the later 1640s made the collection of a tax imposed on the consumption of basic commodities (but not bread) especially resented. While some areas may have been relatively untroubled by such riots, others might experience considerable disorder.[25] In 1647 there was a further outbreak of religious disorder, but this time associated with counter-revolution. In the Revolt of the Prayer Book, large crowds reinstated ejected ministers or compelled the use of the book of common prayer. These disturbances, spontaneously occurring in different regions, were linked to rumours that the army was negotiating with the king for the restoration of the old church.[26]

But while the pressures of civil war conflict produced a second peak of disorders in the later 1640s, these riots against specific grievances did not become the occasion for rebellion. Conflict over the tithe resulted in some riots for example (but how many precisely we have yet to discover) and more tithe-strikes probably, but the politics of the tithe never initiated disorder on the scale that it did in continental Europe.[27] And if the riots of the later 1640s challenged the exercise of authority, they did not automatically signal popular support for a radical attack on the social bases of authority. The largest popular movement of these years, the Clubmen, did not seek to threaten that social order whose hierarchies were seemingly well observed within its ranks.

Ironically the discontinuities between the two peaks of disorder in the early

[23] J.S. Morrill, *The Revolt of the Provinces: Conservatives and Radicals in the English Civil War 1630–1650* (London, Allen and Unwin, 1976), pp. 98–111; J.S. Morrill, 'Mutiny and Discontent in English Provincial Armies 1645–1647', *Past and Present*, LVI (1972), 49–74; D. Underdown, 'The Chalk and the Cheese: Contrasts among the English Clubmen', *Past and Present*, LXXXV (1979), 25–48; R. Hutton, 'The Worcestershire Clubmen in the English Civil War', *Midland History*, V (1979–80), 39–49.   [24] Morrill, *Past and Present*, LVI (1972), *passim*.
[25] C.H. Firth and R.S. Rait (eds.), *Acts and Ordinances of the Interregnum 1642–1600* (3 vols., London, 1911), vol. I, pp. 916–19, 1004–6; D. Underdown, *Pride's Purge: Politics in the Puritan Revolution* (OUP, 1971), pp. 90, 298; Evans, *Norwich*, pp. 170–1; Morrill, *Cheshire*, pp. 195–6. The geography of the excise riot awaits systematic study. While a large number of counties experienced disorder and opposition could be a particular problem in an area like the West Country, some counties seem to have been largely untroubled: J.S. Cockburn (ed.), *Western Circuit Assize Orders, 1629–1648: A Calendar* (Camden Society, 4th series, XVII, 1976), pp. 254, 276, 280; PRO SP 25/169, fols. 5–6; Wiltshire RO, Q/S Gt. Roll, Michaelmas 1659, 10 May 1659; Sharpe, p. 79.   [26] Morrill in *Reactions to the English Civil War*, pp. 111–12.
[27] Morrill in *Reactions to the English Civil War*, p. 110; cf. H. Kamen, *The Iron Century* (London, Weidenfeld, 1971), ch. 10.

and late 1640s suggest that the emergence of more organised radical groupings, like the Levellers and Diggers, coincided with a decline in those forms of disorder which should have provided them with potentially their best opportunities for proselytising. By the later 1640s agrarian disorder had become even more confined to specific areas. The earlier attacks on recusants and malignants had not developed into the feared attack on 'Protestants as well as Papists'. There are isolated examples of attacks by tenants on manor houses and detailed local research may provide more, but the frequency with which a few familiar examples are cited raises doubts as to how common these were.[28] Sequestration and confiscation may have tilted the balance of power in favour of tenants (as incomplete evidence on rent-strikes and arrears suggests) and afforded the odd opportunity for riot, but they did not provide the legitimation nor pretext for wholesale popular plunder.[29] In the English Revolution (some) manorial records were burnt, but not châteaux. For reasons that we look at more fully later, this period did not witness an English rising against seigneurialism.

In the towns, economic discontent provoked tax riots and prompted some to support the radical groups, but harvest failure and popular chafing at the attempted puritan 'reformation of manners' persuaded others to join in the counter-revolutionary political demonstrations that took place in London and other cities.[30] As Peter Clark and Paul Slack note, political upheaval at the centre, popular opposition to high taxation and extreme religious radicalism in many towns meant that the new civil rulers, often differing but in degree from the social composition of their predecessors, were as anxious as their predecessors to exert their authority over the 'meaner sort'.[31]

And despite the tensions and sufferings caused by successive poor harvests in the later 1640s, the urban poor were not brought to the barricades by the demand for Bread and Justice. In fact, grain riots were not only noticeable by their continued absence from the capital; sensitive and previously much troubled

[28] See, for example, I. Roy, 'The English Civil War and English Society', B. Bond and I. Roy (eds.), A Yearbook of Military History, I (1977), pp. 34–5. This is a subject crying out for systematic study. Most of the known attacks on muniment rooms seem to have occurred just after a fortified manor house was taken over by besieging parliamentary troops.

[29] Charlesworth (ed.), Atlas of Rural Protest, p. 41; L. Stone, Family and Fortune: Studies in Aristocratic Finance in the Sixteenth and Seventeenth Centuries (OUP, 1973), p. 151; A.L. Hughes, 'Politics, Society and Civil War in Warwickshire, 1620–1650', unpublished Ph.D. thesis, Liverpool University, 1980, pp. 220, 421–2; Manning, English People, p. 194; Gardiner (ed.), Oxinden Letters, pp. 67–8; B. Schofield (ed.), The Knyvett Letters, 1620–1644 (Norfolk Record Society, XX, 1949), pp. 134, 137; HMC 5th Report, MSS E. Field, p. 388.

[30] P. Clark and P. Slack, English Towns in Transition 1500–1700 (OUP, 1976), pp. 99, 135–6; V. Pearl, 'London's Counter-Revolution' in G.E. Aylmer (ed.), The Interregnum: The Quest for Settlement 1646–1660 (London, Macmillan, 1972); Underdown, Pride's Purge, pp. 323–4; Manning, English People, ch. 10; Gentles, 'Conflict between Soldiers and Civilians'; A. Everitt, The Community of Kent and the Great Rebellion 1640–1660 (Leicester University Press, 1966), pp. 231–59; VCH Suffolk, II, p. 192.   [31] Clark and Slack, English Towns, p. 136.

areas, like Kent and Essex, also escaped the food riot. While the clothing districts of the West Country continued to experience grain riots, there seems to have been a contraction in the geography of the food riot.[32] Famine, even in the conditions of the later 1640s, never became the spur to popular risings.

After the king's execution, social hierarchies trembled but ultimately held firm. Charles's execution had coincided with a third year of harvest failure. Wildman, for the Levellers, had tried to draw on the evidence of food riots in Wiltshire to urge on a reluctant parliament the necessity for reforms to stave-off 'the many-headed monster'.[33] But after 1649 the harvest improved and, despite fears that military provisioning might provoke further disorder, grain riots faded away. Opposition to enclosure continued to flare up in those areas of forest and fen where disorder had been previously pronounced. In parts of the fens, notably Hatfield Chase, running warfare continued between drainers and commoners.[34] There were occasional riots in the western forests where communities of commoners continued the defence of their rights. Where a financially hard-pressed republic attempted to continue the royal policy of disafforestation on former crown lands, their efforts met similar resistance: there were riots in the later 1650s in the forests of Needwood and Sherwood and at Enfield Chase.[35] Elsewhere, attempts at piecemeal enclosure continued to prompt minor disorders.[36] But the overall impression is that the Interregnum witnessed a contraction in the pattern of disorder prompted by traditional popular grievances. Even in forest and fen, riots were less frequent, a silent testimony perhaps to the temporary victory of the commoners. Similarly, what is so far known about the collection of the excise suggests that it occasioned fewer confrontations in the 1650s than in the period 1645–9.[37]

In the 1640s, the army had been both source and focus of disorder because of its indiscipline: in the 1650s it became a cause of resentment and complaint but rarely of disorder, for it was ordered and effective. There were at most times between 10000 and 14000 men in active service in England, scattered in garrisons mainly in London and around the coast and the Scots border.[38]

---

[32] J. Walter, 'The geography of food riots, 1585–1649' in Charlesworth (ed.), *Atlas of Rural Protest*, pp. 72–80.
[33] J. Wildman, *Truth's Triumph or Treachery Anatomized* (London, 1648), pp. 3–4.
[34] Lindley, chs. 4–6; C. Holmes; below, p. 166.
[35] *CSPD 1658–9*, pp. 152, 328; *VCH Staffordshire*, II, p. 353; D.O. Pam, *The Rude Multitude: Enfield and the Civil War* (Edmonton Hundred Historical Society, Occasional Papers, NS, XXXIII, 1977); Sharp, ch. ix.
[36] For examples of minor riots prompted by enclosure in the 1650s, see Somerset RO, Q/SR 90/67, 93.2/72; Coventry RO, City Annals F, fol. 46v.
[37] G.E. Aylmer, *The State's Servants* (London, Routledge, 1973), p. 299.
[38] H. Reece, 'The Military Presence in England, 1649–60', unpublished D. Phil. thesis, University of Oxford, 1981, p. 287.

Garrisoned troops were irritants in various ways: they asserted themselves over and against local governors, demanding custody of the town keys or insisting that senior officers be allowed to attend meetings of the corporation;[39] they frequently set up their own gathered church and welcomed citizens to it;[40] or they protected local separatist groups in the face of civilian hostility – one notable example being the Bristol garrison's succour of the Quakers in 1654–5.[41] Sometimes they intervened to carry out the suppression of popular festivities that the reformation of manners demanded.[42] Occasionally garrisons intervened in local elections.[43] But, despite the barrage of complaints against troops, there is little evidence of street fighting or other violent clashes between soldiers and civilians. Those that did occur, like the events at Enfield Chase, were well reported.[44]

In fact, the existence of well-disciplined and professionally led troops gave governments of the 1650s the opportunity to deal with riotous expressions of dissent by brute force. Agrarian rioters felt the full weight of a military presence when government desired it. Thus troops were used to put down disturbances in the Forest of Dean and Lincolnshire and Cambridgeshire fens.[45] They were called in by the corporation of Newcastle to break a strike by the keelmen;[46] and they enforced sequestration orders.[47] In the summer of 1649, one troop was quartered in each of the five lathes of Kent as direct response to the reports of the meeting of 'disaffected persons'.[48] It established a pattern. Occasionally, insufficient force was applied and disturbances continued, especially where there was considerable community support for the rioters and a difficult terrain for the troops. At Swaffham Bulbeck in 1653, the failure of stationed troops to prevent rioters from destroying the drainage works led a frustrated commander to recommend that a hundred or so inhabitants be pressed for naval service *in terrorem*.[49] But in general, the arrogant order represented by the army inhibited popular resistance as it did royalist resistance. It was not used all the time; that would have strained resources. Troops could maintain order but only while they remained on permanent standby. This probably explains why many scandalous ministers remained in their parsonages despite streams of orders from local and national

---

[39] Reece, 'Military Presence', pp. 126–76.
[40] At Hull, the parish church was divided by a wall, the garrison worshipping on one side and the citizens on the other: *CSPD 1650*, p. 452.
[41] T. Birch (ed.), *Thurloe State Papers* (7 vols., London, 1742), III, pp. 170–2.
[42] Gentles, 'Conflict between Soldiers and Civilians'.   [43] *CSPD 1654*, pp. 331–2.
[44] Pam, *The Rude Multitude*, pp. 10–11.
[45] *CSPD 1649–50*, p. 316; *1651*, p. 286 (and cf. *1656–7*, p. 80); *1650*, p. 218.
[46] *Weekly Intelligencer* for 22 August 1654, cited in Reece, 'Military Presence', p. 182.
[47] *Calendar of the Committee for Compounding*, vol. I, pp. 186, 222, 361, 366.
[48] *CSPD 1649–50*, pp. 253–4.   [49] PRO, SP 18/39/96.

committees dismissing them. Where they had the support of their congregations, it would have taken a permanent military presence to evict them and to sustain a successor. Only in 1659, as a lack of pay again began to lead to a collapse of discipline, did the army become again a force of disorder rather than of resentment.[50]

If the 1650s saw a contraction in the scale and scope of popular disorder, the government's sense of its own insecurities encouraged it to read into reports of often minor disorders 'the beginnings of insurrection'. To the hyperbolic language of its predecessors, the republic added a new political vocabulary which spoke of often minor riots as evidence of 'designs against the Commonwealth'.[51] Men of property continued to fear 'an intended parity' that hurried them into a *de facto* acceptance of republican government. Their fear was less an accurate pointer to the possibilities of popular revolution from below than a reflection of the continuing failure to achieve a political settlement and the emergence of more organised forms of popular radicalism. Caught in a 'moral panic' and witness to many petty acts of insubordination,[52] they could only regard any evidence of disorder as the preliminary rites to the popular rising they had always feared.

From the very outset this 'moral panic' had been fuelled by the unprecedented availability of information about the activities of the 'many-headed monster'. The collapse of censorship and the rapid growth of newspapers and pamphlets at a time of political uncertainty would by themselves have fed this panic. That much of the reporting was just good copy directed at an anxious public fearfully greedy to learn about new disturbances only exacerbated the situation. Never hitherto could gentlemen buy hot from the presses tracts with such titles as *The Last Tumult in Fleet Street Raised by the Disorderly Preachment, Pratings and Pratlings of Mr Barbones the Leatherseller and Mr Greene the Feltmaker*.[53] Such alarmist writings could colour responses to more sober accounts of the marches of thousands of countrymen to present petitions at Westminster, or of disturbances in the provinces. In late 1641 and early 1642, the tempo of such publications quickened,[54] with lurid accounts of atrocities in Ulster spilling over into circumstantial accounts of plots in England and even into plausible but

---

[50] See below pp. 163–4.

[51] See, for example, the attitudes to disorder expression in PRO, SP 25/194, fols. 43–4; /195, fol. 11/ 196, fol. 287.

[52] What probably alarmed gentlemen as much as evidence of collective action by the poor was the growing evidence of plebeian disregard for the niceties of social and religious hierarchies, of which the Quakers' use of 'thou' to address superiors is only the best-known example. This is a subject calling for more investigation; see K.V. Thomas, 'The Place of Laughter in Tudor and Stuart England', *Times Literary Supplement*, 21 Jan. 1977, pp. 77–81.

[53] BL, Thomason Tracts, E 180 (26).   [54] See n. 6 above.

fabricated narratives of popish uprisings.[55] The reality of the early 1640s was bad
enough; rumour made it worse. One prebend of Hereford, preaching on 17 April
1642, solemnly told his congregation that he had certain knowledge that sectaries
now controlled London and had forced the king to flee to the north.[56]

Both sides in the developing political conflict made deliberate and propagan-
dist use of this alarmist literature. The royalists had the easier task, indicting the
House of Commons of 'traitorously endeavouring to subvert the fundamental
laws and . . . to deprive the king of his royal power',[57] and claiming that this
occasioned a breakdown of order. The royalists specifically accused the Commons of wilful encouragement of popular violence and iconoclasm, or more
generally of wilful indulgence of them. Only the restoration of royal authority
could lead to a restoration of order. It became a central prop of royal propaganda
in 1642, most famously in the *Reply to the Nineteen Propositions*,[58] but even
more pointedly elsewhere:

We complained . . . of the multitudes of seditious pamphlets and sermons. And the
declaration tells us, they know we have ways enough in our ordinary courts of justice to
punish those: so we have to punish tumults and riots, and yet they will not serve our turn to
keep our towns, our forests and parks from violence. And it may be, those courts have still
the power to punish, they have lost the skill to define what riots and tumults are: otherwise
a jury in Southwark legally impanelled to examine a riot there, would not have been
superceded, and the sheriff enjoyned not to proceed, by vertue of an order from the House
of Commons.[59]

Equally, however, the managers of the Long Parliament were using the very
threat of a collapse of order to advance the case for an imposed political
settlement. Throughout the winter of 1641–2, the managers whipped up the
hysteria about the massacres in Ireland, and the plans of the papists to spread
their campaign to the mainland. They have been shown to have distorted the
information flowing into them to that end.[60] Besmirching the king as deranged,
incapable of governing, and arguing that anarchy was developing from the king's

---

[55] J. Rushworth, *Historical Collections* (7 vols., London 1659–1701), IV, pp. [398]–[416], 385–421
(page numbers 385–416 are used twice in this edition); K.J. Lindley, 'The Impact of the Irish
Rebellion in England and Wales', *Irish Historical Studies*, XVIII (1972–3), pp. 143–76; Clifton, *Past
and Present*, LII (1971), pp. 25–55; R. Clifton, 'Fear of Popery' in C.S.R. Russell *The Origins of the
English Civil War* (London, Macmillan, 1973) pp. 144–67. For an example of a fabricated papist
rising, see 'A True Relation of a Bloody Conspiracy in Cheshire Intended for the Destruction of the
Whole County' in J. Atkinson (ed.), *Civil War Tracts of Cheshire* (Chetham Society, 2nd series, 65,
1909), pp. 2–4.   [56] BL, Loan MS 29, 173, fols. 237–8.
[57] Rushworth, *Historical Collections*, IV, p. 473.
[58] J.P. Kenyon, *The Stuart Constitution* (CUP, 1962), pp. 21–3.
[59] Rushworth, *Historical Collections*, IV, p. 711.
[60] M. Mendle, 'Mixed Government, The Estates and the Bishops', Ph.D. thesis, Washington
University, St Louis, 1977, pp. 396–432.

incapacity,[61] Pym and his colleagues used the existence of popular disturbances to illustrate the results of misgovernment and to justify further remedial legislation. Thus on 25 January 1642 Pym picked up a theme from a petition of the clothworkers of Essex, which had included the failure to crush popery amongst the causes of the depression,[62] when he predicted an insurrection of the poor if there was no political reform or religious renewal.[63] Five months later, crowds of clothiers sacked the houses of 'papists' and 'malignants', accusing them of being 'the cause of the present troubles and distractions'.[64] Here and elsewhere – in their response to iconoclasm, to lay preaching, even to enclosure riots – there was an ambivalence in parliamentarian attitudes to popular disturbances: they were understandable if reprehensible, to be met not by repression but by the prospect of reform.[65]

That parliament was aware of the damage royalist propaganda could inflict can be seen in the Houses' attempt on 19 May 1642 to vindicate the intimidation of MPs the previous December. Its speciousness stands out:

We do not conceive that Numbers do make an assembly unlawful, but when either the end or manner of their carriage shall be unlawful. Divers just occasions might draw the citizens to Westminster, and other causes were depending in Parliament, and why that should be found more faulty in the citizens than the resort of great numbers every day in the term to the ordinary courts of Justice we know not . . .[66]

Throughout the 1640s and the 1650s the same pattern was to recur. It was always in the interests of newsmen to report in exaggerated detail all manifestations of disorder; and it always suited the polemical purposes of government to exaggerate and to draw lessons from threats to the peace. The manipulation of 'Leveller' plots, of army mutinies, of Quaker plots are the most obvious examples. Historians who rely entirely or principally upon the press give us a reliable guide as to how contemporaries were led to believe in the imminent disintegration of the rule of law. But reality was only in part as it was portrayed at the time.

Propaganda was all the more readily believed, since it not only confirmed gentlemen's beliefs about the real nature of the many-headed monster, but because it also spoke to the deepening social divisions that pre-dated the Revolution. D'Ewes touched on a common fear amongst the propertied classes when he reminded his fellow MPs that, 'all right and property, meum et tuum, must cease in a civil war and they knew not what advantage the meaner sort also

---

[61] J.S. Morrill, 'The Religious Context of the English Civil War', *TRHS*, 5th series, XXXIII (1984), pp. 171–5.

[62] Hunt, *Puritan Moment*, pp. 293–4.

[63] BL, Thomason Tract 200 (21).   [64] See note 17 for sources.

[65] J.S. Morrill, 'The Attack on the Church of England in the Long Parliament, 1640–1642' in D. Beales and G. Best, *History, Society and the Churches* (CUP, 1985), pp. 105–24.

[66] Rushworth, *Historical Collections*, IV, p. 695.

may take to divide the spoils of the rich and noble amongst them, who begin already to alledge that all being of one mould they saw no reason why some should have so much and others so little'. This was a common theme, given a popular (and deliberate) echo in petitions to parliament: 'Necessity dissolves all laws and government, and hunger will break through stone walls', asserted one such petition.[67] In the conditions of the 1640s, the gentry needed little reminding of such proverbial lore.

The real threat of the political conflict was, as D'Ewes observed, that it threatened to explode the deeper tensions latent within a situation of accelerating social and economic differentiation. But, as we have seen, in reality there was a notable discrepancy between actual and projected levels of disorder. This discrepancy suggests the need for a re-evaluation of the traditional view of the civil war period as one which saw a paralysis of political order permitting latent social conflicts to become manifest. We would wish to argue that the breakdown in order was less marked at the level of the local community than at Westminster and that the potential for widespread popular mobilisation in the social and economic changes preceding the Revolution was less great than has been assumed. This resilience of local structures of authority and the containment of disorder have common roots in the pattern of shifting social relationships. Economic change undoubtedly prompted greater popular discontent, but ultimately it created new structures which made possible the containment and even appeasement of that discontent.

If economic changes led to growing popular discontent, it did not of itself create a revolutionary potential. England's earlier omission from the roll-call of European rebellions in the extremely difficult conditions of the 1590s should caution against too facile an equation of economic distress with disorder.[68] A more sensitive assessment of the process and progress of economic change would suggest that there were limits (geographical as much as ideological) to the disorder that popular grievances might prompt. Enclosure could promote riots which in areas with common grievances might achieve extensive coverage, but its ability to prompt a revolt of the countryside was questionable. England remained a society that was local and regional; there seems little evidence to suggest that rural rioters any more than sixteenth-century rebels could have burst the 'natural' boundaries to collective action that this imposed. Moreover, to the extent that agrarian grievances seem to have needed the physical evidence of

---

[67] BL, Harleian MS 163, fol. 541; 'The mournfull Cryes of many thousand poor Tradesmen, who are ready to famish through decay of Trade' in D.M. Wolfe (ed.), *Leveller Manifestoes of the Puritan Revolution* (New York, Thomas Nelson, 1944), p. 278.
[68] J. Walter, 'A Rising of the People? The Oxfordshire Rising and the Crisis of 1590s', *Past and Present*, CVII (1985).

hedges as a goad to riot, then enclosure's patchwork geography and piecemeal timing imposed further limits.

This is not to argue that these limitations were insurmountable. Famine, an effective collapse of local order which permitted the wider dissemination of destabilising rumours, a growing belief in the imminence of a radical millennium or an effective political lead by radical 'vanguard' parties – any of these might have broken down the ideological and physical restraints on wider popular political action. But the fear of popish plots never became the Great Fear of the French Revolution[69] and a radical millenarianism (for reasons which cry out for investigation) never mobilised the rural poor.[70] The bad harvests of the later 1640s led to a heightening of tensions but not to a breakdown of social order. The demographic evidence suggests that by the 1640s England (including previously vulnerable regions like the north-west) had slipped the shadow of a crisis of subsistence.[71] Increased agricultural output, achieved at the cost of heightened potential conflict where it required enclosure and engrossing for its achievement, not only prevented widespread famine but also made possible the continuing effectiveness of crisis relief which made grain available to the poor. These policies seem to have held up well in the later 1640s.[72] As we have already noted, there was a contraction in the areas scarred by food riots at the end of the decade. Despite worries expressed in the economic crisis of the early 1640s, necessity never became great enough in the English Revolution to impel the poor to break *en masse* through the walls of society.

Nor was there a breakdown of order at the level of the local community. There was within seventeenth-century England a process of growing social differentiation.[73] At one extreme this saw the growth in poverty that so alarmed contemporaries (though there is evidence to suggest that historians have perhaps

---

[69] Clifton, *Past and Present*, LII (1971), 159–60; G. Lefebvre, *The Great Fear of 1789* (London, NLB, 1973).

[70] The Fifth Monarchists were predominantly an urban movement dominated by London: B.S. Capp, *The Fifth Monarchy Men: A Study in Seventeenth-Century English Millenarianism* (London, Faber, 1972), ch. 4.

[71] E.A. Wrigley and R.S. Schofield, *The Population History of England 1541–1871: A Reconstruction* (London, Edward Arnold, 1981), pp. 332–55 and appendix 10; R.S. Schofield, 'The Impact of Scarcity and Plenty on Population Change in England, 1541–1871', *Journal of Interdisciplinary History*, XIV (1983), 265–91; A. Appleby, *Famine in Tudor and Stuart England* (Liverpool University Press, 1978), ch. 10; A. Appleby, 'Grain Prices and Subsistence Crises in England and France', *Journal of Economic History*, XXXIX (1979), 865–87.

[72] J. Walter and K. Wrightson, 'Dearth and the Social Order in Early Modern England', *Past and Present*, LXXI (1976), reprinted in Slack (ed.), *Rebellion, Popular Protest and Social Order*, pp. 124–6.

[73] W.G. Hoskins, *The Midland Peasant* (London, Macmillan, 1957), chaps. VI–VII; Spufford, pp. 46–167; J. Thirsk (ed.), *The Agrarian History of England and Wales*, IV (CUP, 1967), pp. 301–6, 396–465; F. Hull, 'Agriculture and Rural Society in Essex, 1500–1640', unpublished Ph.D. thesis, University of London, 1950, pp. 74–81.

exaggerated its depth and character).[74] But the corollary of this was the consolidation of the smaller but more significant growth of the 'middling sort', the yeomen and richer husbandmen in the countryside. The effect of this growing differentiation was to question the validity of the unitary description of those below the level of the gentry as 'the people'. For as a counterpoint to the better-known political conflict between royalist and parliamentarian, there was a developing conflict at a lower level between the beneficiaries and victims of economic change.

As a consequence of this conflict there was a subtle shifting of alliances in the countryside which pre-dated the Revolution. Those groups whose combination of wealth, status and local parish or manorial office allowed them to dominate local communities had provided the backbone of many earlier rebellions.[75] But potential conflict with their poorer neighbours had encouraged them to align themselves with the state in a common attack on a developing 'culture of poverty'. Denied the earlier use of more informal ties of patron and client by their growing pursuit of 'possessive individualism',[76] they turned to local office and an alliance with the gentry as magistrates. This was an alliance eased by an identity of economic interests in service of the market, facilitated by the trend towards enclosure by agreement and cemented where there occurred a shared religion and literate culture. Increasing mobility from the ranks of the yeomen over time and through the avenue of university education had helped to blur the social distinction between parish gentry and wealthy farmers.[77]

Developing political and religious conflict between crown and political nation, therefore, placed the 'middling sort' in something of a dilemma. Like their betters, they resented royalist policies in the 1630s, especially where these seemed to endanger their attempts to impose greater controls over the poor. In the early stages of the Revolution they probably found some forms of crowd action (for example iconoclasm) not unwelcome. But, since the broader political conflict might offer the occasion for the popular attacks on them,[78] they offered

---

[74] J. Walter, 'Social Responses to Dearth in Early Modern England', in R.S. Schofield and J. Walter (eds.), *Dearth and the Social Order* (CUP, forthcoming 1985).

[75] C.S.L. Davies, 'Peasant Revolt in France and England: a Comparison', *Agricultural History Review*, XXI (1973), 130–2.

[76] For the concept of 'possessive individualism', see C.B. Macpherson, *The Political Theory of Possessive Individualism: Hobbes to Locke* (OUP, 1964), pp. 52–61.

[77] The best general discussion of this process is to be found in Wrightson, chs. 6 and 7; for a detailed local study, Wrightson and Levine, chs. 5–7; see also Walter, *Past and Present* (1985); M. Ingram, 'Religion, Communities, and Moral Discipline in Late Sixteenth and Early Seventeenth Century England' (forthcoming). We are very grateful to Dr Ingram for allowing us to see this paper. R. Smith, '"Modernisation" and the Corporate Medieval Village Community in England: Some Sceptical Reflections' (forthcoming).

[78] See, for example, the comments of Thomas May in his *History of the Parliament of England* (London, 1647, repr. Oxford, 1854), p. 112. For popular attacks on puritans in response to their

only reluctant endorsement. Those who sided with Parliament (and we should not assume that there was a natural identity between the 'middling sort' and support for Parliament) wished for political and religious reform, not least to strengthen their position over their poorer neighbours. But they did not seek the radical social and economic reforms that the poorer sort might have sought. To challenge the drift of agrarian capitalism would have been to bite the hand that fed them their profits.

In the English Revolution, therefore, the yeomanry and richer husbandmen were not to play the vital role they had in sixteenth-century rebellions. Rather than use their considerable local power to mobilise a popular movement, they were more likely to use their power to stifle local grievance. Only where these local elites continued to find themselves in conflict with their landlord (or in the Revolution, with army or regime) would they be likely to organise popular action. Thus, the one major area where the 'middling sort' continued to give a lead to popular opposition to enclosure was that of forest and fen. Here imposed enclosure continued to challenge their interests. This was the more so, since the proposed conversion from pastoral to arable economies struck at the pursuit of their market interests which were best served within the context of regional specialisation by their ability to over-exploit the waste and commons. It is their willingness to continue to oppose enclosure that helps to explain the persistence of agrarian disorder in these areas.[79] Some historians have argued that the immediate decades before the Revolution saw a deterioration in the position of the yeomanry that gave them a common interest with the poorer tenants. Much of the evidence for this comes from regions with a history of poor landlord/tenant relationships.[80] But in southern and eastern England the evidence seems to point to growing co-operation between landlord and yeomen.[81]

The incorporation of the 'middling sort' into a state whose presence was becoming more effective at the level of the local community ensured the maintenance of order at a local level. Their presence served not only to suppress disorder but also to ensure that the traditional policies for coping with the problem of the poor did not collapse. In the English Revolution they, not the gentry, became the garrisons of good order. Where local elites succeeded in

attempt to discipline the poor, see B. Manning, 'Religion and Politics: The Godly People' in Manning (ed.), *Politics, Religion and the English Civil War* (London, Edward Arnold, 1973), pp. 92–3, 102–3.

[79] Historians have perhaps been too ready to accept the argument of Buchanan Sharp, based on a simple counting of heads from lists of rioters known to authority, which downplays the role of the yeomen in the western forests, ch. 5. For evidence of the 'middling sort's' role in the fens, see Lindley, p. 256; C. Holmes, below, p. 184.

[80] B. Manning, 'The Peasantry and the English Revolution', *Journal of Peasant Studies*, II (1975), 134–8, where much of the evidence comes from the north of England.

[81] Charlesworth (ed.), *Atlas of Rural Protest*, p. 17.

imposing tighter controls (and we have as yet an incomplete knowledge of the geography of these new patterns of order)[82] they doubtless denied radical groups, if not radical ideas, a toehold in their local communities. Thus, though there is sufficient evidence of popular grievances in outbursts of sedition to give some credence to the threats made in radical petitioning,[83] the possibilities for the collective expression of that discontent in riot were being narrowed rather than extended by social and economic change. Roger Crab's 'labouring poor Men, which in Times of Scarcity pine and murmur for Want of Bread, cursing the Rich behind his Back; and before his Face, Cap and Knee and a whining countenance' were those who had had to accommodate themselves to these changed realities.[84]

Not enough is known about the impact of the Revolution on social and economic relations at a village level to make generalisations safe or secure. But what is known suggests that it might be the case that increases in levels of disorder arose less from conflict *within* local communities than from pressure from without. While we would emphatically reject the view that the English village 'was a place filled with malice and hatred, its only unifying bond being the occasional episode of mass hysteria, which temporarily bound together the majority in order to harry and persecute the local witch',[85] we would not want to go to the other extreme. As other essays in this volume demonstrate, divisions of many kinds could create tensions and create disorder within particular communities. Disputes over land, over common rights, over local rates, over religion, over the performance of social duties could create brief or prolonged disagreements and conflict. Our concern is not with the existence of such tensions so much as with their prevalence during the 1640s and 1650s in comparison with the previous period. This, above all, is impossible to quantify. But despite the existence of new potential sources of internal conflict, our impression is that communal life was not generally more torn by dissension and disorder in the mid-century.

There were three potential new sources of conflict. The first was a direct result of the 'puritan' victory, which brought a renewed drive towards a 'reformation of manners', the imposition of more sober and self-disciplined ways of life: the regulation of alehouses and gaming, of sabbath observance and sexual relations. Pressure for the enforcement of existing legislation and for the introduction of

---

[82] Much of the best evidence for this pattern of changing relationships of authority in the local community comes from a relatively few (and mostly southern) counties.

[83] For some examples of popular discontent, see Wiltshire RO, Q/S Gt Roll Hilary 1647/8, petition of the inhabitants of Westbury; Essex RO, Q/SR 332/106.

[84] Roger Crab, *Dagon's Downfall*, quoted in C. Hill, *Puritanism and Revolution: Studies in Interpretation of the English Revolution of the 17th Century* (London, Secker and Warburg, 1958), p. 307.

[85] L. Stone, *The Family, Sex and Marriage in England, 1500–1800* (London, Weidenfeld and Nicolson, 1977), p. 98.

additional ordinances in all of these areas was a constant feature of the period 1640–60, and was dear to the heart of Oliver Cromwell himself. Court records suggest patchy increases in prosecutions and magisterial initiatives. This was not merely an imposition from outside. In this instance, the survival of petitions from parishes calling for magisterial action is clear evidence of divided attitudes which led to the godly seeking external assistance. But we must beware of making too much even of this evidence. Concern for 'the reformation of manners' was nothing new; most of the specific demands of its proponents derive from legislation unanimously agreed in parliament and consonant with, growing out of, the canon law of the church; pleas for enforcement were characteristic of puritanism, but not their preserve alone; the apparent increase in secular court business may in large part reflect a transfer of business from the defunct church courts.[86]

The second and connected source of additional strain on parishes was the stillborn puritan church order.[87] The old church – its government, liturgy, even the rhythms of its calendar (the celebrations of the great Feasts) – was abolished and proscribed, but nothing was put in its place. A new system, replete with disciplinary procedures, service books, catechisms etc. was legislated for, but the political will at the centre to enforce it crumbled. In the 1650s, successive regimes in practice allowed local self-determination in matters of worship.[88] This led in many – probably most – parishes to the restoration of a watered-down Anglican worship, built around parts of the Prayer Book and Christmas and Easter communions. But in many parishes, godly minorities fought to impose the new order or at least to resist the (illegal) restoration of the old order. Yet all the signs are that violent confrontation between 'anglican' and 'puritan' parties were concentrated in the years 1646–8 when there was some political will at Westminster to introduce the new system. Thereafter, accommodation and compromises were reached: in market towns, the minister in one church would use the Prayer Book and in another the new services;[89] in the countryside, ministers would hold no holy communions at all, an unpopular decision but less inflammatory to the conservatives than of following puritan prescription and opening the communion table only to the godly, and less inflammatory to the godly than a 'promiscuous' communion of all but notorious sinners on the Anglican pattern.[90]

---

[86] The fullest study is in K. Wrightson, 'The Puritan Reformation of Manners', unpublished Ph.D. thesis, University of Cambridge 1973, *passim*; the main points are taken up in Wrightson, pp. 168–170, 181–2, 199–219.   [87] Morrill in *Reactions to the English Civil War*, pp. 103–14.

[88] C. Cross, 'The Church in England, 1646–1660' in G.E. Aylmer (ed.), *The Interregnum*, pp. 99–120.

[89] For an example, see A.E. Preston, *The Church and Parish of St Nicholas, Abingdon* (Abingdon, 1909), p. 97. It is widely true of the towns in at least the south-west and the Welsh borders. We are grateful to Paul Gladwish, Patrick Higgins and Nick Marlowe for advice on this point.

[90] Morrill in *Reactions to the English Civil War*, pp. 105–9.

The third new source of conflict arose from the sequestration of the estates of many – perhaps a quarter – of the gentry for having served the king during the wars. This potentially gave an ideal opportunity to tenants and neighbours to settle scores, by denouncing them to parliamentary authority, uncovering lands which the delinquents were seeking to conceal, spoliating their homes and demesnes. Yet this happened remarkably rarely. Committeemen seem to have relied far more on professional informers than on tenants; looting and mean acts of vandalism cannot be found on any scale. There is plenty of evidence to suggest that successive regimes were concerned to minimise the degree of political ostracism and social humiliation of their defeated opponents. Although ex-royalists were, at least in theory, disfranchised and barred from public office, there was no wider proscription: ex-royalists continued to sit on juries, serve as churchwardens, overseers, constables. Nor is there evidence of political discrimination against ex-royalists in the administration of the poor laws (except that maimed royalist soldiers could not receive state pensions).[91]

In general, these potential new sources of conflict were most likely to divide the 'parish aristocracies' – literate, schooled in Christian teaching, independent proprietors – from labourers, artificers, the poor. In the 1640s and 1650s, as before, relations between the two were uneasy, ambivalent. On the one hand, the latter were dependent upon the former for employment, credit, relief, mediation with county or national authorities; on the other hand, they might find themselves the victims of the former's strengthening relations with the gentry in the extension of agrarian capitalism. Here we would stress that if in the 1640s and 1650s some magistrates and parish notables were increasing the pressure on the poor to conform to their idea of Christian duty, these same magistrates and parish notables were increasing their efforts to provide relief and succour in times of hardship. During the years 1647–9 when grain deficiencies were probably the worst of the century, the full battery of controls on the grain market were employed and a forthcoming study will argue for significant changes in the administration of poor relief in these years.[92] What evidence has been looked at

[91] This is based on a reading of printed quarter sessions records and committee papers and of several unpublished dissertations, as listed in G.E. Aylmer and J.S. Morrill, *The Civil Wars and Interregnum: Sources for Local Historians* (London, Bedford Square Press, 1979), appendices 4, 5. 7. See particularly S.K. Roberts, 'Participation and Performance in Devon Local Administration 1649–1670', unpublished Ph.D. thesis, University of Exeter 1980, chs. 4–5; J.S. Morrill, *The Cheshire Grand Jury* (Leicester University Press, 1976), *passim*.

[92] T. Wales, 'The Structure of Poverty in Seventeenth-Century Norfolk' (University of Cambridge Ph.D. thesis, forthcoming) and his important article, 'Poverty, Poor Relief and the Life-Cycle: Some Evidence from Seventeenth-Century Norfolk' in R.M. Smith (ed.), *Land, Kinship and Life-Cycle* (CUP, 1985, pp. 351–404); Morrill, *Cheshire*, pp. 247–52; J.P. Cooper, 'Social and Economic Policies under the Commonwealth' in Aylmer (ed.), *The Interregnum*, pp. 125–9.

makes the point just as clearly for the towns.[93] While the poor had grounds to be more in conflict with parish elites, they were also becoming ever more dependent upon them; and paradoxically while parish aristocracies felt more vulnerable, it increased their vested interest in the maintenance of order and it may well have increased their solidarity against outside pressures and demands. In stark contrast to the findings of historians of the French, the Russian, the Chinese Revolutions, in England the impression is that the civil war neither created nor fuelled vendettas or blood feuds. We are not aware of more than a handful of cases of inhabitants fighting one another over the issues dividing king and parliament, though many communities sent forth men to opposing armies; and after 1642 divisive actions such as the ejection of a minister most usually followed the arrival of 'foreign' commissioners with interrogatories rather than an initiative from within.

It is our impression, then, that increased levels of disorder owed less to intra-communal strife than to the intrusion of 'outsiders'. The most obvious flashpoints were the arrival of garrisons or the passage of troops; the impositions of new types of taxation; and externally imposed religious change. These were often linked: it was the use of troops to destroy religious images, stained-glass windows, altar rails, service books, or to requisition horses and supplies or to support tax-gatherers, which provoked some of the greatest scenes of violence.[94] Such interventions were especially likely to reinforce local solidarity against the intruders rather than to polarise the community.

Such demands varied, of course, from place to place and from time to time, and there is no simple relationship between the scale of demands and the likelihood of violent resistance. In part this was because the proximity of overwhelming physical force would act as a deterrent. The remarkably low level of violence in London in the 1650s probably owed much to the constant quartering of 3000 or more troops in the centre.[95] But here and elsewhere it also owed something to the ability of 'passive resistance' to limit or to avoid the burdens. Local courts could be used to uphold religious practices banned by the Long Parliament; to indict soldiers for requisitioning horses and supplies and to secure recompense; to undo the work of excisemen.[96] The explicit orders of county committees or parliamen-

[93] V. Pearl, 'Puritans and the Poor: The London Workhouse 1649–1660' in D. Pennington and K. Thomas (eds.), *Puritans and Revolutionaries* (OUP, 1978), pp. 206–32; see also R.W. Herlan's various articles on poor relief in London parishes during the English Revolution, *Guildhall Studies in London History*, II (1976), 43–53; III (1977), 13–36, 179–99.
[94] For iconoclasm, see n. 11 above.   [95] Reece, 'Military Presence', ch. 1.
[96] Aylmer, *State's Servants*, pp. 13–14, 299–302; J.S. Morrill, 'The Army Revolt of 1647' in A. Duke and C. Tamse (eds.), *Britain and the Netherlands*, VI (1977), pp. 59–64. We are grateful to Bill Cliftlands for help with this and many other questions, and for allowing us to see his valuable unpublished paper on the working of indemnity commissioners who investigated these cases.

tary committees could be flagrantly ignored in the knowledge that there was insufficient political will or physical force available to implement the original order.[97] Although the civil wars and Interregnum threw up new bureaucratic bodies with wide powers, most of the fiscal demands were enforced by existing local officials. Such men could get caught in the middle, but they could also mediate or mitigate the burdens, or negotiate distributions of taxation in ways felt to be as equitable as possible. It is surely no accident that there are many more reports of disturbances involving excise (assessed by itinerant agents) than assessment (handled by village constables). Once again, it may be noteworthy that those disorders which produced violence against persons and property were those in which there was direct conflict between local communities and outsiders where the scope for local mediation was very limited – in particular military/ civilian skirmishes, excise riots, the imposition of a minister in place of one forcibly sequestered. The apparent decline of these disorders in the 1650s may be related to the state's relaxation of earlier burdens, and willingness to work through local elites: for example, in at least some areas, parishes 'compounded' with the excisemen and paid a local rate in lieu of the previous assessments backed up by house-searches and distraint; while Cromwell preferred to fill vacant livings in the church with men chosen by the parishioners themselves.[98]

We must not, therefore, exaggerate the extent to which government broke down at a local level. After the war years, when county institutions were suspended for up to four years, there was a return to the old ways and old officers: assizes, quarter sessions, grand juries, churchwardens, overseers. But on top of these familiar institutions and practices were laid new layers of bureaucracy and new forms of control: sequestration committees, assessment committees, commissioners for ejecting scandalous ministers, excisemen.[99] In general, the rhythms of administration at a village level were quickened rather than transformed, reinforced rather than abandoned. Successive regimes from 1646 to 1660 worked through existing structures in their concern with markets and with the poor; they created new structures when they made new demands. It is not surprising that provincial reaction was to cling to the familiar and to reject the unfamiliar which offered nothing and took much.

---

[97] E.g. W.A. Shaw (ed.), 'Manchester Classis Minutes' (Chetham Society, 2nd series, XXII, 1891), pp. 375–95, supplemented by the *CSPD 1650*, p. 442; and W.A. Shaw (ed.), 'Plundered Ministers Accounts' (Lancashire and Cheshire Record Society, XXVII, 1894), pp. 185–7. This is not inconsistent with the point about 'overwhelming physical force'. To be effective, the force had to be at hand and in strength. In many parts of the country it was neither.

[98] E.g., PRO, Chester 24/129 no. 2, grand jury petitions of 27 October 1651, speaking of a 'compositions' for ale made by the jury.

[99] Mather, *American Journal of Legal History* XXIII (1979), 122–3, 133n. For the 1640s, Morrill, *Revolt of the Provinces*, pp. 52–72; for the 1650s, Aylmer, *State's Servants*, pp. 9–17, 305–16.

The resilience of local relationships of authority imposed constraints on the poor's ability to combine which perhaps only leadership from outside would have broken. But effective leadership was not available. Hugh Peter's wish that the army be used to teach the peasants liberty was never realised.[100] The radical sects made too little headway, though exaggerated estimates of their size and militancy created great fear of disaster. Despite the attention paid to them at the time, they constituted a tiny minority of the population. Probably less than 5 per cent attended religious assemblies other than those in their parish church.[101] The flamboyant evangelism of some of the tiny fringe groups provoked responses from their orthodox neighbours.

It is not clear how far the subversive ideas advanced by the sects and taken up, at different times, by groups within the army were responses to the events of the 1640s or the surfacing of subterranean traditions from previous decades and centuries, and irretrievable by us for lack of surviving evidence.[102] It hardly matters. It is hard to be evangelical and secretive. Clearly there was considerable momentum behind the radical ideas during the Revolution. Most striking is the rejection of Calvinist notions of Man and of Grace, an insistence on the dignity rather than on the degradation of Man, of universal access to Grace, and of the need for all men to be free to seek out that Grace without the intervention of church or state; and the political and economic extensions of that liberated doctrine of Man. Yet, powerful and moving as the polemics of the new creeds were, they had very limited impact. In terms of membership, organisation, integration and ability to implement their ideas, they were much less impressive. Violence played little part in their history.

In the 1640s and 1650s, of course, many groups formulated, articulated, disseminated ideas which were profoundly subversive of the social, political and religious order. But those who had subversive *ideas* were not necessarily committed to the use of subversive *means* to impose those ideas. In general, the more subversive the ideas, the less violent the attempt to impose them. Tiny splinter groups like the Ranters and Muggletonians whose ideas were religious and/or individualistic showed little concern with the political implications of their beliefs or for their political implementation.[103] The Fifth Monarchists generally

---

[100] Quoted in C. Hill, *The Century of The Revolution 1603–1714*, 2nd edn (London, Nelson, 1980), p. 161.

[101] A figure proposed by Morrill in *Reactions to the English Civil War*, p. 90.

[102] B. Reay, 'Early Quaker Activity and Reactions to It', unpublished D.Phil. thesis, University of Oxford, 1979, pp. 8–112. C. Hill, 'From Lollards to Levellers' in M. Cornforth (ed.), *Rebels and Their Causes* (London, Lawrence and Wishart, 1978), pp. 49–67.

[103] J.F. Macgregor, 'Seekers and Ranters' in B. Reay and J.F. Macgregor (eds.), *Radical Religion in the English Revolutions* (OUP, 1984), pp. 121–39; C. Hill, W. Lamont, B. Reay, *The World of the Muggletonians* (London, Temple Smith, 1982), *passim*.

eschewed violent preparations for the Second Coming of Christ, and the breakaway group under Venner who tired of waiting passively and planned an insurrection in April 1657 appear to have numbered no more than twenty (Venner did only slightly better in 1661).[104]

The Diggers, too, had only a sketchy organization and hence little ability to proselytise their programme for the communal cultivation of the wastes and commons. The programme, in any case, while it might appeal to the rural poor (cottagers and landless labourers) jarred with an earlier tradition of agrarian protest in which the defence of the commons had been undertaken in support of diminishing individual holdings whose viability only common rights guaranteed. This had led to a growing clash beween indigenous communities and squatters. Where the Diggers appeared as outsiders to a community (as in Surrey and Northamptonshire, though not at Iver in Buckinghamshire) they risked incurring the traditional hostility towards strangers. The Diggers' natural allies, the labourers and cottagers, were the groups with least scope for independent action, and therefore the most difficult to mobilise.[105]

These groups all derived their unity from the labelling of opponents, but even so, should be numbered in scores or hundreds rather than thousands. The most highly 'politicised' of the radicals were, of course, the Levellers. Growing out of the campaign for religious freedom, and coming to believe that there would be no religious liberty until there was political liberty, the Levellers articulated a radical doctrine of political obligation which held that moral authority had been forfeit by all existing political and ecclesiastical institutions. The three leaders at some point in 1646–7 declared the social contract null and void and the nation returned to a state of nature.[106] What was needed was a new social contract, an Agreement of all the People, to put themselves under a new, just and accountable government. This was heady stuff, movingly and extensively canvassed in several hundred tracts, and there was some ability to gather together thousands of supporters and a penumbra of sympathisers willing to petition and to lobby parliament.[107] In London, much of the activity seems to have been organised

---

[104] Capp, Fifth Monarchy Men, passim; C.H. Firth, The Last Years of the Protectorate (2 vols., London, Longmans Green, 1909), II, pp. 208–18. While only twenty took part, over 4700 Quakers were arrested in the wake of the rising.

[105] C. Hill (ed.), Gerrard Winstanley: The Law of Freedom and Other Writings (Harmondsworth, Penguin, 1973), pp. 26–31; K. Thomas, 'Another Digger Broadside', Past and Present, XLII (1969), pp. 57–68; J. Walter, 'The Poor Man's Friend and the Gentleman's Plague' (forthcoming).

[106] For example, see J. Lilburne, Jonah's Cry from the Whale's Belly (London, 1647); R. Overton, Rash Oaths Unwarrantable (London, 1647); W. Walwyn, Outcryes of the Oppressed Citizens (London, 1647).

[107] The best of many books remains J. Frank, The Levellers (Cambridge, Mass., Harvard University Press, 1958); G.E. Aylmer, The Levellers in the English Revolution (London, Thames and Hudson, 1975) is an excellent introduction and collection of key texts.

through (until 1649) sympathetic Baptist churches, although on occasion they canvassed through *ad hoc* and ephemeral committees in the wards of the city.[108] But they never appear to have contemplated raising their supporters in armed insurrections; their 'crowds' above all others seem to have been disciplined and orderly; and even their campaigns of civil disobedience may have been limited to encouragement of those who obstructed the collectors of the excise.[109] For the critical periods of mid- to late 1647 and late 1648 there is no indication that they appealed to the rank and file against the officers, rather than attempting to persuade both of the justice of their programme. They called upon the rank and file to disarm the Grandees in 1649, but they did not explain how they should do so; the agitators had long since lost their power; and there is little evidence that either the so-called Ware mutiny (which was not a mutiny) or the Burford mutiny (which was a mutiny but one disowned by Leveller leaders) were attempts to overthrow the authority of the officers, let alone of the state.[110] There was certainly a rhetoric of violence at times, but the principal thrust of all the leaders (and so unstructured a movement depended upon the decisions of the handful of leaders) was to emphasise 'moral force' rather than 'physical force'. They believed in the self-evident justice of their cause, and assumed that it would capture the hearts and minds of all whose attention could be attracted. There was a potentiality for violence in Leveller determination, but it was never realised. The only exception to this general point is the involvement of Lilburne and Wildman in the fenland disturbances in and around the Isle of Axholme in the early 1650s. As Clive Holmes shows elsewhere in this volume, Lilburne was certainly not averse to breaking the heads or burning the houses of hapless foreign settlers on drained fen. But *pace* Professor Holmes, their role remains mysterious. The fenmen may have paid (and paid lavishly) for the expertise of the Levellers in taking on the enclosers and the law courts, but the ex-Leveller leaders appear neither to have used their presence in Axholme to organise a rural campaign for the Agreement of the People, nor to raise the whole of the fens, and their lasting contribution to the shaping of fenmen's understanding of their plights appears, on present evidence, to be very slight.[111]

Because their organisation was ephemeral, the disillusion and disarray of the leadership in 1649 led to the evaporation of the 'Levellers' as a visible force.

---

[108] M. Tolmie, *The Triumph of the Saints* (CUP, 1977), pp. 138–55, 169–72, 181–4; N. Carlin, 'Leveller Organisation in London', *Historical Journal*, XXVII (1984), 955–60.

[109] See e.g. J. Lilburne, *England's Birthright Justified* (London, 1645).

[110] M. Kishlansky, 'What Happened at Ware?' *Historical Journal*, XXV (1982), pp. 827–40, sorts out that episode. The traditional view of the Burford mutiny was challenged in a paper by Brian Manning at a seminar in Cambridge in 1980.

[111] Lindley, ch. 6; C. Holmes, *Seventeenth Century Lincolnshire* (Lincoln, History of Lincoln Committee, 1980), pp. 198–9, 210–3; PRO SP 18/37/11; below, pp. 166–7, 194–5.

Unlike revolutionary movements in sixteenth-century Europe, they never evolved a cellular structure that could take on a will of its own. So far as our present state of knowledge allows us to determine, the Levellers made little impact beyond London, except in small patches, notably in the Home Counties, and where army garrisons acted as carriers to separatist congregations. It would seem that they failed to make headway in the countryside. Perhaps they never found a way of making their tracts available there; perhaps countervailing propaganda inoculated their natural constituency against their ideas; perhaps they failed adequately to integrate their agrarian programme into their political and religious eschatologies, and into their moving vision of restored human dignity. Their pamphlets do make reference to enclosure, but they never give this important issue the attention it deserved if they were to have hopes of mobilising the rural poor.[112]

The Levellers were a phenomenon of the late 1640s. Although their name and some of their ideas flickered on through the 1650s, it was then much more as a bogey, a phantom menace, than as an actual force. However, the most substantial and, as it turned out, the most enduring of the sects, the Quakers, only emerged in 1652–3. Although, like the other sects (other than the Baptists), their membership was amorphous, casual, it has been plausibly suggested that there were about 40 000 active Quakers by 1660. Once more their ideas were more subversive than their actions, but there was nothing quietist about the early Quaker leaders. Their calculated disrespect for rank and degree, their disturbance of the worship of 'steeple houses' and of the preaching of 'hireling priests', their encouragement of tithe-strikes aroused fear and bewilderment. Amongst orthodox puritans, their dethronement of scripture and proclamation of the universality of grace created bitterness and resentment. But they did not burn down steeple houses, assault hireling priests, organise themselves nationally either in self-defence or to confront the Commonwealth. In fact they were more the victims of violence than the source of it. They were prosecuted under a wide variety of statutes, notably the late Elizabethan vagrancy laws and (ironically) under Marian legislation against field conventicles.[113] But many individual Quakers were set upon and beaten up and some of their larger meetings were broken up by angry crowds, as in Bristol by armed apprentices in 1654.[114] As James Powell told Secretary of State Thurloe on 24 February 1655:

The other cause [of tension] is the comeinge of the Quakers, who with their franticke doctrines have made such an impression on the mindes of the people of this cittie and

---

[112] Morrill, *Past and Present*, LVI (1972), 68–71; BL, Stowe MS 189, fols. 52–5; C. Hill, *The World Turned Upside Down* (London, Temple Smith, 1972), p. 96.
[113] Reay, 'Early Quaker Activity', ch. 3.
[114] Reece, 'Military Presence', p. 152.

places adjacent that it is wonderfull to imagin, and hath also made such a rent in all societies and relations, which, with a publique afront offered to ministers and magistrates, hath caused a devision . . . and consequently many broyles and affronts; these quakers being countenanced by the officers of the garrison . . .[115]

Nothing illustrates better the principal theme of this paper: if we must beware of exaggerating the scale of disorder, we must also beware of underestimating how the fear of disorder filled the minds and affected the actions of those in authority. By 1659, the Quakers had become, in Barry Reay's words, 'the apotheosis of the ecclesiastical and social upheaval that was anathema to the provincial tradition-alists who hearkened back to the old order'.[116]

The regimes of the 1650s survived because they had the perceived power to maintain order. Disheartened, divided, unconfident, the royalists licked their wounds and sought to restore their shattered finances. The lesson of the Penruddock rising was that thousands of royalists could have foreknowledge of a royalist rebellion without disclosing it to the authorities, but only a few hundred would take to arms. Royalist plotters in the 1650s made no effort to harness social and economic ills as part of a broad insurgency.[117] But such acceptance of the Commonwealth and Protectorate *de facto* rested upon a perception of the unity and purpose of the army. In 1659 army unity crumbled. This was in part due to the failure of the late Protectorate to keep expenditure under control: for the first time since 1646–9 army pay was falling seriously into arrears creating indiscipline and rank-and-file restiveness.[118] But it was also due to a bankruptcy of ideas once Richard Cromwell had fallen. From May 1659 on, there was an inexorable withdrawal of co-operation by the gentry as JPs, commissioners etc. With taxes unpaid and orders from Whitehall unheeded, government fell to pieces. Yet still, in the vacuum of power in the winter of 1659–60, there was astonishingly little disorder. Booth's rising was on a bigger scale than Penruddock's but it was still localised and quickly snuffed out by Lambert. In London, apprentices 'did very much affront the soulders as they went up and down the street'[119] and greeted a proclamation on 5 December by pelting the soldiers accompanying the serjeant-at-arms with tiles and lumps of ice.[120]

Yet again, however, the actual disorder and the perceived imminence of the

[115] Birch (ed.), *Thurloe State Papers*, III, p. 170.
[116] B. Reay, 'The Quakers, 1659 and the Restoration of the Monarchy', *History*, LXIII (1978), 212–13.
[117] D.E. Underdown, *Royalist Conspiracy in England* (New Haven, Yale University Press, 1962); P. Hardacre, *The Royalists in the Puritan Revolution* (The Hague, Nijhoff, 1955); A Woolrych, *Penruddock's Rising* (Historical Association Pamphlet G.29).
[118] Reece, 'Army Presence', pp. 45–8.
[119] W.L. Sachse (ed.), 'The Diurnall of Thomas Rugg' (Campden Society, 3rd series, XCI, 1961), pp. 13, 16, 34–5.
[120] A. Woolrych, introduction to R.W. Ayres (ed.), *The Complete Prose Works of John Milton*, (8 vols., 1955–82), VII, p. 145.

total collapse of order are quite different. The political vacuum, the yearning for a restoration of 'the old parliament and a new king' tantalisingly just out of reach, the machinations of a divided and mean army leadership, all made for a total sense of insecurity. In 1640–2 this sense of dread, of the overturning of the natural order, led to the widespread 'catholic' panics and fears. There was no 'papist' conspiracy to slaughter protestants in their beds, despite all the apprehensions of the gentry and others. In 1659–60 there was a precisely similar Quaker panic. Across the country there were rumours of huge marauding bands of Quakers and fears of a God punishing the nation by allowing England 'to be transformed into a Munster'.[121] A central feature of Booth's rising was his proclamation that he was organising a pre-emptive strike against Quakers and Anabaptists.[122] As Barry Reay says, 'The king came back on the crest of a wave of reaction against the "immense and boundless liberty" of 1659.'[123]

This essay should not be read as arguing that the English Revolution produced little disorder. We are concerned only to suggest that a number of easy assumptions have been made by many scholars, and a number of false claims made. As we said at the outset, the disappearance of familiar sources, and their problematical replacement by new types of evidence makes the whole question a treacherous one. No two scholars can claim to have looked at more than a fragment of the sources, certainly not in the light of the conceptual framework developed here. No careful, analytical studies have been attempted of landlord–tenant relations in the wake of the abolition of the prerogative courts and the humiliating sequestration of a quarter of the landlords; of the nature and extent of tithe disputes; of the impact of military service and discipline on one in five of the adult male population; and many similar questions. In an overambitious and doubtless overschematic essay, we have attempted to record our impressions based on independent research which has led us to look at different aspects of these problems from very different angles and for different regions.

But if the violence of civil war led on to an uneasy but far less violent peace, there was no easy return to 'normality'. If scholars have assumed too readily that the English Revolution saw a collapse of order, it is because they have believed the testimony of the governors who were caught up in it. Christopher Hill has rebuked historians of order for falling for the 'illusion of the epoch . . . accepting the standards of the articulate and uncensored classes as though they represented "truth" '.[124] It is a warning which historians of disorder must also beware. We have seen that there were good reasons why contemporaries persuaded them-

---

[121] Reay, *History*, LXIII (1978), 205.
[122] Reay, *History*, LXIII (1978), 198–201, 206–9; 'The Life of Adam Martindale' (Chetham Society, IV, 1845), pp. 135–9.   [123] Reay, *History*, LXIII (1978), 212.
[124] C. Hill in a review article in *Analytical and Enumerative Bibliography*, IV (1980), p. 270.

selves that they lived on the brink of anarchy, in the face of a disintegrating social and legal order. Back in 1641, Sir Thomas Aston wrote that he

looked upon the nobilitie and gentry of this Isle . . . situate as the Low Countries, in a flat, under the banks and bounds of the Lawes, secured from that ocean, the Vulgar, which by the breach of those bounds would quickly overwhelme us, and deface all distinctions of degrees and persons.[125]

The political elite was unsure of itself, unbelieving in the strength of ubiquitous and formalised arbitration procedures, unrecognising the decline of public violence, unaware how deeply (though not universally) ideologies of acquiescence and order had penetrated. Over the next decade they saw most of the landmarks of an ordered society destroyed: monarchy, House of Lords, the *ecclesia anglicana*. It seemed inconceivable that there would not be a descent into chaos. Their preachers anticipated it; their newspapers reported manifestations of disorder (but not of order). Minorities whose rhetoric and inspiration was indeed subversive talked openly about their dreams. Men steeped in classical literature knew that great empires could fall to the vandals; men steeped in the Old Testament knew that God's chosen people were not only led to the land of Canaan but were also made bondmen in Egypt, made captive in Babylon, scattered to the corners of the earth. Such fears prospered, even in the 1650s when Oliver Cromwell, seeing himself as a 'good constable set to keep the peace of the parish',[126] maintained an order more abrasive than, but as effective as, that of the 1630s.

The 'moral panic' of political elites was, in the event, one of the most enduring legacies of the Revolution. It is a generalisation worth pondering that the later a memoir of the Revolution was written by someone living through it, the greater its memory of the disorders. Just as Sir John Oglander, Richard Baxter, Edward Hyde, Denzil Holles retrospectively got it wrong when they spoke of those who ruled as being drawn from the dregs of the people, so they remembered in exaggerated fashion their own anxieties and terrors as the familiar landmarks of their ordered universe were knocked away. Fear of impending anarchy made them give glum recognition to the Interregnum as *de facto* government forestalling chaos, and later inhibited them from a return to arms against their kings and encouraged them to vindictive repression of groups who disturbed their peace of mind. There was disorder in revolutionary England. But there was less than contemporaries anticipated and less than they led themselves and us to believe to have taken place.

---

[125] Sir Thomas Aston, *A Remonstrance Against Presbytery* (London, 1641), sig. A13.
[126] A phrase from Oliver Cromwell's speech of 13 April 1657: T. Carlyle (ed.), *Letters and Speeches of Oliver Cromwell*, vol. III (1871), p. 248.

6

Drainers and Fenmen: the Problem of Popular Political Consciousness in the Seventeenth Century

C. HOLMES

I

On 19 October 1651, the *emigré* Huguenot inhabitants of Sandtoft, the new settlement established on the lands drained by Sir Cornelius Vermuyden on the Isle of Axholme, were approaching their church for the Sunday service. In the churchyard their passage was barred by a number of yeomen from the neighbouring villages, headed by their legal advisors, Daniel Noddel, an Epworth attorney, and John Lilburne, who acted as spokesman for the group. 'This is our common', Lilburne is reported to have said, 'you shall come here noe more unles you bee stronger than wee.'[1] The locals entered the church, the doors of which were guarded by armed men, and Lilburne prayed and preached. The building was then sacked; Lilburne, who had appropriated the house of the French minister, subsequently used the derelict church as a stable and cowhouse. For the unhappy settlers, the incident was the culmination of a miserable year of violence and intimidation. In October 1650 the commoners had smashed their fences, devastated their crops, and seized their cattle; in the following May an all-out assault on Sandtoft had resulted in the destruction of eighty-two houses, a mill, barns, implements and crops. For Lilburne, the incident was the most theatrical moment in more than a year's involvement in the affairs of the Isle, where, from the autumn of 1650, he acted as legal expert, agent and publicist for the commoners in their long-standing feud with the fen-drainers and their French and Dutch tenants.

---

[1] PRO, SP 18/37/11 III p. 5. The incident and its background are described in Lindley, pp. 188–222. Although I disagree with Lindley on several interpretative issues, his narrative, based on a superb command of the sources, is most thorough. In this essay, when discussing specific riots, I will refer the reader to Lindley's account, citing the primary source only where I have taken additional material from it.

166

Lilburne's intervention in the disputes on the Isle in 1650–1 has troubled students of the Leveller movement. His energies, it is suggested, should not have been devoted to so peripheral a cause.[2] But Lilburne's presence has been equally problematic for those historians who have examined the activities and attitudes of the fenmen whom Lilburne, and his Leveller colleague, John Wildman, temporarily led. What drew them to accept the radicals' assistance in their local conflict? Writing in 1954, J.D. Hughes insisted that the alliance between the 'revolutionary section' and the Axholme peasantry was an active one, founded in compatible goals. Not only did Levellers and fenmen share a hostility to the enclosure of common land, but, more generally, 'the radical democratic programme of the Levellers would have an appeal to many . . . peasants' in an area where small farmers were the dominant social group and where there was a lively tradition of religious dissent.[3] Recently Keith Lindley has questioned this interpretation: the alliance, he argues, was 'a temporary expedient serving . . . immediate concerns'. Lindley's evaluation of Lilburne's involvement in Axholme is part of his general rejection of any suggestion that the riots with which the fenmen of eastern England greeted drainage attempts throughout the seventeenth century had any broad ideological motivation. 'Fenland rioters', he writes, 'did not give expression to political feelings, but contented themselves with drawing attention to specific grievances of immediate concern.' Nor were the fenmen 'politically educated' in the course of their often extended struggles; their experiences, Lindley concludes, 'produced little in the way of heightened political consciousness'.[4]

Lindley's evaluation, founded as it is upon a thorough command of the evidence concerning the riots, compels respect. And yet the presence of Lilburne and Wildman on the Isle of Axholme is disquieting, not easily explained within the confines of an argument that refuses to credit the fenmen with 'political consciousness'. Even if the alliance with the Leveller leaders was no more than a tactical move, designed to pressure the drainers through parliament and the law courts, it surely suggests an awareness of central politics, and perhaps of the legal and constitutional concerns that were thought to exercise the national rulers at Westminster.

How might this latter suggestion be tested? The historian seeking some insight into the *mentalité* of the fenman naturally turns to the documentary evidence

---

[2] P. Gregg, *Free-Born John* (London, Harrap, 1961), pp. 308–9; H.N. Brailsford, *The Levellers and the English Revolution* (London, Cresset Press, 1961), p. 610; H. Shaw, *The Levellers* (London, Longmans, 1968), p. 89.

[3] J.D. Hughes, 'The Drainage Disputes in the Isle of Axholme and Their Connection with the Leveller Movement: a Re-examination' *The Lincolnshire Historian*, II (1954), 13–45, especially 14, 24–6. See also B. Manning, *The English People and the English Revolution* (London, Heinemann, 1976), pp. 292–3 for a similar argument.   [4] Lindley, pp. 65, 194, 253, 257–8.

concerning his conflict with the drainer. But the sources present major critical problems of which historians of early-modern 'popular' movements in general are only just becoming aware.[5] Basically the struggles in the fenland generated two classes of documents both directed to the central authorities. First, there are representations from the drainers describing the riots in an effort to secure assistance in their suppression; second, attempts by the fenmen to justify their actions and to denounce the tactics of their opponents. Both groups, I would argue, are more revealing about their writers' sense of the interests of the body they are addressing, than about either the events they purport to describe, or the ideals which motivated those involved in the defence of their commons.

The dispute in the Isle of Axholme, which lasted for over a century, provides an excellent series of complaints from the drainers to the central authorities. The concern for *audience* informs every aspect of the structure and substance of these documents. It is not merely a rhetorical veneer, but dictates the choice of incident which is detailed, and of the language and actions of the rioters which are emphasised. In the 1620s the element of seditious conspiracy is dwelt upon: expressions of *lèse-majesté* ('they cared neither for god nor the king') were assiduously reported; the covert organisation of the fenmen and their efforts to secure the insurrectionary support of neighbouring communities were detailed.[6] Emphases changed significantly during the civil wars and Interregnum. From 1645 to 1648 the drainers insisted that the rioters, a benighted rabble, were damaging a public project of prodigious benefit, thus occasioning 'much losse to the Commonwealth'.[7] Under the Rump the drainers sought to make political capital from the fenmen's Leveller affiliations, elevating the riots, as Lindley writes, 'into preliminaries for a national insurrection and a violent change of government'.[8] Representations to the centre took another tack during the Protectorate. The most effective appeal for governmental assistance came, ostensibly, not from the drainers but from their tenants, 'poor Protestant strangers'. The latter asserted that their fundamental motive for emigration had been their 'not haveing libertye to exercise the Protestant Religion in their native Contryes', and then provided a lurid account of the attacks on Sandtoft church

---

[5] Sharp, pp. 5–6, 136–55, 261–6, insists that contemporary suggestions of elite leadership in riots against forest enclosure are an attempt to play upon the paranoia of the Caroline government which was more ready to move against disturbances involving men of substance; they are not accurate social description. Yet Sharp's argument that forest artisans expressed sentiments 'approaching class hatred' (pp. 8, 264) is based on evidence, from the same or similar documents, which is equally designed to arouse central concern.

[6] PRO, SP 16/113/38 I; S.R. Gardiner (ed.), *Cases in the Courts of Star Chamber and High Commission* (Camden Society, NS, vol. XXXIX, 1886), pp. 59–65.

[7] HLRO, Main papers, 1645 15 Nov., the petition of Peter Berchet *et al.*; 1645/6 21 March, the petition of the participants; *LJ*, vol. VIII, p. 36.

[8] Lindley, pp. 193, 258; Lindley recognises that the 1650–1 accounts are 'polemical'; but he fails to realise that this is true of all the drainers' evidence.

both in 1651 and again, after its repair, in January 1656. In a splendidly Miltonic conclusion the tenants remind Cromwell that his 'zeale for God's glory engaged you to soe great a tendernesse for the distressed protestants in Savoy', and plead for similar consideration.[9] In addition to appealing to the Protector's religious sensibilities, the petitions also regaled him with a selection of political comments attributed to the fenmen. The choice of statements displays an exquisite editorial sense of the sensitivities of a government deeply concerned with its own legitimacy: the commoners, it was reported, said 'they will defend their Common with theyr swords which they say they may as lawfully doe as the Lord Protector may the government hee hath taken upon him'.[10] At the Restoration the drainers, noting that they too had been 'unduly kept out of their inheritances,' emphasised that the fenmen had eagerly supported parliament in the civil war, 'takeing upp armes against their King your glorious father', and then provided Charles II with a rich vein of evidence of continuing anti-monarchical sentiment on the Isle. 'If there bee the king's laws', William Jervase was reported as saying, 'God's curse light upon his heart, for that it was likely hee would bee a traitor as his father was.'[11]

Representations to the government from the drainers in other fenland areas, though there is no series as full as that from Axholme, suggest an equally careful attention to the concerns of the particular audience. Sir William Killigrew and his colleagues, whose drainage scheme in the Lindsey Level was attacked in 1641–2, played upon the *amour propre* of the House of Lords, tender in this period, with reports of the derision with which the Lords' orders were received and the fenmen's unfavourable comparisons of the upper House with the Commons.[12] Cruder, but effective, was the report to the Privy Council in 1690 that the locals who had gathered to petition against the Deeping Fen drainage operation were papists and sectaries vowing to restore James II.[13]

The fenmen, in their addresses to Whitehall or Westminster, also display an acute sensitivity to the assumptions and concerns of their rulers which vitiates the easy use of these documents as evidence of local attitudes. The appeals demonstrate that the fenmen's agents had a sophisticated understanding of central politics, but, with their chameleon-like shifts of emphasis attuned to the perceived audience, they can reveal little of locally held values. Representations

[9] PRO, SP 18/126/57: see also SP 18/129/144.

[10] PRO, SP 18/128/80; also SP 18/129/144 IV, V.

[11] HLRO, Main papers, 1660 26 June, the affidavit of Nathaniel Reading; the certificate of the sheriff of Yorkshire. See also Main papers, 1660 23 Aug., the petition of the participants.

[12] HLRO, Main papers, 1641 4 June, the petition of Matthew Clerk; 1641 8 Sept., the affidavits of Jasper Heiley, and of Anthony Lingwood *et al.*; 1642 9 May, the petition of Sir William Killigrew; 1642 23 May, the certificate of Sir Edward Heron.

[13] Lady Elizabeth Cust, *Records of the Cust Family of Pinchbeck, Stamford, and Belton* (London, privately printed, 1898), p. 245.

before 1642, to king or Lords, follow a conventional pattern: the fenmen abased themselves, stressing their poverty and inexperience; then, almost apologetically, raised their legal claim, dwelling upon both the local employment of force and chicane by the drainers and their more insidious machinations at the centre whereby the government has been misinformed about the benefits, feasibility and legality of the drainage operation.[14] The tone changed dramatically in the Interregnum, particularly in the fenmen's addresses to the Rump. These present an aggressive assertion of and demand for their legal and constitutional rights, rights in defence of which, the petitioners insisted, parliament had prevailed upon them to take up arms in the civil warres. 'By the whole current of your declarations, the end of the late wars was to maintain, defend, and secure our properties and fundamental legal rights', the fenmen of the Lindsey Level adjured the Rump in 1650: then, citing the Grand Remonstrance and the Rump's manifestos of 9 February and 17 March 1649, they reminded MPs of their promise to 'maintain the good old laws and customs of England, the badges of our freedom, the benefit whereof our ancestors enjoyed long before the Conquest'.[15] The same hortatory tone was adopted by petitioners from the Great Level; so the commoners of the Soke of Peterborough hoped to 'enjoy the benefit of your Declarations to maintaine our Proprieties, according to the Great Charter and Petition of *Right*'.[16] Local representations were quickly adjusted to the religious concerns of the Barebone's parliament in 1653. The author of the *Anti-Projector* blessed the 'Divine Providence' which had cut short the Rump's corruption and recalled that the fenmen had contributed not only military support to the cause, but 'the praiers of a numerous godly pretious people': Daniel Noddel, having detailed the Rump's injustices perpetrated at the expense of the Epworth commoners, expressed his assurance that 'the fear of God is amongst you, to distribute righteousness to all the people of the Commonwealth'.[17] At the Restoration the petitions, while expressing the most sedulous respect for central authority, insisted on the technical legal arguments against particular schemes, and, more generally, on the threat the drainers' proceedings represented to property rights.[18] This latter theme dominates discussion after the

[14] See, for example, PRO, STAC 5/A2/18, the answer of Robert Curlys *et al.*; BL, Add. MS 33466 fol. 25; HLRO, Main papers, 1641 4 May, the petition of Thomas Abbott *et al.*
[15] *Two petitions presented to the supreame authority of the nation from . . . Lincolnshire; against the Old Court-Levellers, or Propriety Destroyers, the Prerogative Undertakers* (London, 1650), pp. 6–7; see also, for another example, *The Pick-lock of the Old Fen Project* (London, 1650), p. 15.
[16] *The Humble Petition of the Inhabitants of the Soake of Peterborough* (London, 1650), p. 2.
[17] *The Anti-Projector or the History of the Fen Project* (London, n.d. – but 1653); Daniel Noddel, *To the Parliament of the Commonwealth of England . . . the declaration of Daniel Noddel* in J. Tomlinson, *The Level of Hatfield Chase* (Doncaster, J. Tomlinson, 1882), p. 270.
[18] HLRO, Main papers, 1660 15 Dec., the petition of Simon Maw *et al.*; 1663 1 June, the petition of Robert Ryther *et al.* 1677/8 1 Feb., the petition of the inhabitants of Uffington and other towns; *The Case of the Manor of Epworth . . . Concerned in the Bill for an Act Settling the Level of Hatfield Chase* (London, 1661).

Revolution of 1689: in 1701 counsel for the fenmen of the Lindsey Level, attacking a drainage bill before a parliamentary committee, denounced it as establishing 'the most arbitrary proceedings in the world. It invades the properties of thousands of people.'[19]

Of course, not all the information provided by these two classes of documents is tainted by their essentially polemical purpose. It was not in the interests of the drainers to falsify the dates upon which riots occurred, for example, and in consequence we can speculate about the relationship between riot and the ritual year. Football games were favourite affirmations of traditional communal rights in the enclosed fen: so in the spring of 1642 it was reported that the fenmen 'throwing out a football and playing at it drove it against a new house . . . and because it stood in theyr way, pulled it downe . . . and so have they pulled down many'.[20] Some of these games can be established as occurring on the traditional feast days associated with village football play: Shrove Tuesday in Long-Sutton in 1643; Plough Monday in Deeping Fen in 1699.[21] Riots, without the accompaniment of the symbolic game, took place on other feasts; Ascension Day in the Lindsey Level (1642), May Day in Wildmore Fen (1663).[22] But the fenmen did not restrict their action to the ancient feasts; a good opportunity, or a blatant provocation, could become the occasion for action.[23] Nor should we necessarily assume that the occasional association of riot with the ritual calendar is informed by a visceral sense of customary rights as opposed to an understanding of law.[24] Feast days were often associated with the exercise of rights guaranteed by law, as in Wildmore Fen where the 'drift' of the cattle of outsiders which had strayed onto the common took place on May Day.[25] More generally, community action required for the maintenance of ancient drainage works was officially an-

---

[19] HMC, *Manuscripts of the House of Lords*, NS, vol. IV (1908), p. 217: see also the broadside, *The Case of the Lindsey Level on Behalf of the Country* (1698). The power of this rhetoric is demonstrated by the drainers' attempts to appropriate it; see William Killigrew's two tracts, *The Property of All English-men Asserted in the History of the Lindsey Level* (London, 1705), and *A Short Answer to a Paper, Intituled Reasons Humbly Offered to the . . . Commons . . . Against a Bill brought in by Sir Robert Killigrew* (no date or place), p. 3.

[20] Bodleian, Tanner MS 63, fol. 16. See also PRO, SP 16/392/45 I for the June 1638 game in which the men of Ely, Littleport and Lakenheath proposed to assert their common rights in Whelpmore fen.

[21] HLRO, Main papers, 1642/3 7 Feb., the affidavit of John Reade (Sutton); PRO, PC 2/77 pp. 309–10; *Reasons Humbly Offered to bring in a Bill to Confirm the Decrees of Draining Lindsey Level* (no place or date) (Deeping).

[22] The letter of May 1642 reprinted in Killigrew, *Property of All Englishmen*, pp. 13–15 (Lindsey Level); PRO, SP 29/75/15 (Wildmore).

[23] In August 1641 the riot in the West Fen was timed to coincide with the assizes when most of the JPs were away at Lincoln (PRO, SP 16/484/8): the great riot in Axholme on 31 May 1660, in which two men died, was provoked by a semi-military action commenced by the drainers' agent (HLRO, Main papers, 1660 26 June, the affidavit of Nathaniel Reading).

[24] B. Bushaway, *By Rite: Custom, Ceremony and Community in England, 1700–1880* (London, Junction Books, 1982), pp. 5–14, provides an interesting introductory discussion.

[25] PRO, E 134 10/11 Charles I, Hilary 27.

nounced in the fenland churches 'uppon some festivall daye . . . for the good knowlidge of the commoners'.[26]

This kind of information requires not only a sensitive reading, but a structural context within which it can be understood. The latter is even more necessary in the deployment of documents which have an evidently polemical purpose. This essay will attempt to suggest and test a model, derived from an analysis of the broad pattern of the fen riots, which may provide such a context and so advance discussion concerning the 'political consciousness' of the natives of the region, and, perhaps, provide some explanation of Lilburne's presence in Sandtoft churchyard in the autumn of 1651.

II

After 1600 five major drainage schemes were resurrected; in Wildmore Fen, in the Isle of Axholme, in the Ancholme Level, in Deeping Fen and in the Great Level. All these operations had been established under Charles I, but were abandoned in the face of popular attacks during the civil war. Of these five, the Wildmore and Axholme projects were, from the drainers' perspective, failures. The Wildmore scheme was an attempt by London-based entrepreneurs, acting for the Earl of Stamford, to drain and enclose 4000 acres in the fen. The matter was handled with considerable dexterity. The favourable disposition of the crown was secured with a gift of a quarter of the enclosed land; *douceurs* proffered to officials like Secretary Bennett and to selected peers ensured that warrants from the Privy Council and the House of Lords were at the drainers' disposal. Landowners with a claim to common in the fen were guaranteed allotments in the enclosed lands in return for their consent to the undertaking; local farmers were offered favourable leases; the 'meaner sort' were employed in the construction of the drainage works at inflated wages. Yet despite these adroit manoeuvres designed to secure central favour and local acquiescence, the operation was interrupted by a series of riots in 1663 and 1664 and was eventually abandoned.[27] In Axholme, Sir Cornelius Vermuyden had secured a grant of 7400 acres from the 13 400-acre common of the manor of Epworth. Two days after Charles II entered London, Nathaniel Reading, the drainers' vigorous and unscrupulous local agent in the Isle, attempted another Restoration, launching a quasi-military offensive designed to recover the original allotment. His action was the prelude to sixty years of lawsuits and appeals to king and parliament,

---

[26] A.E.B. Owen (ed.), *The Records of the Commissioners of Sewers in the Parts of Holland, 1547–1603*, vol. II (Lincolnshire Record Society, vol. LXIII, 1968), p. 136.

[27] Lindley, pp. 225–7; PRO, SP 29/74/65; 29/71/23, 95; 29/75/2; 29/107/69; 29/159/48.

punctuated by intermittent local violence. Not until 1719 was a truce concluded, whereby the drainers secured title to only 2800 acres of their original claim.[28]

The other three operations were far more successful. A general drainage project for the marshland in the Ancholme valley was undertaken by Sir John Monson for a grant of 5827 acres. Loud complaints immediately arose from some of the affected villages that the scheme adversely affected the old drainage patterns and so worsened the quality of their lands, complaints which seem to have been warranted. In 1662 Monson's workmen were abused and threatened by the men of Winterton, and the cargraves, communal officers responsible for the village's drainage works, were accused of building banks which interrupted Monson's larger scheme. Yet despite these mutterings the issue was fought out, not in the fields of Winterton, but in the courts at Westminster.[29] Riots occurred in the Great Level, where the Earl of Bedford and his associates in the drainage were granted 95 000 acres, but they were localised: at Mildenhall and Peterborough in the 1660s, at Holywell in 1678. And in each of these cases the object of attack was neither the engineering works nor the participants' allotment in the fen, but the enclosures made after drainage by lords of the manor.[30] This was invariably a tense, problematic issue. Henry Warner, who organised the Mildenhall resistance in the courts and in the fen, asked rhetorically whether he had done 'any otherwise then what any other honest man might . . . doe', given that the townsmen had 'probable cause of . . . contestinge their rights against the lord of the mannor?' This question is apposite, for the judges at Westminster were deeply divided about the legality of the Mildenhall enclosure.[31] The Deeping Fen drainage had been one of the first schemes to be attempted (1602), though, incongruously, it was technically one of the most difficult. The post-Restoration project, whose backers received half of the fen, 15 000 acres in all, was badly mismanaged, and the operation of the works only drained the participants' allotment at the expense of flooding the remaining common and the other lands of the surrounding towns, and of destroying the local river transportation network. Local resentment surfaced noisily in 1678 and again in 1690. Yet only in 1699, after three decades' experience of the technical incompetence and

---

[28] Lindley, pp. 233–52.

[29] Lindley, pp. 227–9; Lincolnshire RO, Monson 7/17/46; 7/18/5; PRO, E 134 17 Charles II, Easter 14; E 178/6301.

[30] Lindley, pp. 230–1; HLRO, Main papers, 1678 4 May, petition of the inhabitants of Hallowell-cum-Needingworth.

[31] PRO, E 134 36 Charles II, Michaelmas 44: for the legal arguments, see Roger North, *The Lives of Francis North, Baron Guilford . . . the Hon. Sir Dudley North . . . and the Hon. and Rev. Dr. John North* (3 vols., London, Henry Colburn, 1826), vol. I, pp. 129–30; *The English Reports* (176 vols., Edinburgh, Green & Son, 1900–32), vol. LXXXV, pp. 503–14 (1 Wms. Saund, 346–53); vol. LXXXVI, pp. 245–54 (1 Ventris 383–98); vol. CXXIV, pp. 1060–4 (Vaughan 251–8).

broken promises of the drainers, did the fenmen resort to violence, doing £100 000 worth of damage to the engineering works, houses and outbuildings on the participants' allotment.[32]

So in Wildmore and Axholme the violent opposition to drainage schemes was immediate and continuing, and it ultimately obliged the drainers to abandon or severely modify their plans. In the other three areas opposition ran largely in legal channels; riots were either directed to peripheral matters or occurred after a long delay. What distinguishes these two diverse experiences? One obvious difference is that the three successful schemes were established by parliamentary legis- lation: the attempts of those involved in the Wildmore and Axholme operations to secure statutes in their favour failed, and the drainers' claims were warranted only by agreements, legal rulings and the orders of Commissioners of Sewers dating from the 1630s.[33]

Can we assume that there is a correlation between the absence of major riots against certain post-Restoration schemes, and the fact that these had received legislative approval? Any argument that the relationship is one only of chance, substantially meaningless, would have to explain the eagerness of the drainers to obtain such parliamentary assistance. Not only the Wildmore and Axholme participants, but the heirs to the claims of Sir Anthony Thomas in the East and West Fens, and of Sir William Killigrew in the Lindsey Level and the Holland Fen, sought legislation resurrecting these projects. Thomas's heirs abandoned the struggle quickly; the Killigrew family, more tenacious, badgered parliament for nearly half a century: but in both cases the failure to secure Westminster's approval ensured that the schemes did not get beyond the drawing-board.[34]

The drainers themselves sought legislative warrant, but does this necessarily indicate that parliament's approval was a crucial element in the local acceptance of a scheme? In particular, it could be argued that parliament was simply recognising, and giving its statutory seal of approval to, drainage operations which stood a good chance of success; those for localities where the plans seemed technically viable; where drainage was agreeable to the interests of local land- owners; where the populace had been cajoled or crushed already. Projects that lacked these characteristics were rejected. Legislation did not silence local opposition; rather, it was the prior existence of a consensus favouring drainage in

---

[32] Lindley, pp. 232–3: for 1678, see HLRO, Main papers, 1677/8 1 Feb., the petition of the inhabitants of Uffington and other towns; *Reasons Humbly Offered to the Consideration of the Parliament* (no place or date); for 1690, Cust, *Records of the Cust Family*, p. 245.

[33] For the successful legislation, see *The Statutes of the Realm* (9 vols., London, Record Commission, 1810–22), vol. v, pp. 499–512 (Great Level); pp. 559–68, 687–9 (Deeping); Lincolnshire RO, Monson 7/17/31 (Ancholme). For the proposed Axholme legislation, see Lindley, pp. 239, 241; HLRO, Main papers, 1661 24 May, draft act for Hatfield Chase: for Wildmore, HLRO, Main papers, 1664/5 17 Feb., draft act for Wildmore Fen.

[34] For the attempt to resurrect these schemes at the Restoration, see Lindley, pp. 223–4: for the

the affected area that ensured both the passage of legislation and the success of the scheme.

The hypothesis is not supported by the history of the various drainage bills offered for parliament's approval. The glimpses we can catch of the often opaque process whereby proposals were accepted or foundered do not suggest that the Houses were swayed by considerations of the technical feasibility of a scheme, or of its local acceptability and social consequences. Parliament might feel obliged to provide mechanisms for the expression of the concerns of 'the Country'. But neither these sentiments nor the conflicting claims of the national interest in 'so public and beneficial a work' and of private property, the rhetorical staples of debate',[35] seem to have been crucial to the final disposition of a bill. Central to this were the manoeuvres of small cliques of deeply engaged MPs. Those with a vested interest in the success of a project duelled with their colleagues who either favoured alternative schemes or who feared that drainage operations would reduce the rentals of their 'high country' estates, since, as one of them was assured, an acre of drained fen would become 'as good as three hereabouts'.[36] This process did enable MPs themselves or those gentlemen with influence at Westminster to advance their own individual interests, either by private negotiation with the drainers or by the addition of provisos to the proposed legislation.[37] But it did not guarantee serious discussion of more general concerns. Sir Robert Carr was a powerful advocate for 'my fenn men' against the Lindsey Level scheme; yet it was not the 'very much reason' of his speeches in the Commons that dashed the bill in 1668, but his skilled manipulation of the procedures of the House and his intimacy with Charles II and his ministers. Similar conditions appertained at the end of the century: bills were defeated by their opponents' readiness to bribe the speaker and to win the votes of uninvolved MPs by promising reciprocal assistance for *their* pet projects.[38]

Killigrew family's later endeavours to re-establish the Holland Fen and Lindsey Level projects, see Killigrew, *Property of All English-men*, pp. 16–21; Lincolnshire RO, Fane 3/1/A/2, 3, 5, 6.

[35] For examples, see *CJ*, vol. IX, pp. 206–7; HMC, *Manuscripts of the House of Lords*, NS, vol. IV (1908), pp. 215–19.

[36] Sir Charles Hussey, who led the opposition to the Killigrews in 1661–3, backed an alternative scheme (*CJ*, vol. VIII, pp. 352, 528: PRO, SP 29/403/123; Lincolnshire RO, 2 Anc. 10/1/2); the same is true of his son, Sir Edward, in the 1690s (Lincolnshire RO, Monson 7/12/80). This latter document also provides direct evidence of the organised opposition of the 'high country' MPs, but their self-serving attitudes had been complained of by the drainers for a century: see *APC, 1597*, pp. 367–8; CUL, EDR A/8/1 p. 119 (1606–7).

[37] For a private arrangement, whereby the prospective drainers of the Holland Fen secured the goodwill of the Earl of Bridgewater, see Lincolnshire RO, Fane 3/1/A/5; for provisos, see those added to the Ancholme legislation, in favour of Lord Bellasis, Sir Edward Rossiter and Sir Michael Wharton (Lincolnshire RO, Monson 7/17/31).

[38] Killigrew's *Property of All English-Men*, pp. 16–18, provides an account of 1667–8 and the 1690s. For Carr, see also *CJ*, vol. IX, pp. 206–7; C. Robbins (ed.), *The Diary of John Milward* (CUP, 1938), pp. 128, 140, 185, 238, 246, 255: Carr's phrase is from PRO, SP 29/291/41.

The passage or failure of the drainage legislation proposed after 1660 owed little, it seems, to any careful investigation of the merits of the particular project at Westminster. The general acceptability of a scheme within the affected locality was not a precondition for parliamentary action. Indeed, it would seem, to return to the argument advanced earlier, that the local acceptance of certain post-Restoration drainage schemes, as measured by the absence of violent disruption, is a product of the parliamentary sanction which they enjoyed.

The drainers who badgered parliament after 1660 looked for more than a legislative seal of approval upon a *fait accompli*. Acts of parliament provided advantages which enhanced the potential success of their schemes. These advantages may be distinguished, for analytical purposes, as being of two kinds. First, legislation might provide immediate and practical benefits, such as clauses establishing a machinery of government or punishing opponents. Secondly, less tangibly, it could provide legitimacy.

The practical assistance which the drainers might derive from legislation is most apparent in the 1663 Act for the Bedford Level. A stong administrative organisation was established, with clearly defined responsibilities and privileges. A clause forbidding other Commissioners of Sewers to 'intermeddle' within the Level freed the corporation from the danger of interference by rival authorities. The operation was given formidable legal protection. The destruction of drainage works carried a penalty of triple damages and, if deliberate sabotage, was made a capital offence; those who attacked 'the hedges, ditches, or fences' that enclosed the improved land were liable to a £20 fine or three months' imprisonment. The local concerns and grievances that might have fuelled such attacks were not neglected, however. A special tribunal, the Commissioners of the Fens, was established, with the power to adjudicate boundary and enclosure disputes, and to relieve those whose lands were damaged by the drainers' operations. The commissioners, under the presidency of the rising lawyer, Francis North, appear to have acted with expedition and fairness, and to have won the respect of 'the country people'. Since the Act declared that the commissioners' decisions 'shall be final' the possibility of review by the central courts, and thus of disputes becoming enmeshed in litigation, was removed.[39] The benefits enjoyed by the drainers in the Bedford Level must have been the envy of their counterparts in the Isle of Axholme, whose attempt to secure similar legislation in 1660–1 had proved abortive. The Axholme drainers were continuously involved in suits with the commoners in the entire range of central courts. Robert Popplewell, the post-Restoration solicitor for the commoners, brought up his chorus of octogenarian witnesses, his 'Affidavit men', 'almost every term for a great number of years'

---

[39] *Statutes of the Realm*, vol. v, pp. 499–512; North, *Lives of the Norths*, vol. I, pp. 74–5; *The English Reports*, vol. LXXXII p. 116 (1 Siderfin 296).

until they became a standing joke among the lawyers in Westminster Hall. But the fenmen did not content themselves with 'battling the participants at law'.[40] The drainers were confronted not only by incessant suits, but by incessant violence in the Isle, against which, they argued, they were inadequately protected by the law, at least until the passage of the Riot Act.[41] The drainers' difficulties were further enhanced, and no doubt their opponents encouraged, by their extended feud with the local Commissioners of Sewers concerning the assessments to be levied upon their lands for the upkeep of the drainage works, and the payment of the commissioners' officers. When the matter was brought to the attention of the House of Lords in 1678 the parties complained wearily of their 'long and tedious disputes', of '14 yeares controversie', but the issue was to drag on for another decade.[42]

The clear authority which the drainers enjoyed within the Bedford Level by their Act, and the protection from disruption by riot or litigation, contrast markedly with the situation in Axholme. Yet legislation did not necessarily incorporate such practical advantages. Neither the Act for the Ancholme Level (1661) nor the first Act for Deeping Fen (1665) provided the drainers with either the administrative machinery or the legal protection embodied in the Bedford Level Act.[43] The Deeping drainers made several attempts to improve upon their original legislation. In 1670 they secured a clause making those guilty of the malicious destruction of their works liable for damages (a far milder penalty than that in the Bedford Level legislation).[44] But their attempts to gain corporate status and to free themselves from the interference of the local gentry acting as Commissioners of Sewers failed in 1678 and 1685. The parliamentary hearings on these occasions reveal a convoluted situation akin to that in Axholme, in which uncertainty as to the locus of authority had been compounded by growing anger and mistrust between the drainers and the commissioners.[45] Yet, despite these administrative conflicts and the technical inadequacies of the drainers'

[40] C. Jackson (ed.), 'The Stovin Manuscript', *Yorkshire Archaeological and Topographical Journal*, VII (1881–2), 224.

[41] For the Riot Act, see Jackson (ed.), *Yorkshire Archaeological and Topographical Journal*, VII, p. 213. For the drainers' earlier complaints concerning the inadequacies of the law, see their undated broadside, *An Answer to the Case of the Commoners of the Manor of Epworth . . . published in Opposition to the Bill for Making the Statutes of Edward I and Edward VI against Destroying Improvements more Effectual.*

[42] HLRO, Main papers, 1678 12 June, the petition of Nathaniel Reading, and attached documents.

[43] Lincolnshire RO, Monson 7/17/31; *Statutes of the Realm*, vol. V, pp. 559–68.

[44] *Statutes of the Realm*, vol. V, pp. 687–9: the drainers began to press for this legislation in 1668; Robbins (ed.), *Diary of John Milward* p. 212; HLRO, Main papers (parchment), 1668 1 May, engrossment of the Deeping Fen Act.

[45] HLRO, Main papers, 1677/8 1 Feb., supplementary Act for Deeping; HLRO, Committee book 3, *sub* 1677/8 28 Feb.; Spalding Gentleman's Society, MS MJ B1, five unfol. letters of 1 Jan. to 2 Mar. 1678; *Reasons Humbly Offered to the Consideration of the Parliament* (no date or place): for 1685, see *HMC, Eleventh Report, Appendix 2* (1887), pp. 310–12.

works, it was not until 1698 that the fenmen of Deeping invaded the lands, half of their ancient common, granted the drainers by the 1665 statute.

The legislation for the Ancholme and the Deeping projects suggest that statute was not valued solely for the practical benefits which parliament could accord the drainers. A similar conclusion seems appropriate with respect to the attempts by the pre-civil war drainers to secure statutory backing for their operations. In 1605 it was decided that the 'articles and conditions agreed uppon' by the Commissioners of Sewers to establish Lord Chief Justice Popham's operation in the Great Level 'shoulde be prayed to be confirmed by Acte of Parliament', despite Popham's own insistence that the authority of the commissioners was quite sufficient.[46] More remarkable are the provisions in some of the Caroline schemes for legislative ratification 'whensoever a parliament should be called': this in a period when the Privy Council had publicly accepted Popham's argument concerning the sufficiency of the commissioners' decrees and was vigorously backing the drainers' operations in the localities.[47] The intention in all these cases was to secure, by parliament's approval, 'full and final confirmation', *legitimacy*, for the schemes. An Act of Parliament, one of the drainers' propagandists wrote in 1653, is presumed 'to provide for the good of the whole, and to compel every man so to use his owne as it may be serviceable to the common good'; an Act 'wherein all men's consents are included' is 'for publick good', and 'it is an unheard of boldnesse' to challenge the veracity of matters of fact 'declared by them in the Act itself'.[48] The need to assert these constitutional platitudes so overtly may reflect the little conviction they inspired in relation to the legislation at issue in 1653, the Rump's Act for the Bedford Level, passed three months after the abolition of the monarchy and the upper House. However, we can see the power of such ideas in a less tainted context in 1666. The villagers of Winterton complained that the Ancholme Level project had harmed their lands, and a group of local gentlemen were empowered to investigate their claim. A minority report backed Winterton: there was clear evidence that the lands were flooded by Sir John Monson's works and land values had fallen sharply. The majority opinion favoured Monson. The 1661 legislation had categorically asserted that Winterton's lands had been subject to flooding and were improved by Monson's

---

[46] PRO, SP 14/26/38; BL, Hargraves MS 33, fols. 215–17v.

[47] S. Wells, *The History of the Drainage of the Great Level Called Bedford Level* (2 vols., London, R. Pheney, 1830), vol. II, p. 122; Lincolnshire RO, Monson 3/9/130. For the role of the Privy Council in this period, see M. Albright, 'The Entrepreneurs of Fen Drainage in England under James I and Charles I: An Illustration of the Uses of Influence', *Explorations in Entrepreneurial History*, VIII (1955–6), 51–65; M. Kennedy, 'Charles I and Local Government: The Draining of the East and West Fens', *Albion*, XV (1983), 19–31.

[48] *An Answer to a Printed Paper Dispersed by Sir John Maynard Entitled the Humble Petition of . . . Isleham* (no date or place), pp. 2, 3.

operations: this statement, 'admitted by the Act of Parliament itself', was irrefutable.[49]

I suggested that an examination of the pattern of riots after 1660, when only those operations lacking statutory warrant were subject to immediate, fierce and sustained attack, might illuminate the issue of the 'political consciousness' of the fenmen. The drainers, I have argued, believed that legislation was crucial to the success of their project, in part because it might provide practical assistance, but also because it endowed their operations with a legitimacy superior to that of Council directives or decrees of Commissioners of Sewers. The fenmen's pattern of action suggests that they accepted the force of the 'full and final confirmation' embodied in statute, and the theory of parliamentary sovereignty that sustained it. This conclusion, of course, is an inference from action; there is little direct evidence to support it. But the conviction it carries may perhaps be enhanced by undertaking another line of analysis; by establishing more precisely the social identity of the generalised 'fenmen' who struggled with the drainers in the seventeenth century.

III

In the general conclusion to his study of the riots generated by the Caroline forest enclosures in western England, Buchanan Sharp argued that artisans were 'engaged most intensely' in early modern popular disturbances, and that they provided leadership to the other major constituent of the rural proletariat, the landless labourers. Lindley, testing this assertion in the fenland context, found it inadequate and preferred the 'Mousnier model' which Sharp had criticised. Lindley emphasised the activities of the local gentry, who 'condoned or actively encouraged violent behaviour'; their 'central role' explains the 'scale and persistence' of the anti-drainage riots. It is my sense that both these polar interpretations, echoes of the Porchnev–Mousnier debate, are wide of the mark. In the seventeenth-century fens, as in Norfolk in 1547, it is the activities and attitudes of the yeomen and richer husbandmen that are crucial.[50]

This is not to deny the involvement of either the landless poor or of the gentry of the region in the riots and associated transactions. Labourers (and their wives) invariably provided the bulk of the muscle-power to level fences, fill ditches and destroy houses, barns and implements. Occasionally members of this group might emerge as influential leaders during the riots. The charismatic Edward

---

[49] PRO, E 178/6301, the report of Molineux Disney *et al.*

[50] Sharp, pp. 3, 5–6, 257–8; Lindley, pp. 255–7: for an excellent review of the earlier debates on this issue, which emphasises the role of the 'middling sort', see C.S.L. Davies, 'Peasant Revolt in France and England: A Comparison', *Agricultural History Review*, XXI (1973), 122–34.

Powell, the labourer leader of the 1638 disturbances at Ely, who asked 'if one might not be inspired (and why not he) to doe the poore good?' and who claimed to have 'ordinarie accesse and speeche with the king' ('they are told the king . . . leaned on his shoulder and wept when he heard his relation'), was an exceptional individual.[51] But others from the same social stratum, if more shadowy figures, exercised considerable influence: Thomas Welles, 'daylabourer', whose speech in Deeping church provoked the attack on Lovell's operations in 1603; Edmund Clipsham, labourer, of Freiston, 'Captain' of the 500 men who levelled the enclosures in the West Fen in 1636.[52] The involvement of artisans and labourers in the fenland riots, or even the occasional emergence of a leader from their ranks, is not at issue: the question is of their capacity for effective action independent of other social groups.

Some contemporary accounts argue that the rural proletariat had taken the initiative in certain incidents, but much of this evidence is suspect. It was often in the interests of the fenmen's representatives, in their appeals to the central government, to distance their legal claims from violent actions that might arouse sympathy for the drainers. So the opponents of Killigrew's proposed legislation for the Lindsey Level during the Interregnum denied *their* involvement in the riots of 1641–2: these were an irrational outburst, regrettable but understandable, by the 'poor commoners . . . being of weak capacity and understanding' answering the oppression and threats of the drainers.[53] A similar line of argument, and the attendant condescension, informs Lilburne's account of the events at Sandtoft in 1650. The destruction was the work of 'the poorer sort', frustrated by the delays and chicanery of the drainers: 'in their rage', wrote Lilburne, 'the multitude did foolishly throw down many poor houses . . . but that folly of the multitude none of the most discreet commoners . . . do justifie'.[54] Lilburne's premonition that the Sandtoft riot would harm the commoners' cause at Westminster proved correct. The Rump's committee of investigation dwelt almost exclusively upon the incident in their report: that document became both the justification for the omission of the Sandtoft rioters from the 1652 Act of Oblivion, and dictated the attitudes of the various regimes that succeeded the Rump to the situation on the Isle. Yet neither of the writers, both local men, who publicly attacked the committee's report in 1653 and 1654, attempted to duplicate Lilburne's analysis: the riot was depicted as a communal response to the 'bloody, barbarous, and inhumane massacres and tyrannies exercised upon us' by the drainers, not as the work of the poorer elements on the Isle alone.[55]

[51] PRO, SP 16/392/45 I; 16/409/50.   [52] Lindley, pp. 33–4, 88–9.
[53] *A Relation of the Proceedings and Causes of Complaint between the undertakers . . . and the Owners and Commoners* (no date or place), p. 13: see also *A Breviate of the Cause Depending, and Proofes Made Before the Committee of the Late Parliament for the fens* (London, 1651) p. 9.
[54] John Lilburne, *The Case of the Tenants of the Manor of Epworth* (London, 1651), p. 9.
[55] John Spittlehouse, *The Case and Appeale of the Inhabitants . . . of the Manor of Epworth*

Perhaps the facts were too well known to permit the comfortable elision of responsibility effected, though with as little historical justification, by Killigrew's Interregnum opponents as they reflected on the events of a decade earlier.

If we discount such tactical attempts to shift responsibility for destruction on to the shoulders of the, conveniently anonymous, 'poorer sort', then we are left with few examples of independent action by artificers or landless labourers in the fenland. Events in Soham in early June 1629 are akin to those that Sharp described for the western forests. Negotiations to establish a 2000-acre enclosure for the lord of the manor were proceeding smoothly with the 'better sort' until rudely interrupted, first by the 'mutinous words' of those inhabitants 'who neither had houses nor land and hardly any chattels of their owne', and then by a volley of stones. In 1632 'the rude rabble' of Soham were again in action, levelling the lord's enclosure, though on this occasion the Council was deeply suspicious that they had acted with the connivance of the village elite. A 1701 petition from the Deeping area suggests the existence of a similar division between the 'middling sort', prepared to compromise with the drainers, and the landless poor, eager to resort to violence.[56] But these incidents of independent initiative are isolated, and, in themselves, hardly demonstrate a capacity for sustained action in the lower orders.

Events in the fenland do not support the contention that the landless poor, artisans and labourers, were 'most intensely' involved in riots. Yet the alternative argument, which emphasises the role of the gentry in 'formenting and guiding' popular disturbances, seems equally flawed. It rests upon the interpretation of evidence in the light of a model of social structure and relationships which, questionable in general, is extremely dubious with respect to the fens.

Of course, the local gentry opposed drainage schemes which ran counter to their interests. So, before the civil war, they appealed to the central authorities against the drainers' operations, and, despite the heavy-handed attempts of the Caroline Privy Council to force them to abandon 'vexatious suits', they battled incessantly in the courts.[57] Their sentiments might also lead them, as magistrates, to refuse to act vigorously against popular disturbances: with William Lockton Esq., of Swineshead, they might insist on every trivial legal technicality to avoid

(London, 1653); Noddel, *Declaration*, and his *To the Parliament of the Commonwealth of England . . . the Great Complaint of about 1200 Freeholders* (1654) in Tomlinson, *Hatfield Chase*, pp. 258–70, 271–6.

[56] PRO, PC 2/78 pp. 78–9 (Deeping): Lindley, pp. 40–1; PRO, E 178/5171 – the report of Robert Henley *et al.* (Soham, 1628): Lindley, pp. 83–6 (Soham 1632). The Council's suspicions of the village elite's connivance in the riots appear in their order that 'The principall freeholders and copieholders' should be responsible for the arrest of the rioters, and in their angry response when only one of the latter was captured (PRO, PC 2/42 pp. 32, 49–50, 99–100; PRO, SP 16/219/1 1).

[57] For petitions to Council or parliament, see Lindley, pp. 93, 94–5, 109; for litigation, Lindley, pp. 87, 90–2; Kennedy, *Albion* xv (1983), 29.

punishing rioters – 'by god's blood, neighbours, you shall not be wronged'.[58] Yet it is hardly legitimate to infer from such activities – petitions, suits, even magisterial inaction – that the gentry were, perhaps covertly, 'masterminding local resistance'. Lindley's argument depends upon an unexamined assumption about social relations, akin to the conception of early modern French society held by Mousnier. It supposes a 'society of orders' linked by vertical loyalties, in which a deferential peasantry, incapable of independent action, were moved by the promptings of their local lords.[59] The model is hardly appropriate to the seventeenth-century fenland, however. Contemporaries noted the 'want of gentlemen here to inhabit' in the Lincolnshire fens, and their complaints have been substantiated by the best modern study of the economy and social structure of the region.[60] The situation in the Isle of Ely was similar: in 1674 the proportion of substantial gentlemen to the general population in the fenland parishes was half that in the southern part of Cambridgeshire. The unhappy consequences for the maintenance of social order on the Isle were emphasised by an anonymous early seventeenth-century commentator: 'the governors or justices of peace within th'isle not beinge of soe great lyvinge, wealth, and cowntenance as in other places, and the povertye there in exceeding great abundance . . . [the populace] . . . are readye to take any occasion to contempne authoryty'.[61] The fenmen's want of deference in the face of authority may have been enhanced by the fact that many of the greater gentry were newcomers to the region, the purchasers of royal, monastic or ecclesiastical lands, who then sought to exploit their new acquisitions at the expense of the natives. Sir Miles Sandys, who, as an Ely man sardonically wrote, 'for our punishment planted himself in this countrie', engaged in a bitter campaign of legal intimidation against his Willingham and Stretham tenants, in the course of which '14 of the gravest, auncientist, and most harmlesse men' were harassed in the courts, 'untill he gott his unreasonable desires'. He was only the most notorious of a group of aggressive *parvenus* in the fenland: Sir John Aylmer of Revesby, Sir Edward Heron of Surfleet and Sir Thomas Josselin of Littleport all pursued similar policies.[62]

---

[58] HLRO, Main papers, 1641 8 Sept., affidavits concerning the Donington riots; for other examples, see Lindley, pp. 94–5, 98–9, 226.

[59] Lindley, p. 63. C.S.L. Davies perpetrates a similar evidential leap when he states that Oliver Cromwell 'took part in the Fenland riots'; the evidence refers to Cromwell's plan to raise money to fund suits against the drainers (*Agricultural History Review* XXI (1973), 127).

[60] J. Thirsk, *English Peasant Farming* (London, Routledge, 1957), p. 47.

[61] BL, Add. MS 33466 fol. 290: in 1674, houses with ten or more hearths represented 1.39% of the total number of entries for the hundreds of Armingford, Chilford, Longstowe, Radfield, Thriplow, Wetherley and Whittlesford: 0.6% in the fen hundreds of Ely, Wisbech and Wichford (discounting the towns of Ely and Wisbech). If we recalculate the figures for six or more hearths, the figures are 5.43% and 2.97% respectively. The hearth tax figures are from *VCH Cambridge and the Isle of Ely*, vol. IV, pp. 277–9; vol. V, pp. 277–8; vol. VI, pp. 280–2; vol. VIII, pp. 271–2.

[62] CUL, EDR A/8/1 p. 143: CUL, EDR A/8/1 pp. 142–5 presents an account of Sandys's activities. For

The limited numbers of gentry within the fens, and the tensions between many of them and their tenantry should warn us against the easy transmutation of the elite's opposition to drainage into their leadership of popular riots. Nor do the few instances of direct gentry involvement in the disturbances confirm the model of a society of orders and deferential social relations. The men directly involved were invariably parochial gentry, barely distinguishable from their yeoman neighbours from whose ranks their families had, in some cases, recently risen.[63]

Joan Thirsk has noted, of the Lincolnshire fen village: 'Its aristocracy was not a single squire and his family, but a substantial group of middling-rich yeomen.'[64] It is the activities of these men, and others of the 'middling sort', in the organisation of local opposition to the drainers throughout the fenland, which have been overlooked in the debate concerning the respective roles of the rural proletariat and the gentry elite. The involvement of this village aristocracy is very apparent in a number of well-documented riots. On 13 August 1629 the men of Haxey attacked Vermuyden's workmen. The recollections of the latter are of a huge crowd engaged in filling the ditches and burning equipment, of blood-curdling threats both verbal and symbolic (the erection of a mock gallows) and of a fair measure of casual violence. Their testimony, while it dwells on confusion and terror, does indicate that the riot was a communal action co-ordinated by the yeoman elite. Two of the wealthiest villagers, Vincent Tankersley and Hezekias Browne, with another yeoman, Vincent Scott, led and encouraged the rioters; more significantly, Browne, another yeoman, and the village constable told the unfortunate workmen that 'if they would leave their work they would appease the multitude, or els they might goe on at their perill'. On 15 August the labourers, protected by armed men, returned to their works. The Haxey villagers again attacked and were driven off when one of their number was shot dead. But, before the guards opened fire, the commoners' leaders sought to parley with them: on this occasion the constable and Hezekias Browne were joined by another yeoman and by a local lawyer, John Newland, the bailiff of Epworth manor.[65] This balance of forces was to recur in other Axholme disturbances. So on 25 June 1647 after a week of rioting, Daniel Noddel, the fenmen's attorney, sword at his side, waited in Haxey Carr with several hundred of his clients armed with clubs and forks. Noddel sought, so he claimed, to negotiate with the drainers; they believed that he intended to prevent their recovery of lands the fenmen had occupied. Fifty of Noddel's retinue were mounted; the eight whose

Aylmer, see PRO, STAC 8 39/4, 5; 137/16; 186/27; 212/5, 11: for Heron, PRO, STAC 8 195/11; 199/3: for Josselin, PRO, STAC 8 189/9.
[63] Lindley, pp. 106–7, 179, 181, 200, 225–6.
[64] Thirsk, *English Peasant Farming*, p. 47.
[65] Lindley, pp. 72–5; PRO, SP 16/113/38 I–IV; Gardiner (ed.), *Cases in the Court of Star Chamber*, pp. 59–65.

names are known were substantial yeomen from Epworth, Haxey and Owston.[66]

In 1660, trying to list those involved in the riots that had wracked Axholme since 1642, the sheriff of Yorkshire listed thirteen men then concluded, rather lamely, 'and most of the inhabitants of the Isle of Axholme'. A similar situation confronted Sir Edward Heron, sheriff of Lincolnshire, in the spring of 1642 in the drained fens in the Holland region of the county: he and the JPs could not halt the rioters, 'they beinge all or the most parte of the inhabitants thereabouts and the . . . outrages committed by a generall combination of approbation of that parte of the cuntrey'.[67] In the riots in this area in 1640–2, as with those in Axholme, it seems that the co-ordination of communal activity was undertaken by 'the middling sort'. There was a measure of gentry involvement in this region, certainly greater than that on the Isle of Axholme. Lady Dymock and Robert Cawdron Esq., who had petitioned the Short Parliament against Lindsey's scheme, were accused of encouraging attacks on the enclosures in the summer of 1640; next year William Lockton flagrantly abused his magisterial authority to protect the rioters.[68] But these members of the established gentry elite did not exercise a preponderant influence. In 1642 sheriff Heron was certain that Thomas Hall of Donington was the most influential man in the area; he 'had much power among the multitude'. Hall was a gentleman who was to achieve some eminence in the country during the Protectorate, but he came from a solid local yeoman family. Hall had been summoned before the Privy Council in 1639 and 1640 for attacking the enclosures; in 1641 he was the fenmen's agent in London, opposing the attempts of Lindsey and Killigrew to secure statutory confirmation and parliamentary protection for their operations.[69] In Hall's town, Donington, the organisation of direct action in 1641 was undertaken by yeomen and other men of some substance. 'One of the cheife incouragers to these rioters' was Henry Carre, mercer. Carre and others summoned the poorer members of the community, promised them wages, and instructed them 'when to meete and on what ground they shall committ the ryotts'; carts were hired to carry off the drainers' crops, which were stored in Carre's barns. The wages and cart-hire indicate the existence of a common fund which was also used to fee counsel – local attornies like Posthumus Preistman of Bourne, who employed his technical skills to challenge the legal validity of the warrants by which the drainers sought to quell the disturbances – and to pay the charges of those convicted. When Carre and his Donington colleagues had costs assessed against

[66] Lindley, pp. 152–5; *LJ*, vol. IX, pp. 428–9; PRO, SP 18/37/11 I, III p. 3. Details on the status of Axholme rioters are largely derived from the 22 Dec. 1641 poll tax certificate from the wapentake of Manlack, in HLRO, Main papers.

[67] HLRO, Main papers, 1660 26 June, the certificate of the sheriff of Yorkshire; Main papers, 1642 23 May, the certificate of Sir Edward Heron.

[68] Lindley, pp. 109, 111, 124–5.   [69] Lindley, pp. 106–7, 110, 122, 131, 164.

them by the Lords they pleaded for a mitigation on the usual grounds, they were 'men of small estates and lives by husbandry'. The drainer, Sir William Killigrew, would have none of this; most of those convicted 'are sufficient men, and the rest maintained in their disorders at the chardge of the townes where they are inhabitants'. Such 'sufficient men' also support the riots, if less directly, in their capacity as jurors; at Spalding sessions John Colson swayed his fellows against the conviction of some Pinchbeck rioters, 'for it is our owne case'.[70]

The leadership of the 'middling sort' is hardly surprising, for it was in their immediate economic interests to oppose the drainers. In the 1650s, in their appeals to Westminster, the Axholme and, particularly, the Lindsey Level drainers argued that their operations had been genuinely beneficial to the poor. A few tame labourers were brought up to London to testify that wages had fallen dramatically and unemployment risen since the drainage operations had been wrecked: 'the poore cry out mightily since the improvements layd downe and say they are all undone'. The village elite, they claimed, had forced them, by threats, into contributing to the common fund and taking part in riots; 'the rich had . . . done so much that they durst doe noe more and the pore should doe something'. In the Lindsey Level, Sir William Killigrew organised a petition from the poorer commoners in favour of the statutory re-establishment of the project. In this, and in his propaganda in general, he emphasised that the pre-drainage situation had favoured the rich. An unstinted common had allowed those with capital to purchase and fatten cattle for the market, and so 'eate out the poore commoners with their great stocks'.[71] Killigrew's argument, that the rich 'do oppose us that they may still oppresse the poor commoners', cannot be accepted without qualification. It is too obviously a variant on the long-standing debate concerning the social consequences of drainage, its rhetoric adjusted to the supposed reformist concerns of the Rump – Killigrew's opponents ironically remarked the incongruity of the 'Leveller-like' stance adopted by the old courtier and cavalier.[72] Yet Killigrew's charges were not pure invention. Pre-drainage surveys and suits in the fenland indicate that some individuals were feeding very substantial herds on the commons. Dr Thirsk has calculated that Mary Jenkinson of Heckingon, who testified that she kept sixty cows, eight oxen, thirty horses, twenty young cattle and a thousand sheep in the fen, was making free use of 600

---

[70] Lindley, pp. 113, 123, 125–6, 132: HLRO, Main papers, 1641 25 Oct., the petition of Henry Carre *et al.*; Main papers, 1641 15 Nov., the petition of Henry Carre *et al.*, and the attached petition of Sir William Killigrew.

[71] PRO, SP 18/37/11 III p. 20; 18/129/144 VII (Axholme): for Killigrew, see *Certaine Papers Concerning the Earl of Lindsey His Fennes* (no date or place), p. 5; William Killigrew, *Answer to the Fenne Men's Objections* (London, 1649), p. 16; *The State of the Case Concerning the Late Earle of Lindsey's Drayning the Fennes* (no date or place), p. 7; BL, Add. MS 21427 fol. 207.

[72] See the double broadside, *A Paper Delivered and Dispersed by Sir William Killigrew* (London, 1651) – the answer, section 2.

acres of grazing: her situation was not unique.[73] Such opportunities were severely restricted after drainage. In the West Fen, when Sir Anthony Thomas, the drainer, had taken his allotment and royal patentees had enclosed nearly 5000 acres by virtue of the crown's supposed rights as lord of the soil, the fenland left to the commoners barely supported an eighth of the pre-drainage herds.[74]

IV

I have argued that it was the 'middling sort' of the fenland villages – minor gentry, yeomen, richer husbandmen, some tradesmen – who played the crucial role in organising the local resistance, including riots, to the drainers' activities. The latter threatened the traditional pattern of land utilisation which had been very much in their interests. It is this group, then, whose 'political consciousness' must explain the pattern of post-Restoration opposition, with its apparent regard for the principle of legislative sovereignty. This suggestion would not have surprised some knowledgeable contemporary observers, who also re-marked on the legal experience and interests of the village elite in the fens. Sir Edward Heron's attempts to exploit his manorial rights in the fens and saltmarsh of Surfleet entailed extended conflict with the villagers, particularly the Burton family – men whose 'addition' in the documents of the period wavers between 'gent' and 'yeoman'. In a 1625 suit the Burtons claimed that, poor and inexperienced, they had been duped into a disadvantageous agreement by the chicanery of Sir Edward, an eminent lawyer. Heron's interrogatory to witnesses expresses incredulity at their newly affected humility: 'whether be John . . . and Zachary Burton simple and ignorant men? . . . whether it is not in generall speech that John Burton doth take uppon him to tell the law and statutes unto others in the countrey?'[75] Francis Taverner, who inherited a fifty-year old dispute with the men of Haddenham, made a similar point in 1653. 'Many of the inhabitants had competent estates, who wanting full employment in tillage, they, of antient custome make it a part of their recreation to discourse of law cases'; a nice twist to the old canard that the fenmen, as pastoralists, were given to 'all slowthe and idlenesse'.[76]

It was suggested by one acute commentor, an anonymous Yorkshireman, that

---

[73] Thirsk, *English Peasant Farming*, pp. 31–9, 112–17, especially pp. 38, 113: see also PRO, E 13425/ 26 Elizabeth, Michaelmas 30 (Thomas Thewe of Kirton's using over 400 acres of grazing in Holland fen).

[74] Thirsk, *English Peasant Farming*, pp. 118–19; PRO, DL 44 1166 – the 12.5% figure is that which can be calculated from the detailed returns from Mavis Enderby and Halton Holgate; the Hareby figure is 11%; Bolingbroke, 10%.   [75] PRO, E 134 1 Charles I, Trinity 13.

[76] Francis Taverner, *A Vindication of the Jurie who . . . gave their verdict . . . against the inhabitants of Haddenham* (London, 1653), p. 18: the particular 'idleness' charge quoted here was levelled by James I in 1606 (BL, Add. MS 35171 fol. 206), but it is a commonplace of drainer propaganda.

the fenmen's legal experience was forged in their battle with the drainers. Vermuyden's initial deployment of the authority of the Privy Council and the law courts against the locals of necessity obliged them, 'Sir Cornelius having shown the way to White-hall', to become rapidly conversant with governmental norms and institutions.[77] The sense of the fenmen's undergoing an often uncomfortable political and legal education is compelling. The village elites were ultimately to be involved not only in organising local resistance, but, as at the time of the Short Parliament, in preparing petitions to the king or Commons, canvassing for the election of sympathetic MPs, feeing counsel and undertaking lawsuits and co-ordinating action with sympathetic gentlemen.[78] The fact, sardonically noted in the early eighteenth century, that the prime beneficiaries of the fenland disputes had been 'the gentlemen of the law' who 'reaped a long and plentiful harvest', is evidence for the same process.[79] But the fenmen's post-drainage involvement with Whitehall and Westminster, while it grew in volume and intensity, did not represent the dramatic shift in horizons that the Yorkshire observer supposed. The fenmen had considerable practical acquaintance with the law and legal institutions, apparent at least a generation before 'that monster of a man', Sir Cornelius Vermuyden, stalked into their region. This experience, gained in official and community roles, as much as their economic interests, explains the readiness of the village elites to lead their communities against the drainers.

The official institution, peculiar to the fenland, in which the legal and political awareness of the village elite was formed was the jury of sewers. The traditional works defending the fens from inundation were the formal responsibility of the Commissioners of Sewers. The orders of these local gentlemen for repairs and the concomitant levies were based upon the verdicts of jurors who were charged to list the defects in the ancient works and to assign responsibility for their maintenance.[80] Despite some suggestions, usually found in exhortations to the jurors, that their investigations were perfunctory and their verdicts motivated by a concern to save their own and their neighbours' pockets,[81] overall the work was

---

[77] *The State of That Part of Yorkshire, Adjacent to the Levels of Hatfield Chase, Truly Represented by a Lover of His Country* (York, 1701), p. 6.

[78] Lindley (p. 109) provides a good account of the ferment in the fenland in the spring of 1640. For another telling example, see the account of the August 1649 meeting at Donington, where six gentlemen, and five yeomen representing the 'towns', debated their responses to the proposals of Sir William Killigrew and his backers in the Rump (*Certaine Papers Concerning the Earl of Lindsey His Fennes*, pp. 2–3).

[79] From an account attributed to Abraham de la Pryme, printed in Tomlinson, *Hatfield Chase*, p. 101: see also Jackson (ed.), *Yorkshire Archaeological and Topographical Journal*, VII (1881–2) 223–34.

[80] There is a good general account of the function of the sewers' juries in A. Mary Kirkus (ed.), *The Records of the Commissioners of Sewers in the Parts of Holland, 1547–1603*, vol. I (Lincolnshire Record Society, vol. LIV (1959)), pp. xxvii–xxx.

[81] [Robert Bissell], *Instructions for Jury-Men on the Commission of Sewers* (London, 1664), pp. 31–2: Lincolnshire RO, Massingbred (Gunby) 6/7/2 no. 8.

conscientiously performed. The jury foreman who both consulted those 'very skillful' in questions of drainage and hired a boat to examine the banks and drains before presenting his verdict, was not untypical.[82] The juries were formed from members of the village elites: they were the 'most substancyall personnes of the inhabitantes within . . . south Holland', the Holland commissioners assured Burghley in the 1580s, 'the best frehoulders and inhabitants within that part of the cuntrie'.[83] They were also experienced men, 'grown grey in this employment'; a juror's youth or short residence in the area might be questioned.[84].

The juries' verdicts were supposed to embody traditional practice 'accordying to ower olde ancient custome usyd tyme with owte mynde of man', but by the late sixteenth century the old works were increasingly ineffective as a consequence of the silting up of the outfalls of the fenland rivers.[85] The Commissioners of Sewers debated schemes for improvement long before the general drainage undertakings of the Caroline period, debates which grew hot as local and individual interests clashed. In consequence the courts of sewers increasingly operated in a politicised atmosphere, most apparent in attempts by cliques of commissioners to pack or browbeat juries.[86] However, the jurors cannot be seen simply as the cat's-paws of gentry faction. They were invited to consider the evaluate schemes for improvement, and their verdicts on these demonstrate a high level of technical expertise, such as that displayed by the jury for the soke of Burgh in their support for the Clowes Cross project early in the seventeenth century.[87] Conflict, and the consequent presence of lawyers at the courts of sewers, obliged the jurors to become more acquainted with legal technicalities; 'all punctilioes imaginable, though . . . never so slight and trivial' had to be observed if their verdicts were to survive formal challenge.[88] A growing popular awareness of the legal limitations under which the Commissioners of Sewers were obliged to act appears in an incident in 1602. In that year the Commissioners of Sewers proposed the building of two new cuts to improve the drainage of the area between the rivers Witham and Glen. A Holland jury of sewers was enthusiastic, but their colleagues from Kesteven preferred an alternative scheme. Despite this

---

[82] CUL, UA CUR 3/3 no. 72.

[83] Owen (ed.), *Commissioners of Sewers in the Parts of Holland*, vol. III (Lincolnshire Record Society, vol. LXXI (1977), p. 85; BL, Lansdowne MS 41 fol. 195v.

[84] [Bissell], *Instructions for Jury-Men*, pp. 1, 64; CUL, UA CUR 3/3 unpaginated material between fols. 2 and 5, jury list of 17 April 1619.

[85] Kirkus (ed.), *Commissioners of Sewers in the Parts of Holland*, vol. I, pp. 104, 137; for the ineffectiveness of the traditional works, see H.C. Darby, *The Draining of the Fens* (CUP, 1956) pp. 11–22.

[86] One such squabble has been well analysed by M. Kennedy, 'Fen Drainage, the Central Government, and Local Interest: Carleton and the Gentlemen of South Holland', *Historical Journal*, XXVI (1983), 15–37. For attempts to manipulate the sewers' juries, see CUL, EDR A/8/1 pp. 127–8; Lincolnshire RO, Alford Court of Sewers, 1630–40, fols. 110v, 112v–113.

[87] BL, Add. MS 35171 fol. 44v.

[88] [Bissell], *Instructions for Jury-Men*, p. 54; see also CUL, UA T/xii/3 pp. 7–8.

the commissioners went ahead with the project and laid an assessment on the Kesteven towns. Resistance, led by members of the sewers jury and other minor gentlemen and yeomen, was immediate; payment was refused and attempts to distrain for the tax repelled. But the Kesteven men did not content themselves with local action; they petitioned the Council and, after raising a common purse, consulted 'certen men learned in the lawes', who agreed with their contention that the commissioners' action was illegal under the Statute of Sewers.[89]

The confidence apparent in the readiness of juries of sewers to discuss the technical merits of drainage schemes or to question the legality of the commissioners' actions may stem from a reconceptualisation of their role apparent in the late sixteenth century. The jury's status was elevated: from a practical device for discovering defects and assigning responsibility they became the voice 'of the country'. This usage develops in the context of gentry conflicts, as a riposte to those who sought to impose their particular schemes without the warrant of a jury verdict.[90] Yet the actions of seventeenth-century juries, and the rhetoric they occasionally employed,[91] suggest that the notion had been internalised by their yeomen membership. Certainly the king's lofty order in 1630, that, to avoid 'partiall and unsafe' verdicts, the commissioners should act without the assistance of a jury, was deeply resented. Sewers proceedings by jury, wrote an anti-drainer pamphleteer, was one of the 'indubitable priviledges . . . preserved to the free people therein concerned':[92] it was certainly an important institution shaping the fenmen's politico-legal experience in the early seventeenth century.

The transformation of the role of the juries of sewers was, in part, the product of a crisis in the fenland, the growing inefficiency of its traditional drainage system. Another crisis, the increased pressure on the common of the region, obliged the village elites to organise communal action which also brought them into contact with the national legal system.

The use of common fen and marsh had always required complex regulation. In the West Fen and Wildmore management was undertaken by juries drawn from all the towns that took common in the fen; in other areas each village made its own arrangements.[93] Such by-laws, once made, required limited adjustment

---

[89] PRO, STAC 5/A2/18; PRO, SP 13/G/18; Lincolnshire RO, Spalding Sewers, 460/3/33, 35; 460/5/82.

[90] Owen (ed.), *Commissioners of Sewers in the Parts of Holland*, vol. III, p. 86; D.H. Willson (ed.), *The Parliamentary Diary of Robert Bowyer, 1606–1607* (Minneapolis, University of Minnesota, 1931), p. 149; PRO, SP 14/110/75; BL, Lansdowne MS 160 fol. 149.

[91] BL, Add. MS 33466 fols. 137–41.

[92] For Charles's order, see Albright, *Explorations of Entrepreneurial History*, VIII (1955–6), 57; for examples of the legal argument against it, see *Two Petitions Presented to the Supreame Authority*, p. 3; *The State of the Case Concerning the Late Earl of Lindsey's Drayning*, p. 18.

[93] C. Brears, 'The Fen Laws of Common', *Lincolnshire Notes and Queries*, XX (1928–9), 58–64, 74–7; H.E. Hallam, 'The Fen Bylaws of Spalding and Pinchbeck', *Lincolnshire Architectural and Archaeological Society Reports and Papers*, X (1963–4), 40–56.

when the resources of the common sufficed to meet the demands of the users. A witness recalled that the stewards of the manor of Armtree simply asked the jurors whether they wished to continue 'theire anciente paines and orders' for Wildmore Fen, 'who have answered "yea" and so adiorned the court'.[94] By the late sixteenth century the complacent routine concealed a growing tension as the balance of resources and demand shifted. Pressures from within the region – natural population increase and the desire of those with capital to take advantage of the market opportunities for large-scale stock-rearing – were compounded by external forces. Poor migrants descended on the fens, attracted by its commons; lords saw the opportunities to profit from the full exercise of dormant manorial rights.

One consequence of increased pressure on the fenland's resources was a rash of disputes. Basically, these fall into two categories. First, villages squabbled over boundaries and inter-commoning: so the men of Haxey sought to monopolise their local fens, and exclude their Misterton neighbours whose use of the common, previously tolerated, was thought to have become excessive.[95] Second, the fenmen fought the enhanced exploitation of dominal rights by their manorial lords. The most objectionable of these, in that it exacerbated the problem of overstocking, was brovage, whereby the lord claimed the right to take unlimited pasture in the fen which he might sell to outsiders. But other issues, concerning the extent of the demesne or customs governing copyhold tenure, for example, could also arise.[96]

In such disputes collective action was organised by the village elite. In a 1619 complaint to Star Chamber, Sir Thomas Josselin, who was attempting to extend the jurisdiction of his manor of Littleport, depicted his opponents, the men of Upwell and Welney, in the stereotyped language of popular insurrection. They were the 'basest and unrulye people'; he demanded exemplary punishment to discourage others from riot, to which 'the mutynous people in those parts are but too prone'. Yet his account describes, not mindless violence, but a co-ordinated communal response to his interventions. The villagers, organised by yeomen, held meetings, raised a common purse and hired men to guard their cattle from Josselin's agents.[97] The elements of collective action which emerge complete in this case can be detailed in the activities of other fenland communities. At Haddenham in 1618 the general meeting to discuss resistance to a tax levied by

[94] PRO, E 134 11 Charles I, Michaelmas 39, deposition of Thomas Bookey.
[95] PRO, E 134 39 Elizabeth, Easter 14. For other boundary disputes, see PRO, E 134 13 James I, Trinity 4; Michaelmas 19; 14 James I, Easter 11 (Crowland/Deeping): PRO, E 134 5 James I, Easter 23 (Doddington/Somersham): PRO, E 134 12 James I, Michaelmas 6 (Hatfield/Crowle).
[96] For brovage, see Thirsk, *English Peasant Farming*, pp. 111–15; for an excellent account of the complex ramifications of a village/lord dispute, see Spufford, pp. 121–7.
[97] Lindley, p. 39; PRO, STAC 8 189/9.

the Commissioners of Sewers took place in church after the service, 'as usuallie in other busines concerning the whole parish they had done'.[98] Fund-raising often involved the deployment of the official network of collection; at Haddenham the constables levied the money; at Epworth those who were reluctant to pay were threatened with suits in the manor court.[99] The commoners' actions occasionally took forms more obviously significant of their sense of corporate identity than the raising of money or hiring guards. In Wildmore in the 1590s three men were appointed 'by consent' to drive brovage cattle from the fen; later, 'the inhabitants of Horncastle Soake, free and rightfull commoners . . . did chuse twoe publique persons, whoe in theire owne rightes and in the rightes of the inhabitants of the . . . Soake', impounded the sheep of 'divers great rich men' who were abusing their right of common.[100]

Some disputes over boundaries and manorial rights were settled locally, but a good number brought the commoners' leaders into the orbit of the national legal system – and not always as defendants in Star Chamber investigations of alleged riots. The village elite might collaborate in the collusive actions in equity designed to guarantee negotiated settlements; such agreements often recognised and reinforced their local authority.[101] Yeomen can also be found in more aggressive roles, instigating actions against both the intrusions of their neighbours and the aggrandisement of their lords. In 1610 three yeomen of Hale sued the lord of Swineshead in the Star Chamber in a dispute over inter-commoning. In the 1590s Haxey's suit in the Court of Exchequer against Misterton concerning their boundary in the fen was orchestrated by two yeomen, Robert Medley and John Torksey; the latter's son, William, was one of the community's leaders against Vermuyden forty years later. Seth Pavy, yeoman of West Deeping, sued at Common Law to uphold the Deeping freeholders' rights in Goggisland Fen, denied by the men of Crowland.[102] Such dealings with the courts and with lawyers developed the fenmen's consciousness of legal title in the common, apparent in their concern for the preservation of the community's deeds and case documents. When Vermuyden's scheme was mooted in the Isle of Axholme, Francis Thornhill of Misterton, a minor gentleman, who had custody of the 'wrytings, orders, and copies of orders' concerning earlier boundary suits,

[98] PRO, STAC 8 27/8.　　[99] PRO, E 134 9 James I, Trinity 2; 21 James I, Michaelmas 9.

[100] PRO, E 134 10 Charles I, Michaelmas 66; 10/11 Charles I, Hilary 27; 15 Charles I, Trinity 1.

[101] See the systems of communal government of the fens established in Sutton and in Cottenham: PRO, C 3 456/76, 77; W. Cunningham (ed.), 'Common Rights in Cottenham and Stretham in Cambridgeshire', in *Camden Miscellany*, vol. XII (Camden Society, 3rd series, vol. XVIII, 1910), pp. 173–252, especially pp. 208–9: for the later history of Cottenham's system, see J.R. Ravensdale, *Liable to Floods: Village Landscape on the Edge of the Fens, 450–1850* (CUP, 1974), pp. 68–9.

[102] PRO, STAC 8 168/15 (Hale): PRO, E 178/5412 – Attorney-general v. Torksey & Popplewell; Lindley, p. 76 (Haxey): PRO, E 134 13 James I, Trinity 4 (Deeping).

carefully poured over these documents with 'some of his neighbours', all yeomen. At Haddenham, the village elite, locked in a contest with an aggressive tithe-farmer, paraded before their lesser neighbours 'black boxes with writings with great seales . . . cominge, as they say, from the kinge, thereby perswadinge the inhabitants to pay noe tythes'.[103] The sense of the legal documents as icons, both symbols and guarantees of abstract rights, is yet more apparent in the manor of Epworth. The tenants of that manor claimed, and eminent lawyers concurred, that a mid-fourteenth-century deed of the then lord, John de Mowbray, barred his successors from making any further improvement on the commons. The deed was enshrined in Haxey church: as Daniel Noddel wrote:

The manner of keeping this deed hath been in a chest bound with iron in the parish-church of Haxey, being the greatest town within the mannor, by some of the chief freeholders, who had the keeping of the keys, which chest stood under a window, wherein was the portraicture of Mowbray set in ancient glass, holding in his hand a writing which was commonly reputed to be an emblem of the deed.[104]

The powerful sense of right, symbolised by the Mowbray deed, among the Epworth commoners was obviously exceptional. There were considerable variations in the degree to which fen villagers were prepared to insist, whether in court or by violence, upon their rights. The century long conflict of the Epworth men contrasts sharply with the muddled passivity of their counterparts at Long Sutton, at least until 1642, in the face of the depredations and duplicity of the court-backed vultures (including, of course, Sir Cornelius Vermuyden) who settled hungrily upon their 7000 acres of saltmarsh.[105] Each local situation was no doubt the product of a complex interaction of circumstances, but one variable, which also provides an additional indication of the locals' legal experience and understanding, emerges with some clarity: the predominance of copyhold or freehold tenure. Dr Lindley has remarked the contrast between the resistance Vermuyden faced at Epworth, with the acquiescence of the tenants of the neighbouring manor of Crowle, 'onely coppyholders', to the loss of a third of their common.[106] Similarly, resistance was generally less vigorous in the Isle of Ely, where copyhold predominated, than in the fens north of Boston, an area of freehold tenure.[107]

It is fashionable to argue that copyholders had as secure a tenure as did

[103] PRO, E 178/5412 – Attorney-general v. Torksey & Popplewell; PRO, E 134 9 James I, Trinity 2.
[104] Noddel, *Declaration* in Tomlinson, *Hatfield Chase*, p. 262.
[105] The complex situation at Sutton is set out best in Bodleian, Bankes MS 66/4; HLRO, Main papers 1640/1 23 Feb., articles of agreement concerning Sutton; 1641 19 Apr., petition of the inhabitants of Sutton; 1642/3 7 Feb., letter to Lord Willoughby.
[106] Lindley, pp. 79–83; PRO, E 134 9 Charles I, Michaelmas 56.
[107] Thirsk, *English Peasant Farming*, pp. 41–4: in addition to the sources that she cites, see also the survey of the manor of Heckington, PRO, E 178/5429.

freeholders. The men of Crowle, who in the 1570s were prepared to pay the Earl of Lincoln a substantial sum for their enfranchisement, or those of St James Deeping, who, a century later, found their traditional rights being undermined by an unscrupulous lord, would have been less assured on this point.[108] Early in the seventeenth century, an acute observer of the social structure of the Isle of Ely noted that the substantial farmers of the area were all copyholders, who, despite their wealth and status, could easily be pressured by their lords.[109] His general insight was no doubt based on the particular activities of the predatory Sir Miles Sandys, who, from the late sixteenth century, had pursued a skilful policy of manorial blackmail. Claims to agistment were revived, as were demands for labour services; heriots, and fines at the transfer of copyholds, were declared to be arbitrary. Such demands were only dropped when the tenants agreed to Sandys's enclosing a substantial proportion of the fen common.[110] Copyholders in the Isle, like those of Moulton in south Holland, might not admit to having 'any doubt . . . of the goodnes of their right and title', but their uncertainty emerges in their readiness 'to purchase their peace and to avoyde suits in lawe'.[111] They lacked the sense of absolute legal and moral right which informs the language and actions of the Epworth freeholders or the freeholders of Waddingham, who, in 1640, insisted on their right to sue the drainers despite the proscription of the Privy Council, 'it being the freedome of a free borne subiect to take his fitting action wherein he ought not to be restrained'.[112] In the light of the copyholders' concessions to lords and drainers in return for a secure title, such affirmations seem more than a rhetorical flourish.

The legal insecurity of the village elite in regions where copyhold tenure predominated was not the only reason for the comparatively limited resistance such areas offered to the drainers. Frequently the copyholders' search for security had already undermined the basic village unity which was essential to successful opposition, before the drainers' appearance. Throughout the fenland, right of common was technically vested in 'householders . . . dwellinge upon any auncyent house'; the occupants of newly built cottages had no right to common, but were permitted its use, 'which we connive at, otherwise they would go abegging'.[113] But the cottagers' interests were often neglected when the lords

[108] PRO, E 134 37 Elizabeth, Hilary 22; 28/29 Charles II, Hilary 17; 29 Charles II, Easter 14. For the argument of the strength of copyhold right, see E. Kerridge, *Agrarian Problems in the Sixteenth Century and After* (London, Allen and Unwin, 1969).   [109] CUL, EDR A/8/1 pp. 63–4, 67.

[110] Spufford, pp. 121–7; PRO, E 134 3 James I, Michaelmas 34; 1655/6, Hilary 20 (Willingham): Cunningham (ed.), 'Common Rights' pp. 261–87; PRO, E 134 3 James I, Michaelmas 30 (Stretham). Other lords followed Sandys's lead – e.g. at Over (PRO, E 134 1654, Michaelmas 22).

[111] PRO, E 134 1 James I, Michaelmas 4; 11 Charles I, Michaelmas 6; 11/12 Charles I, Hilary 18.

[112] PRO, C 3 422/15.

[113] PRO, E 134 44/45 Elizabeth, Michaelmas 29; *To the supreme authority . . . the . . . petition . . . of Isleham* p. 5.

obliged their copyholders to accept a settlement. In 1624 the lord of Sutton, the Dean and Chapter of Ely, reached agreement with the tenants (a process presided over by the maleficent figure of Sir Miles Sandys). In return for a substantial allotment in the 4000 acres of fen and an increased rent of £40, the Dean and Chapter agreed that copyhold fines should be fixed. The parties then proceeded to divide the remaining fens: 14 acres to be held in several by each commonable house; 1 acre of fen for every 2 in the arable lands of the village. It was initially suggested that each new cottage should receive 2 acres, but this was eventually abandoned; the copyholders took an increased allotment, the cottagers were given only the use of a small common.[114] This is the background to the powerful petition of the 'poore inhabitants' of Sutton to the Rump, 'being the instruments under god to be the deliverance of the poore out of the hand of his rich neighbour'.[115] The petitioners prefaced their complaint with a quotation from the book of Proverbs (19:4): 'wealth maketh many freindes, but the poore is seprate from his neighbour'. This may stand as a commentary upon the enhancement and the formalisation of social divisions which occurred when the village elite's doubts concerning their legal title led them to co-operate with their lords, and which dissipated the possibility of communal resistance such as that which the drainers faced in Epworth.

V

I have argued that a structural analysis of the pattern of fenland riots after 1660 can free the historian, concerned with the question of local 'political conscious-ness', from dependence upon the partial and interested accounts skilfully de-signed for consumption by the central authorities. The fenmen's actions, acceding to schemes established by parliament while assailing those that lacked legislative warrant, suggests a fairly sophisticated awareness of legal and consti-tutional norms. This was not simply a product of the intensive education in the ways of the centre which the fenmen received from the inception of the drainage schemes in the 1630s. The village elites, those who 'engaged most intensely' in the fenland's resistance, had already experienced the courts, lawyers and the values that informed the legal system as community leaders and officers, at the level of both village and *pays*, well before the advent of Vermuyden. It is in this context, to come full circle, that we can best understand Lilburne's presence at the head of the men of Epworth in Sandtoft churchyard. The locals' acceptance of his

---

[114] PRO, C 2 James I/E 7/39; C 3 456/76, 77. A similar situation occurred at Soham after 1666, when the cottagers were allowed only the use of a small common by the 'bounty and charity' of the lord (PRO, E 134 35 Charles II, Michaelmas 54).

[115] HLRO, Main papers (1649), petition of the inhabitants of Sutton; Lindley, pp. 142–3, 256.

leadership was not fortuitous or merely tactical. Leveller ideals on the franchise and on executive authority, emphasising broad participation and decentralisation, were founded in an experience of local instructions which was certainly cognate with the fenmen's traditions of self-government.[116] Similarly Lilburne's emphasis on the ancient nature right of freeborn Englishmen resonated with the men of Epworth's affirmation of their freehold rights – 'the mane and great privileges' embodied in the Mowbray deed (*their* Magna Carta) which they fought to defend for a century.

[116] Manning, *English People and the English Revolution*, pp. 302–6; K.V. Thomas, 'The Levellers and the Franchise' in G.E. Aylmer (ed.), *The Interregnum: the Quest for a Settlement* (London, Macmillan, 1972), p. 61.

7

Gender, Family and the Social Order, 1560–1725

S.D. AMUSSEN

Yea, God hath so disposed every one's severall place, as there is not anyone, but in some respect is under another.[1]

William Gouge's stress on the ubiquity of hierarchy in early modern England would rarely have been challenged by his contemporaries. Gouge assumed that the family was a mirror of society. The parallel between order inside and outside the family was obvious to writers in late Elizabethan and early Stuart England; Matthew Griffith began his *Form for Families* by arguing that 'there be two things which a Christian should especially desire, and endeavour to approve himself; namely, both a good servant to God, and a good Subject to the King; and my scope in this Manual, is to teach both'.[2] Griffith and Gouge assumed, as did all political and social theorists before Locke (as well as many after), an analogy between the structure of authority in the family and the state.

The familial analogy, while commonplace, is problematic. It means that the distinction between 'family' and 'society' was absent from early modern thought. Most historians have accepted the twentieth-century view of the family as a private institution separate from public life and public order. The campaign against scolds and dominating women discussed by Professor Underdown shows that this is not so. The family defined the ideals of the gender system, as relations between husband and wife provided a model for all relations between women and men. Patriarchal political theorists also made the family the basis of political order and many others assumed the familial analogy. Lockean political theory at the end of the seventeenth century defined the family as private. This theoretical transformation followed, however, the transformation of social practice. This chapter will examine both the implications of the familial analogy, and its changing role in the enforcement of order in early modern England.

[1] William Gouge, *Of Domesticall Duties: Eight Treatises* (3rd edn, London, 1634), p. 5.
[2] Matthew Griffith, *Bethel: or a Forme for Families* (London, 1633), fol. A6.

196

I

The seventeenth century literary sources which discuss the analogy between the family and the state fall into two separate categories. Patriarchal political theorists described the king as a father, and located the origins of political power within the family, but they did not discuss the quotidian implications of such an analogy. Gouge, Griffith and other writers of household manuals described the fathers of families as having the same powers in their families that kings had in the state, but never developed the political implications of their theories. This reluctance is understandable. While political thought was interested in the nature and origin of kingly power within the family, household manuals were concerned with the variety of roles that family members took in relation to each other – as husbands and wives, parents and children, masters and servants. Political theory focused on immutable natural relations; household manuals described social – and therefore mutable – family relations. They must therefore be discussed separately, before the connections between them can be properly understood.

Patriarchal political theory assumed that the origins of political society determined the nature of political society and political obligation. It also argued that political authority originally belonged to fathers, and was therefore natural. Thus, Sir Robert Filmer in *Patriarcha*, the best-known expression of the theory, argued that

not only Adam, but the succeeding Patriarchs had, by right of fatherhood, royal authority over their children . . . 'That the patriarchs . . . were endowed with kingly power, their deeds do testify' . . . I see not then how the children of Adam, or of any man else, can be free from subjection to their parents. And this subordination of children is the fountain of all regal authority, by the ordination of God himself.[3]

With royal power derived from fatherhood, the obligation to obey was supported by appeals to the fifth commandment, to 'Honour they father and thy mother'. When the royalist Lord Capel was executed in 1649, he asserted that:

I die, I take it, for maintaining the fifth commandment, enjoined by God himself, which enjoins Reverence and Obedience to Parents. All Divines, on all hands, tho' they contradict one another in many several opinions, yet most Divines do acknowledge that here is intended magistracy and order; I have obeyed that Magistracy and that Order under which I have lived, which I was bound to obey.[4]

---

[3] Sir Robert Filmar, *Patriarcha and other Political Works*, P. Laslett (ed.) (Oxford, Basil Blackwell, 1949), p. 57; for a full account of patriarchal thought, to which I am greatly indebted, see G.J. Schochet, *Patriarchalism in Political Thought*, (New York, Basic Books, 1975).
[4] Quoted in Schochet, *Patriarchalism*, pp. 91–2.

The patriarchal theory of political obligation was not fully articulated in England before the reign of James I, and then developed along with absolutist theory and practice. In the words of the treatise *God and the King* in 1615: 'For as we are born sons, so we are born Subjects.' The familial analogy was not unique to defenders of absolutism, however. It was so commonplace that it was necessary to explain its rejection, not its acceptance. During the Putney Debates Henry Ireton used the fifth commandment to defend property qualifications for the franchise; Colonel Rainborough did not reject the analogy, but responded that 'the great dispute is, who is a right father and a right mother?' It was only the interpretation of the analogy that differed.[5]

The comparison of the king to a father had some resonances that were peculiarly English. The moral and disciplinary authority of fathers, common to all western Europe, was strengthened by the English legal system. After the passage of the Statute of Wills in 1540, there were almost no restrictions on the distribution of property by the father to his children. In 1669 Edward Chamberlayne remarked that this legal freedom 'keeps the Children in great awe'.[6]

In the 1640s, royalist contract theorists added to the image of king as father the analogy between the relationship of king and people to that between husband and wife: once the marriage had been entered into, it was indissoluble, as was the contract between king and subjects. The analogy between the family and state thus often supported an authoritarian-absolutist, and usually a divine right, theory of monarchy: political theory allowed no resistance of subjects, any more than household manuals allowed the resistance of wives or children.[7]

The political and social implications of the parallel between the state and the family can be seen in an unorthodox use of the metaphor. In 1648 Elizabeth Poole, a poor widow, prophesied to the Council of the Army. Her arguments show the diffusion of patriarchal theory and its appropriation by an uneducated woman. She argued that while the army held kingly power, the king remained its 'Father and husband, which you were and are to obey in the Lord', even though

---

[5] Quoted by Schochet, *Patriarchalism*, pp. 88–90; A.S.P. Woodhouse (ed.), *Puritanism and Liberty* (London, Dent, 1938), pp. 60–1.

[6] Edward Chamberlayne, *Angliae Notitiae: or, The Present State of England* (2nd edn, London, 1669), pp. 458–9, 461; for inheritance, see S.D. Amussen, 'Inheritance, Women, and the Family Economy: Norfolk, 1590–1750', unpublished paper; Amussen, 'Governors and Governed: Class and Gender Relations in English Villages, 1590–1725', unpublished Ph.D. thesis, Brown University, 1982, ch. 5; also discussion of the meaning of the Statute of Wills in A. Macfarlane, *The Origins of English Individualism* (Oxford, Basil Blackwell, 1978), pp. 83–4.

[7] For a full discussion of the uses of the analogy during the civil war, see M. Shanley, 'Marriage Contract and Social Contract in Seventeenth Century England', in *Western Political Quarterly*, XXXII, 1 (1979), 79–91. The connection between state and family provided the context for the puritan debate on divorce, for if divorce were possible, so too was the dissolution of established government.

he had forgotten his 'divine father-hood and head-ship'. Poole sought to protect the person – and the mystique – of the king. Her reasoning was clear:

And although this bond be broken on his part; You never heard that a wife might put away her husband, as he is the head of her body; but for the Lord's sake suffereth his terrour to her flesh . . . And accordingly you may hold the hands of your husband, that he pierce not your bowels with a knife or sword, to take your life. Neither may you take his.[8]

Poole's discussion of the king as 'father and husband' was unusual in emphasising the husband; this allowed a more ambiguous analysis. These ambiguities justified some resistance, but the limits of the resistance demonstrate the power conferred by the analogy. While Poole wished the king to be tried and convicted 'in his conscience', she could go no further.

The governing classes of England, including political thinkers, assumed that the state was upheld by a hierarchical social structure. Wealth and social position determined the nature of participation in government. Sir Thomas Smith believed that the beginning of the commonwealth was the family, 'the first and most natural beginning and source of cities, towns, nations, kingdoms, and of all civil societies'. Smith's analysis of the types of commonwealth is followed by his description of the social hierarchy of England – which precedes the discussion of parliament and the king or queen.[9] The speed with which the Levellers were suppressed after the execution of the king in 1649 demonstrates both the determination of those in power to maintain social order and their fear that a change in the political order could change the social order.[10]

Political order involved more than national and county government. Towns and villages had governments to defend and maintain. Social unrest and class conflict threatened that political order.[11] Throughout the early modern period the political order of individual villages was challenged and defended in interactions between local notables and their social inferiors which we will examine later in this chapter. Villages and towns were collections of households, governed by those with the most property. An orderly village consisted of well-governed households: if a household were ill-governed, the local notables had to discipline it.[12]

The notion that the family is the cornerstone of social order remains to this day, but the connection between the family and political order does not. John Locke was the first to deny the analogy. He argued both that a father's power was

---

[8] Elizabeth Poole, *An Alarum of War* (1648), BL, E555 (23), pp. 3, 5–6.
[9] Sir Thomas Smith, *De Republica Anglorum*, L. Alston (ed.) (CUP, 1906), p. 24, *passim*.
[10] D. Underdown, *Pride's Purge: Politics in the Puritan Revolution* (Oxford, Clarendon Press, 1971), pp. 266–8; C. Hill, *The World Turned Upside Down* (London, Temple Smith, 1972), p. 56.
[11] For an example of how local events could threaten the whole government, see J. Walter, 'Grain Riots and Popular Attitudes Toward the Law' in Brewer and Styles, pp. 47–84.
[12] For an example of such paternalism in action, see Wrightson and Levine.

not political, and that a marriage contract was negotiable and terminable. These distinctions were of enormous political and theoretical significance, but while the first reflected changes in social practice which had already occurred, the second was generally ignored.[13] While the familial analogy did not disappear from political thought, it was no longer an unquestioned assumption.

Discussions of the family in household manuals also reflected the political and social significance of order within families. After Gouge described the family as a 'little commonwealth', he added that it was 'a school wherein the first principles and grounds of government and subjection are learned . . . inferiours that cannot be subject in a family . . . will hardly be brought to yield such subjection as they ought in Church or Commonwealth'.[14] Griffith summarised the duties of all members of the household saying that 'They must fear God and the King and must not meddle with them that be seditious.' These are assertions, not arguments; as political theory assumed the family, household manuals assumed politics.[15]

The family described by the household manuals was composed of people in complementary and distinct relationships.[16] While the male head controlled the household, his roles as husband, father and master were distinct. Some of the power relations within the family were simple, but others were ambiguous. Ambiguous relations within the family undermined the analogy between the family and the state.

The simplest relations were those of parents to children and masters/mistresses to servants. The superior was responsible for educational and moral direction of the inferior, in return for honour and obedience. There was little distinction between servants and children; both were subject to the physical and moral authority of their parents/mistresses. Education was stressed for both: superiors were expected to hold daily prayers and Bible readings, to teach reading and writing as well as work skills and to correct misbehaviour. The master of the household was legally and morally responsible for all his dependents: he had to ensure that they were catechised weekly, and was often held responsible for maidservants who became pregnant while in his service.[17] The

---

[13] See Shanley, *Western Political Quarterly*, XXXII, 1 (1979), 79–91.

[14] Gouge, *Domesticall Duties*, p. 17.   [15] Griffith, *Bethel*, pp. 429–30.

[16] For the purpose of this paper, family and household are used interchangeably, which is consistent with seventeenth-century practice. The manuals that described domestic relations were concerned with co-residence, not kinship: they usually assumed resident children, and treated servants as part of the family. The head of the household was expected to discipline those who lived with him, and in practice had no power over adult children.

[17] Canon LIX, 'Constitutions and Canons Ecclesiastical, 1604', in E. Cardwell (ed.), *Synodalia: a Collection of Articles of Religion, Canons, and Proceedings of Convocation in the Province of Canterbury from the Year 1547 to the Year 1717* (2 vols., OUP, 1842; reprinted by Gregg Press, Farnborough, Hants., 1966), vol. I, pp. 280–1; for pregnant servants, see C/S3/45, Examination of Jane Taylor of Brancaster; also Giles Moore, *The Journal of Giles Moore*, R. Bird (ed.) (Sussex Record Society, vol. LXVIII, 1971), pp. ix, 173, 349.

master was expected to maintain order in his household to contribute to the order of the community.

The relationship between husbands and wives, however, posed recurring problems for commentators on family relations. Theoretically, the husband ruled his wife, and she obeyed him in all things; he provided wise government and the necessities of life. At the same time she was joined with him in the government of the household, and was often responsible for the day-to-day education and supervision of both children and servants. Simple subordination of women to their husbands was thus an inadequate description of their relationship: in the words of Dorothy Leigh, 'if she be thy wife, she is always too good to be thy servant, and worthy to be thy fellow.'[18] The exchange of deference and obedience for protection between husband and wife was problematic on both sides; theorists believed that both women and men often failed in their duties. Gouge complained that 'among all other parties of whom the Holy Ghost requireth subjection, wives for the most part are most backward in yielding subjection to their husbands'; Matthew Griffith lamented the number of women who supported their families while their husbands spent 'in whoring, idleness, drunkeness, gaming that which should bring comfort to their posterity'.[19]

The major problem of conjugal relations in household manuals was the extent of a husband's authority over his wife. This can be seen in discussions of a husband's right to correct his wife. William Whately argued that a man could beat his wife 'if she give just cause, after much bearing and forbearing, and trying all other ways, in case of utmose necessity', but that beatings should not be administered 'for those weaknesses which are incident even to virtuous women'.[20] Gouge, on the other hand, argued that a wife was too closely associated with her husband's authority to be beaten by him: it would be like his beating himself. If correction were necessary, a husband should 'refer the matter to a public magistrate'. Gouge considered beating the least effective method of correction available to a husband.[21]

Most household manuals were written by puritan clergymen. For them the family was a spiritual institution. The father was a king, but he was also in some ways a minister to it; young men and women were asked to choose their spouses primarily for spiritual affinity. The puritan belief in the spiritual equality of the elect existed in tension with assumptions about social hierarchy. This struggle between equality and subordination is clearly seen in William Gouge's treatise.[22]

---

[18] Dorothy Leigh, *The Mother's Blessing* (London, 1616), p. 55.
[19] Gouge, *Domesticall Duties*, p. 24; Griffith, *Bethel*, pp. 292–3; cp. Thomas Gataker's complaint of those who 'live, like drones, on their wives labours, wasting all that is gathered together by their industry': *Marriage Duties Briefely Couched Togither* (London, 1620), pp. 45–7.
[20] William Whately, *A Bride-bush, or A Direction for Married Persons* (London, 1623), pp. 106–7.
[21] Gouge, *Domesticall Duties*, pp. 394–7, esp. 396.
[22] The logical conclusion of spiritual equality emerged during the civil war: see K.V. Thomas,

Gouge, the puritan rector of Blackfriars, in London, dedicated *Of Domesticall Duties* to his parishioners, who had listened to it as sermons before publication. In his dedication he acknowledged that when he had preached, 'much exception was taken' to limits on the wife's ability to dispose of family property 'without, or against, her husbands consent'. Gouge was addressing an urban audience in which economic activity – often independent – on the part of wives was normal. Gouge repeated the limits on the proscription, but remained defensive. Later in the dedication he tried once again to escape the logical implications of a wife's subjection to her husband:

When I came to deliver the husbands duties, I shewed, that he ought not to exact whatsoever his wife was bound unto (in case it were exacted by him) but that he ought to make her a joint governor of the family with himself, and refer the ordering of many things to her discretion, and with all honourable and kind respect to carry himself toward her . . . That which maketh a wives yoke heavy and hard is an husbands abuse of his authority: and more pressing his wives duty, than performing his own . . . I so set down an husbands duties as if he be wise and conscionable in observing them, his wife can have no just cause to complain of her subjection . . . This just apology I have been forced to make, that I might not ever be judged (as some have censured me) an hater of women.[23]

In spite of the initial apology, the tension between equality and subjection recurs throughout the treatise. The husband 'is as a king in his own house', yet the subjection of the wife 'is no servitude'. While husband and wife should be equal in 'Age, Estate, Condition, Piety', a husband could be older than his wife 'Because he is an head, a governor, a protector of his wife'; on the other hand, 'if a man of great wealth be married to a poor woman, he will think to make her as his maid-servant, and expect that she should carry her self towards him as beseemeth not a yoke-fellow, and a bed-fellow'. Gouge expected husbands to yield to their wives' requests, and 'They must observe what is lawfull, needfull, convenient, expedient, fit for their wives to do, yea, and what they are most willing to doe before they be too peremptory in exacting it.' Both husband and wife were responsible for the property of the family, 'because the wife is by God's providence appointed a joint governor with the husband of the Family, and in that respect ought to be an help in providing such a sufficiency of the goods of the world, as are needfull for that estate wherein God hath set them'.[24]

Gouge was aware that the position of the wife in the family was unattractive for women, and addressed the hypothetical question: 'If the case be such betwixt man and wife, it is not good to marry.'

'Women in the Civil War Sects' in T. Aston (ed.), *Crisis in Europe, 1560–1660* (London, Routledge, 1965), pp. 317–40; also Hill, *World Turned Upside Down*, esp. ch. 15.
[23] Gouge, *Domesticall Duties*, pp. 2, 4.
[24] Gouge, *Domesticall Duties*, pp. 188–90, 260, 270–1.

This is no good inference; for all the seeming-hardness of a wife's case is the lewdness of an husband, who abuseth his place and power; and not in that subjection which is required by God. For if an husband carry himself to his wife as God requireth, she will finde her yoke to be easy, and her subjection a great benefit even unto her self.[25]

The assertion that subordination was a 'benefit' to women assumed female inferiority – in the words of Edmund Tilney, men possessed 'more capacity to comprehend, wisdom to understand, strength to execute, solicitude to prosecute, patience to suffer, means to sustain, and above all, a great courage to accomplish, all which are commonly in a man, but in a woman very rare'.[26] Insofar as the conflict between co-operation and subordination was resolved, it was done by setting up a model which resembled 'limited' monarchy: women should be consulted in their own sphere, but the husband knew best.

Gouge expected women to be modest, submissive, chaste, thrifty and wise. It is unlikely that all these attributes were ever combined in one person. Although on marriage women generally lost legal control over their property, income and bodies, wives played a significant role in the family economies of early modern England. In the kitchen, dairy and brew-house they supervised production; they sold their own cheese, ale and eggs in the market, where they purchased other necessaries for their families. Neither laws nor sermons could undermine the significance of wives to the family. And while women's position in society was based on their position in the family, so was men's. Sir Thomas Smith argued that yeomen – the lowest group with a stake in society and a role in its government – had to 'be married, and have children, and as it were have some authority among his neighbours'.[27] The position belonged to the head of the family.

Ambiguous social relations were not unique to the family. Furthermore, household manuals could undermine the absolutist doctrines of patriarchal political theorists. If the household were a little commonwealth, the connections between households became problematic: the godly household might withdraw into itself rather than associate with sin. Furthermore, the ambiguity of conjugal relations made a simple analysis of authority impossible. The analogy between the family and the state was an analogy, not an equation. Yet it ensured that events within the family were never without social significance. The family was, at least until the late seventeenth century, an institution whose internal relationships were important to society.

The analogy between the family and the state was not the exclusive province of the gentlemen, lawyers and clergymen who wrote about society, politics and the family. Its significance lies in its diffusion, primarily through the church. The

---

[25] Gouge, *Domesticall Duties*, p. 343.
[26] Edmund Tilney, *A Briefe and Pleasant Discourse of Duties in Mariage, called the Flower of Friendshippe* (London, 1571), fol. Ei.   [27] Smith, *De Republica Anglorum*, p. 45.

Elizabethan homilies on obedience, marriage and brawling echoed conventional conceptions of social relations. The homilies reflected official – and widely shared – assumptions about the need for obedience, deference and submission. Sermons reinforced the messages of the homilies. Even sermons which disagreed with government policy projected a conception of government, law and order that was unifying rather than divisive.[28]

The church had another means of inculcating hierarchical notions in the catechism. All those below the age of sixteen were to be catechised weekly by the rector, vicar or curate. This responsibility was taken seriously, especially before 1640: rectors and vicars were presented for failing to catechise, as were masters who failed to send their children or servants to be catechised.[29] The catechism which appeared in the Prayer Book of 1559 was a relatively brief statement of the articles of faith and their meaning, so many ministers wrote fuller versions. The analogy between the family and the state appeared in all discussions of the fifth commandment. According to the 1559 Prayer Book, this meant that the catechumen ought

to love, honour and succour my father and mother; to honour and obey the King and all that are put in authority under him; to submit myself to all my governors, teachers, spiritual pastors and masters: to order myself lowly and reverently to all my betters: . . . to learn and labour truly to get mine own living, and to do my duty in that state of life unto which it shall please God to Call me.

The state and social hierarchy were deduced from fathers and mothers. The Westminster Assembly's Shorter Catechism of 1644 said that 'The fifth commandment requireth the preserving the honour, and performing the duties, belonging to every one in their several places and relations, as Superiors, Inferiors, or Equals.'[30]

The familial metaphor in political writings, and the political metaphor in familial writings was a commonplace in the manuals and treatises which poured from the presses of Elizabethan and early Stuart England. The failure of writers to integrate the two did not negate the implications of the analogy; for the theoretical writers they were critical for constructing a coherent argument. The analogy helped define order and hierarchy in early modern England. Household-

[28] K. Debus, 'Discovering a National Consciousness in Pre-Civil War England: A Structural Approach to the Problem', unpublished honours thesis, Cornell University Department of History, 1983.
[29] See, e.g., NRO, visitation articles in P.D. 62/33 (Bacton, 1631); DEP/28, William Ellyet, Cler., John Toolye and Thomas Bygott con Silvester Oldman, Gent., fols. 444–5v; also 'Interrogatories, July 1560', and 'Interrogatories for the Diocese of Norwich, 1561' in W.H. Frere (ed.), *Visitation Articles and Injunctions of the Period of the Reformation*, Alcuin Club Collections XIV–XVI (3 vols., London, Longmans, 1910), vol. III, pp. 87–93, 101–7.
[30] Quoted in Schochet, *Patriarchalism*, pp. 78, 79.

ers were to keep order in their families: their wives should be meek, submissive and chaste, their children orderly, their servants chaste and honest. Yeomen and gentlemen were to maintain orderly villages, making sure that the disorderly were corrected. The failings of inferiors, if uncorrected, provided a criticism of their superiors.

The mutual duties and responsibilities described by these works should have assured that early modern England was a deferential, orderly society. There is no room in this model for the drunk, the thieving or the riotous, the unchaste wife or the insolent servant. Any such were quickly corrected and disciplined. Yet historians are increasingly aware – as people then were – of the challenges to order, and the extent of disorder in the century leading up to 1640. In the face of this disorder, the question which must now be addressed is how the theoretical parallel between the family and state affected the enforcement of order in practice in early modern towns, villages, and families.

II

In 1630, the corporation of Thetford, Norfolk, decided that

Walter Salmon, Gent., one of the Burgesses of this Burrough is become altogether unable for to undergo the said office and have for diverse years now last past neglected to do those duties & offices which he as a Burgesse ought to have done. And also where the said Walter have now lately lived incontinently and thereby become infamous in the public notice of the World to the great disreputation of the Corporation & to the Scandal & disgrace of other the Burgesses there, That he the said Walter shall from henceforth be removed & degraded from the dignity & office of a Burgesse within the said Burrough, save only that he the said Walter shall still retain & have the immunities of a free man.[31]

The corporation had tolerated Walter Salmon's refusal to perform the duties attendant on his position, and only acted when his sexual behaviour caused the other burgesses embarrassment. Their action demonstrates that they were aware, as were the writers of household manuals and political theory, that 'the personal is political'. Salmon's sexual misdemeanours undermined respect for other burgesses. Laziness, in this case, was more acceptable than sin.

How typical is the action of the Thetford corporation against Walter Salmon? What types of disorder exercised the governors of the towns and villages of England? Between 1560 and 1640 they frequently brought the disorderly before the courts. The increased frequency of prosecution is itself significant. The rules and regulations under which the prosecutions took place were not repealed in 1660 nor (for the most part) were they first enacted in 1560, but between 1560 and

---

[31] NRO, T/C1/4, Thetford Corporation Book, p. 95, 13 August 1630.

1640 offenders were more likely than before or after to be prosecuted for them.
The people who were prosecuted were vagrants and beggars; they played dice,
cards or other 'illegal games'; they drank excessively, kept an alehouse without a
license or allowed other men's servants to drink in their homes; they bore and
fathered bastards, committed adultery or seduced their servants; women scolded
and brawled with their husbands and neighbours; they allowed their children to
run around the church during sermons, sat in the wrong seat in church or argued
with others about who should sit where; the poor insulted their social superiors,
or refused to behave reverently in church or fell asleep during the sermon. These
prosecutions reflect a breakdown in the maintenance of order, since the machinery of prosecution encouraged informal settlement of disputes, not prosecution.[32] The position of the parish elites responsible for prosecution may have
been particularly insecure during this period: inflation, social mobility and an
active land market meant that those who were prosecuting were not far removed
from their neighbours – and their disorderly neighbours may have delighted in
remembering that once they had been equals.

Offences against the social order fall into three major categories. Some were
derived primarily from a moral notion of appropriate behaviour: this includes
particularly those relating to drinking and gaming; others disrupted 'class'[33]
relations between superiors and inferiors: such were cases of begging and
vagrancy, disputes about church seats and insults to those of higher status;
finally, there were those which disrupted the gender order – relations of women
and men as family members, servants or neighbours: these were offences relating
to adultery and bastardy, scolding, and the family disorder present in domestic
violence, desertion and divorce. We will be concerned chiefly with these last two
categories. Both class and gender were hierarchical power relations, based on the
different responsibilities and characters of the participants. These relationships
were not exclusive: the relationship between a master and his maidservant
involved both gender and class. Yet such categories provide a schematic structure
within which to analyse the challenges to order and the responses to them. It was
assumed that the class and gender hierarchies would never conflict, and there was
enormous anxiety when they did so. Elite women occasionally had power over
men; all men – no matter how poor – had power and authority over their wives.[34]

[32] For a full discussion of these issues see Wrightson in Brewer and Styles, pp. 21–46; Wrightson and
Levine; W.H. Hunt, *The Puritan Moment: The Coming of Revolution in an English County*
(Cambridge, Mass., Harvard University Press, 1983), chs. 2–3; these patterns parallel the
prosecutions for violent crime: see J.S. Cockburn, 'The Nature and Incidence of Crime in England,
1589–1625: A Preliminary Survey' in Cockburn, pp. 49–71.

[33] I am using the word 'class' here in a non-technical sense, to refer to relations within the socio-
economic hierarchy rather than social groups defined by their relation to the means of production.
Its use does not indicate either the existence of a class society in the period or of class conflict.

[34] See Amussen, 'Governors and Governed,' pp. 259–61; also C. Carlton, 'The Widows Tale: Male
Myths and Female Reality in Sixteenth and Seventeenth Century England', *Albion*, x (1978), 118–
29.

The social order of gender relations, as we have seen, prescribed distinct behaviours for women and men, wives and husbands. Women were expected to be chaste, patient, docile and submissive while men had authority and power, at least over their own wives. These characteristics, based on ideal conjugal relations, were applied to the behaviour of women and men outside the family as well as within it. This explains the attention paid to scolding women, disorderly women and even witches.[35] In most sexual offences men and women are, of course, equally guilty. But the consequences of illicit sexuality were different for women and men, and the type of attention paid to them, and the ways they were punished, differed correspondingly. The gender system defined a set of relationships conditioned by difference.

The most obvious sexual offence was represented by the women who bore illegitimate children. Illicit pregnancy accounted for from one-fifth to over one-half of all sexual offences presented to the archdeaconries of Norfolk and Norwich during sample years between 1572 and 1681.[36] Bastard-bearers raised other problems for villages in addition to the fear of having to support the child. The mother of the illegitimate child had no place in village society; her family had no head to ensure order and provide property or legitimacy. Sexual offences other than bastardy could also be disruptive of the ideal gender order. Premarital sexuality could lead to inappropriate marriages, to the distress of family and neighbours. Extra-marital sexuality disrupted families: a husband was not governing his household if his wife committed adultery, and he was not a loving and faithful husband if he did the same. The skimmington ritual which was directed against the henpecked husband included (usually) horns, the symbol of the cuckold. If the wife rejected her subordination to her husband, she might also reject sexual fidelity.

Village notables, parish priests and anyone else could preach, punish and admonish, but sexual offences still occurred. The offenders were declared deviant and undesirable, but they did not disappear. They were a constant reminder that the real order of society was different from the ideal. Not all challenges to the gender order were so overt. One more subtle problem was the disagreement between women and men over the standards for women's behaviour. Many women did not emphasise obedience to husbands either in their own reputations or in their evaluations of each other.

[35] Underdown, above, pp. 120–1.
[36] The low came in the archdeaconry of Norfolk in 1663, when pregnancy-related offences accounted for 1.1% of the total presentments, and all sexual offences 6.3% of the total; the highest proportion of pregnancy related offences was 1614–15, when 10.2% of the presentments were pregnancy-related, and only 18.9% of the presentments focused on sexual offences. Usually pregnancy-related offences made up between $\frac{1}{3}$ and $\frac{1}{2}$ of all sexual offences presented to the courts. The sample years were NRO, ANW/2/8, 15, 27, 58, 74, 84, 85 (1572, 1581, 1589–90, 1614–15, 1638–9, 1678–81), and ANF/1/1, 2, 5 (1560–61, 1590, 1667). The situation in Norfolk differs, it appears, from that in Lancashire: see W.J. King, 'Punishment for Bastardy in Early Seventeenth Century England', *Albion* x, 2 (1978), 130–51, esp. 137, 149.

When women defended their reputations through defamation suits in the ecclesiastical courts, they were most concerned with their reputation for chastity, not for submissiveness, obedience or being a good housewife. When Alice Fysher watched Olive Grymwood draw water from Fysher's well, and taunted 'You use it [the water] sluttishly and you wash your corrupt clowtes [clothes?] in it', Grymwood did not complain; instead Fysher complained that Grymwood had responded by calling her 'a whore and an arrant whore and go play cock sodden again'.[37] When mistreatment of a husband was alleged in an insult, it was in the context of adultery. Thomas Rayner of Cawston alleged that Margery Suffield had pushed her husband out of the house in his shirt, that she was a 'drunken sottish whore', and that she had a man with her in her chamber.[38] This pattern is not explained by law, since the insults complained of by men covered a far wider range of behaviour. Men worried about insults to their social position, their honesty or sobriety as well as about their sexual behaviour. The 'sexual' insults complained of by women and men had social implications: to be a whore or whoremaster, for instance, threatened the parish with a bastard or disrupted another household.[39]

Women also refused to condemn each other for breaches of obedience when these became issues in litigation. When Thomas London, Gent., of Norwich left nothing to his wife Mary in his will, she sued to gain access to the property which she saw as hers by right. Thomas London's friend Christopher Layer testified that London had been mistreated by his wife and her children: he had been misled about the extent of her estate, and she and her children failed to give him 'due respect'. Two women neighbours, however, asserted that she had always behaved herself 'very lovingly loyally and well' towards her husband, and had 'a very due care and respect of him'. Both sides may have been right: 'due respect' was in the eye of the beholder.[40] Similarly ambiguous language was used by a witness when Samuel Bridgewell accused his wife of adultery in 1706: a maidservant testified that 'she never saw her commit or omit anything whereby

[37] NRO, DEP/31, Alice Fysher con Olive Grymwood, fols. 6–6v (1600).
[38] NRO, DEP/39, Suffield mul. con Rayner, fols. 333–33v, 336–36v.
[39] This is based on the defamation cases appearing in NRO, DEP/15(15), 16, 17, 18, 19, 20 (21a), 22, 23, 24, 31, 37, 42, 46, 47, 49, 53 (1572–5, 1577–83, 1579–80, 1580–1, 1581–2, 1582–3, 1586–7, 1587– 9, 1589–90, 1600–1, 1617, 1635, 1661–4, 1664–6, 1671–5, 1692–1703); the exceptions – accusations of being a scold, or of having been ducked or the target of a charivari – are unusual, and even when most common (before 1590) they never account for more than 10% of the defamation cases brought by women. Amussen, 'Governors and Governed', pp. 252–67; J.A. Sharpe, *Defamation and Sexual Slander in Early Modern England: The Church Courts at York*, Borthwick Papers, 58 (University of York, St Anthony's Press, 1981), finds the same patterns in the causes of cases and the differences between women and men that I have found in Norfolk, and makes it clear that the ecclesiastical courts continued to adjudicate many suits which were theoretically within the province of the common law: pp. 15, 27–8.
[40] NRO, London con London, DEP/40, fols. 272–73v, 295, 300–3, and DEP/41 138v–39, 147v–48, 281.

her said husband . . . might be justly provoked to treat her roughly or unkindly, or whereby he might become jealous of her virtue and chastity'.[41] 'Just provocation' is, like 'due respect', imprecise. These conflicts suggest that men may have expected more of their wives than their wives were willing – or able – to give. Women appear to have developed a consensus about their obligations to their husbands which reflected the nature and extent of their role in the family economy. Emphasis on wifely obedience first appears in testimony by other women after 1700 – and then in urban upper bourgeois families where their economic role seems to have diminished earliest. In these families the conflict that seemed so clear to others would have been a less present concern.[42]

Wives did not consciously decide to focus on the sexual dimensions of marriage. They confronted the same conflict between co-operation and subordination which Gouge had failed to resolve, and women lived with the conflict daily. Their solution – not to discuss their roles as housewives or the non-sexual dimensions of their roles as wives – avoided contested areas. While their refusal to focus on the non-sexual aspects of their relations with men was not disruptive, it provided a covert critique of relations within the family.

One final aspect of gender relations reminded local notables of the gap between the ideal and the real. This is the incidence of domestic violence and family breakdown. Violence was complained of by both wives and neighbours.[43] Desertion was often an unofficial solution to conjugal conflict. It is impossible to assess the frequency of informal separations in early modern England, but fragments of evidence show it to be a frequent end to unhappy marriages. Separations were often followed by consensual unions or bigamous remarriages, which only came to light if someone who knew of the earlier marriage informed the authorities or surviving spouse.[44]

Domestic violence undermined the notion of the family as an orderly, wisely

[41] NRO, DEP/54, 1706, Mary Bridgewell con Samuel Bridgewell, testimony of Elizabeth Gay.
[42] NRO, DEP/58, July 1724: Mary Hubard ux. con Peter Hubard vir; especially unusual is the testimony of Mary ux Lawrence Bond and Elizabeth ux John Sporle. For the economic role of women, see A. Clark, *Working Life of Women in the Seventeenth Century* (London, Routledge, 1919): her analysis, though somewhat exaggerated, reflects changes that can be detected in women's work in the period; see also Amussen, 'Inheritance, Women, and the Family Economy', unpublished paper.
[43] While women themselves often complained of violence from their husbands, most of the complaints about women beating their husbands came from neighbours.
[44] Amussen, 'Governors and Governed', esp. pp. 228–41; between 1560 and 1725 there were at least twenty-one suits for divorce before the Consistory Court of Norwich; six were brought by men, all alleging adultery (four of these occurred before 1590); fifteen were brought by women, which all alleged adultery, violence or economic deprivation – and only one adultery only; most indicate an earlier period of separation; for the role of neighbours in detecting bigamous marriages, see e.g. NRO, DEP/34, John Burroughs con Brooke, fols. 386–7v, DEP/53, Watson als. Thorpe mul. con Thorpe vir (1690); for consensual unions, see C/S3/47 (1666), Examinations of John Blacklock of Gayton and C/S3/57 (1686), Examination of John Brown.

governed unit. Even after villages had withdrawn their gaze from many aspects of family life, it led to intervention by neighbours and families. Neighbours could intervene directly, or alert the wife's family to what was going on: in 1600 the family of Anne Gosling of Bedingham, Norfolk, knew that her husband had severely beaten and injured her the day after it happened – her father was told by a neighbour at Loddon Market, five miles from Bedingham. A century later John Robinson's neighbour Mistress Cooke interrupted when he was beating his wife by telling him that 'he was a very ill man to beat his wife at that rate'.[45] If such interventions were unsuccessful, neighbours might complain to the justices of the peace, hoping that respected government officials would be more effective in reforming violent villagers.[46] Desertion and the more formal solution of a separation *a menso et thoro* obtained from the church courts had the same structural effect as bearing an illegitimate child, but the woman was perceived as innocent, and the lack of a male household head more 'legitimate' than in the household of a bastard-bearer.

Relations between husbands and wives, and the social relations of the sexes in general, raised a series of problems for the local notables of early modern England. The reality of gender relations rarely conformed to theory, but there were no direct challenges to the gender order. No one questioned women's subordination to their husbands – they just sometimes refused to give it. The general acceptance of the gender order stands in marked contrast to the attitudes toward the class order.

III

The connection between gender and class behaviour becomes explicit in petitions to the justices of the peace. The petition was, in many ways, the ideal form of protest. It allowed a village to complain of all the offences of troublesome neighbours, not just crimes. More than one-half of the sixty-two petitions which came before the quarter sessions and assizes for Norfolk between 1600 and 1669 complain of the violence or contentiousness of the person involved.[47] More than one in five petitions complain of the abuse or neglect of family responsibilities, more than one-third of alehouse offences, one-third of the abuse of economic relations.

The petitions demonstrate that those who offended the standards of the

---

[45] NRO, AYL/17, 45–47; DEP/53, 1696, Robinson mul con Robinson vir, testimony of Rebecca Mallowes.

[46] Amussen, 'Governors and Governed', pp. 232–7.

[47] The petitions against disorderly villagers end in 1669, in both quarter sessions and assizes; the reason for this is unclear, but it is probably that the need for such action ceased to exist: the disorderly could be dealt with less formally.

gender system were also likely to break the code of class relations. Simon Keeper of Newton-next-Castle Acre, who was the object of petitions in both 1615 and 1623, mistreated his mother and prevented others from helping her, and also encouraged quarrels and lawsuits between his neighbours.[48] Matthew Loose, who was 'at continual strife with his wife, often beating her and seldom quiet with her', was also 'disobedient to all authority'. In 1621 Simon Woodrow of Great Fransham not only threatened his pregnant wife, but also killed his neighbour's cattle and left fences open to the common so that he could impound the beasts which entered his land. Robert Johnson of Northwold, who 'heinously railed upon his wife', was a common drunkard who had assaulted the constable and attacked the parson in the churchyard. In 1622 Henry Eaton of Holme Hale fathered a bastard on his maidservant, then encouraged her to abort it or charge another with its paternity. The case concerned the community because Eaton's treatment of his servant could not otherwise be controlled.[49] The behaviour of villagers inside and outside the family could encourage disorder and challenge notions of appropriate relations between husband and wife, master and servant, rich and poor or neighbour and neighbour.

Some challenges were more direct. Richard Sheepheard, 'a desperate tinker', often came home drunk 'and in that humour hath divers times beaten his wife and her children'. Like Simon Keeper, he encouraged lawsuits, often initiating a suit only to drop it when the victim had gone to the expense of preparing a defence. He refused to pay rent for his town house, and abused the churchwardens and other inhabitants with 'such fearful blasphemies, oaths, reproaches and threatnings' that his neighbours were afraid he would set fire to their homes. The poor who received charity – including housing in a town house – were expected to be grateful for the beneficence of their neighbours. Sheepheard refused the deference and respect which held the socially stratified communities of early modern England together.[50]

Deference was also refused by words. Insults threatened the reputations of local notables. Some insults involved using a term of abuse to a social superior that would have been defamatory in any case, as when Thomas Copping called a gentleman a 'common drunkard'. But often these insults were claims of equality: in 1615, William Byrde of West Lynn refused to pay a poor rate because of the idleness of Humphrey Guybon, Esquire, a justice of the peace; Byrde was alleged

[48] NRO, C/S3/20,24, Petitions against Simon Keeper of Newton-next-Castle Acre.
[49] NRO, C/S3/23A, Holme Hale vs. Henry Eaton; C/S3/26, Articles against Matthew Loose; C/S3/23, Articles against Simon Woodrow; C/S3/28A, Articles against Robert Johnson.
[50] NRO, C/S3/26, Articles against Richard Sheepheard, late of West Winch, now of Castle Acre; cp. Barnard Shipabarrow, probably of Outwell, Norfolk, who refused to work except for extortionate wages, followed no regular trade, and 'there is not any evil vice usually amongst men that he hath not part thereof' (C/S3/15, 1606).

to have said that 'he is as good a man as he [i.e. Guybon]'. Henry Weavers claimed superiority when he told Mr Miles Lynn, a parson, in 1613, that 'I am a better man than thou art, knave parson, a turd in thy teeth.'[51] After the Restoration the defamation cases brought by men reflect a greater interest in protecting social position. The claims of equality disappeared, but local notables were increasingly touchy about any insult.[52]

Parsons were especially likely to be the targets of criticism and claims of equality. The position of the parson in the social order depended on his office, not his wealth or birth, and was therefore increasingly anomalous. Social position was usually based on wealth and property, but the parson was set apart by his role and education. The status terms of gentleman, yeoman and husband-man remained in use throughout the seventeenth century, and masked changes in the basis of social position. The key to these changes is the word usually used to describe character, 'credit'. Credit implied honesty, but it also described financial solvency. The word as used by wealthy villagers was often ambiguous; it allowed an equation of wealth with worth. The confusion is telling. Poorer villagers rarely used 'credit' against their fellows in the way their superiors did when they dismissed someone as of 'little credit or reputation'. Credit was a contested concept in seventeenth-century villages.[53]

The nature of the social hierarchy and the disputes over it can also be seen in conflicts over church seats. Seating in churches reflected, to a certain extent at least, the social hierarchy of the community. One kind of dispute arose over the extent to which it did so, another over the right to control seats. All such disputes persisted through the seventeenth and into the eighteenth centuries. In Swaffham in 1636, Robert Theodorick had been placed in a seat in the church which many of his neighbours felt was too high for him, 'he being an oatmealmaker and a man of no great credit'. Nothing was done until a year later, when Theodorick brought a barber, 'a man of mean condition', into the seat; some of the 'chief inhabitants' demanded that both men be removed from 'a seat fit for the best man of the parish'. Theodorick did not deserve the seat, but the situation was

---

[51] NRO, DEP/28, Thomas Spooner, Gent, con Thomas Copping, fols. 422, 525–6, 530; C/S3/20, Examination of Thomas Anderson of West Lynn, Laborer; DEP/36, Mr Miles Lynn cler. con Henry Weavers, fols. 124–9.

[52] A fuller discussion of this process can be found in Amussen, 'Governors and Governed', pp. 266–7, 305–10.

[53] Amussen, 'Governors and Governed', pp. 248–52, 312–18, 342–6. The position of the clergy is challenged by the emergence of dissent after the Restoration. There is some evidence for this in the defamation cases surveyed in n. 39. After the Restoration, men make up a smaller percentage of those bringing defamation cases, but clergymen bring a larger proportion of all cases brought by men. Before 1640, men bring 55% of all defamation cases (N = 196), with clergymen as 8% of all male plaintiffs. After the Restoration, men bring only 35% of all defamation cases (N = 114), but clergymen account for 18% of the cases brought by men.

aggravated by his attempt to reshape the symbolic hierarchy of the town, though Theodorick never claimed to be entitled to his seat.[54] When the churchwardens of Bawdeswell went to Margaret Skener during morning prayer in 1608 and sought to move her 'to certain new seats by them erected under and near the clock where the poor and such as took almes did sit', she protested, asserting that since her husband contributed to the town charges she deserved her place. Others believed that since he was not a householder, she should not 'be ranked and seated with others much her betters'. This was a disagreement about the criteria for status in a village, and it fuelled numerous disputes.[55]

The conflicts between different criteria are explicit in a dispute in East Bilney in 1668. Christopher Crowe, JP, was the chief inhabitant of the parish, and sat in the first seat in the church. The next seat was occupied by some of Crowe's servants, along with William Breame and his family; in the third seat sat William Wiscard and his family. The dispute arose because Wiscard's family was too large for his seat, and some of them moved up to the second seat. Crowe and Breame claimed that continuous occupancy gave them ownership of their seats. Wiscard countered that as the second wealthiest inhabitant he deserved the seat. The dispute reflected the competing claims of wealth and tradition.[56] Disputes about the criteria by which villagers were seated reflect the different systems of ranking – from the more traditional one of status to a more 'modern' one based on wealth and, eventually, class. They all assume, however, that seating in church should reflect a hierarchy.

Disputes in which one family claimed ownership of a particular seat in church reflect the anxiety of many local notables about maintaining their position. These first emerge in the late 1610s, when social mobility began to be more restricted, and continue into the eighteenth century. These disputes involve the front of the church; almost all take place in market towns and pastoral villages where larger local elites made conflict over position more likely than in more sharply polarised arable villages. In 1634, William Grudgefield, Gent., of Fressingfield, Suffolk, asked Francis Sancroft sen. and his nephew Francis Sancroft jun., Gents., to move from the seat they had occupied for the previous ten years to make room for Grudgefield's servants. The two families were of similar status, but Grudgefield was a newcomer to the parish, and the Sancrofts had been there for generations. At issue were Grudgefield's control of access to

---

[54] NRO, DEP/43, Robert Theodorick con John Bride, fols. 78v–80v, 81v–84, 98–102v; Theodorick may have been given his seat as a kinsman of Thomas Theodorick, who served as churchwarden and feofee of the town lands, and was therefore part of the local oligarchy.

[55] NRO, DEP/35, Skener con Leman and Pescod, fols. 202b–202c, 247v–249.

[56] NRO, DEP/48, William Breame con William Wiscard, Mr Christopher Crowe con William Wiscard, fols. 113–19v, 129v–32.

the seat, and where the Sancrofts ought to sit. The Sancrofts were widely respected; their seat reflected the status they were thought to deserve.[57]

Conflicts over church seats reflect the stresses present in a finely graded social system. Even after the period of dramatic social change, the slow development of agricultural capitalism continued to transform social relations in English villages. Conflicts were inevitable when the class order was made visible and concrete each week. That order, theoretically based on function, increasingly reflected an emerging capitalist society – exemplified by Wiscard's claim to a seat on the basis of his wealth. Ultimately, conflicts over church seats affirmed the social order; while the details were called into question, the order itself was not.

IV

Not all challenges to, or conflicts over, the gender and class orders required, or even permitted, a reaction. But most disruptive actions by villagers brought responses from authorities or neighbours. Many responses were informal: most English villages were relatively small, and their informal shaming rituals were effective.

Initially, villagers observed their neighbours. The personal information that often emerges in disputes, as well as defamation suits, demonstrate that villagers also gossiped about each other: many defamation suits were attempts to stop a rumour before it became part of the victim's 'common fame' and reputation.[58] Observation and gossip not only shaped reputation, but also shamed people and defined particular behaviours as deviant. It might not be possible to stop women from bearing bastards or to force men into controlling their wives, but it was possible to ensure that these things were not seen as normal. Shame was provided more formally through charivari, quasi-judicial duckings, and placement in the stocks. Charivari in England were usually directed at families where the woman was allowed by her husband to dominate, beat or cuckold him. Ducking was the

---

[57] Statements about elites are based on the analysis of wills left by yeomen in the NCC: I am grateful to Nesta Evans of the University of East Anglia for sharing her research with me; for social mobility, see L. Stone, 'Social Mobility in England, 1500–1700', Past and Present, XXXIII (1966), 16–55; NRO DEP/41, William Grudgefield Gent. con Francis Sancroft Sr. & Francis Sancroft Jr., Gents, fols. 524–65; Fressingfield is in the pastoral area of Suffolk: Looking Back at Fressingfield (Fressingfield Workers' Education Association, Fressingfield 1979), pp. 29, 33, 35–6; the Sancrofts had only recently attained the status of gentlemen: Francis Sancroft Jr's father described himself as a yeoman, though his son was to be Archbishop of Canterbury.

[58] See the separate suits brought by Roger Watson in NRO, DEP/24 against Thomas Corpe, Thomas Newark, and Thomas Richardson, fols. 97–8, 174–5 and 314v, 180–1 and 183–4: all are in response to the same allegation that he had been taken with a whore in Norwich and whipped for it, though the victims of the suits lived in various places around Norwich – Hethel, Hethersett and Swainsthorpe; even when the insult occurs in an argument, such arguments were rarely private and the insults then can become part of local gossip.

punishment for scolds – women who stepped out of the modesty and submissiveness which was supposed to characterise them, and instead argued and fought with their neighbours, particularly their social superiors. The stocks were usually used for drunkards or brawlers.[59]

In some disputes a broad range of responses was used: Robert Dey, the rector of Cranwich in 1595, was accused by his former servant Elizabeth Purkey of fathering her child. While she was pregnant she was married (at the instigation of Dey's brother-in-law) to Robert Bate, a young thatcher. When part of the dowry that Bate had been promised failed to materialise, Elizabeth Bate entered Cranwich church during evening prayer, deposited her child and declared that Dey could provide for it. Dey was presented to the church courts for fornication, and responded with a defamation suit against Bate and those who supported her allegations. Depositions revealed that a previous servant, Agnes Greene, had alleged that Dey had attempted to seduce her; Dey's defamation suit against her was halted when a local JP convinced Greene to keep silent. Dey initially sought to control the damage to his reputation by making sure that Bate got married (an informal response); when she shamed him (another informal response) he responded formally, with a lawsuit; simultaneously, however, he was subject to formal disciplinary proceedings. In the case of Agnes Greene, her gossip (informal) was stopped by his lawsuit (formal) only when mediated by a local justice (informal). Not only do the responses constantly move between the formal and informal, but the dispute itself straddles the line between gender and class relations. Robert Dey used his power as a master (class) to seek and obtain sexual (gender) favours. Illicit sex between servants and masters involves both class and gender.[60]

The conflicts between Robert Dey and his servants demonstrate that formal responses to breaches of gender or class order were available. A JP might try to frighten offenders into good behaviour, or bind them over to keep the peace and to appear at the next quarter sessions. This process followed brawls, minor trespasses, family disputes and other everyday events – moral, class or gender offences. If this process failed, villages could make petitions to the justices in quarter sessions, or begin a prosecution in quarter sessions or ecclesiastical courts on particular charges.

There was a large overlap between the jurisdictions of the quarter sessions and ecclesiastical courts; both dealt with scolds and drunkards, domestic disorder and sexual offences. Punishment in the ecclesiastical courts was usually public

---

[59] Underdown, above, pp. 123–32.
[60] NRO, DEP/28, Ex officio con Robert Dey, Robert Dey con Leonard Poole, Richard Dey, Robert Bate, and Elizabeth Purkey alias Bate, fols. 3–11v, 25–7v, 89–91v, 235–42, 244v–5v, 247–51v, 253–6.

penance – an institutionalised shaming ritual. In the secular courts punishments ranged from a fine, to whipping, the stocks and imprisonment. Gender offences appeared legitimately in both courts. Most prosecutions in the ecclesiastical courts were the result of presentments made by villagers – the churchwardens and questmen – in response to questions from the archdeacons. These referred to attendance at church, taking Communion, behaviour in church, the behaviour (and orthodoxy) of the rector or vicar, the church fabric and the personal morality of the parishioners. In the last category they were asked about fornicators, adulterers, bastard-bearers, scolds ('in breach of Christian charity'), drunkards, bigamists and almost anyone else that could be imagined. The articles remained the same, but over the course of the seventeenth century the presentments did not. Before the civil war, the ecclesiastical courts played a major role in social control; after the civil war, gender, class and moral offences were rarely presented to the church courts. By the end of the century visitations dealt almost exclusively with issues of church fabric and defaults of the vicar, and were irrelevant to social order. There were occasional presentments for adultery or pregnancy, but the drunkards, scolds, bigamists, separated couples and those who slept in church disappeared.[61] Similarly, though the quarter sessions continue, the petitions against disorderly neighbours disappear after 1669. Why?

Many people in the early seventeenth century thought that society was falling apart; this belief was confirmed by scolding women, the poor, vagrants and day-to-day social tensions. In spite of this, the gender order was never challenged explicitly, and the inferiority of women never denied. The existence of the gender hierarchy was secure. But the class hierarchy was challenged: the criteria for determining status, the conception of the moral superiority of the wealthy and inferiority of the poor were all called into question. The radical groups of the civil war challenged the class order, not the gender order.[62]

The period between 1560 and 1640 saw rapid population growth, inflation and massive transfers of land. The governors of England, from parish officers to those in parliament, sought to impose order on a society which was changing, and apparently disintegrating, before their eyes. In their attempts to impose order on society, they were aided by the commonplaces of political and social thought. The analogy between family and state, gender order and class order, offered an effective response to disorder. By insisting on the proper gender order, local notables could effectively reaffirm the social order, since no one had ever called the power relations of the family into question. The public nature of

---

[61] This analysis is based on the records of the archdeaconries of Norfolk and Norwich; the evidence presented by Wrightson and Levine suggests that it would hold true for the quarter sessions as well, but the Norfolk records are not complete enough to test that assumption. See note 36.

[62] Hill, *World Turned Upside Down.*

familial relations was a tool for the local notables of early modern England in their attempts to defend and protect the society in which they held power. This effort was successful, and even if the threat was less than they had feared, the dimensions of the fear itself should not be underestimated.

Between 1640 and 1660 the political order of England suffered a civil war, but it was not accompanied by social revolution. The dreaded disaster did not occur. In the aftermath of the civil war and Interregnum, the governors of England became more tolerant, but they also became more adept at intervening before a problem threatened their position. After the Restoration, when population began to decline, prosperity returned, and the social hierarchy became more secure, it was no longer so necessary to enforce order in families. There was a residual concern with the parents of bastards and domestic violence, but the hysteria of the earlier period is absent.[63] Faced with the same lists of questions from the archdeacons, gender and class offences disappear from the records. It is possible that these offences had disappeared. It is more likely, however, that they no longer threatened the social order. In a sense, the local notables of early modern England had begun to declare the family 'private' in the thirty years before Locke did.

This examination of the ideological construction of the concept of order in its social context reveals the mutual shaping of social theory and social practice. Between 1560 and 1640 social theory and social practice were congruent. Patriarchal political theory supported the notion of the family as a social institution, and thereby provided a means to maintain order when it was most threatened. After the Restoration many theorists continued to assume the familial analogy, but it was no longer central to social control. When Locke defined the family as private, he did so only after it had ceased to play a significant role in the public maintenance of the social order.

[63] One sign of this is the changing targets of English charivari: in the eighteenth century the domineering wife is replaced by the violent husband. See E.P. Thompson, 'Rough Music: Le Charivari Anglais', *Annales ESC*, XXVII, 2 (1972), pp. 285–312.

8

The 'Moral Economy' of the English Crowd: Myth and Reality

J. STEVENSON

The social history of the early modern period has been transformed in recent years by the attempt to explore and explain the popular culture of the common people through their rituals, celebrations and protests. The last of these has become one of the most important windows onto the world of otherwise largely inarticulate sections of the population. Hence for a generation or more British scholars have followed a path first trodden by the *Annales* school in using popular disturbances and movements not only to investigate the ideas and beliefs of the people concerned, but also to reconstruct their assumptions and attitudes and to place them in the context of larger-scale processes of social and economic change.[1] Few concepts have proved more influential in this exploration than E.P. Thompson's notion of the 'moral economy', in which Thompson argued that the activities of English crowds in the eighteenth century indicated an 'extraordinary deep-rooted pattern of behaviour and belief' – a 'moral economy' – which legitimised popular actions against those who transgressed customary practice. For Thompson the crucial task was to 'decode' these actions and their ceremony and symbolism in order to reveal the underlying assumptions of what he called the 'plebeian culture', assumptions which frequently ran contrary to those of the propertied and those in authority.[2]

It is no small tribute to the power of Thompson's arguments, and the literary ability with which they have been expressed that they have, in one form or another, become part of the intellectual luggage of a whole generation of social historians – by no means all of them sympathetic to Thompson's perspective on

[1] See J. Stevenson, *Popular Disturbances in England, 1700–1870* (London, Longman, 1979), pp. 1–16; R.J. Holton, 'The Crowd in History: Some Problems of Theory and Method', *Social History*, III (1978), 219–33.

[2] E.P. Thompson, 'The Moral Economy of the English Crowd in the Eighteenth Century', *Past and Present*, L (1971), 76–136.

social history in general and his reading of the history of this period in particular.[3] The purpose of this essay is not to indulge in facile revisionism, but to explore the degree to which Thompson's highly persuasive analysis bears up to the results of more than a decade of further scholarship and can still be regarded as an accurate guide to the ideology and attitudes in the early modern period.

I intend to proceed in three stages, first to place Thompson's perception of the 'moral economy' in the context of his own and other writing in the field of popular culture; secondly, to examine its relationship to what we now know about the causes and distribution of the disturbances upon which Thompson focused for his evidence about the existence of the 'moral economy', namely food riots, and, thirdly, to assess the nature of the qualifications which emerge for the interpretation of the nature of the 'popular' or 'plebeian culture' in this period.

I

Thompson's notion of the 'moral economy' must be seen within the context of the burgeoning of interest in popular movements, riots and crowds which was pioneered by George Lefebvre, whose work as early as 1934 provided one of the first serious attempts to treat the role of the crowds and mobs of the French revolutionary era as a serious historical phenomenon. After the Second World War a number of historians began to give more serious attention to the ideology of popular movements. Amongst the pioneering works in this area were E.J. Hobsbawm's *Primitive Rebels* and the studies by G. Rudé, *The Crowd in the French Revolution* and *Wilkes and Liberty*.[4] The work of Rudé not only followed Lefebvre in placing the hitherto despised 'mob' into the context of the political life of revolutionary Paris and Hanoverian London, but also added a new dimension to their significance; Rudé provided a greater understanding of the composition, nature and ideology of the eighteenth-century 'mob'. His reconstruction of crowd events such as the Wilkite disturbances of the 1760s, using court records and newspaper accounts, enabled him to identify some of the 'faces in the crowd'. Contemporary stereotypes of the 'mob' as the 'rabble', composed of criminals, unemployed and ne'er-do-wells – stereotypes frequently repeated by subsequent historians – were demonstrated to be highly misleading. Analysis of the participants in some of the larger disturbances in eighteenth-century London, for example, often thought the home of the 'mindless mob' *par excellence*, were found to represent a fairly typical cross-section of the working population: people in work rather than unemployed; a range of journeymen and

---

[3] For example, see my *Popular Disturbances*, p. 3.
[4] E.J. Hobsbawm, *Primitive Rebels: Studies in Archaic Forms of Social Movement in the 19th and 20th Centuries* (Manchester University Press, 1959) and G. Rudé, *Wilkes and Liberty* (OUP, 1962).

masters, drawn from the various crafts, and even a sprinkling of professional people. Rather than being dominated by the vagrant poor or the rootless young, by the standards of the day they were composed of the relatively law-abiding rather than the criminal. Moreover, when examined closely, many 'riots' were revealed as disciplined and highly ritualised forms of protest, in which the populace acted in accordance with a coherent set of beliefs and values. Rudé argued that by the eighteenth century the so-called London 'mob' showed an emphasis upon its 'rights' and 'liberties', intermingled with recurrent themes of 'No Popery' and popular chauvinism.[5]

Rudé was also one of the first historians to turn his attention to the country food riots of England and France, suggesting that they too were frequently selective, disciplined and, often, highly ritualised forms of protest with the rational objective of purchasing food at what were seen as 'just' or 'fair' prices.[6] Eric Hobsbawm's interpretation of industrial protest in Britain pointed in a similar direction. In his essay in *Labouring Men*, published in 1964, Hobsbawm's study of the Luddites placed them within the context of a rational process of 'collective bargaining by riot' – one of the means by which workmen in the eighteenth and nineteenth centuries, and even earlier, could bargain and negotiate with their employers.[7]

The effect of these studies was to rescue many forms of collective protest and disorder from the incomprehension and condescension with which they had been treated in the past. With social historians already establishing the rationality of many activities regarded as 'senseless' and some, such as Rudé, beginning to attempt to see the activities of the eighteenth-century 'mob' as precursor of the more self-consciously political and more formally organised political and labour movements of the late eighteenth and nineteenth centuries, the way was open for a more thorough and systematic study of protest movements. E.P. Thompson's *The Making of the English Working Class*, published in 1963, offered the beginnings of this exploration. Although its primary aim was to examine what Thompson saw as the critically formative period for the development of a 'working class consciousness' – namely the period between the 1780s and the 1830s, in doing so, Thompson articulated some important views about the nature of popular culture at the end of the eighteenth century. In *The Making of the English Working Class*, Thompson described 'the phenomena of riot and the mob' as part of the 'sub-political' tradition which flowed into the early working-class movement: '. . . we must realize that there have always persisted popular

[5] See G. Rudé, *The Crowd in History: A Study of Popular Disturbances in France and England, 1730–1848* (New York, John Wiley, 1964), pp. 47–65.
[6] Rudé, *Crowd in History*, pp. 33–46.
[7] E.J. Hobsbawm, 'The machine breakers' in Hobsbawn (ed.), *Labouring Men* (2nd edn London, Weidenfeld and Nicolson, 1968), pp. 5–22.

attitudes towards crime, amounting at times to an unwritten code, quite distinct from the laws of the land.'[8] The distinction between this 'unwritten popular code' and the legal code was particularly sharp at the end of the eighteenth century, but it was a 'commonplace at any time'. Moreover, 'the resistance movement to the laws of the propertied' took not only the form of 'individualistic criminal acts', but also a tradition of riot and 'turbulence'. Thompson drew attention to the two different forms this 'riotous action' might take:

that of more or less spontaneous popular direct action; and that of the deliberate use of the crowd as an instrument of pressure, by persons 'above' or apart from the crowd.[9]

For Thompson, the former had not received the attention it deserved. Its importance was that 'it rested upon more articulate popular sanctions than the word "riot" suggests'. The most common example was the food or price 'riot', evidence of which could be found in England and Wales from the 1520s until the 1840s. These were rarely undisciplined occasions of mere uproar and looting, but were 'legitimized by the assumptions of an older moral economy, which taught the immorality of any unfair method of forcing up the price of provisions by profiteering upon the necessities of the people'. In both urban and rural communities, a 'consumer-consciousness' preceded other forms of political or industrial conflict, in which the price of bread became 'the most sensitive indicator' of popular discontent. Hence such 'riots' were to be seen as 'popularly regarded acts of justice', analogous to the French concept of 'taxation populaire'. These actions, for Thompson, indicated an extraordinarily deep-rooted pattern of behaviour and belief which was legitimised by the old paternalist moral economy. The final years of the eighteenth century, as demonstrated by the extensive food riots of 1795–6 and 1800–1, witnessed 'a last desperate effort by the people to reimpose the older moral economy as against the economy of the free market'.[10]

These disturbances were, then, of major significance. The most common form of 'mob' action – disturbances associated with the price of food – revealed a stratum of values and customs which had been largely overlooked by historians unconcerned with the rationale and motivation of the people involved in them. A preoccupation with 'order' in the simple-minded sense of the absence of overt conflict or an explanation based solely on predictable and spasmodic reactions to the price of bread or other foodstuffs seriously undervalued the significance of these events. Hence, the food 'riot' – hitherto written off as the almost inevitable companion of bad harvests, dearth and high prices – became a major source for the exploration of popular culture, analogous to the arcane worlds of carnival,

[8] E.P. Thompson, *The Making of the English Working Class*, rev. edn (London, Penguin, 1968), p. 64.   [9] Thompson, *The Making*, p. 67.   [10] Thompson, *The Making*, p. 63.

heresy, magic and witchcraft through which other historians had sought to
penetrate the *mentalité* of the population at large. Food disturbances occupied a
central role, for, as well as being the most frequent occasions of popular action,
they revealed a network of values and attitudes which was similar to those found
in other incidents, as 'behind every such form of popular direct action some
legitimizing notion of right is to be found'.[11]

These ideas took on a new dimension in Thompson's *Past and Present* article
of 1971. In part Thompson set out to reinterpret 'popular actions' along lines set
out by himself, Rudé and others. In particular he singled out for criticism the
'crass economic reductionism' of those who sought to explain popular disturbances in 'spasmodic' and 'mechanical' terms, including economic historians,
such as W.W. Rostow, whose 'social tension chart' sought to correlate outbreaks
of social disturbance and popular agitation with the fluctuations of the trade
cycle and movements in the price of bread. The attempt to sophisticate and
quantify statistical evidence of this kind merely concluded investigation at the
exact point at which it could become of value and interest in explaining the values
and moves of the people concerned. To the 'spasmodic' view of popular disorder,
Thompson opposed his own:

It is possible to detect in almost every eighteenth-century crowd action some legitimizing
notion. By the notion of legitimation I mean that the men and women in the crowd were
informed by the belief that they were defending traditional rights or customs; and, in
general, that they were supported by the wider consensus of the community.[12]

The food or price riot was the classic expression of this 'consensus', for while
food riots were triggered off by identifiable external factors, notably rising
prices, distress and malpractice by middlemen, they were also informed by a
popular consensus as to what were legitimate and illegitimate practices in the
processing and marketing of food. This consensus was grounded upon a
consistent traditional view of social norms and obligations and of the proper
economic and social functions of the various parties within the community, a
view which Thompson argued constituted the 'moral economy' of the poor in
eighteenth-century England.

The food riots of the eighteenth century therefore were a symptom of the
conflict between a traditional set of values relating to a vital area, food, primarily
bread and bread grains, and the aggressive commercial capitalism of the farmers
and middlemen in the food trade. In this conflict an older, paternalistic model of
marketing and manufacturing was being pushed to one side. Legislation against
monopolistic practices by the middlemen, regulation of the market-place to
permit the local population to purchase food before the larger dealers came into

[11] Thompson, *The Making*, p. 73.   [12] Thompson, 'Moral Economy', pp. 76–8.

action, and municipal price regulation through the Assize of Bread could all be seen to be under pressure by the eighteenth century. Similarly the body of regulations known as the *Book of Orders* which the government had sought to enforce in the Tudor period in times of scarcity and which gave priority to the needs of the consumer was no longer applied. In the face of these changes Thompson argued that a traditional frame of reference still dominated the attitudes of some sections of the authorities in the eighteenth century: forgotten and completely overtaken in good years, it was to flicker into life in years of dearth, seen, for example, in the proclamations against monopolistic offences, belated attempts to enforce the Assize, and authoritative denunciations against the operations of the middlemen.[13] Most significantly, however, they were to be found expressed in the actions of the crowd themselves. Thompson, properly, noted a particularity in the attacks of the crowd against selected targets, writing:

one may suggest that if the rioting or price-setting crowd acted according to any consistent theoretical model then this model was a selective reconstruction of the paternalist one, taking from it those features which most favoured the poor and which offered a prospect of cheap corn.[14]

This model, however, was less 'generalised' than that of the paternalists. It was individuals: farmers, millers, bakers and popular scapegoats such as the Quakers, who were the victims of popular disapprobation, and especially provocative incidents, such as the movement of corn out of a region or abroad in times of scarcity, which were most likely to provoke disorder. Thompson has called the economy of the poor 'still local and regional, derivative from a subsistence economy', one which reflected a popular memory of the operation of the *Book of Orders* long after it had passed out of effective use. The forms of popular action were remarkable more for their restraint than their disorder, in which there can be no doubt that the actions of the crowd were 'approved by an overwhelming popular consensus', a consensus that prices *ought*, in times of dearth, to be regulated by the authorities in order to restrain the activities of farmers and middlemen, any indeed who sought to profit from the operation of the market at the expense of the local consumer.[15]

Here lies the heart of Thompson's case about the nature and significance of the actions of the English crowd in the eighteenth century, that they represent part of the long-drawn-out resistance of an older moral economy of provision based on the needs of the consumer to the profit-orientated world of *laissez-faire*, and in which the food riots of the eighteenth century represented the popular reaction to the transition to 'the extortionate mechanisms of an unregulated market economy'.[16]

[13] Thompson, 'Moral Economy', pp. 95–8.   [14] Thompson, 'Moral Economy', p. 98.
[15] Thompson, 'Moral Economy', p. 98.   [16] Thompson, 'Moral Economy', pp. 132–4.

II

By the eighteenth century, England possessed a highly sophisticated trade in foodstuffs, of which the trade in corn was easily the most important. During the eighteenth century the corn trade continued to develop as population growth and urbanisation put increasing strain upon the food supply of the whole country.[17] London had been a major importer of foodstuffs, especially corn, for centuries, drawing its supplies from an increasingly wide area of the country. In the early eighteenth century it was estimated that almost four-fifths of the internal corn trade of England was devoted to supplying the capital. London consumed upwards of a million quarters of wheat a year by the end of the eighteenth century, representing about a seventh of the total crop. By 1700, London drew its grain from beyond the Home Counties and the metropolitan grain market influenced the whole of south-eastern England except for the Trent valley and parts of the south-west. London's tentacles spread out even further during the eighteenth century, following the lines of the turnpike system, coastal shipping routes and the growth of river and canal improvements. In years of scarcity London dealers could be active in the coastal districts of Yorkshire and the north-east, in Cornwall and in the upper Thames valley and south Midlands. East Anglia, however, remained the principal granary of the capital. Over sixty market towns, usually sited on rivers, specialised in the marketing of corn for the capital. Coastal shipping brought grain from small ports on the coasts of Essex, Norfolk and Suffolk and places such as Wells, Blakeney, Lynn, Ipswich and Yarmouth shipped huge quantities of grain to London. For more specialised produce, London's reach stretched even further. Cattle bought in Wales and on the Scottish border found their way to Smithfield market, while a tight ring of cheese factors operated in Somerset and Derbyshire to supply the London market.[18]

The London market played a crucial part in creating a national trade in foodstuffs during the seventeenth and eighteenth centuries. For much of the period up to 1750, it was the main focus of population growth in the country as a whole, serving to enlarge the market for basic necessities, improve production

---

[17] See A.H. John, 'The Course of Agricultural Change, 1600–1760' in L.S. Pressnell (ed.), *Studies in the Industrial Revolution* (London, Athlone Press, 1969); T.S. Ashton, *An Economic History of England: The Eighteenth Century* (London, Methuen, 1955), p. 86; N.S.B. Gras, *The Evolution of the English Corn Market* (Cambridge, Mass., Harvard University Press, 1915), pp. 109–24.

[18] On the corn trade to London see O.A.K. Spate, 'The Growth of London, A.D. 1660–1800', in H.C. Darby (ed.), *An Historical Geography of England before A.D. 1800* (CUP, 1936), pp. 541–2; F.J. Fisher, 'The Development of the London Food Market, 1540–1640', *ECHR*, V (1935); and A. Everitt, 'The Marketing of Agricultural Produce' in J. Thirsk (ed.), *The Agrarian History of England and Wales*, vol. IV, *1500–1640* (CUP, 1967), pp. 507–16.

and stimulate specialisation.[19] An expanding market for foodstuffs provided what E.A. Wrigley has described as 'revolutionary changes in agricultural practice, at first within a limited radius of the city, but by the beginning of the eighteenth century over a large part of England'.[20] The capital's impact upon the country was to stimulate the development of a transport network which gradually created a more unified national market for foodstuffs and grain in particular. The availability of coastal transport had always meant that regional autarchy was less marked in England than in parts of the continent. Although considerable differences in price could occur between districts into the eighteenth century, no area was so far from the coast or other sources of supply that it could suffer a complete breakdown of its food supplies.[21]

Nonetheless, until the eighteenth century, England remained a series of only loosely related regional economies. J.E. Thorold Rogers distinguished six price regions for grain at the end of the seventeenth century. One was based on the Thames valley and region, including places such as Hitchin and Wycombe. The eastern counties, comprising Cambridgeshire, Bedfordshire, Essex, and parts of Hertfordshire, Suffolk, Norfolk and Huntingdonshire comprised another. The Midlands provided a less definite area, but comprised the region west of the eastern counties, between the Trent and the Thames. The south included the area between Kent and Devonshire, including parts of Surrey. The south-west included Falmouth, Plymouth, Bristol and the valleys of the Severn and Wye. The north contained the markets north of the Trent.[22] N.S.B. Gras simplified this pattern into two groupings, the metropolitan and non-metropolitan areas, using price tables for the period 1691–1702. The metropolitan area was determined by the availability of coastal and river transport, as well as the developing turnpike system.[23] The cheapness of waterborne transport also meant that the grain market of south-eastern England was also part of a European market which included the Channel and Biscay coasts of France, the Low Countries and the Baltic. A.H. John has argued that prices in Danzig, Bordeaux, Biscay and London moved in similar patterns, so that significant differences could show up between the metropolitan market and the still largely local markets of the north and south-west.[24]

---

[19] See F.J. Fisher, 'London as an "Engine of Economic Growth"' in J.S. Bromley and E.H. Kossmann (eds.), *Britain and the Netherlands*, vol. IV (The Hague, 1971), pp. 3–16; E.A. Wrigley, 'A Simple Model of London's Importance in Changing English Society and Economy, 1650–1750', *Past and Present*, XXXVII (1967), pp. 44–70. [20] Wrigley, *Past and Present*, XXXVII (1967), p. 50.
[21] E.L. Jones, *Seasons and Prices* (London, George Allen and Unwin, 1964), p. 58; P. Bowden, 'Agricultural Prices, Farm Profits, and Rents' in Thirsk (ed.), *Agricultural History*, pp. 609–16.
[22] J.E. Thorold Rogers, *A History of Agriculture and Prices in England, 1259–1793* (CUP, 1866–1900), vol. VII; John 'Course of Agricultural Change', pp. 126–7.
[23] Gras, *Evolution of the English Corn Market*, pp. 121–2.
[24] John, 'Course of Agricultural Change', p. 141.

By the mid-eighteenth century the effects of improving transport and the growth of provincial newspapers, which published London prices, began to reduce the differences between regional averages. The degree of uniformity varied considerably. L.A. Clarkson has remarked that it would be a mistake to think that even by 1750, England was 'a truly national market', writing: 'Ignorance, conservatism, and inadequate communications, still contrived to fragment the country into a number of only loosely integrated regional economies.'[25] Nonetheless, by 1772 Arthur Young was impressed by the degree of uniformity of prices in England. Moreover, a unified national market did not necessarily mean the ironing out or price difference between the regions. Differences in prices between regions were not inconsistent with the existence of a national market. Such differences would reflect local conditions, whether of scarcity or abundance in relation to immediate requirements. More important in determining the existence of a national market was the rate of change of prices and the speed of reaction between different areas. Using the prices for London and Eton, Winchester and Lincoln, in the period 1723–62 and 1754–93, Grainger and Elliott concluded that, taken over a long period, prices did tend to move in a highly connected way. In short-term fluctuations, however, the divergences were greater. Significantly, the two southern markets were more highly connected in both long- and short-term fluctuations. This would reflect the greater unity of the grain market in southern England: Lincoln being still only loosely tied in with the metropolitan area. This is confirmed by more impressionistic evidence that the Lincolnshire area still remained an autonomous market for much of the eighteenth century, though gradually being brought into line with the rest of the country if the long-term market movements were examined.[26]

The most important difference in prices lay between the coastal areas, which were relatively accessible to the sea and therefore more closely tied into a national market, and the inland counties where transport difficulties were often reflected in erratic price movements. This transitional situation in the corn market was reflected in the system of making returns of average prices in order to regulate the import and export restrictions. Until 1804 returns were taken separately for twelve 'maritime districts' of England and Wales. These districts were considered as independent of each other for the purposes of foreign trade and ports were opened or closed in them by reference to the price in the local district. In 1804 it was decided to regulate the entire foreign corn trade of England by one internal price, the aggregate of the twelve maritime districts. When

[25] L.A. Clarkson, *The Pre-Industrial Economy in England, 1500–1750* (London, Batsford, 1971), p. 123.
[26] C.W.J. Grainger and C.M. Elliott, 'A Fresh Look at Wheat Prices and Markets in the Eighteenth Century', *ECHR*, xx (1967), 257–65.

Scotland was brought into this system in 1805, Great Britain was officially regarded as a national market.[27]

But many local differences remained. In some areas different corn measures were used, making the determination of averages difficult. Even at the end of the eighteenth century there was much popular resistance to the Winchester measure and customary weights continued to be used.[28] More important was the growth of the manufacturing areas as fresh regional markets, often based on a local port, which provided a counter-pull to the metropolitan market. Arthur Young recorded that it was impossible to determine prices solely by their distance from the London market, for the state of local agriculture, the existence of a large manufacturing population, and the position of local transport also played a crucial part.[29] The older manufacturing districts, such as the cloth towns of the West Country, had their own catchment area. The south-western area was influenced both by these traditional markets and the growing port of Bristol. In the early eighteenth century Defoe commented that Warminster was the biggest wheat market outside London.[30] As the century went on, the burgeoning manufacturing centres of the Midlands and the north created their own catchment areas for food. Hence even by mid-century, dealers from Lancashire were active as far afield as southern Scotland and North Wales.[31]

The eighteenth-century consumer lived in an increasingly sophisticated economy in which the chain between the consumer and the primary producer of food was becoming more complex. Professional middlemen were gaining an importance in the grain trade throughout the century and attenuating the chain of supply. The grain trade showed this development as clearly as any other. At the consumers' end, the main difference showed itself in the decline of home baking. Considerable variation existed between town and country and between north and south. At the end of the century, many country areas and parts of the north continued as home-baking areas. Eden quoted budgets from the Lake District

[27] C.R. Fay, 'Price Control and the Corn Averages under the Corn Laws', *Economic Journal*, I (1929) pp. 149–54; D.G. Barnes noted the relatively crude system for administering the corn bounty system prior to 1773; price levels were determined on a county basis twice a year by the Justices of the Peace at quarter sessions. The price derived from their enquiry was then returned to the local customs officer at neighbouring ports: see D.G. Barnes, *A History of the English Corn Laws* (London, Routledge, 1930), pp. 16–17.

[28] See W.H. Beveridge, *Prices and Wages in England*, vol. I (London, Longmans, 1939), p. xxix; Thompson, 'Moral Economy', p. 102.

[29] Gras, *Evolution of the English Corn Market*, pp. 95–9.

[30] Gras, *Evolution of the English Corn Market*, p. 124; John, 'Course of Agricultural Change', p. 127.

[31] J.P. Dodd, 'South Lancashire in Transition: a Study of the Crop Returns of 1795–1801', *Transactions of the Historic Society of Lancashire and Cheshire*, CXVII (1965), p. 97; D.J.V. Jones, *Before Rebecca* (London, Allen Lane, 1973), p. 1. North Wales also attracted dealers from Dublin: see G. Nesta Evans, *Social Life in Mid-Eighteenth Century Anglesey* (Cardiff, Welsh University Press, 1936), p. 132.

and the north-east which confirmed that families still bought bread grains or flour to bake into bread. Even an industrial town as large as Manchester was reported to have only three professional bakers in 1804. In the industrial areas, however, there was a movement towards professional baking and the greater intervention of middlemen. People who had once bought grain direct from the farmer and took it to the miller to turn into flour, now bought flour from a retail flour dealer. The farmer increasingly sold his grain to a corn factor, who in turn sold it to a miller. The latter sold it to a flourman who supplied the flour dealer. In the most highly developed areas, notably London, another link in the chain was occupied by the professional baker. M.D. George has commented of eighteenth-century London that it 'had reached a stage of industrial development where spinning, weaving, baking, brewing, and candle-making were no longer done by housewives'. Eighteenth-century Londoners were consumers, totally dependent upon a range of middlemen for the supply of basic necessities, above all for their staple diet of wheaten bread. In country districts, the process was less complete. E.P. Thompson quotes a return of Northamptonshire parishes in 1757 which reveals that only fourteen out of twenty-seven parishes making returns had a resident baker.[32]

The degree of specialisation in the food trade had gone a considerable way even before 1700. A study of the grain trade from north-east Kent to London in the early eighteenth century has concluded that most of the major developments had taken place which characterised a *laissez-faire* system. Grain was brought on regular schedules by cart or on Kentish 'hoys', boats of 40 to 60 tons, and unloaded at Bear Key, until 1750 'the greatest corn market in Europe'. In 1750 a covered Corn Exchange was set up in Mark Lane, where sale of grain could be by sample to a small group of prominent factors. Defoe described the changed condition of the London market in 1738: 'Instead of the vast number of horses and wagons of corn on market days there were crowds of farmers, with their samples, and buyers such as mealmen, millers, corn buyers, brewers, etc., thronging the market.' In London the day of the regulated public corn market 'had long passed'.[33]

[32] Thompson, 'Moral Economy', pp. 105–6; Dodd, 'South Lancashire in Transition', p. 106; M.D. George, *London Life in the Eighteenth Century* (London, Penguin Books, 1966), p. 172. The rise of professional baking is more noticeable in the case of Norwich, a city of some 13 000 inhabitants at the beginning of the sixteenth century, rising to 30 000 by 1700. The number of freemen bakers rose from 21 in 1525 to 32 in 1569. Admissions of bakers to freemen status rose from a total of 89 between 1500 and 1603 to 318 between 1660 and 1749, when they represented the largest group of admissions in the food and drink trades, displacing the butchers. See J.F. Pound, 'The Social and Trade Structure of Norwich, 1525–1575', pp. 141, 143 and P. Corfield, 'A Provincial Capital in the Late Seventeenth Century: the Case of Norwich' in P. Clark (ed.), *The Early Modern Town: a Reader* (London, Longman, 1976) p. 261.

[33] D. Baker, 'The Marketing of Corn in the First Half of the Eighteenth Century; North-East Kent', *Agricultural History Review*, XVIII (1970).

The organisation of marketing had become more complex with a proliferation of middlemen. Mealmen and flourmen entered the processing side of the trade and became millowners and millers. Farmers moved into milling and malting, whilst carriers of coastal and inland traffic became factors and merchants. Millers bought their own supplies direct from the farmer and sometimes moved into the baking trade. In Essex and Kent, the large millers expanded their operations during the eighteenth century, building new mills and becoming substantial entrepreneurs, often buying grain at Mark Lane and selling flour to large-scale professional bakers. The overall direction was towards a self-regulating market economy with an increasingly complicated and attenuated chain between consumer and producer.[34]

In line with these developments, the government had largely stepped out of regulation of the internal trade in corn. This had a long history before 1660, but after that date was of relatively little significance. Tudor policy accepted the mechanism of the market, but regulated the grain trade in accordance with a clear set of priorities, notably the London market, the supply of the armed forces and the poor in times of scarcity. Corn dealers were permitted to operate in 1552 providing they were licensed by three justices of the peace. The Privy Council took considerable pains to inform itself about the state of the corn market and regulating exports. In 1587 the *Book of Orders* urged local officials to make enquiries into the grain supply in their area. These instructions were reissued in subsequent periods of scarcity up to the civil war. Thereafter, however, government control waned. In 1663 the medieval statutes against monopolistic offences were practically abolished, although only finally repealed in 1772 as the culmination of a debate about the efficacy of the Tudor legislation.[35] By the middle of the eighteenth century, the laws against monopolistic offences were widely regarded as a hindrance to the production of grain and the supply of the large urban centres. In 1757 the *Gentleman's Magazine* observed that the laws against forestalling, engrossing and regrating were 'so antiquated and the circumstances and manner of living of all ranks of people so alter'd, that a vigorous execution of them would rather contribute to famish than feed in many places great numbers of the poorer sort'. The good harvests of the first half of the century encouraged the relaxed attitude of the government towards the activities of the middlemen. The government and local justices, however, retained the right to reimpose anti-monopolistic regulations in times of scarcity. But in spite of pressure from consumers, attempts to reimpose more traditional forms of control found only temporary favour.[36]

[34] C.R. Fay, *The Corn Laws and Social England* (CUP, 1932), pp. 56–7.
[35] Clarkson, *Pre-Industrial Economy*, pp. 176–7; Thompson, 'Moral Economy', pp. 89–94.
[36] Barnes, *History of the English Corn Laws*, pp. 32–3.

Similarly, the old paternalistic framework of price control, surviving in many towns in the form of the Assize of Bread, became increasingly irrelevant to the operation of the food market.[37] The Assize set a price for a fixed size and quality of loaf. Its original aim was to protect the consumer from the exploitations of the middleman, at a time when his operations were regarded with great suspicion. A number of places continued to set the Assize during the eighteenth century, perhaps the most important example being London, where the Assize was not finally abolished until 1822.[38] But long before then the Assize had been under attack and also became widely ignored, even in places where it continued to be set. The Assize was unable to keep up with the developments in the corn trade and the specialisation in the milling and baking industries. For example, it often suited the large millers of the capital to buy grain, grind it into different grades and sell it off separately at whatever price the market would bear. The difficulty of setting an Assize price which reflected these complexities was one of the factors which led to its decay. Bakers often found they could not buy and make bread from the finer grades of flour at the Assize price, leading to widespread evasion of the law and ill-feeling in the trade when prosecutions were undertaken. By the middle of the century it was widely accepted that the Assize was incapable of coping with the growing complexity of the trade and some voices were raised in favour of abolition. Parliament, however, would not go so far as this and magistrates were left with the option of setting the Assize as they wished. Arthur Young in 1790 claimed that 'Magistrates are very much embarrassed to fix the assize of bread . . .' The Webbs concluded that by the end of the eighteenth century, the system had become virtually a dead letter. Where the Assize remained, it was principally seen as a check upon the grosser forms of profiteering.[39] Thus Charles Smith commented in 1764 that 'in large towns and cities it will be always necessary to set the Assize, in order to satisfy the people that the price which the bakers demand is no more than is thought reasonable by the magistrates'.[40] Even detractors of the Assize admitted its usefulness in times of scarcity; as late as 1814 Frankland Lewis feared the removal of a control which 'in times of scarcity . . . had preserved internal tranquillity'.[41] In times of scarcity, however, the Assize was forced to reflect the market price for grain or risk driving the middlemen out of the trade altogether.

The regulation of the external trade by government was important from 1660 to 1814. Before the middle of the seventeenth century, the principal concern of the government was with protecting the consumer and the specific interests, such as

[37] S. and B. Webb, 'The Assize of Bread', *Economic Journal*, XIV (1904), pp. 196–218.
[38] The Assize was partly dismantled in the London area by an act of 1815, 55 Geo. III c. 49.
[39] Webb, *Economic Journal*, XIV p. 209n.
[40] C. Smith, *Three Tracts on the Corn Trade and Corn Laws*, 2nd end (London, 1977), p. 30.
[41] *Hansard* (1814), XXIX. 637.

the supply of London and the armed forces. From 1660, however, England was a grain-exporting country and exports were stimulated by bounties. In 1689 bounties were paid on the exports of each of the four grains, wheat, barley, rye and oats. The bounty on wheat was 5 shillings per quarter, so long as the price of wheat at home, effectively in the county of origin, did not rise above 48 shillings. Imports were regulated by a sliding scale of duties. These laws operated with little disturbance until the middle of the eighteenth century, when they became the subject of intense debate. None the less, the system of helping the producer to dispose of a surplus when prices were low and of keeping out foreign imports until the price was high remained the basis of the laws governing the foreign trade in corn until the corn laws of 1814 and 1815. From mid-century, dwindling exports and the rise of population gave rise to revisions in the law, notably in 1773, which reduced the price levels at which bounties were paid on exports and duties collected on imports. The Acts of 1814 and 1815 abolished the export bounty and made export free at all times. It also replaced the sliding scale with an absolute prohibition of imports before prices reached a fixed level, 80 shillings in the case of wheat. Between the end of the seventeenth century and the beginning of the nineteenth, the sole function of government in relation to the foreign trade was temporarily to suspend or lower duties on imports or prohibit exports, usually in times of scarcity. The government therefore had some role to play, but it was one which it was only called upon to perform in times of emergency. The import–export trade was otherwise left free to operate under the existing regulations with minimum government interference.[42]

So-called food 'riots' covered a wide, but well-defined, range of activities, such as stopping the movement of grain, forcible seizure and resale of food, often at 'fair' or 'just' prices, the destruction of mills and warehouses, the spoiling of foodstuffs and various kinds of tumultuous assembly to force dealers or local authorities to reduce prices. In its classic form the food riot could be found in many parts of western Europe between the seventeenth and the twentieth centuries. It was usually characterised by a high degree of discipline amongst the rioters, the use of ritual elements and concentration upon those specifically concerned with the trade in foodstuffs and the setting of prices.[43] The origins of food rioting in England is still somewhat obscure. R.B. Rose, in one of the pioneering articles on this subject in 1961, could find no evidence of a price-fixing riot before 1693 and tentatively suggested that the first authentic example took place in Oxford in the April of that year, when 'the poor . . . by clamouring,

---

[42] Barnes, *History of the English Corn Laws*, pp. 285–7; see also R.B. Outhwaite, 'Dearth and Government Intervention in English Grain Markets, 1590–1700', *ECHR*, XXXIV (1981), pp. 389–406.

[43] See C. Tilley, 'Collective Violence in European Perspective' in H.D. Graham and T.R. Gurr (eds.), *Violence in America* (New York, Bantam, 1969), pp. 16–19: Rudé, *Crowd in History*, pp. 33–8.

brought the price of corn from 9s to 6s 2d'.[44] In fact, more recent researches have pushed the history of food rioting and price-fixing much further back. There is evidence of food rioting as early as the 1520s, and groupings of disturbances have been found in 1527, 1551, 1586, 1595–7, 1605, 1622–3, 1629–31, 1647–9, 1662–3, 1674, 1681, and 1693–5.[45] Lack of firm evidence about food riots earlier than the 1520s may well reflect more the inadequacy of the source materials than the absence of disturbances of this type. Certainly, examples of price-fixing riots can be found in the sixteenth century. The Proceedings of Star Chamber record an incident in Southwark in 1595:

Attorn [ey] R [egina] v [ersus] Hoskins *et al* [iis] to the number of 300 apprentices for gathering themselves together in Southwark on a market day, and there taking away from divers persons both fish and butter which they disposed of at their pleasure; and they took upon them the office of Clerk of the Market and did abate the price of victuals and set them at lower rates than the owners did usually sell them; and they did also cause one Poultrie to make open proclamation that no persons should sell any butter at their houses or inns but that they should bring it into the open market by 9 o'clock the next day, to the end they might sell it at such rates as they pleased . . .[46]

Recent writers have suggested that there were at least forty and perhaps as many as seventy incidents of food rioting between 1585 and 1660 which can be verified from the records of central and local government. Although this total is regarded as an underestimate, they have concluded that the years of dearth in early modern England 'were not marked by widespread rioting'.[47] Whatever the conclusions reached by a definitive study of popular disturbances in the sixteenth and seventeenth centuries, it seems likely that they will not substantially alter this picture. Food rioting certainly took place in seventeenth-century England, but it never reached the scale which it was to achieve later. Available research suggests that food riots only became common towards the latter part of the seventeenth century, accompanying periods of high prices in the mid-1670s, mid-1690s and 1708–9. But it was during the eighteenth century that food riots became most pronounced, occurring with increasing frequency as the century wore on and only dying out in the first half of the nineteenth century. A number of nation-wide waves of food rioting have been identified after 1714 and related to periods of harvest failure or trade depression, such as those of 1727–9, 1739–40, 1756–7, 1766–8, 1772–3 and 1783. The years of the French Revolution and the Napo-

[44] R.B. Rose, 'Eighteenth Century Price Riots and Public Policy in England', *International Review of Social History*, VI (1961), pp. 276–7.

[45] See Stevenson, *Popular Disturbances*, p. 90 n.2, for further references; also A. Charlesworth (ed.), *Atlas of Rural Protest in Britain, 1548–1900* (London, Croom Helm, 1983), pp. 63–80.

[46] BL, Proceedings in Star Chamber, Harleian MS. 2143, fol. 57ff.

[47] J. Walter and K. Wrightson, 'Dearth and the Social Order in Early Modern England', *Past and Present*, LXXI (1976), p. 26; Charlesworth, *Atlas of Rural Protest*, pp. 72–80.

leonic Wars also witnessed major periods of disturbances in 1792–3, 1795–6, 1800–1, 1810–13, 1816–18. Thereafter, food roots were a feature of particular parts of the British Isles. By the mid-nineteenth century, the tradition of popular food riots in Britain was virtually dead, though it survived in other parts of Europe until the twentieth century.[48]

Two features stand out in the incidence of food rioting in England, the influence of the communications network and the distribution of the manufacturing population. A substantial proportion of all disturbances took place at ports, market towns or trans-shipment points. This factor seems to have operated whether disturbances occurred in relatively prosperous or marginal areas. Indeed, one of the heaviest concentrations took place in East Anglia, where grain was frequently being moved by cart or barge to the capital. As early as 1565, the town of Cambridge protested to the Privy Council about grain being moved to London. Again, in 1581 there were complaints against the effects of water transport moving grain from country areas. These complaints multiplied with the development of the transport network in the seventeenth and eighteenth centuries, gradually affecting a wider range of areas.[49]

Equally important, however, was the presence of a large non-agricultural population, dependent upon local market towns for supply and vulnerable to rapid fluctuations in price. For much of the eighteenth century, colliers were the most important such group. The Kingswood colliers, for example, proved one of the most persistent groups of food rioters, taking part in almost every major wave of food riots. The Cornish tinners were another prominent group active during the period, participating in every wave of disturbances. Riots broke out in Cornwall in 1709, 1727–9, 1737, 1748, 1757, 1766, 1773, 1795–6, 1810–13, 1831 and 1847. Similarly, clothworkers formed another group with a persistent history of food disturbances from the sixteenth through into the early nineteenth centuries. The textile centres of Yorkshire, East Anglia and the West Country were amongst the frequent participants in popular disorder.[50]

The incidence of food rioting, however, was shifting. In the seventeenth century, food riots were most common in East Anglia, the Thames valley, and the cloth towns of the West Country. This pattern remained well into the first half of the eighteenth century, for relatively few disturbances took place in the north until the middle and end of the century. By the Napoleonic Wars the manufacturing areas of the north and Midlands were more frequently disturbed, a pattern

[48] M. Beloff, *Public Order and Popular Disturbances, 1660–1714* (CUP, 1938), pp. 63–4; Rudé, *Crowd in History*, pp. 36–7; Rose, *International Review of Social History*, VI, pp. 283–4; Stevenson, *Popular Disturbances*, pp. 91–4; Charlesworth, *Atlas of Rural Protest*, pp. 80–118.
[49] Gras, *Evolution of the English Corn Market*, pp. 109, 124, 127–8; Beloff, *Public Order*, p. 73; Stevenson, *Popular Disturbances*, pp. 94–6.
[50] Stevenson, *Popular Disturbances*, pp. 96–7; Charlesworth, *Atlas of Rural Protest*, pp. 63–71, 79.

confirmed in the post-war disturbances of 1816–18. The food disturbances of the Regency period were the last really widespread waves to occur in England. Thereafter food riots became confined to two principal areas: the remoter marginal areas of the British Isles, including the south-west and some of the poorer urban slums. There were food riots in Cornwall in 1830–1, in 1847 (as well as in the Scottish Highlands) and in Devon in 1867. In urban areas, there were attacks on food shops in Manchester in 1826 and in other parts of Lancashire in 1829. Provision shops were looted in the Potteries in 1842, and in Liverpool in February 1855. Unemployment and distress also led to similar events in east London in 1855, the winter of 1860–1 and again in 1867.[51]

In many ways the English food disturbances conformed to the classic pattern mentioned earlier. The transportation or storage of food in times of scarcity was often prevented by the populace, and the food resold at 'fair' prices. On other occasions the disturbances could take the form of assemblies in the market-place to compel the dealers to reduce their prices to a 'just' level; sometimes the intimidation was directed at the local authorities to compel them to intervene in the marketing of provisions. Stopping the movement of grain and preventing its export was particularly common, while mills were the tangible symbol of the middlemen and were extremely vulnerable to attack by outraged crowds. The spoiling of food was often the means of showing the anger, or even contempt, of the populace for the activities of the middlemen. Corn and flour was scattered over the floor of market-places or tipped into rivers, growing corn trodden into the fields, cheeses rolled through the gutters and vegetables thrown from their carts. The destruction of sacks, breaking of mill machinery and dams or weirs all played a part in punishing the dealers.[52]

Although there were instances of pilfering and violence, the most remarkable feature of these food disturbances was the element of ritual and restraint. The great majority of food disturbances exhibited strong ceremonial and ritual elements. Mobs were frequently headed by someone blowing a horn, beating a drum or carrying a flag or other emblem such as a loaf of bread. In using these ceremonial devices, the people concerned were often showing their sense of the legitimacy of their actions, endowing them with a ritualism which put them within the context of a form of 'popular justice'. Accordingly, the resale of food was often followed by a return of the money (and even the sacks) to the dealers from whom it had been taken. Even the destruction of food was often carried out with an orderly deliberation far removed from the frenzied looting that was feared by the authorities. The general run of disturbances were directed at property rather than persons. Threats were certainly made, especially to unpop-

[51] Stevenson, *Popular Disturbances*, pp. 96–7; on Kingswood, see Brewer and Styles, pp. 85–127.
[52] Stevenson, *Popular Disturbances*, pp. 102–6.

ular dealers or to dealers as a group, but they were rarely carried out. English crowds appear to have killed no one deliberately, certainly in the various food disturbances which occurred from the beginning of the eighteenth century to the beginning of the nineteenth, although several food rioters were killed by authorities and a number executed.[53]

As food disturbances became more common they tended to be concerned with foods which were not essential, such as meat and butter. Although hardly 'luxuries', they illustrated that these were not always riots of desperation by starving men and women, but displayed a wider 'consumer consciousness' and resistance to high prices over a range of commodities. They were 'price' riots, rather than reactions to famine, more plausibly placed within the context of scarcity, high prices and resentment than of major demographic crises. Commodities included: meat (Redruth, St Austell: 1766; Wisbech, Coventry, Portsea: 1795; Oxford, Nuneaton: 1800; Brandon: 1816); cheese (Exeter, Coventry, Oxford: 1766; Seaford: 1795; Nuneaton, London: 1800); butter (Stourbridge, Kidderminster: 1767; Bury St Edmunds: 1772; Liverpool: 1793; Wells, Aylesbury, Deddington: 1795; Oxford, Banbury: 1800; Carlisle: 1812; Callington: 1847). Other price riots involved green vegetables, salt, fish, bacon, malt and also household commodities such as candles and soap. These were usually treated in much the same way as grain or bread, with attempts to 'fix' the price and spoiling the goods if this was not complied with.

III

How well then does Thompson's analysis of a 'moral economy' of the crowd fit in with what we know about the evolution of the grain trade and the occurrence of food disturbances after the middle of the seventeenth century? It appears that within a general acknowledgement of the potential value of such a concept, some qualifications have to be made. The term 'crowd' is one which clearly has some relevance in upgrading the status of popular disturbances from the actions of a mindless rabble to the more rational and calculated activities which closer investigation has revealed. There seems, however, some reason to regard 'crowd' as being a rather evasive description of the participants in food and price riots. It has already been acknowledged by Thompson and others that English food riots stand apart from those elsewhere in Europe in being primarily the protests of urban workers. Thompson's association of the 'moral economy' at different points in his 1971 article with, variously, the 'crowd', the 'poor' and, at one point, the 'commonweal' offer an insight into the confusions that can occur. Of the 'crowd', it is perhaps sufficient to say that it is a very elusive concept, one which

---

[53] Stevenson, *Popular Disturbances*, pp. 105–6.

almost begs definition. In some cases it is clearly used in the sense of a synonym for the 'common people', for Thompson a forerunner of the 'plebeian culture' which he went on to discuss in subsequent articles.[54]

There are dangers, however, in the classification of seventeenth- or eighteenth-century popular disturbances as being the work of the crowd in the sense of a representative section of the common people as a whole. As we have seen, food riots were scarcely that; they were, in fact, the protests of a minority section of the population – the urban dweller. Nor moreover are we dealing with the protests of a uniform section even there – some towns and villages witnessed disturbances, others did not. Indeed the recent work by Andrew Charlesworth, John Bohstedt and David Rollinson has taken us a good deal further in identifying the sort of community in which food rioting might occur. Charlesworth, for example, has noted some of the factors which encouraged or checked the growth of food rioting in particular regions. By no means all colliers, for instance, saw the food riot as the most appropriate response to the economic and social changes occurring in seventeenth- and eighteenth-century England and the differentiation between the responses of *similar* groups of workers forms a significant qualification on attempts to identify a coherent 'moral economy'.[55] David Rollinson's detailed investigation of the proto-industrial county of Gloucestershire also imposes a useful perspective in an area where there was a complex interplay of industrial and agricultural workers, landowners and early industrialists. He has argued that 'for much of the eighteenth century moral economy riots were exclusively the function of industrial districts', and that such riots may have reflected more than a subsistence ethic, but were 'tied into a long-term effort to defend a marginally rising standard of living'.[56] John Bohstedt's recent study of riots and community politics at the end of the eighteenth century has also suggested the complexities of motive and context which lay behind some of the areas most likely to experience food disturbances.[57]

There is too a curious aspect to the timing of the major outbreaks of food rioting in England and Wales, namely that they appear to have occurred at least

---

[54] There is a huge literature on the 'crowd' and its definition; for an introduction see Holton, *Social History*, May (1978); Stevenson, *Popular Disturbances*, pp. 7–9. Thompson's major discussion of the 'plebeian culture' can be found in 'Patrician Society, Plebeian Culture', *Journal of Social History*, VII (1974), pp. 382–405; 'Eighteenth-Century English Society: Class Struggle Without Class?', *Social History*, III (1978), pp. 133–65.

[55] Charlesworth, *Atlas of Rural Protest*, pp. 64–71.

[56] D. Rollinson, 'The Intensification of Community, Society, and Economy in seventeenth- and eighteenth-century Gloucestershire', unpublished D.Phil. thesis, University of New South Wales, 1981, pp. 122–4.

[57] J. Bohstedt, *Riots and Community Politics in England and Wales, 1790–1810* (Harvard University Press, Cambridge, Mass., 1983), esp. pp. 27–68.

fifty years after the marketing and legislative changes which are supposed to be their occasion. The largest outbreaks of food rioting, such as those in 1766 and 1795–6 clearly came not when people were being exposed to the market mechanism and the withdrawal of government intervention in the grain trade for the first time, but long afterwards. In a sense then, Thompson has telescoped the coming of marketing changes and the outbreak of food rioting. The existence of an active market in grain and other foodstuffs, whether national or regional, pre-dates, often substantially, the disturbances which are said to have arisen from its operation.[58] This means we are not dealing with a straightforward reaction to the onset of market capitalism in the food trade. If that had been the case, there should have been many more food riots, much earlier.

This brings us, finally, to the value of Thompson's general notion of the 'moral economy'. It is, as indicated at the outset, one which struck a chord with many people working in the field of popular movements. It was a highly suggestive phrase because it enshrined the view of the intrinsic rationality of popular protests made familiar by Rudé and others. The 'moral economy' presupposed a set of attitudes and assumptions – in this case relating to the marketing and sale of food. But while the idea that food protests were rational activities may hold, there can be some dispute as to how much can be read into them. Do the food riots of the seventeenth and eighteenth centuries reveal a coherent moral economy of the type Thompson suggested, one in which the necessity of providing food at a fair price took precedence over private profit? There is clearly something in this argument, as the nature of many food riots clearly suggests a demand for 'fair' prices and an end of malpractice. There is a danger, however, of approaching these food disturbances too naively and invoking too rigid a notion of popular assumptions and attitudes. There is, for example, some evidence that in asserting a 'fair' price for food, rioters did not 'fix' prices at a constant level, but took account of overall changes in prices. Clear evidence from the earlier part of the eighteenth and seventeenth centuries is difficult to find, but by the end of the century it is plain that a more flexible attitude was being taken. As John Bohstedt has argued about Devon food riots:

It is often said that food rioters looked backward and sought to restore the 'just price'; that they were trying to enforce ancient forms of market regulation while the magistrates were increasingly becoming converted to laissez faire doctrines; and that rioters were resisting the new strains placed on local supplies by urban areas and a growing national system of food marketing. First of all, rioters did not base their claims to legitimacy on ancient paternalistic practices. Nor did they seek to restore the 'just price' of some prior golden

---

[58] E. Fox Genovese, 'The Many Faces of Moral Economy', *Past and Present*, LVIII (1973), pp. 162–3; Bohstedt, *Riots and Community Politics*, pp. 211–12.

age. In Devon, for instance, the rioters of 1795 merely sought the prices of the previous year, while in 1801 the prices they set in their contracts were compromises between 'normal' and crisis levels.[59]

This suggests that price-fixing riots should be seen more as a gesture of displeasure at exploitation and malpractice and within the context of their particular communities rather than part of a generalised statement of a 'plebeian culture'. Certainly, if anything like a 'moral economy' can ever be said to have existed, it was remarkably flexible and adaptive to change.

These qualifications have some profound implications in relation to our understanding of popular attitudes in the context of the social and economic changes which were occurring in England and Wales between the sixteenth and eighteenth centuries. We need not go all the way with Alan Macfarlane in arguing that from at least the thirteenth century the majority of ordinary people were 'rampant individualists . . . economically "rational", market-orientated and acquisitive' in arguing that the detailed history of food rioting substantially qualifies any attempt to see it as a social sympton of the 'Great Transformation' – a reaction to market capitalism and the social consequences it is alleged to have brought about.[60] Ironically, in supplanting a 'spasmodic' view of food rioting, I would contend that Thompson created an overrigid framework of his own, one in which the works of Tawney and Dobb clumped a little too heavily into view and one which, valuable as it has proved, may now be in danger of obscuring more than it reveals.[61]

[59] Bohstedt, *Riots and Community Politics*, p. 211.
[60] A. Macfarlane, *The Origins of English Individualism* (Oxford, Basil Blackwell, 1978), pp. 163, 198–200.
[61] Tawney is cited in Thompson, 'Moral Economy', p. 132; see also M. Dobb, *Studies in the Development of Capitalism* (London, Routledge, 1946).

Index

239

Index of places